D0162043

Photo: Harry Heleotis

The Multicultural Imagination

Psychoanalysis has tended to ignore the importance of "race" within the unconscious. In *The Multicultural Imagination* Michael Vannoy Adams investigates the deep-seated, unconscious origins and effects of racism or "colorism" and argues that "race" is as important as any other aspect of the unconscious.

The author presents case material from patients for whom "race" or color is a significant social and political concern which impacts on them personally. In the therapeutic dialogue and in dreams, these patients struggle to establish an effective individual identity in relation to whatever collective "racial" identity may have been either imposed on them or adopted by them. *The Multicultural Imagination* challenges the essentialist view that restricts all individuals to this kind of collective identity. The book uses various analytic perspectives in both the Freudian and Jungian traditions to cover topics such as "whiteness" and "blackness," the "cultural unconscious," the "civilized" and the "primitive."

Focusing on Jung's visits to Africa and his nightmares about the color complex of whites and blacks, Michael Vannoy Adams offers a re-reading of Jung's theory of the collective unconscious—one that includes cultural differences. With reference to the work of Frantz Fanon and Alice Walker, the author shows how questions about universal, human principles have continued to inform thinking about "race."

This book exposes the unconscious attitudes that have stood in the way of an authentically multicultural imagination. It encourages psychoanalysts and psychotherapists to recognize the importance of "race" or color within the unconscious and will interest those working in other fields, including cultural studies and "racial" and ethnic studies.

Michael Vannoy Adams is a psychotherapist in private practice and Senior Lecturer in Psychoanalytic Studies at the New School for Social Research, New York.

Written in an engaging personal style, Adams's book tells us how our unconscious handles the "racial" categories of black, white, or otherwise. It helps us to think about a difficult problem for which there are no easy answers.

Tzvetan Todorov, author of *On Human Diversity*

With passionate commitment and intellectual panache, *The Multicultural Imagination* offers something that has been missing from debates on ethnic and "racial" difference. Adams's move from "race" to "raciality" is as important as the earlier move from sex to sexuality. He succeeds in utterly repositioning the unconscious as a contributor to social and political processes of healing and reconciliation between different groups of people.

Andrew Samuels, author of *The Political Psyche*

The Multicultural Imagination

"Race," Color, and the Unconscious

Michael Vannoy Adams

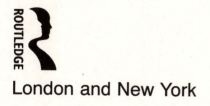

London and New York

LONGWOOD COLLEGE LIBRARY
FARMVILLE, VIRGINIA 23901

BF
175.4
.R34
V36
1996

First published 1996
by Routledge
11 New Fetter Lane, London EC4P 4EE

Simultaneously published in the USA and Canada
by Routledge
29 West 35th Street, New York, NY 10001

© 1996 Michael Vannoy Adams

Phototypeset by Intype London Limited
Printed and bound in Great Britain by
TJ Press (Padstow) Ltd, Padstow, Cornwall

All rights reserved. No part of this book may be reprinted
or reproduced or utilized in any form or by any electronic,
mechanical, or other means, now known or hereafter
invented, including photocopying and recording, or in any
information storage or retrieval system, without permission
in writing from the publishers.

British Library Cataloguing in Publication Data
A catalogue record for this book is available from the British Library

Library of Congress Cataloging in Publication Data
Adams, Michael, Vannoy, 1947–
    The multicultural imagination: "race," color, and the unconscious/
    Michael Vannoy Adams.
    p. cm.
    Includes bibliographical references and indexes.
    1. Psychoanalysis and racism. 2. Race—Psychological aspects.
    3. Race awareness. 4. Psychoanalysis—Philosophy. 5. Pluralism.
    I. Title.
    BF175.4.R34V36 1997
    155.8'2—dc20   96–7561
                                                                      CIP

ISBN 0–415–13837–X (hbk)
ISBN 0–415–13838–8 (pbk)

LONGWOOD COLLEGE LIBRARY
FARMVILLE, VIRGINIA 23901

For my multicultural family:
Una Chaudhuri
Nathaniel Lee Grotowski Adams (Jes Grew)

> "Yes, Nathan."
> "You said that you were going to teach me how to catch it."
> "Catch what, Nathan?"
> "Jes Grew."
>
> Ishmael Reed, *Mumbo Jumbo* (1972: 151–2)

Sonu Rita Jessie Adams
James Edmund Couch Adams (Kim Sang Chul)
Sandra Adams Leatherwood (Kim Jung Ai)

And to the memory of my father and mother:
Ethalmore Cox Vannoy Adams
Jessie Smith Adams

LONGWOOD LIBRARY

1000288657

Contents

Acknowledgements

One person, above all others, has been a true friend: Andrew Samuels, Professor of Analytical Psychology in the Psychoanalytic Studies Programme at the University of Essex and an analyst with the Society of Analytic Psychology in London. I know no one who has such a generous spirit.

I also wish especially to thank Martin Stanton, Director of the Centre for Psychoanalytic Studies at the University of Kent at Canterbury, for the support that he has always so kindly offered.

A number of colleagues at the New School for Social Research have been important to me—in particular, Sekou Sundiata, David Shapiro, Donald M. Scott, and James Miller.

I should also like to thank the former Dean and Associate Dean of the Graduate Faculty of Political and Social Science—Alan Wolfe and Richard Gaskins—who, when the New School established a Psychoanalytic Studies Program in 1992, supported me as Coordinator of that program. I appreciate the opportunity to have served in that capacity during the first three years of the program.

From 1986 to 1991, I was Associate Provost of the New School. I wish to thank Provost Judith B. Walzer and President Jonathan F. Fanton for the opportunity to serve in that position. It was a privilege—and always a pleasure—to work with Provost Walzer. I especially value the confidence and respect that she has accorded me.

I should also like to thank Dean Beatrice Banu of Eugene Lang College, who has supported me as Chair of the Mind, Nature, and Value academic concentration in that division of the New School.

A grant from the Faculty Development Fund of the New School enabled me to present portions of research in the United Kingdom during the summer of 1994 at the Centre for Psychoanalytic Studies at the University of Kent, the Psychoanalytic Studies Programme at Middlesex University, the Psychoanalytic Forum of the History and Philosophy of Science Programme at Cambridge University, the seventh international conference of the London Convivium for Archetypal Psychology at Cumberland Lodge, and the Society of Analytical Psychology in London. I wish to thank xii Acknowledgements

Martin Stanton, Bernard Burgoyne, Teresa Brennan, Noel Cobb, Jean Knox, and Andrew Samuels for arranging those presentations. Martin Stanton originally suggested that I should present this material in the United Kingdom and invited me, as an Honorary Research Fellow of the Centre for Psychoanalytic Studies, to be a resident scholar at the University of Kent.

I presented other portions of research at the tenth international conference of the Association for the Study of Dreams in Santa Fe in the summer of 1993 and at the C.G. Jung Institute Analyst Training Program of Pittsburgh in the winter of 1994. I wish to thank Carol Schreier Rupprecht and Stanton Marlan for organizing those presentations.

Members of the Jungian community in the United States have provided valuable support. James Hillman in particular has been an influence and an inspiration. I also wish to thank Paul Kugler, Marga Speicher, Beverley Zabriskie, Yoram Kaufmann, Ann Belford Ulanov, Aryeh Maidenbaum, Robert Bosnak, Thomas Kirsch, Stanton Marlan, Harry W. Fogarty, Donald Kalsched, Joseph Wagenseller, David Morgan, Richmond K. Greene, Alan Jones, Susanne Short, Maurice Krasnow, Virginia Bird, Stephen A. Martin, Laurel Morris, V. Walter Odajnyk, Warren Steinberg, Armin A. Wanner, Jane White Lewis, Richard C. Lewis, Polly Young-Eisendrath, Betsy Halpern, Gertrud Ujhely, Laurie L. Schapira, Georgette K. Kelley, Janet Careswell, Charles Boer, Jay Sherry, and Michael Perlman.

Over the years, many other individuals have been personally important to me: Jay Milner, W.W. Rostow and Elspeth Davies Rostow, the late Michael Polanyi, the late Marcus Cunliffe, Kathleen Raine, Tzvetan Todorov, Jerzy Grotowski, Lee Leatherwood, Bush Bowden, Dick Benson, Gad Alpan, and Harry Heleotis.

I especially thank those individuals who have granted me permission to use personal and other material in this book.

I should also like to thank Edwina Welham, who commissioned this book for Routledge.

Several individuals read all or a large part of the manuscript in draft. I thank them for comments and criticisms: Andrew Samuels, Sekou Sundiata, Kirkland Vaughns, David Shapiro, Donald M. Scott, Judith B. Walzer, Paul Kugler, Beverley Zabriskie, Robert Bosnak, Thomas Kirsch, Jeffrey Seinfeld, Alan Roland, Martin Schulman, and Tzvetan Todorov.

I, alone, of course, am ultimately responsible for the ideas and opinions in this book.

Finally, I thank Una Chaudhuri. No words can express how much I value the constant love and intellectual and emotional support that she provides. She is, in the truest sense, my multicultural imagination.

Michael Vannoy Adams
New York City, 1995

Preface

There are three principal dimensions to this book: theoretical, historical, and clinical. In addition, the book necessarily involves another dimension that motivates this project. The immediate context of the project comprises experiences of events over the past five decades, a decisive half century during which I and we all, personally and collectively, have become much more aware of just how multicultural we are. These experiences constitute a certain psychical reality that deserves not to be forgotten (or repressed) but to be shared with and interpreted by others. This is, after all, a psychoanalytic book. I therefore offer a "psychobiographical" account of the origins of this project. I know that this is an unexceptional account. Many others will have had similar experiences. The very commonality, it seems to me, is what endows them with relevance.

TEXAS AND THE BACKSIDE OF ABRAHAM LINCOLN

I was born and raised in Texas. I grew up in Bonham, a small town named after one of the defenders of the Alamo—James Butler Bonham, who was sent for reinforcements but who returned empty-handed to die with the other "heroes." I moved away from Texas in 1972 and now live in New York City. I consider myself a New Yorker—but I also still consider myself a Texan.

Few Texans identify themselves as "Southerners." Most regard themselves as "Southwesterners," as I do. The myths and symbols in the imagination of Texas are very different from those in the imagination of the "Deep" South. Texas did join the Confederacy (in spite of the efforts of Sam Houston, who, after accepting the surrender of Santa Anna at the battle of San Jacinto, had been elected president of the Republic of Texas and, after that nation became a state in the Union, had been elected governor—he resigned rather than take an oath of allegiance to the Confederacy), but Texas had no significant effect on the Civil War—and little economic interest in it. As a small child, I played with gray and blue toy soldiers, including a General Lee and a General Grant. I asked my mother to make me a Confederate uniform. In loving secrecy, she sewed a costume with a border of gold braid. The cloth she used, however, was blue. (My mother had not the slightest interest in the Civil War, nor had my father, nor had any other adult I ever knew in my hometown—except, that is, for Edwardine Crenshaw Couch, a very dignified old lady lawyer who walked about town with the aid of a gold-headed cane. My father was a postal clerk. One day, Mrs Couch appeared at the post office to buy stamps. A new purple four-cent, first-class stamp had just been issued. It bore the head of Abraham Lincoln. As my father told the story, Mrs Couch refused to buy the stamp because, as she said, "I will never lick the backside of Abraham Lincoln.")

That my mother, to my dismay, had mistakenly made my uniform out of blue cloth did not keep me from wearing my costume proudly—and pretending that it was gray. In my make-believe battles, the Rebels always defeated the Yankees. I knew intuitively, however, that the Confederacy had been in the wrong and the Union in the right. I knew this because I knew that slavery had been wrong. Who could not know that, not acknowledge that? I played civil war, not cotton plantation. If, along with my gray and blue toy soldiers, I had also had black toy slaves, I wonder what the effect would have been. I doubt that my conscience, childish as it was, could then have countenanced any victories of the South over the North. I would no longer have been able to pretend.

"US" AND "THEM": THE BLACKEST LAND AND THE WHITEST PEOPLE

I do not remember exactly when I put these childish things behind me, but I do remember 1954. That was the year of *Brown vs. Board of Education*; it was also the year that I entered first grade. In my segregated hometown, white students attended the "Bonham" schools—black students, the "Booker T. Washington" school. Three years later, in 1957, the schools in Little Rock were forcibly integrated. For some Texans, Arkansas was too close for comfort. Each day after school, I played baseball with a friend in his backyard. I remember overhearing his mother one afternoon declare, in no uncertain terms: "*My* children will never sit next to *them*." Not until my senior year—twelve years after the Supreme Court decision—was the Bonham high school finally integrated. Even then, for that year, integration was voluntary and unidirectional: black students in their senior year in the Booker T. Washington school were given the option of transferring to and graduating from the Bonham high school; three did. The three of "them" sat next to "us," without incident. The following year, all twelve grades in my hometown were peacefully integrated.

In 1977, while I was working at the circulation desk of the University of Illinois library in Urbana, a young boy approached me and requested a book by an author whose last name happened to be "Bonham." Unfortunately, that book was not among the millions of volumes in that library. While searching in the card catalog under "Bonham," however, I chanced on what to me was an item of great personal curiosity: a copy of the rules, regulations, and curriculum of the Bonham Public Schools (1910) for the session 1910–11. In that year, my father had been in the fourth grade. I immediately went into the bookstacks and looked up the document. For anyone with an interest in the history—and putative decline—of public education in America in this century, this is an impressively provocative ninety-five-page source. One might well wonder how many public schools today are capable of such a beautifully literate, even eloquent statement of educational principles and purposes. One page, however, gives a different kind of pause. This is the page on which the superintendent submitted an annual report on the school year of 1909–10. He presented statistics under three columns: "White," "Col'd" (an abbreviation of "Colored"), and "Total." There were 962 students in the white schools, 184 students in the black school. The value of all property in the white schools was $97,300; in the black school, $3,910. That is, the property value per white student was $101; per black student, $21: a five-to-one ratio. There were 850 books in the library of the white schools, 75 in the library of the black school. That is, there was not quite one book per white student and less than half a book per black student. So much for "separate but equal" education in America in the first decade of the twentieth century.

Bonham was hardly exceptional. I want to state emphatically that while I lived there my hometown was no more racist than other towns or cities in America—North, South, East, or West. By no means was it the most overtly racist town in northeast Texas. That dubious honor, it seemed to me, belonged to Greenville, a nearby town that for many years posted a notorious sign for all to see: "The Blackest Land and the Whitest People."

ORA WALKER, FRANK RAYFORD, AND "BLUE" VANCE

I have other memories. One is of Ora Walker, a black woman who for a time took care of me after school, while my mother worked. Her brother Wiley, who was especially impressive to me because he was the only person I knew who had ever lost an arm in an automobile accident (my mother used to invoke him as an example when she would warn me to keep my arm well inside the open window of our car), plowed my grandfather's fields with a team of mules. I remember Ora Walker as a woman who loved a little white boy and cooked him tart apple pies and peach cobblers that made his mouth pucker in delicious delight. One day, I eagerly came home from elementary school with a present for my mother, who was not yet home from work. My teacher had taught us how to make notepads for our mothers. We had dutifully followed her instructions, tracing the outline of a female figure, coloring it with crayons in strict conformity with the image that the teacher had provided as a model, then glueing a notepad to it. When I got home, I proudly showed the notepad to Ora Walker. In my innocence, I repeated what my teacher had said: "It's a Negro Mammy." It was then that I received my first lesson, from a real teacher, in what racism is—and how it hurts. Ora Walker simply said, "I never want to hear you say that again."

In high school, I sang in the choir. My mother, who admired my father's voice and imagined that I, too, had talent (until I proved her wrong), arranged private lessons for me. Bonham was not just one town. There were towns-within-the-town: what whites called "nigger-towns," with names like "East End," "Sunshine," and "Locksborough," where blacks lived. My voice teacher was a black man, Frank Rayford, who lived in "Tank Town." As a young man, he had studied opera in Paris. I remember the day I first met him—and the impression his house made on me. The outside of the house could hardly have been more different from the inside. The wooden, clapboard exterior was unpainted and unprepossessing; it looked neglected, as if it were a sign of just how impoverished the owner was. The interior, however, was furnished with a piano, an extensive collection of opera records, and a shortwave radio on which my voice teacher listened to classical music from as far away as Europe. It may be, of course, that the difference between outside and inside was a matter of choice, that it merely reflected that my voice teacher had chosen not to keep up external appearances at the expense of what really mattered to him—his music. Even then, however, I wondered whether there was more to it than that. Was the difference between outside and inside an indication of ingenious duplicity on the part of my voice teacher? Would an exterior as fine as the interior have been interpreted as an ostentatious display, a provocative assertion of equality (or even superiority)?

I also remember coming home from university at winter intersession one year. Like many towns, my hometown held a contest at Christmas and awarded prizes for houses that were judged to have the best decorated exteriors. A friend of mine, also home on vacation from university, and I drove around town looking at all the houses. That year, there was a new entrant in the competition: a black man, "Blue" Vance. In a gesture that must have been an allusion to his name, he had covered every square inch of his house with blue lights—it was an astonishing, amazing sight. My friend and I drove past his house over and over again. We knew that he would win first prize. There was absolutely no doubt in our minds. We were outraged when it was announced that he had been awarded second prize, second place—which we righteously interpreted as his being "kept in his place."

MEXICO AND "REMEMBER THE ALAMO!"

When I was growing up, there were other colors besides "white" and "black" in Texas: "brown," for example—which meant Mexicans. My hometown in northeast Texas, very near the Red River, could hardly have been farther from the Rio Grande. The only Mexican I was aware of as a child was a man who for a short time sold tamales from a cart. Merely to find a restaurant that served Mexican food, or what was later called "Tex-Mex," we had to drive all the way to Dallas. An uncle and aunt of mine did once take me on a trip to south Texas, to the "Valley," to visit relatives and see the citrus groves, where the men and women who picked the orange and grapefruit and lemon trees were called pejoratively "wetbacks." We went across the border to shop in the markets. My mother had cautioned me against any misimpression that the bordertowns were at all representative of "Old Mexico" (as she called it).

As a young woman in the 1930s, my mother had taught English for a year at a school in Torreón. That was an experience that she never forgot—and often fondly remembered. When I was in high school, we made a family trip one summer to Mexico. We drove across the border, across the mountains to Monterrey, then west to Saltillo and Torreón. For my mother, this was a final, nostalgic return to the days of her youth. In Saltillo, we visited the home of a man, then in his late sixties, who in his youth had romanced my mother with a tennis racket. (His wife—and my father—seemed to me rather awkward at this reunion.) In Torreón, we visited two of her former students. One, a man, seemed to own the town, he was so wealthy. He insisted that we stay as a courtesy at the hotel he owned; he also owned a factory and a bank. His daughter had just been married to the son of the governor of Coahuila. The house was full of extravagantly luxurious wedding presents. His son was a priest, who argued liberation theology with his father. My mother's other former student, a woman, had been a nationally prominent concert violinist. She took us to lunch at a restaurant, where she rose from her seat to serenade us, to the applause of all those around us—she was famous. These memories are, for me, radically different from any "Remember the Alamo!"

"INDIANS" AND ARROWHEADS: LAYERS OF COLLECTIVE EXPERIENCE

There was also the color "red'—which meant "Indians." Although Bonham is so far north that it is only ten miles from the border with Oklahoma, in my childhood there were, at least to all appearances, no Indians living in my hometown. This did not mean, however, that no Indian influence was felt. The Bonham high school football team was named the "Warriors"—and a mascot in a feather bonnet performed war dances at half-time. The high school yearbook was named the *Coushatta*, after the Alabama-Coushatta Indians who had once inhabited the area. I felt the Indian presence more personally. My family moved to my grandfather's farm after his death in 1959. Indians had once lived on that land. My mother would reminisce about her childhood and recall how her father used to plow up "bushel baskets" of arrowheads on his eighty acres. When I was a child, after fresh rain had fallen and washed away layers of earth from the side of a hill near the railroad tracks that crossed the farm, arrowheads would be exposed. I would walk along, my head down, looking intently for them. I had a large collection of Indian arti-facts, and my father and mother would take me arrowhead hunting to other sites as well. My mother, an amateur artist, painted a portrait of an Indian chief on a wooden plaque to which I proudly glued my arrow-heads for display.

I had a fantasy of becoming an archaeologist—as both Freud and Jung had. If I now reflect on the origins of my interest in psychoanalysis—or "depth psychology"—I would trace the interest back to that source in childhood. Horizontal space has always been an important factor in the imagination of Texas, which was the largest state in the nation when I was a child. (It is said that, in conversation, Texans never stand face-to-face but always side-to-side, looking out on the vast expanse.) For me, it was not the drilling of oil wells but the searching for an Indian presence that added a vertical dimension to my imagination. The Texas land on which I grew up has meant for me, psychically, not only breadth but also depth—the uncovering, the discovering, of layers of collective experience underneath my own personal experience.

KOREA IN TEXAS: THE ADOPTION OF ANOTHER CULTURE

When I was 9 years old, my father and mother adopted my sister and brother, two Korean-American war orphans, one just 5 years old, the other not quite 5. Rex Ray, a Baptist minister from Bonham, who, along with his wife, had for many years been a missionary, first in China, then in Korea, personally arranged for the adoption of my sister Sandra (Kim Jung Ai) and my brother James (Kim Sang Chul). The only famous and influential person from my hometown was Sam Rayburn, Speaker of the House of Representatives. "Mr Sam," as he was known locally, intervened in my parents" behalf, sending cablegrams to Syngman Rhee, the presi-dent of the Republic of Korea, urging him to cut red tape and expedite the adoption process. Mrs Couch prepared and submitted all the necessary legal documents, handled all the correspondence (whether she used any purple, four-cent, first-class Abraham Lincoln stamps, I do not know, but she may have). On the night of January 10, 1958, the plane carrying my sister and brother all the way from Korea, those thousands of miles, finally arrived in Texas.

At the time my parents adopted my sister and brother, my father was 57 years old, my mother, 51. It was no simple, easy thing for a man and a woman of that age successfully to integrate two young children from another country, another culture, who spoke another language, into a small, rural Texas town of 7,000 population—but they did. In all those years, I never knew of any overt prejudice or discrimination in my home-town against either my sister or my brother—with one exception: the father of one of my brother's high school girlfriends forbade his daughter, in no uncertain terms, to continue dating an "Oriental."

Of course, if my sister and brother had been black, rather than Korean-American, my parents' efforts at integration would have been far more difficult, probably impossible. The fact that my sister and brother were "foreign" made it difficult for anyone who might have had racist incli-nations to reduce them to familiar "racial" categories. They simply did not conform to the prevalent local notions of the "other," the "opposite." (The dominant "racial" opposition was black–white, not foreign–domestic.) In terms of color, my sister and brother were not "yellow" but "half-white." They were also already "part-American"—Korean-American—orphaned children fathered by American soldiers.

ROOTS AND BRANCHES OF A MULTICULTURAL FAMILY TREE

During my lifetime, my entire family has gone—or come—from "Anglo-Saxon" to Asian-American. One of my uncles, a professor of rhetoric at Auburn and Georgia Tech, was also the self-appointed family genealogist. At family reunions, he would unfurl scrolls on which he had carefully inked the family tree. (When he would do that, my father, with a twinkle in his eye, would whisper to me, "*I* prefer to live in the present.") My uncle traced my father's side of the family back to England. The Adamses had immigrated to America in the 1700s and settled in Virginia—and then had moved to Georgia and, finally, in 1849, to Texas. I doubt that they could ever have imagined how multicultural the family would even-tually become.

Not only are my sister and brother Asian-American—so are my wife, who is Indian (from India, that is), our biological son, who is Indian-American, and our adoptive daughter, who is Indian. To complicate (and enrich) matters even more, my wife is Sikh-Hindu (her father was a Sikh, and her mother is a Hindu: such marriages were by no means uncommon until relatively recently, when unscrupulous politicians in India have fomented communal antagonism and incited religious fundamentalism in a cynical, deliberately divisive effort to gain or maintain power). Suddenly, in only one generation, I and all the members of my family have a very personal interest in the success of multiculturalism.

PSYCHOANALYSIS AND MULTICULTURALISM

I do not believe that psychoanalysis can, by itself, realize the promise of multiculturalism, but I do believe that it has a valuable, potentially unique contribution to make to the endeavor. What is distinctive about psychoanalysis is its emphasis on the unconscious. A genuinely multicultural psychoanalysis would provide us with an opportunity to inquire into the "raciality" (as we already have done with the sexuality) of the unconscious. This book is an effort on my part to try to determine what the "racial" contents of the unconscious have been—and are.

In researching this question, I have been struck by the fact that the word "race" occurs so infrequently in the indexes of psychoanalytic books and journals. With the exception of anti-Semitism, racism is not a topic that has attracted much psychoanalytic attention. Part of the explanation is that sex excited the interest of so many psychoanalysts for so long; another reason is that so few psychoanalysts have been "non-white." Perhaps the most important reason, however, is that psychoanalysis has still not adequately taken into account the cultural dimension of the psyche. I do not mean merely other cultures, in the sense that Alan Roland (1988) advocates "cross-cultural" psychoanalysis. I mean the presence and influence of cultural factors in the psyche. Although psychoanalysis is no longer exclusively "intrapsychic" (if it ever was) but is now also "interpersonal," "object relational," "interactional," or "intersubjective," it remains insufficiently cultural. With some exceptions, it continues to regard culture as an "extrapsychic" factor. Perhaps even more important than the "family romance" in psychoanalysis has been what I would call the "individual romance"—the emphasis on the individual in relation to other individuals, not in relation to culture. As Roland notes, "Western individualism, with its emphasis on strong outer ego boundaries and individual autonomy," is a bias that has prevented psychoanalysis from satisfactorily addressing cultural issues, including significant cultural differences (1988: 227).

Freud had very little to say about "race" in the white–black sense. An exception to this rule occurs in a letter to Wilhelm Fliess. Freud expresses regret at the brevity of a vacation: "In three weeks it will all be over; and then the worries begin again whether some negroes will turn up at the right time to still the lion's appetite" (1985: 368). Peter J. Swales (forthcoming) notes that this "racial" joke by Freud equates patients with blacks and the psychoanalyst with a hungry lion that voraciously devours them. Ernest Jones explains the context as follows: "The consultation hour was at noon, and for some time patients were referred to as 'negroes.' This strange appellation came from a cartoon in the *Fliegende Blatter* depicting a yawning lion muttering 'Twelve o'clock and no negro' " (1953 1: 151). This remark, of course, has no status in psychoanalytic theory, but for someone who wrote a book on jokes and the unconscious, it does reveal a certain attitude toward both blacks and patients. Although Freud only occasionally addresses "racial" relations theoretically, he does so momentarily when he discusses group psychology. He observes that in intimate, durable relations between individuals "aversion and hostility" are almost invariably present. The same is true of relations between groups. "Closely related races," Freud says, "keep one another at arm's length." In the case of groups with "greater differences," there is often "an almost insuperable repugnance" that one group feels for another group—for example, "the Aryan for the Semite" or "the white races for the colored" (*SE* 18: 101). In this instance, the same Freud who jokes that psychoanalysts are to patients as lions are to blacks suggests that Aryans are to whites as Semites are to blacks. That is, in this analogy, Freud the Semite is implicitly in the same insuperably repugnant position as a black. Both are objects of racism.

Similarly, Jung compares himself to blacks, or as he put it on at least one occasion, to "niggers." He recounts how a black African medicine man lamented that he had had no dreams since the arrival of the British. What the *laibon* meant was that the ostensibly "superior intelligence of the white man" had suddenly rendered redundant the knowledge, or guidance, that black Africans had previously obtained from dreams. White Europeans simply presumed to "know," without any guidance from the unconscious. Jung says, however, that dreams do guide him, and, in that respect, "I am as primitive as any nigger, because I do not know!" (*CW* 18: 286, para. 674). On Jung's use of the word "nigger," the editors of Jung's *Collected Works* comment: "This offensive term was not invariably derogatory in earlier British and Continental usage, and definitely not in this case" (*CW* 18: 286, para. 674n.). Derogatory or not, the word functions in this instance as a means for Jung to associate himself with black Africans and to dissociate himself from white Europeans. Was Jung a racist in the white–black sense? Some have argued that he was (Dalal 1988). I would only say that what ultimately interests me is not whether Jung, Freud, or any other psychoanalysts in the past were racists but whether psychoanalysts and psychotherapists in the present and future are and will be effective multiculturalists. Jung had much more to say about "race" than Freud did—some of it disconcerting, some of it inspiring; Frantz Fanon had a lot to say about it. The time is now right for us to begin to analyze (and I do mean "analyze," not "moralize") the "raciality" of the unconscious. We may be surprised by what we find there. If the word "unconscious" means anything, we will be.

I hope that this book will find an audience among Freudians, Jungians, and every other school of psychoanalytic thought, as well as among representatives of every other therapeutic profession, including psychiatrists, clinical psychologists, clinical social workers, counselors, and other mental health workers—and among all others who have an interest in multiculturalism. I hope that the book will have an impact on both the theory and practice of psychotherapy—and not only a clinical but also a cultural influence.

I am an American, and this is in a very real sense an American book. The book offers an "American" perspective on "race," color, and the unconscious. This perspective has all of the limitations and advantages of what Clifford Geertz calls "local knowledge" (1983). The feeling-tone of the "color complex" in America is different from the feeling-tone in, for example, Britain. Although both Britain and America are multicultural countries, the histories are different. In Britain, the dominant historical factors are colonialism and imperialism; in America, slavery. I do not believe that there is less racism in Britain than in America. I merely mean that history has "colored" racism differently in Britain and America. In America, "race" is fundamentally a white–black issue.

Freud had a notorious bias against America. For example, Jones quotes Freud as having said, "America is a mistake; a gigantic mistake, it is true, but none the less a mistake." Jones also recounts an anecdote, courtesy of Marie Bonaparte, that he considers a humorous example of Freud's anti-Americanism:

> An amusing instance of this prejudice transpiring was when in one of his fanciful moods he predicted the extinction of the white race in a few thousand years and its probable replacement by the black one. Then he jocularly added: "America is already threatened by the black race. And it serves her right. A country without even wild strawberries!"
>
> (1955 2: 60)

This is anti-Americanism with a vengeance. Americans—that is, white Americans—will get what they deserve when African-Americans finally render them extinct. Freud was wrong about wild strawberries—they do exist in America; as a child I used to pick them and eat them on my grandfather's farm. I hope that Freud is also wrong about the future of relations between whites and blacks in a multicultural America.

A NOTE ON TERMINOLOGY

In the course of the book, I define many of the terms that I employ. For example, I state that I use "self" and "other" in a very ordinary way—although I am well aware that there are "many selves" (Redfearn 1985) or "multiple selves" (Mitchell, S.A. 1993). I do note that Jungians use the term "self" (which they often capitalize as "Self") in a quite distinctive way, but I do not employ it in that sense in this book. When I use the term "ego," I tend to employ it not as Freud defined it (as "reason" in relation to the "reality principle") but as "self-image," or "identity." For me, the ego is also, as Jung says, an "ego-complex"—an at least partly unconscious feeling-toned set of ideas in association with the "I." The ego is often quite defensive, although it can also be receptive. In a sense, this book is about the potential receptivity of the self-image to other-images, whether they be images of external others or internal others. For me, what is most important is not *that* the ego is defensive, but *how* it is defensive. I mean not merely which "defense mechanism" the ego happens to employ on a particular occasion but what specific attitude the self has toward the other. Does the self hate the other, fear the other, envy the other, resent the other? Similarly, *how* is the ego receptive? Does the self love the other, desire the other, revere the other, respect the other?

I also define such terms as "race," racism, "racial" identity, and the "raciality" of the unconscious in the course of the book. One term, "psychical reality," seems, however, to require a more immediate definition. Freud variously contrasts psychical reality with material, factual, practical, or external reality. For example, he asserts that *"psychical* reality is a particular form of existence not to be confused with *material* reality" (*SE* 5: 620). Sometimes he equates psychical reality with fantasy. Fantasies, he says, "possess a reality of a sort." The sort of reality that they possess is *"psychical* as contrasted with *material* reality, and we gradually learn to understand that *in the world of the neuroses it is psychical reality which is the decisive kind"* (*SE* 16: 368). Freud thus equates fantasy, or psychical reality, with neurosis. He declares: "We may lay it down that a happy person never phantasizes, only an unsatisfied one" (*SE* 9: 146). Although I agree with Jung that the recognition of the existence of psychical reality is "the most important achievement of modern psychology" (*CW* 8: 354, para. 683), I consider the definition that Freud provides to be inadequate to the extent that he equates it with neurotic reality. I believe that it is obvious that happy as well as unhappy people fantasize continuously, sometimes neurotically, sometimes not— and that the imagination can be not only distortive or even destructive but also creative. As Jung says:

> It is true that there are unprofitable, futile, morbid, and unsatisfying fantasies whose sterile nature is immediately recognized by every person endowed with common sense; but the faulty performance proves nothing against the normal performance. All the works of man have their origin in creative imagination. What right, then, have we to disparage fantasy?
>
> (*CW* 16: 45, para. 98)

"Reality" is not given; it is constructed, or created, in and through fantasy. "The psyche creates reality every day," Jung says. "The only expression I can use for this activity is *fantasy*" (*CW* 6: 52, para. 78). This is what I mean by *the fantasy principle* and *the psychical construction of reality*. To me, "psychical reality" is a neutral term that describes how we imagine ourselves and others.

* * *

As I was correcting the page proofs and preparing the indexes for this book, there appeared on the front page of the *New York Times* a three-column photograph of the charred remains of the New Light House of Prayer, an African-American church in Greenville, Texas, with the Reverend Chester Thomas inspecting the damage. Subsequently, the Greenville Hotel, a vacant building across the street from the Katy Railroad Depot, was also burned. Coincidence or not, it was from the hotel and the depot that a banner proclaiming "The Blackest Land and the Whitest People" hung in Greenville. At the latest counting, more than 30 African-American churches in the South have been burned in the last year and a half (Labaton, 11 June 1996: B, 7).

M.V.A.
June 1996

Chapter 1

Pluralism, racism, and colorism

This is a book about "race," color, and the unconscious. It is also a book about the prospects for a multicultural psychoanalysis.

Some individuals will have a special interest in the clinical dimension of the book. In chapter 12, I discuss case material from contemporary patients, both "black" and "white," who consider "race" a significant issue. In chapters 13 and 14, I also present interpretations of "color-change" dreams—that is, dreams in which the dreamer or other figures in the dream change color or "race." Color-change dreams are not, of course, the only kind of dream in which "race" assumes prominence for both whites and blacks, as well as for people of other colors. Consider the following four dreams of a "white" man:

> My son and I are in New York City. There's a Ku Klux Klan rally on the steps of a church. Whites (and one black) are standing, arms folded, on the steps. They're holding signs and firebrands. Then my son and I are inside the church. We have to change clothes. At some point, I realize that there could be some ugly, dangerous incident—say, a bombing of this church in retaliation for the rally. I urge my son to get dressed quickly.

> I walk back to my apartment building. Along the way, I'm passing and avoiding these hellish dark streets and alleyways where homeless blacks are sleeping, possibly lurking. Back at the apartment building, upstairs is a kind of down-and-out "share" place. In this room I see a new but cheap chrome telephone of modern design. A black roomer has bought it. I look at it, push the buttons. Then I go into my wife's and my room. I start telling my wife that I'm going to buy this labor-saving household device. "It's a 'scapegoat,' " I say. That's the generic name of the device.

> I'm doing volunteer work in Africa in a country where the king is autocratic. He kills his opponents, tortures them mentally and physically to death. The end of the process is a system of wooden troughs that fill with shit sludge, loose brown fecal matter. A white man from America

tells me that the black rulers toward the middle of Africa tend to be far more oppressive and cruel than white dictators on the coast of Africa. (The black rulers cruelly oppress their own people.) I'm working at the end of this shit sludge process, in the troughs. After a while, I suddenly realize that for some time I've been handling this fecal matter. It occurs to me that I've been working in this stuff with my hands and arms unprotected. There are blood products in these fluids—AIDS is in Africa. I wash, then rush into a hospital that's right there on the grounds. I go up to a foreign doctor from a European country and explain the situation. He takes me into a room and asks another, local doctor whether they have "stick" (by which he means a special detergent soap for washing before surgery). The local doctor says no and acts indifferent. Then the foreign doctor takes a surgical instrument and starts shaving the hair from one of my hands. He looks at me inquiringly. I say something about how I will withstand the pain. Suddenly, he cuts into the flesh around my wrist and peels back the skin. I hadn't expected this. I realize that he's looking to see whether the fecal matter—or how much of it—may have soaked through the skin.

My wife and I are strolling through some shops. We finally come to this one shop. My wife says, "You'll like the wood carvings here." (She's being ironical.) Just then, we come into a section where I see, up above on the right, on a kind of second floor, a display of large wooden animals—African ones: lions, tigers, elephants. They're hideous. We laugh. Then there's this big, real, live elephant asleep in the room. A black man is on top of the elephant. He gets the elephant to wake up. My wife and I are laughing to each other that the elephant is drowsy. When the elephant wakes up, however, it traps another black man in its legs. The black man gets free. Then the elephant gets another black man. It looks each time as if the elephant may have killed or maimed, severely injured, one of these men. One black man looks as if he's lying there injured. The other two black men leave all these men, women, and children in this area with the elephant. My wife and I are standing back behind a little fence, a circle, a ring. Then everyone starts running to escape from the elephant. Three little black children are in the middle of the ring. They're too young, too small, too weak. They have no one. One stumbles and falls. I leap into the ring, grab them, pick them up, run with them out of the ring to safety.

I shall not attempt to interpret these dreams. I will merely note that one person of whatever color may have an incredible variety of dreams of persons of another color, of another culture. One and the same person may dream of white supremacists and black bombers; homeless blacks and scapegoat devices; oppressive black African rulers, AIDS, and shitty, bloody matter under the skin; African animals, mayhem with a rogue elephant, and the rescue of black children. (In order to know all that "race" or color may mean to a dreamer, we need to interpret more than a single dream in isolation; we need to interpret many dreams, ideally a longitudinal series.)

Color-change dreams interest me because they directly pose questions of "racial" identity. Consider, for example, the following dream of an Asian-American woman, a "brown" woman:

I'm walking on a street. I see a figure coming toward me. I realize that it's Richard. He's huge, as tall as he is but much fatter than in real life. As I'm talking to him, I realize that he's becoming white, getting lighter— even as I look at him. Then there's this semi-articulated questioning about it and response from him—a nonverbal exchange about his condition. I'm asking him how he got this way. He stands there with raised eyebrows, open hands, palms up, and says, "Hmmmm"—as if to shrug and say, "Well, it's too complicated to explain." I'm astonished at his getting lighter. I can't explicitly, awkwardly say, "Richard, you're becoming white." I want to say that, but I can't, so I say, "Richard, you're like me." He puts his hands up to his face in horror. He hasn't realized it until now. (Because I've said it, he knows, but I handled it wrong.) He would have had to lie: put on a whole act about being angry and shocked, instead of quietly acknowledging it and moving on. He had become my color.

In the dream, a black man changes color, becomes the color of the brown woman, the dreamer. The dreamer and Richard were in the same profession. In fact, the dreamer had been a mentor to Richard. She had helped him obtain a job. The dreamer felt ambivalent about Richard. "He exemplifies something fine, a good ideology (which I don't think I do, really), but he irritates and annoys me," she said. "His ideas and attitudes about race are a chip on his shoulder—he's always complaining about people's racism, even when I don't think it's justified." She considered Richard "a neurotic, a semi-crazy person." She was, however, also "proud of him, proud of what he's worked on, proud of how he's gotten jobs, proud of how he has a high opinion of himself." She acknowledged that "I don't know him very well." The dreamer had immigrated to America from Asia ten years ago. There she had always "felt much lighter by contrast" than here. She felt "more attractive" in Asia, where being "fairer" than others meant being more attractive. She liked being fair. "I have never agonized about it or worried about my color the way some people do about theirs," she said. "I like being my color." In America, however, she was not fair: "Here I am very, very often aware of being the only non-white in a group." Her sense of "racial" identity—and of "racial" aesthetics—was relative to her cultural location. "Here," she said, "the prevailing norm is not to my advantage—there it is." She concluded: "What that means is that I experience myself as changing color."

In the dream, Richard had not actually become white—he was becoming whiter, or lighter, "becoming gray, as I watch," the dreamer said. "He was becoming nondescript, like me—neither black nor white, a sort of 'nothing' shade, an 'in-between' a 'light-black' or 'dark-white.' " She felt that "in America there are only two colors, white and black, and to be in-between is not to have an American identity—you can be American only if you're white or black." For the dreamer, "racial" identity was a legitimation crisis. "I'm not legitimate," she said. "My identity doesn't figure in any real-world thing—it's exotic, it's a joke, it's a non-identity." Being neither white nor black in America did have a certain advantage. It meant that she was "off the hook with all that racism crap." It meant that "I can't be accused of being a racist." Being brown, or in-between, was "a kind of safe place but also a kind of non-place, a place of irrelevance." In the multicultural imagination, color-change dreams like this one demonstrate all of the unconscious ambivalences and ambiguities of collective "racial" identity in relation to individual identity.

SELF AND OTHER: THE ZERO-SUM GAME

As I use the word "psychoanalysis," it includes the Freudian, Jungian, and all other schools of thought that, in spite of theoretical and practical differences, acknowledge the existence and the influence of the unconscious. What qualifies a therapy as psychoanalytic is neither the number of sessions per week and minutes per hour nor the sort of furniture, couch or armchair, in a room but an explicit recognition of the profundity of the psyche. What distinguishes psychoanalysis from other psychologies is that it is a "depth psychology," a psychology of the unconscious. I advocate a nonsectarian, nonpartisan, nondogmatic psychoanalysis that does not reduce differences in theory and practice to cults of personality but that encourages free and open critical inquiry and amicable, dialogical relations among all schools of thought.

In a sense, the word "multiculturalism" in the title of my book is a misnomer. One might accurately say that this is actually a book about biculturalism, about psychical relations between only two cultures, two "races," two colors: the white and the black. I do, I readily acknowledge, emphasize the white–black opposition. What is of immediate concern to me are the souls not only of black folk but also of white folk. This book is about the bigotry of everything white that, as W.E.B. Du Bois says, countenances "that personal disrespect and mockery, the ridicule and wanton license of fancy, the cynical ignoring of the better and the boisterous welcoming of the worse, the all-pervading desire to inculcate disdain for everything black, from Toussaint to the devil" (1903/1993: 13). The white–black opposition provides only one among many possible perspectives on the problem of "race" and racism. It is, however, the extreme example, and, in that respect, it serves as a paradigmatic case, a model for critical inquiries into other examples of prejudice and discrimination. I hope that this book will induce, perhaps inspire, others to scrutinize instances that are simply beyond the scope of this book.

If I could have a dream and fulfill one wish, it would be to encompass what I call *the diversity of diversity*—but that aspiration appears to me, at present, impossible. At least it seems to be beyond my own ability; it may be beyond anyone's. We have only begun to address the issue of diversity, of "self" and "other," in all its immensity. In one lifetime, we can have significant contact with only a few cultures besides our own, and to imagine that we can know even a few intimately well—that is, well enough not to render ourselves ridiculous in some vicarious, even perversely voyeuristic effort, as if we were merely sightseeing in some foreign territory or, worse, slumming in some ghetto—is to delude ourselves. Try as we may to become cosmopolitan, even with the best of intentions we inevitably remain provincial. The effort to transcend the limitations of our own accidental circumstances, to diversify our own "selves" in contact with "others," is fraught with difficulty. As the T-shirt defiantly asserts: "It's a Black Thing. You wouldn't understand." Or, as the poet and performance artist Sekou Sundiata contends: "It all depends on the skin you're livin' in."

Erik H. Erikson eloquently articulates the humanist position. As members of a nation, class, caste, sex, or "race," he says, we all have identities that "at the very minimum comprise *what one is never not*." As Erikson defines this "never not" identity, it is the inevitable, paradoxical basis of the very possibility of a transcendent, human identity. "What one is never not," he declares, "establishes the life space within which one may hope to become uniquely and affirmatively what one is—and then to transcend that uniqueness by way of a more inclusive humanity" (1969: 266). Such inclusivity is not a naive universalism that immediately asserts that we are all fundamentally human. Rather, it is a project that acknowledges what we are never not, affirms what we become, in process, as unique individuals, and ultimately comprises the prospect of a more comprehensive human identity through contact with a diversity of other cultures, other "races," other colors.

Communication between self and other is not impossible, but it is, as the history of "racial" relations amply demonstrates, extremely difficult. Although the self—"white," "black," or any other color—may desire contact with the other, it may also fear the consequences of it. The self may be afraid that the encounter is a zero-sum game in which any gain of identity from the other must necessarily result in an equal, or equivalent, loss of identity from the self. That is, the self may fear losing itself.

At the extreme, this is an intense fear of a potentially overwhelming experience in which self might suddenly, irreversibly, and unrecognizably become wholly other. This fear may amount to dread at the prospect of the self being entirely supplanted by the other. Such fear may result in phobia, paranoia, or panic: in such a defensive reaction that the self avoids all contact with the other or flees any too intimate encounter. The self may even attempt to dominate the other, rather than be dominated— or annihilate the other, rather than be annihilated. It is the "different" (or at least the ostensibly different), not the similar or identical, that evokes such responses. As the philosopher Horace M. Kallen says, "Sometimes we protect ourselves by ostracizing that different, sometimes by coercing, indenturing, or enslaving it, sometimes by liquidating it" (1956: 16). (There are, of course, many other possible, more moderate responses, but they all require a much less anxious, much less apprehensive attitude on the part of the self toward the other—toward the different.)

I believe that the zero-sum game is inadequate to the facts of identity formation and transformation because it does not acknowledge *psychical resilience and elasticity*. I prefer a more expansive, a more inclusive vision of communicative possibilities between self and other. The self is more resilient and more elastic than we may sometimes imagine (so, too, is the other). Identity formation and transformation entail not mere zero-sum gain and loss but multiplication of cultural possibilities in the construction of a resilient, elastic, multicultural self that expands to include the other. An encounter with the other can have a multiplier effect on the self. We may eventually contain multitudes. In contact with the other, even as we gain identity, we may still retain or maintain identity. (In the process, we may lose something, too, but it need not be ourselves; it may be only the bias that we project, consciously or unconsciously, onto the other.)

PSYCHICAL, PSYCHOANALYTIC, AND CULTURAL PLURALISM

The issue of diversity, in all of its ambiguities and ambivalences, seems to me to epitomize the contemporary, collective identity crisis. A differentiated psyche—I would say, a diversified psyche—is a psychoanalytic ideal. It also happens to be the multicultural ideal, and it is on that basis that I believe psychoanalysis and multiculturalism have something important to offer each other. A unified, or integrated, psyche is another psychoanalytic ideal. Psychoanalysis advocates a psyche in which the parts are not segregated but are integrated into a whole. In this respect, psychical integration has a purpose similar to or identical with that of "racial" integration. I should emphasize, however, that integration, whether psychical or "racial," is not an effort to render the separate constituents of any unity indistinguishable. The parts that separately constitute the whole remain distinct. Integration respects the differences among the parts, within the whole. The Jungian analyst Andrew Samuels has recently described psychical pluralism as an effort "to hold unity and diversity in balance"—that is, "to hold the tension between the one and the many," or between the whole and the parts (1989: 1).

Whereas Samuels emphasizes the pluralism of the psyche, the Freudian analyst Robert S. Wallerstein emphasizes the pluralism of psychoanalysis. Wallerstein addresses the historical trend toward pluralism within psycho-analysis as an institution. He notes that since the divergence of Jung and other dissenters from Freud, the International Psychoanalytical Associ-ation has managed to accommodate institutionally a variety of different perspectives—among them, Freudian, Kleinian, Lacanian, and Kohutian perspectives. The Jungian perspective is the exception to this rule. Insti-tutionally, it remains separate from the International Psychoanalytical Association. (For Jungian analysts, there is a comparable organization, the International Association for Analytical Psychology.) As Wallerstein observes, Jungian analysis "has endured worldwide as an alternative therapeutic system" (1988: 5–6).

Wallerstein does not so much advocate pluralism as acknowledge it. Thus he says that "we do indeed have several, or even many psychoanaly-ses today, and not one." As for Jungian analysts, Wallerstein mentions that they have recently "reappropriated the label psychoanalysis, calling themselves Jungian psychoanalysts and implying that only political and organizational issues, reflections of bygone struggles, keep them in a world apart." Although he states that he is "not in a position to have an adequately informed opinion on the psychoanalytic credentials of Jungian theory," he then immediately implies that Jungian analysis in all prob-ability does not qualify as a version of psychoanalysis (1988: 12). The evidence, such as it is, that Wallerstein cites for this tentative conclusion is one article by a Jungian analyst who argues that the doctoral disser-tation that Jung published in 1902 indicates that Jung had no capacity to appreciate the decisive importance of psychical conflict. "It is on the basis of evidence of this kind," Wallerstein says, "that I would in the end answer for myself whether Jung's psychology is truly a *psychoanalytic* psychology or not" (1988: 13). The obvious implication is that Wallerstein would answer in the negative: Freudian, Kleinian, Lacanian, Kohutian, and other perspectives are properly psychoanalytic; the Jungian perspec-tive is not.

Although I admire what Wallerstein says about psychoanalytic plural-ism as both fact and ideal, he perpetuates the historical exclusion of Jungian analysis. What Jung published almost a century ago, when he was only 27 years old, five years before he even met Freud, is hardly cogent evidence that contemporary Jungian analysis is not true psychoanalysis. In spite of psychoanalytic pluralism, it is evidently very difficult to let certain bygones be bygones. In a reply to Wallerstein, Samuels (1988) rejects the notion that Jungian analysts should call themselves psychoanalysts instead of analytical psychologists. As a pluralistic alternative, he recommends "depth psychology" as a comprehensive rubric for the unity that comprises the diversity of both psychoanalysis (for example, the Freudian, Kleinian, Lacanian, and Kohutian perspectives) and analytical psychology (the Jungian perspective). I should not like to quibble, but, for me, "depth psychology" is synonymous with "psychoanalysis"—that is, with all of the different schools of psychoanalytic thought, including the Jungian school—and the name "analytical psychology" is simply a rather infelicitous artifact of what seems, in retrospect, an absurdly acrimonious, quite unnecessary dispute between Freud and Jung: a conflict that to this very day compromises the integrity of psychoanalysis both as an institution and as a discipline that purports to be scientific.

It is not only psychical and psychoanalytic pluralism that concerns me. Any inquiry into multiculturalism must address what Kallen calls "cultural pluralism." In contrast to diversity, Kallen says that unity is "a future formation," an extension of "present imaginations" (1956: 47–8). That is, cultural pluralism is diversity in continuous process toward unity. Cultural pluralism describes "the ways that people who are different from one another do, in fact, come together and move apart." Kallen equates pluralism with democracy (which he identifies with the very idea of America). It epitomizes, he says, "the cultural ideal natural to a free world." For Kallen, cultural pluralism is a differentiated federation, "a federal union of diversities, not a diversion of diversities into undifferentiated unity" (1956: 51–2). Cultural pluralism is not so much "a unity discovered" as "a unification desired" (1956: 57). What interests Kallen is not an abstract intellectual concept but rather "the concrete intercultural total which is the culture of America" (1956: 98).

Cultural pluralism is thus a diversification, or differentiation, in continuous process toward a unification that is never a present actuality but always a future potentiality. To the extent that multiculturalism emphasizes multiplicity and appears to privilege diversity over unity, it may not seem to qualify as authentic cultural pluralism. It seems to me, however, that multiculturalism is perfectly consistent with cultural pluralism, at least as Kallen describes it. In both multiculturalism and cultural pluralism (or "interculturalism", as Kallen calls it), unity is no more (nor less) than an ideal to which diversity may aspire, as cooperation and consensus are ideals to which competition and conflict may aspire.

"RACE," RACISM, AND "RACIAL" PLURALISM

Throughout this book, I place the noun "race," the verb "racialize," the adjective "racial," and the adverb "racially" within quotation marks. From one position, of course, which the cultural anthropologist Ashley Montagu mentions, "One cannot combat racism by enclosing the word ['race'] in quotes" (1952: 284). Although the practice may belabor a point, I do so as a constant reminder that "race" is "so-called," that no such thing exists in any reality except the psychical reality of racists, as well as the theoretical reality of certain biologists and physical anthropologists.

"Race" is not a physical—that is, a biological—reality. It is an unscientific or pseudoscientific concept with potentially insidious consequences. I agree with the cultural critic Tzvetan Todorov, who observes that although racism exists, " 'race' itself does not exist" (1986: 370). If there are no "races," then, in the strict sense, there can be no "racial" pluralism. In a defense of affirmative action against recent attempts to abolish it, the sociologist Orlando Patterson offers an operational definition of "race." According to Patterson, "race" in the white–black sense has three meanings. First, it "refers to physical appearance." Blacks agree with whites, Patterson says, that this reference "should be a matter of no importance." Second, however, for blacks "race" refers to "surviving an environment in which racism is still pervasive." Patterson argues that the content of the character of blacks is the result of survival in spite of the adversity of racism. In this sense, "race" remains significant as a function of the persistence of racism. Third, "race" in America "connotes something positive: the subcultural heritage of African-Americans that in spite of centuries of discrimination has vastly enriched American civilization out of all proportion to the numbers, and treatment, of the group creating it." Although "race" does, operationally, have these three meanings, only the first is strictly a "racial" definition (in terms of differences in physical appearance, insignificant as they are). The second and the third are, respectively, characterological and cultural definitions. Because of—and in spite of—racism, blacks have developed a survival character and a rich culture (or "subculture")—both of which are vitally important to the multicultural project that Patterson calls "ecumenical America" (1995, 7 August: A, 13).

There is ethnic pluralism, but it is simply a variety of cultural pluralism. There is also a pluralism of physical differences (none of which, of course, are significant in any psychical sense), but there is no pluralism of "races" for the simple reason that there are no "races," as such. It is only the irrational persistence of racism, which categorizes people on the basis of insignificant physical differences such as skin color, that lends any credence to the notion of "racial" pluralism. There is multiculturalism, but there is no "multiracialism." If there were no racists, there would be no "racial" segregation and no necessity for any attempt at "racial" integration. It is cultural pluralism, not "racial" pluralism, that is the decisive issue. "Race" and "racial" pluralism obscure and confuse the issue, deflect attention from the diversity of diversity, the multiplicity of cultures that are the basis of all truly significant psychical differences between self and other.

Anything thought, felt, or done on the basis of "race," whether this thinking, feeling, or doing be positive, negative, or merely neutral, is by definition—or at least as I define the term—"racist." I thus reject the distinction that some individuals, including Todorov (1993: 90–1), employ between "racialism" as an ideological (or, I would say, more inclusively, a psychological) formation and "racism" as a behavioral formation. Racists are not simply racialists who put a "theory" into practice. I define "racism" to be any categorization of people on the basis of physical characteristics (such as skin color) that are indicative of putatively significant psychical differences, *whether these ostensible differences are positive or negative, honorific or defamatory.* By my definition, anyone who believes in the existence of "races" and categorizes people on that basis is a racist. This is, of course, a very broad definition that not everyone would accept. Some would argue that only negative categorizations are racist. Others would argue that, even if blacks categorize whites negatively on the basis of "race," they are not *effectively* racists, because they are not in a position of *power* to exercise "racial" domination over whites.

Todorov notes that, although biologists do acknowledge the physical differences that do so patently exist among us, contemporary biology "no longer uses the concept of race." As obsolete, even disreputable, as "race" may be as a biological concept, it is a pervasively influential notion, or preconception, that continues to condition the perception of physical differences. For racists, the only significant physical differences are, as Todorov says, "the immediately visible ones"—prominent among them, skin color (1993: 92). "Races" exist only in a virtual, psychical reality that racists propagandize on the basis of very obvious physical differences that are utterly insignificant as indicators of any psychical differences. This virtuality does not prevent racists from a presumption that "races" are real—and, of course, they are "real," if only psychically, to them.

UNINFORMATIVE CATEGORIES AND EMPTY SIGNIFIERS

For racists, colors function as natural, rather than cultural, categories. Physical differences such as skin color serve as indicators of ostensible psychical differences. As I have previously said:

> I am not denying that natural categories exist. I am merely asserting that they exist at a level of generality so abstract that they convey hardly any concrete information. It is this paucity of information that tends to render these categories ineffectual and irrelevant. Natural categories such as "racial" ones (in contrast to cultural categories such

as ethnic ones) are so vague and elusive that virtually the only purpose they serve is an utterly trivial and inconsequential one—or a vicious one, as an excuse for invidious distinctions and an opportunity for prejudicial projections.

Cultural categories are much more readily accessible as sources of pertinent information. Because it is difficult if not impossible to discuss natural categories to any satisfactory effect, it is especially significant that cultural categories afford such an impressively ample explanation of the diversity of the psyche. There is simply no need to resort immediately to natural categories to account for the existence of these differences.

(Adams 1991: 254–5)

People differ much more culturally than they do naturally, and there is no necessary connection between psychical differences and physical differences. The reason that natural categories like color are so useless (except to racists, for whom they are all too useful) is that they convey very little, if any, information about significant psychical differences. In this respect, the colors white and black—as in the white–black opposition that racists employ—are especially uninformative.

In one sense and one sense only have "racial" categories ever conveyed any significant information about psychical differences. For example, in the very first encounter between white Europeans and black Africans, the fact that these two peoples had existed separately for so long, for so many centuries, continents apart, meant that there happened to be an initial coincidence between natural (or "racial") differences (such as skin color) and cultural (or ethnic) differences. At that moment, there was a statistical probability that such physical differences as "whiteness" and "blackness" were more or less accurate indicators of psychical differences. Although these psychical differences were the result of cultural (not "racial") differences, skin color happened to be a rather reliable predictor of psychical differences. To the extent that racists subsequently (through, for example, the institutions of slavery, "Jim Crow" segregation, apartheid, or ghettoization) perpetuated the separate existence of whites and blacks, physical differences remained, historically, an indicator of psychical differences. The maintenance of psychical differences on the basis of "race" was, of course, the principal motivation for the separate and unequal discrimination against blacks by whites. Only in that respect has there been historically a *de facto* (not a necessary) connection between physical differences and psychical differences. (I should also emphasize that this historical coincidence between physical differences and psychical differences was never any necessary indicator of superiority and inferiority. In contrast to "difference," which is a strictly descriptive category, "superiority" and "inferiority" are evaluative categories that are always relative to some extrinsic, *ad hoc* criterion. In what context, from what perspective, is one group ostensibly superior and another inferior?)

As Michael Rustin, a sociologist and one of the few commentators to address the issue of "race" from a psychoanalytic perspective, says:

> In the racial case, virtually no differences are caught by "black" or "white", except those which are the effects of something else—culture, nationality, the experience of discrimination or of oppression: the result of hostility to the racial category as such. These differences are in the main the product, perhaps over a long period of history, of the irrational regard (and actions) of the other. This is paradoxically the source of racism's power. It is the fact that this category means nothing in itself that makes it able to bear so much meaning—mostly psychologically primitive in character—with so little innate resistance from the conscious mind.
>
> (1991: 63)

In short, it is cultural categories, not natural categories like color—ethnic, not "racial" categories—that provide abundant evidence of significant psychical differences. Counterintuitively, it is the low informational value of a category like color that enables racists to endow it with such high projective value. The relative poverty of color as an indicator allows it to be used—or abused—by racists who empower it with a wealth of significance and project it uncritically.

Rustin is not naive about the incorrigibility of racism. He does not minimize the difficulty of ameliorating—or eliminating—racism. He does not regard racism as an "ideological formation" that is directly amenable to conscious efforts at manipulation and alteration (1991: 73). He considers racism a psychological formation, a very deep structure indeed— an unconscious projection, a peculiarly intractable problem with an origin in a paranoid-schizoid developmental split between "good" and "bad" objects.

Although this object relations perspective seems to me ultimately too restrictive in theoretical and practical scope—and too developmentally reductive (I mean that it does not adequately take into account other factors, adult rather than infantile factors and collective rather than personal factors)—I appreciate the emphasis that Rustin places on the unconscious. Rustin suggests that while we develop conscious strategies and tactics to resist racism, we need to analyze the unconscious sources and vicissitudes of racism. Otherwise, the effort promises to be a mere exercise in futility. There is much that I admire in what Rustin says about "race" and psychoanalysis. I agree with him, for example, that the ultimate objective should be not an "anti-racist" position (which, by continuing to posit the existence of a "racist" other, necessarily perpetuates the white–black opposition) but a truly "non-racial" psychical reality (1991:

78). Although as I define "racism," there are black racists as well as white racists, it is white racism that requires the deepest psychological analysis. White racism is not just a scheme to deny certain people social, political, and economic rights. It is a mental (and moral) illness that we need to psychoanalyze.

Rustin approaches the topic of "race" semiotically. He notes that " 'race,' as such, is an empty signifier." This semiotic perspective does not imply that the signifier "race" has no signified, or meaning. "Race" has many meanings, which have been projected, both consciously and unconsciously, onto the other. Projection is, of course, a variety of reference. When a psychical content has been projected onto the other, that content has been referred (or transferred) to the other. When "race" has been projected onto the other, that other has been referred to as a "race." If the signifier "race" has both a signified and a referent, then how is it empty? According to Rustin, "race" is a signifier with no basis in scientific fact, "no rational foundation" (1991: 79). It is empty because it has no scientifically specifiable referent, no relation to any rationally determinate object in external, or physical, reality (however many unscientific and irrational referents it may have).

ARBITRARY CONSTRUCTS: COLOR, COLORISM, AND PEOPLE OF COLOR

In contrast to "race," color does exist—and so does colorism. Of course, the color of the skin is not the only physical feature that racists—separatists and supremacists, white or black, or any other color—refer to in the effort to distinguish themselves invidiously from others. In the most facile way, they "racialize" noses, eyes, lips, hair, and other organs, including the sexual organs. The color of the skin, however, is a conspicuous, perhaps the most prominent, referent of the signifier "race." For this reason, colorism is an especially pernicious variety of racism. What is so curious is that color difference, relative to the obvious similarities between people, as well as any number of other, more substantive differences between them, is such a trivial physical fact yet such an emphatic signifier. Freud notes that, paradoxically, "it is precisely the minor differences in people who are otherwise alike that form the basis of feelings of strangeness and hostility between them" (*SE* 11: 199). He does not explain this peculiarity except to say that it is an expression of narcissism. He simply observes that "the intolerance of groups is often, strangely enough, exhibited more strongly against small differences than against fundamental ones" (*SE* 23: 91).

For the cultural critic Henry Louis Gates, Jr, "racial" colors are not objectively real. "Who," he asks, "has seen a black or red person, a white, yellow, or brown?" If "black," "red," "white," "yellow," and "brown" are not absolutely empty signifiers, they are at the very least egregiously gross signifiers that do violence, rather than justice, to the incredible diversity of colors in external reality. As Gates says, "These terms are arbitrary constructs, not reports of reality" (1986: 6). (Perhaps we should also place "color" and all terms for colors within quotation marks.)

Gates apparently believes that what we need is a more accurate perception of the vast array of actual colors in external reality. If, rather than the arbitrary constructs "white," "black," "red," "brown," and "yellow" that we project onto people, we had more reliable reports of external reality, we would then presumably be in a position to appreciate exactly how fallacious it is to employ colors to categorize people as "races." This is one strategy and tactic that we might apply to the problem of colorism. An alternative, one that I tend to prefer, would emphasize not external reality but psychical reality. Perhaps what we need is a more imaginative vision of the immense variety of possible colors in psychical reality: all of the imaginable hues, shades, casts, tints, tones, and values.

From this perspective, the oppositional categorizations of colorism constitute a failure of imagination. It may be that what we need are not more reports of external reality but more arbitrary constructs—many, many more, as many as we can imagine, an innumerable number more than merely the five colors that Gates so aptly criticizes as inadequate— so that, by a *reductio ad absurdum*, the categorization of "races" in terms of colors eventually seems the preposterous fallacy that it, in fact, already is.

Like Gates, Naomi Zack also observes that although " 'black' and 'white' purport to categorize people racially on the basis of their skin color," few Americans "have skin the actual colors of objects that are accurately described as having black and white surfaces." She remarks that, from a certain scientific perspective, "black and white are anomalous." The science of optics defines "black" as "the perceptual experience of the absence of all colors from the visible spectrum" and "white" as "the perceptual experience of the presence of all colors from the visible spectrum." If black is optically an absence of color, then the designation "people of color," at least in reference to "blacks," is a contradiction in terms. As Zack says, "These optical facts make a joke out of the use of the sobriquet 'of color' for all non-white people" (1993: 169).

The Jungian analyst James Hillman (1992) quite properly notes that "we are all 'people of color.' " As long as we categorically oppose "white" people to "black" people (or to "red," "brown," or "yellow" people), however, we will continue to regard only some people as people of color. The category "people of color" excludes whites on the dubious basis that whiteness is colorless—while blackness, redness, brownness, and yellowness are colorful. The category is attractive to those who historically have been the victims of racist exclusion, often on the assumption that they were, in some "racial" respect, deficient in comparison with whites. There is thus an ironic aspect to the contemporary appeal of the category, for it affords a sense of solidarity among so-called black, red, brown, and yellow people, who now, for once, exclude so-called white people as "racially" deficient—at least in terms of skin pigment.

It is as if a psychoanalytic person of color—say, a black Freud—were suddenly to declare with a vengeance that pigmentation (rather than anatomy) is destiny. Just such an assertion, along with anti-Semitic remarks, is precisely what has earned notoriety for Leonard Jeffries, the controversial professor of African-American Studies at the City College of New York, for whom "the skin pigment melanin is the secret ingredient that makes blacks physically and mentally superior to whites" (Kriegel 1990, 3 May: A, 27).

In all probability, the source for this notion is the "theory" that the psychologists Alfred B. Pasteur and Ivory L. Toldson espouse about black soul and black expressive behavior, which includes "natural rhythm." Although they are not psychoanalysts, they propose a "Freudian" interpretation. According to Pasteur and Toldson, blacks are mentally healthier than whites because they are more behaviorally expressive and less defensively repressive. Most blacks "would probably have gone crazy" as a result of the oppression that they have suffered, had they not evolved a special capacity for behavioral expression (1982: 8). In effect, the "white man's burden" is the white man's unconscious. Whites are more repressed than blacks and therefore more unconscious—and, presumably, more neurotic. "The black/African mind," Pasteur and Toldson contend, "is one that appears not to be burdened by a massive unconscious area" (1982: 16).

A primary factor in black behavioral expression is ostensibly melanin, which is present not only in the skin, hair, and eyes but also in the brain, in the *substania nigra*. Pasteur and Toldson assert that melanin "appears to noticeably determine the quality of black expressive behavior, of *soul*" (1982: 30). They maintain that melanin possesses extraordinary qualities— that it is "impervious to destruction" and "unalterable by time." They cite a professor of dermatology who evidently says that "melanin in abundance, as in blacks, produces a superior human being, both mentally and physically" (1982: 31). This same authority also apparently considers "melanin to be the factor that accounts for black athletic superiority"— and not only that but also, at least potentially, for black longevity. According to the professor, in the absence of oppression, "blacks should live twice as long as whites," all because of the presence of melanin (1982: 34). Pasteur and Toldson conclude that the available evidence implies that "blacks are indeed more emotional, feeling, sensitive, and more soulful than whites as a result of their more heavily melanized pigment cells" (1982: 35). They declare that "the remarkable adaptation of blacks" not only to the natural environment but also to "slavery and oppression" is a consequence of "the sheer abundance of melanin in their bodies" (1982: 36). We have to infer, they say, that "the feat of black survival has been made possible by melanin quantity," which is basic "to black expressive behavior" (1982: 37).

Pasteur and Toldson—and Jeffries—thus present a "psychodermatological" perspective on "race" and racism. By a pseudoscientific appeal to pigment, they reverse the usual colorist valuation that white is superior and black inferior. They insist that a quantitative chemical factor, melanin abundance, produces a qualitative behavioral effect, the expression of black soul and all that it implies in a psychical sense. Pigmentation, they argue, assures that mental and physical superiority over whites is the evolutionary destiny of blacks. A truly "non-racial" (rather than a merely anti-racist) position, however, would repudiate all such racist imputations and would include everyone under the rubric "people of color." Whatever behavioral (and psychical) differences there may be between blacks and whites, however expressive blacks may be and however repressive whites may be, any significant differences are the result of culture (or ethnicity), not of nature (or "race")—and certainly not of melanin.

Chapter 2

Whiteness and blackness, nature and culture

If the very basis of the "logic" of racism is a patently false premise (that certain physical differences such as skin color are indicative of significant psychical differences), then why is racism so apparently incorrigible? This seems to me the fundamental enigma of racism. Although racism is demonstrably preposterous, it is also remarkably tenacious. "Race" is such a sensitive topic that many individuals are understandably reluctant to say anything even potentially controversial about it. They hesitate because of trepidation that what they might say could result in incomprehension or, worse, misconstrual. Historically, there are so many examples of individuals who, even if we credit them with the most innocent or benevolent of intentions, have said things that seem to us problematic or offensive, it is no wonder that individuals are apprehensive, even utterly silent on the issues of "race" and racism. I do not recommend imprudence of the sort that Jung exhibited in the 1930s when he raised the issue of possible collective psychical differences between Jews and "Aryans," Germans, Christians, or Europeans: he defiantly declared that "the first rule of psychotherapy is to talk in the greatest detail about all the things that are the most ticklish and dangerous, and the most misunderstood" (*CW* 10: 539, para. 1024). That, to me, is not the first rule of psychotherapy; the "basic rule" of psychoanalysis is not for the self to talk but for the self to listen, to invite the other to talk.

The question, however, remains: why does racism (or colorism) endure in spite of all efforts to eradicate it, especially when it is so obviously an erroneous conflation of mere external, surface appearances with internal, depth realities? One possible explanation is that there is, in all of us, a propensity (that is, a "natural" inclination) to racism. Are there factors in either "human nature" or "environmental nature" (or at the interface between the two) that predispose us to be racist? Is there a natural proclivity or susceptibility to racism? Even to entertain such a possibility is, of course, to offer racists an opportunity to misappropriate it for nefarious purposes. From a Jungian perspective, however, the mere fact that certain attitudes may be "natural" does not mean that they are

incorrigible. For Jungians, psychotherapy or psychoanalysis is, like alchemy, an *opus contra naturam*—that is, a "work against nature." The
therapeutic or analytic process is, by definition, an "unnatural act."

In the attempt to explain racism, is "culture" the necessary and sufficient condition, or is "nature" also a factor? Is racism simply a cultural
artifact, merely the accidental historical product, for example, of colonialism, imperialism, and slavery, or is it also, in some peculiar sense, a
natural fact? Are prejudice and discrimination on the basis of skin color
simply a convenient excuse for "whites" to exploit and dominate
"blacks?" Is the colorism of some blacks who apparently prefer, as Spike
Lee documents in the film *School Daze*, "light" skin over "dark" skin
simply the internalization, under duress, of the historically racist values
of some whites? Are there non-colorist cultures, or do all cultures tend
to be colorist in the white–black, light–dark sense? Is there something
about "whiteness" and "blackness," "lightness" and "darkness," that
tends to influence us all to misapply them in racist ways to something as
superficial as skin? Do the colors "white" and "black" have a natural,
universal, essential, or "archetypal" significance? Or are all colors, as
Edward Shils asserts, meaningless in themselves? Although Shils is a
sociologist, he discusses color as a physicist might:

> Color is just color. It is a physical, a spectroscopic fact. It carries no
> compellingly deducible conclusions regarding a person's beliefs or his
> position in any social structure. It is like height or weight—the mind
> is not involved. Yet it attracts the mind; it is the focus of passionate
> sentiments and beliefs. The sentiments color evokes are not the senti-
> ments of aesthetic appreciation. Nor does color have any moral signifi-
> cance; color is not acquired or possessed by leading a good or bad life.
> No intentions are expressed by color; no interpretations of the world
> are inherent in it; no attachments are constituted by it. The mind is
> not at work in it, and it is not a social relationship. It is inherently
> meaningless.
>
> (1967: 279)

Shils does not believe that any aesthetic, moral, social, or other meanings
inhere in colors. Rather, it is we who endow color with meaning. Yet
even Shils says that color is mentally (or psychically) attractive and
evocative, as if something inherent in it exerts an influence on us.

Contemporary attempts to explain racism tend to regard it as a strictly
cultural rather than, in any sense, a natural phenomenon. The assumption
is that no one is racist by nature but only by culture—by certain untenable
attitudes that are entirely arbitrary and conventional. Why, if it is so
unnatural, is racism so obstinately intractable, so apparently resistant to
logical, moral, ideological, social, and political suasion? Is racism, as the
culturalist explanation contends, simply an accident of history, or is there

more to it than that? These questions seem to me difficult ones. I am unsure that they even have answers.

Freud was fond of comparing himself to Copernicus, who decentered the earth as Freud decentered the ego (*SE* 16). What was important about the Copernican revolution was that it demonstrated, once and for all, that only from a naive (Freud would also say, a narcissistic) perspective does the earth *appear* to be at the center of the universe. The Copernican revolution was an irreversible triumph of intuition over sensation, of reality over mere appearance. Strictly phenomenally, the sun appears to revolve around the earth, when actually the earth simply rotates on an axis while it revolves around the sun. The Copernican revolution thus exposes just how deceptive certain appearances can be. Before Copernicus, a "natural," or purely phenomenal, perspective seemed entirely adequate. Now we realize just how unsatisfactory it is. It seems to me possible that at least one of the bases of racism is also a deceptively "natural," naive, and narcissistic perspective that privileges surface appearances over depth realities. If so, nothing less than another "Copernican revolution," an *opus contra naturam* that would decenter the color "white," is now in order. To begin to address the nature–culture, white–black issue, I wish to present for consideration what I regard as provocative speculations on "whiteness" and "blackness" by a number of individuals—the historian Winthrop C. Jordan, the cultural critic Tzvetan Todorov, the Jungian analyst James Hillman, and the novelist Herman Melville—who contribute, in various ways, to the controversy over the significance of color.

WHITE OVER BLACK

Jordan provides a culturalist account of the white-over-black encounter between the English and Africans in the sixteenth century. "The most arresting characteristic of the newly discovered African was his color," Jordan says. "Travelers rarely failed to comment upon it; indeed when describing Negroes they frequently began with complexion" (1968: 4). The very first impression of the English was the "blackness" of Africans. The description of Africans as "black" was an exaggeration, "which in itself suggests that the Negro's complexion had powerful impact" on the perceptions of the English. "Blackness," Jordan asserts, "became so generally associated with Africa that every African seemed a black man" (1968: 5).

According to Jordan, part of the explanation for this hyperbole is that the primary contact of the English was with West Africa and the Congo, "where men were not merely dark but almost literally black" (1968: 6). Suddenly, one of the lightest peoples encountered one of the darkest peoples, with the result that "black" seemed to the English an entirely adequate descriptive term. Although some of the English did accurately perceive the variety of complexions among Africans—not only black but also yellow and other colors—the white–black opposition, in this instance, dominated the encounter between self and other.

In addition, Jordan notes, the English, as northern Europeans (in contrast to southern Europeans) were probably more apt to endow "the concept of blackness" with special significance. "No other color except white," he contends, "conveyed so much emotional impact." Well before the encounter with Africans in the sixteenth century, the English had already assigned a variety of negative aesthetic and moral values to the word "black." To be black was to be dirty, ugly, evil, deadly, devilish. To be white was to be clean, beautiful, good, lively, and godly. "No other colors so clearly implied opposition," Jordan remarks (1968: 7).

As a historian, Jordan does not attempt to offer any ultimate explanation for the white–black opposition. He does not argue, for example, that it was in any sense natural for peoples with lighter skin to oppose themselves to peoples with darker skin. Nor does he maintain that the white-over-black value judgment has any universal implication or any general application. He describes a local case at a quite particular time and place, the initial contact between the English and Africans. Jordan details the circumstances—the vagaries of history—under which certain "whites" first experienced certain "blacks" and judged them to be inferior in both aesthetic and moral terms. The consequence of the encounter, he suggests, was contingent on preexistent cultural values that the English conventionally associated with the color black—and, by extension, arbitrarily associated with the "black" skin of Africans.

WHITE–LIGHT–DAY VERSUS BLACK–DARK–NIGHT

In contrast to Jordan, Todorov suggests that the white-over-black value judgment is virtually universal. Whereas Gates mentions five colors, Todorov mentions three. Todorov asserts that "the most popular classification works with three races: white, yellow, and black." In this classification, yellow occupies an intermediate position between the extremes of white and black, with the result that, for racists, "there are only two real races, or rather two poles, white and black, between which all the races are arrayed." Todorov says that the reasons for this polarity may not all be a function of culture. That is, the white–black opposition may not be entirely arbitrary or conventional. According to Todorov, factors in nature may influence the formation of this "racial" dichotomy:

This opposition may have captured attention for reasons that have to do with universal symbolism: white–black, light–dark, day–night pairings seem to exist and function in all cultures, with the first term of each pair generally preferred. The history of humanity being what it is, the exemplary racism, racism par excellence, is thus that of whites toward blacks.

(1993: 95)

That is, it may not be merely an accident that this "racial" opposition exists, since white tends to be associated universally with such ubiquitous natural phenomena as light and day, while black tends to be associated with dark and night. The possibility that factors in nature may predispose us all to a symbolically universal, racist polarization of whiteness and blackness, I should note, is hardly central to what Todorov has to say about human diversity. He does not emphasize the polarity, as if it were simply a natural fact, utterly resistant to cultural influence; he merely mentions it in passing.

If, however, almost all cultures do, indeed, privilege the associations "white–light–day" over the associations "black–dark–night," then this is suggestive, although hardly definitive, evidence that a general preference for white over black may not be a choice without a certain constraint. Todorov does not attempt to explain why so many cultures apparently judge white, light, and day more valuable than black, dark, and night. He simply observes that, historically, they have evidently done so. The implication, however, seems to be that it is improbable that this value judgment would be so prevalent unless nature conditioned culture in ways that may be either gross or subtle. Such a conclusion is inimical to what is perhaps a rather presumptuous notion that we entertain about freedom of choice as it applies to us. Are we, in fact, as free to choose to be either racist or non-racist as we suppose we are?

What is the nature of black, dark, and night? What exactly is it about them that seems to countenance racist projections? Does the "actual world" that we inhabit as humans naturally incline us to prefer white, light, and day over black, dark, and night? Does the connection between sight and light on a planet like the earth that rotates in relation to a star like the sun happen to predispose us through evolutionary adaptation to feel certain emotions about the dark that disconcert us? Is it that it is easy for us to see in the light of day and hard for us to see in the dark of night, so that, by nature, the diurnal seems positive and the nocturnal negative? For example, is it that we are naturally—that is, instinctually—afraid of the night, the dark, the black? Do we (and especially people with "white" skin), by a fallacious but virtually inexorable extension of a spurious logic, then tend naturally to fear people with "black" skin and, quite literally, to denigrate them? We might speculate about a "possible world," an alternative world the very opposite of the one that we inhabit. Would we then prefer black, dark, and night over white, light, and day and tend to be racist in reverse?

The Jungian analyst Robert Bosnak distinguishes between what he calls images of "African" blackness and images of "Thanatos" blackness. Images of African blackness are not universal; they are stereotypical images that the self may employ in either a positive or a negative "racial" (or racist) sense and project onto an other. In contrast to African blackness, Thanatos blackness "has to do with the night—and the fears that come up in the night." According to Bosnak, Thanatos blackness "has nothing to do with race." Images of Thanatos blackness are universal; they are archetypal images:

> Night and fear and death and also romance and love—all the things that are related to night—are transcultural. Something about the night does something to humans, makes us afraid, makes us imagine. That is another kind of black than the racial black. There will be thanatic black figures in the dreams of people from all kinds of different races.
> (Adams 1992: 25)

The problem would seem to be that racists do not distinguish, as Bosnak does, between these two very different kinds of blackness. Instead, racists conflate African blackness and Thanatos blackness, "racial" blackness and nocturnal blackness, and project fear of the dark night onto "black" people.

CULTURAL HYBRIDIZATION: COMMUNICATION AS TRANSLATION

What possible solution does Todorov propose to the problem of racism? If racism is in part—perhaps in large part—a function of nature, then it is a problem considerably more difficult to eradicate than we may naively suppose it to be. To combat racism effectively, we need to know exactly how incorrigible it is—and why. Todorov is, in this respect, apparently more pessimistic than I am about the persistence of racism. "Is it bound to disappear in the coming years—as everyone, or almost everyone, appears to hope?" he asks. "We may be allowed our doubts" (1993: 95). According to Todorov, the only possible, practical solution is a natural— in this case, a sexual one. To eliminate racism, we would evidently have to eliminate "races." Thus Todorov declares: "The solution involves racial mixing, that is, the disappearance of physical differences" (1993: 96).

If all physical differences between "races" were eventually to disappear through sexual intercourse and "interracial" procreation, then racists would have no basis for "racial" classifications. Presumably, in some indefinite future, we would all, through literal miscegenation, become nondescript. We would all become the same "race"—that is, no "race" at all, only a "human race," with no physical differences, including no differences in color. There would no longer be any physical differences that could serve racists as indicators of ostensible psychical differences. "Racial" mixing would simply render racism obsolete.

I consider this an unnecessarily extreme, utopian (or dystopian) position. Personally, I would abhor—and I believe that Todorov would, too—the disappearance of all physical differences. Although the members of my own family—myself, my brother, and my sister—all proudly have "racially" mixed marriages with "racially" mixed children, what Todorov calls in another context the "cultural hybrid" seems to me just as viable a solution as any natural hybrid. It is in this sense that Todorov regards Malintzin, Doña Marina, or La Malinche (the indigenous woman who, as a translator for the Mayans, the Aztecs, and the Spaniards during the conquest of Mexico, facilitated communication) "as the first example, and thereby the first symbol, of the cross-breeding of cultures" (1984: 101).

In this respect, we do not need literal miscegenation but metaphorical hybridization: an encounter in which self and other have an opportunity to achieve what Todorov calls nonviolent communication rather than violent confrontation. "Nonviolent communication," Todorov notes, "exists, and we can defend it as a value" (1984: 182). He says that "we want *equality* without its compelling us to accept identity; but also *difference* without its degenerating into superiority/inferiority." That is, we do not want self and other to be equal only on the condition that they become identical—nor do we want them to remain different only on the condition that the self is superior and the other inferior. The ultimate objective is to experience "difference in equality" (1984: 249). This may be easier said than done, but however difficult it may be, Todorov contends that it is through cultural hybridization that we may eventually accomplish it.

In addition to the natural (or sexual) solution, Todorov thus offers a cultural (or communicative) solution to the problem of racism. Whereas literal miscegenation would obliterate all physical differences, cultural hybridization would simply experience physical differences for what they are: nothing more nor less than an external reality, a mere appearance, that has no necessary connection to any psychical reality. The result would be what I call *indifference to difference*—that is, indifference to physical difference as any indicator of psychical difference. The cultural hybrid would be indifferent to how physically different we may happen to be. "Race" or color would simply be psychically irrelevant.

The emphasis would be on strictly psychical differences and on the possibilities of communication between self and other. For Todorov, translation is decisive. The self needs to learn to speak the "language" of the other. Effective communication between self and other requires not only verbal but also cultural fluency. The cultural hybrid is a mediator who articulately, even eloquently, translates the psychical differences—the psychical idioms—between self and other. However much racism may be a natural problem, the hope would seem to be for a cultural solution, one that might include sexual intercourse but that would emphasize communicative intercourse. (Sexual relations can, of course, be a variety of communicative relations between self and other.)

ARCHETYPAL WHITE SUPREMACY

Like Todorov, Hillman also argues that there is a virtually universal (or, since he is a Jungian analyst, an archetypal) preference for white over black. Evidence demonstrates, he asserts, that it is not only white Europeans and white Americans but also black Africans who judge white to be more valuable than black. In this sense, he says, we are all white supremacists. According to Hillman, the universality of this value judgment "suggests that dilemmas in society attributed to ethnic bigotry have sources that are fundamentally difficult to modify." (He does *not* say, I should emphasize, that they are impossible to alter.) The difficulty is that "the fantasy of white supremacy," which imagines white to be superior and black to be inferior, "is archetypally inherent in whiteness." Hillman defines the archetypal as the "geographically distributed, temporally enduring, and emotionally charged" (1986: 29). What motivates Hillman is a determination not to minimize what he considers to be a fundamental difficulty in modifying the racist imagination. In this respect, the objective is to "indicate a psychological mode of ameliorating the archetypal curse of supremacy beyond the usual and necessary societal measures" (1986: 30).

Hillman presents a variety of evidence: ethnographic, etymological, lexical, mythological, alchemical, historical, and literary. All of these sources cumulatively tend to privilege white over black. For example, Hillman cites the anthropologist Victor Turner, who describes the color classification of certain black Africans, the Ndembu of Zambia. Turner discusses three colors: white, red, and black. "Of the three," he says, "white seems to be dominant and unitary, red ambivalent, for it is both fecund and 'dangerous,' while black is, as it were, the silent partner, the 'shadowy third,' in a sense opposed to both white and red, since it represents 'death,' 'sterility,' and 'impurity'" (1967: 68).

To the Ndembu, white tends to have a positive value, black, a negative value. "Even human beings, Negroes though they are, are classified as 'white' or 'black' in terms of nuances of pigmentation," Turner notes. "There is here an implied moral difference and most people object to being classified as 'black'" (1967: 69). Turner lists "the basic senses" of white and black in the Ndembu color classification (1967: 69–71):

White
goodness

making strong or healthy
purity
to lack (or be without) bad luck or misfortune
to have power
to be without death
to be without tears
chieftainship or authority
when people meet together with ancestor spirits
life
health
begetting or bringing forth young
huntsmanship
giving or generosity
to remember
to laugh
to eat
to multiply
to make visible or reveal
to become mature or elder
to sweep clean
to wash oneself
to be free from ridicule

Black
badness or evil, bad things
to lack luck, purity, or whiteness
to have suffering or misfortune
to have diseases
witchcraft or sorcery
death
sexual desire
night or darkness

Turner summarizes the white–black, positive–negative oppositions of the Ndembu in a serial array:

> A brief survey of the senses attributed by informants to "white" and "black" respectively indicates that these can mostly be arrayed in a series of antithetical pairs, as for example: goodness/badness; purity/ lacking purity; lacking bad luck/lacking luck; lacking misfortune/misfortune; to be without death/death; life/death; health/disease; laughing with one's friends/witchcraft; to make visible/darkness, and so forth.
>
> (1967: 74)

Turner merely reports these associations; he does not state that they are evidence that this color classification is a function of any inherent—that is, any natural—order of things. He does not say that it is collectively intrinsic to either the conscious or unconscious of the Ndembu in particular or of black Africans in general. Hillman, however, concludes that such a consistent classification of white and black in terms of positive and negative is an indication that whiteness has had archetypal supremacy over blackness in the psyches of both whites and blacks.

Perhaps I should note that Hillman is not the only analyst to present evidence that at least some black Africans tend to regard the color black as negative. The Freudian analyst Wulf Sachs recounts a dream in which John Chavafambira, a black South African medicine man, or *nganga*, interprets whiteness as good luck and blackness as bad luck, even death:

> *I am given four white pills. Very small and very white. These pills are to clean my body and blood. White eggs and white pills always bring luck. Your medicine is wonderful medicine. All people now will be talking about me and I will get very rich. It's not lucky to see black in a dream, because black means dead people.*
>
> (1947: 133)

Although this dream is evidently a transference dream in which the dreamer receives from Sachs, a white "medicine man," or psychoanalyst, white pills to clean or cure him, the fact remains that Chavafambira classifies the color black negatively in contrast to the color white. This classification seems not to be simply an idiosyncratic personal preference on the part of Chavafambira but an interpretation with a basis in pervasive collective notions about the significance of blackness and whiteness. (This one example is, of course, merely suggestive. It proves nothing conclusive about whether such collective notions are natural or only cultural.)

THE WHITE SHADOW AND SHADES OF WHITENESS

Hillman identifies three primary associations to the color white: (1) heaven, divinity, and spirituality; (2) innocence, purity, and perfection; (3) femininity, effeminacy, and vulnerability. (Of course, in a culture that emphasizes masculinity and heterosexuality, this third association to the color white is hardly a positive value.) The archetypal problem with whiteness, Hillman contends, is its own unconsciousness, which apparently prevents it from recognizing its own shadow, which is not black but white—and potentially psychopathological. He declares that *"white casts its own white shadow"* (1986: 38).

According to Hillman, the problem is that we assert an opposition between whiteness and blackness rather than acknowledge differences between whiteness and blackness. "Differences neither compete, contradict nor oppose," he says. "To be as different as night and day does not require an opposition of night and day." Differences simply contrast. White and black are not opposites in any ontological sense. It is we who oppose them, we who unimaginatively perpetrate the white–black opposition. Our opposing them "does not entail an ontic necessary opposition, that in their nature and being black and white are opposites" (1986: 39).

White is a color that presumes that it is never wrong but always right (morally and otherwise); it is a light that shines so bright that it blinds the eye—obliterates all differences, all other shadows, all other shades of color. The differences within blackness and within whiteness are just as important as any differences between them. For example, Zack notes that "in the old lower South," the skin colors of people of mixed "race" were called " 'coffee,' 'almond,' 'almond shell,' 'piney,' 'honey,' 'ivory,' 'mahogany,' 'tan,' and so on" (1993: 72). Similarly, in commenting on the complexities of complexion, Hillman says that he has it on authority that "American black vernacular is full of shades for so-called black people: yellow, brown, dusky, coffee-colored, blue-black, even pink." Although so-called white people also have many shades—for example, "ruddy, pearly, tanned, peaches-and-cream or sallow"—this variety, however, "collapses to the one category": to the putative uniformity of white. As Hillman says, whiteness "rejects distinctions" (1986: 40).

In contrast to this undifferentiation, what Hillman proposes is an inquiry into "the varieties of whiteness." Rather than assume that there is only one kind of white (and no degrees of it), he asks: "What *sort* of white in this dream, in that behavior: deathly? bridal? lamblike? milky? Which *shade* of white: blinding? ashen? silvery?" According to Hillman, the differentiation of white is a fundamentally difficult project because white is archetypally oppositional. Although white and black are not opposites, are not "inherently opposed," the color white opposes itself to the color black: there is an archetypal predisposition in whiteness "to imagine in oppositions." If, as Hillman maintains, *"the supremacy of white depends on oppositional imagining"* (1986: 41), then any ultimate equality among colors will depend on the possibility of differential imagining.

MODERNISM AND REFERENTIALITY, POSTMODERNISM AND REFLEXIVITY

We will not be able effectively to address the issue of white supremacy, Hillman suggests, until we are able to imagine differentially rather than oppositionally—and this effort will require a postmodernist, reflexive optics rather than a modernist, referential optical illusion. Instead of referring to objects in the external world, we will all, white and black, need to reflect further on ourselves—and on whiteness itself. Modernism assumed that consciousness referred to "something literal, opaque, outside itself—the referent." In the final analysis, however, it "could not escape the white of its own eyes." It had to admit that consciousness "is supremely solipsistic": that perception of the object in external reality is mediated—and often obscured, or occluded—by a projection onto it of a whiteness that exists only in the mind's, or the imagination's, eye. In pursuing a referent external to consciousness, modernism was merely "desperately seeking the obscure object of its desire." Eventually, modernism had to acknowledge what Hillman calls a "double delusion": that consciousness "does not really require another" but simultaneously "really does refer to another." In an effort to avoid this paradox, modernism "had to invent the unconscious in order to remind consciousness that it could never be as white"—that is, as objective—"as it wished" (1986: 53). The conscious–unconscious opposition was thus not so much a discovery as an invention, an attempt to perpetuate a pretense: the objectivity of the conscious. In the process, modernism relegated subjectivity to the unconscious.

Although, in contrast to modernism, postmodernism denies referentiality (and affirms reflexivity), it does not deny the existence of the object in external reality. Postmodernism is epistemologically, not ontologically, skeptical. "To deny the referent," Hillman notes, "is merely to state that what's out there is not knowable as referent or ever to be referred to as referent." Paradoxically, this unknowability "affirms the thing," preserves and protects the object as such, which we can never be sure we know. The object does not become known by reference to it. "The knower becomes known through the statements of his knowing," Hillman says. In effect, postmodernism reverses the old racist epithet: "Now, it's the overseer in the woodpile, *is* the woodpile" (1986: 54).

There is no knowledge without a knower, no object without a subject. In postmodernism, there is no subject–object opposition. From this perspective, a psychoanalysis that would effectively challenge the supremacy of whiteness, the supremacy of consciousness, would eschew the white–black, conscious–unconscious oppositions (in fact, all oppositions whatsoever, including the subject–object, self–other oppositions) and, instead, emphasize differences in degree rather than kind. It would accentuate the nuances.

The solution that Hillman proposes to the problem of racism requires reflection and imagination—or reimagination. According to him, we all need to reflect on the white of our own eyes, the white of our own imagination's eye, the white overseer in our own woodpile, in order to see how we have unconsciously projected a white shadow onto objects in external reality and uncritically opposed whiteness to blackness. Whiteness is not pure consciousness, or pure objectivity; it has its own unconsciousness, its own subjectivity. There is no psychical purity any more than there is any "racial" purity. Whiteness has reigned archetypally supreme for so long only because it has denied the differences that do exist within it. Just as there are many different degrees of blackness and not just one kind, so there are many different degrees of whiteness. If, for once, we were to reimagine whiteness—that is, if we were to imagine it differentially (rather than oppositionally in relation to blackness)—then there would be hope for color equality and no more white supremacy.

A WHALE OF A WHITENESS

It is not only Todorov and Hillman who inquire into the very nature of the color white. In *Moby-Dick*, Melville—or, rather, Ishmael—also contemplates the enigmatic effect of whiteness. Jung considers *Moby-Dick* "the greatest American novel" for the vision that it affords of the collective dimension of the unconscious (*CW* 15: 88, para. 137). *Moby-Dick* is a novel of immense psychoanalytic importance (Adams 1982, 1983, 1984/85, 1988). It is also a novel of multicultural importance. Although "race" is not the dominant theme of the novel, *Moby-Dick* is a "book of color."

What, Ishmael asks, is a man's skin color? "It's only his outside," he concludes. Ishmael declares that a man can be honest in any sort of skin (Melville 1851/1988: 21). He also repudiates the racism of those who regard him and Queequeg as improper companions—"as if," he notes ironically, "a white man were anything more dignified than a whitewashed negro" (1851/1988: 60). Ishmael thus offers a commentary on the superficiality of skin color; in this instance, whiteness is a mere gloss on blackness. Under the surface and at a depth, whites are nothing better, nothing more, than blacks.

It is in "The Whiteness of the Whale" chapter, however, that Melville devotes most attention to the color white. The chapter includes only one mention of the apparently universal "racial" preference for white over black. Ishmael says of whiteness that "this pre-eminence in it applies to the human race itself, giving the white man ideal mastership over every dusky tribe" (1851/1988: 189). Is this a racist comment by Ishmael—or by Melville? Is this an affirmation that whites are ideally the "racial" masters of blacks (who are presumably, by an extension of this logic, ideally slaves), or is it merely an assertion that such mastery is only an ideal of racist whites? The word "ideal" is, at the very least, ambiguous— although the prior, unambiguously anti-racist remark by Ishmael about whiteness as mere whitewash is obviously inconsistent with any racist idealization of a white–black, master–slave discourse.

What Ishmael says about "race" and the color white—and what he may or may not mean in that respect—is hardly what is most significant about the chapter. Melville addresses whiteness from what is, in effect, a phenomenological perspective. Ishmael believes that there is some essence to the phenomenon of whiteness. He posits something essential in the very nature of whiteness. It is this essential something, so difficult if not impossible to describe, that so engrosses Ishmael.

The white whale evokes in Ishmael a horror that is "vague, nameless" and "so mystical and well nigh ineffable" that it all but defies comprehension. "It was the whiteness of the whale," he says, "that above all things appalled me." (The whiteness of the whale appalls Ishmael in the sense that it horrifies him, but, if Melville is in all probability capable of a pun that is consistent with the imaginative intent of the novel, the whiteness of the whale may also appall him in other senses. For example, it may pale him, or whiten him, so that Ishmael is almost as white, or as pale, as the whale is. It may also pall him in the sense that it depletes and depresses him, or perhaps even deadens him, as a shroud drapes a coffin and corpse—an image that Ishmael does eventually mention in the chapter.) In desperation, Ishmael says that he can hardly hope, except by "some dim, random" effort, to attempt to explain the effect that the whiteness of the whale has on him, although he must try to do so (1851/1988: 188).

In many instances, Ishmael observes, it seems as if whiteness were "imparting some special virtue of its own" to objects. He provides many examples of how whiteness endows objects with positive value, but he also provides many more examples of how it invests them with negative value. Actually, it is more accurate to say that he describes how some essence in whiteness enhances both positive and negative values that are already present in objects. However much whiteness, in association with objects that are "sweet, and honorable, and sublime," may seem to suggest that the color has an essentially positive value, this notion is, in fact, a fallacy. Thus Ishmael says of whiteness that "there yet lurks an elusive something in the innermost idea of this hue, which strikes more of panic to the soul than that redness which affrights in blood." Although this something in the qualitative aspect of whiteness may elude description, it nevertheless seems to exert an extreme influence and sensationally to increase the negative value of objects. "This elusive quality it is," Ishmael elaborates, "which causes the thought of whiteness, when divorced from more kindly associations, and coupled with any object terrible in itself, to heighten that terror to the furthest bounds." What is it, he asks, but whiteness that makes certain horrible objects "the transcendent horrors they are?" (1851/1988: 189).

Ishmael admits that individuals with only "common apprehension" do not regard "this phenomenon of whiteness" as he does, "as the prime agent in exaggerating the terror of objects otherwise terrible." He also concedes that individuals of "unimaginative mind" do not experience any of the terror that "to another mind almost solely consists in this one phenomenon, especially when exhibited under any form at all approaching to muteness or universality" (1851/1988: 193). (By "muteness," Melville probably means an experience of whiteness that is felt but that is not—and perhaps cannot be—expressed.)

Ishmael wonders why whiteness "appeals with such power to the soul"—why it is paradoxically not only "the most meaning symbol of spiritual things" but also "the intensifying agent in things the most appalling to mankind." He speculates on the reasons why whiteness in association with certain objects has such an effect on them—and on us:

> Is it that by its indefiniteness it shadows forth the heartless voids and immensities of the universe, and thus stabs us from behind with the thought of annihilation, when beholding the white depths of the milky way? Or is it, that as in essence whiteness is not so much a color as the visible absence of color, and at the same time the concrete of all colors; is it for these reasons that there is such a dumb blankness, full of meaning, in a wide landscape of snows—a colorless, all-color of atheism from which we shrink?

Perhaps, Ishmael conjectures, it is "the great principle of light," which "for ever remains white or colorless in itself," that accounts for the dread of whiteness. Ultimately, he simply says that "of all these things the Albino whale was the symbol" (1851/1988: 195).

ESSENTIALISM, RELATIVITY, GUILT BY ASSOCIATION, AND PROJECTION

Melville does not attempt to propose a solution to the problem of racism. That is not the particular purpose of the chapter. Rather, Melville has a more general, phenomenological interest. He ponders the nature of whiteness, in itself, in association with objects. As Ishmael describes the essence of whiteness, it is a certain intensity. The nature of whiteness is to function as an intensifier. According to Ishmael, whiteness—like no other color—intensifies the effect that objects, either positive or negative, have on us. The chapter surveys various associations of whiteness with objects and, in the process, subverts any notion that whiteness has an essentially positive value. In the context of racism, this is hardly an inconsequential contribution.

In effect, Melville both essentializes and relativizes whiteness. If whiteness has no essential positive (or negative) value but only an essential intensity in association with positive and negative objects, then the value of whiteness is always relative to the value of objects. Nothing is either good or bad about whiteness, but associating it with good or bad objects intensifies that goodness or badness and, by a fallacious logic, makes whiteness itself seem good or bad. If a whale seems horrible, then a white whale will seem even more horrible; if a person seems horrible, then a white person will seem even more horrible; if a "race" seems horrible, then a white "race" will seem even more horrible—until whiteness acquires guilt by association and itself seems a horror.

What if Melville had included in *Moby-Dick* a chapter on blackness? What might the result have been then? In a critical appreciation of Nathaniel Hawthorne (to whom, incidentally, he dedicates *Moby-Dick*), Melville does discuss blackness. He commends Hawthorne for an unsentimental attitude toward human nature. There is not only a light side to the soul but also a dark side, "like the dark half of the physical sphere." This darkness is "a blackness, ten times black." Melville is uncertain whether "this mystical blackness" is, for Hawthorne, simply a means to an aesthetic end, which is "the wondrous effects he makes it to produce in his lights and shades," or whether there is some unconscious, psychical reality to it—a blackness "perhaps unknown to himself" in the very soul of Hawthorne. Be that as it may, the source of "this great power of blackness" in Hawthorne is an association with "Innate Depravity and Original Sin." That is, "this black conceit" is, for Hawthorne, a dominant moral device. In Hawthorne, "the blackness of darkness" is so pervasive that it all but excludes the lightness of whiteness (1850/1987: 243). Melville argues that this morally dark side produces a *chiaroscuro* effect in relation to the morally light side of human nature:

> Now it is that blackness of Hawthorne, of which I have spoken, that so fixes and fascinates me. It may be, nevertheless, that it is so largely developed in him. Perhaps he does not give us a ray of light for every shade of his dark. But however this may be, this blackness it is that furnishes the infinite obscure of his back-ground.
>
> (1850/1987: 244)

In this discussion of blackness, Melville does not, as he does in the chapter on the whiteness of the whale, adopt a phenomenological perspective. He does not inquire into the essence of blackness. Nor (although he moralizes blackness) does he "racialize" it. Although, in this instance, both Melville and Hawthorne associate blackness with innate depravity and original sin, neither of them projects, as racists do, this negative value onto people who happen to have "black" skin. They both refrain from any such projection. What interests them is not the "racial" darkness of so-called black people but the moral darkness of so-called white people.

Racists believe that blackness has an essentially negative value. They seem to employ a certain syllogism: blackness has a negative value (in opposition to whiteness, which has a positive value); some people have black skin; therefore, all people who have black skin have a negative value. Is whiteness, as Ishmael suggests, alone among all colors an intensifier, or is the essence of blackness, like that of whiteness, also a certain intensity in association with objects? Does blackness also acquire guilt by association with objects that have a negative value, and do racists then fallaciously project that negative value onto other objects that have a positive (or a neutral) value—for example, onto all black people, or, as Ishmael says, onto "every dusky tribe?"

Moby-Dick is a book about the fallacy of projection: about the sheer insanity of it. Captain Ahab monomaniacally projects onto the white whale—which has only animal instinctuality—a human, perhaps even a divine or demonic, intentionality. For Starbuck, the white whale is only "a dumb brute" that dismembered Captain Ahab "from blindest instinct" (1851/1988: 163–4). For Captain Ahab, it is not the whale's actual whiteness that appalls him but rather the whale's possible consciousness that maddens him. Captain Ahab presumes that the white whale is as capable as he, as a man, is—or as a god or a devil is—of malice. He believes that the white whale intended, quite maliciously, to devour him or at least to dismember him. He projects onto the white whale "the sum of all the general rage and hate felt by his whole race" (1851/1988: 184).

Malice is not, however, an attribute of the white whale but merely an attribution by Captain Ahab, who feels rage and hate and projectively surmises that the white whale must have the capacity to feel them, too. Bunger says to Captain Ahab that "what you take for the White Whale's malice is only his awkwardness." The white whale "never means to swallow a single limb" (1851/1988: 441). Captain Ahab, however, believes that the white whale did mean to swallow at least one leg. The result of this projection, of course, is a malicious quest from which Ishmael alone— and quite by accident—survives to tell the story. By extension, any projection—be it onto a whale, a person, or a "race"—is fraught with peril, for it may redound to the detriment, perhaps even to the utter destruction, of the individual responsible for it.

COLOR THEORY

Traditional color theory considers some colors "primary" (most often, red, yellow, and blue) and others "secondary," "tertiary," and so forth. Patricia Sloane (1989) notes that there are two different, incompatible definitions of what is primary. In one definition, the primary colors are those that, in mixture, can produce all other colors; in the other, they are colors that a mixture of other colors cannot produce. By neither definition is white or black a primary color. In fact, traditional color theory regards absolute white and absolute black as noncolors: white, because it reflects all wavelengths of light; black, because it absorbs all wavelengths. (Alternatively, color theory identifies black, white, and gray as achromatic colors.) According to Sloane, the absolutist definition of white and black as "noncolors" is a simplistic idealization inadequate to actual visual experience. For her, white and black are colors like all other colors. The exclusion of black as a color, she says, "rests on the syllogism that light waves cause colors, yet do not cause black, which consequently cannot be a color." Sloane reverses this logic. She argues that "because black *is* a color, light waves do not cause all colors" (1989: 88).

If, as Sloane contends, black is a color "because we see it as a color," then this emphasis on sight as the criterion of color problematizes both the electromagnetic, or wavelength, theory of color and, perhaps more importantly, the ostensible opposition between white and black. "Oppositeness of color," she asserts, "is not a visual concept." Like Hillman, she rejects the notion that white and black are opposites onto-logically. According to Sloane, oppositional white–black logic is not a visual but a strictly psychical or symbolic function:

> When the world is interpreted as a collection of opposites (black and white are among the pairs of opposites), each pair is imagined to consist of a positive member poised against its negative twin. In psychological association and in symbolism, positives may be freely interchanged, as may negatives. Black, for this reason, is said to symbolize (or suggest) night, darkness, the void, Satan, evil. In our society black is rarely associated with day, light, salvation, God, goodness, or other concepts more intimately linked with white. Gray has few symbolic associations, an omission I consider significant. A world seen predominantly in terms of black or white, true or false, allows little room for the continuum of ambiguities, for that which is more or less true, or neither exactly black or white.

If white is regarded as positive, then black, "reduced to no more than an antipode of white, is defined almost totally in negatives." Implicit in the oppositional white–black logic is a positive–negative, superior–inferior evaluation. Sloane says that "the negative member of each opposed pair is subtly devalued, flagged as less worthy of respect or serious attention." She states, in unequivocal terms: "Oppositeness is a value system" (1989: 89).

Like Todorov and Bosnak, Sloane speculates that the symbolism of color is "a supplement to the symbolism of light." Whether the symbolism of light and dark is absolutely universal, or archetypal, it is at least "international." It is a symbolism that "appears in many cultures." In this respect, Sloane cites the intimate association between color symbolism and the "moral imperatives" of the Bible. While white is a symbol of "purity," black is a symbol of "death," "mourning," "sexual provocativeness," and "sin." Not only Judeo-Christian tradition but also Islamic tradition associates black symbolically with sin:

> Islamic legend says that the sacred black stone of Mecca was white when it fell from heaven. The stone, incorporated today into the masonry of the Ka'aba, became black—rather than blue or green—

from the sins of the human beings who touched it. Why was the stone sent? Evidently to remind human beings of the blackness of their deeds, for which they could expect to be punished.

(1989: 120)

The symbolic "purity" of white also influences "racial designation, an elaborate code that only nominally refers to skin color." Like Gates, Sloane says, "Nobody's skin is actually black, white, yellow, or red." That visual fact, however, hardly prevents the construction of "idioms that can be mistaken for (or turned into) racial slurs." As Sloane remarks, by certain linguistic conventions "white intentions are pure; black motives are evil" (1989: 190–1).

The perception of color is relative to the immediate physical context of the color—that is, relative to the other color or colors around it. Thus Josef Albers emphasizes "interaction of color," or what he calls "seeing what happens between colors" (1975: 5). For example, a white figure on a black ground appears deceptively larger than a black figure of the same size on a white ground. What is much more important, however, in terms of "race" and racism, is that the perception of color is also relative to the psychical context (which includes the cultural context). In this sense, perceptions are a function of conceptions—or preconceptions. Concepts do not determine percepts, but they do constrain them. Benjamin Lee Whorf says that "our linguistically determined thought world not only collaborates with our cultural idols and ideals, but engages even our unconscious personal reactions in its patterns and gives them certain typical characters" (1956: 154). I would say that our conceptually constrained sight world engages our unconscious personal (and collective) reactions and gives them certain stereotypical characters. That is, I would emphasize the interaction of color and culture, or seeing what happens between colors and cultures. Whorf introduces "a new principle of relativity, which holds that all observers are not led by the same physical evidence to the same picture of the universe, unless their linguistic backgrounds are similar, or can in some way be callibrated" (1956: 214). I prefer to say that different conceptual backgrounds tend to result in different pictures of the universe. If a culture conceives (or preconceives) people "racially" in terms of white and black (or white, black, red, brown, and yellow), then individuals in that culture will tend to be unable to perceive all of the gradations in skin color that actually do exist. Individuals will tend to see only a difference in kind rather than differences in degree—or, worse, in the case of white and black, see only an "opposition" that is, at least implicitly, an invidious valuation. A cultural background also includes various conceptions, or associations, that constrain perceptions. Among the "modern American color associations" that the color consultant Faber Birren presents, the color white is associated with "normality" and the color black with "negation" (1961: 143). Birren notes that the color white in association with skin color is simply an arrogantly racist affirmation of white supremacy. " 'White' expresses the vanity of the Caucasian race," he says. "To say that a man is white is an American-ism dating back to 1877, when it was supposed to cast aspersion on red men and black men" (1961: 170). Whether or not the "white" man appears as a cultural concept on the American scene only as recently as the nineteenth century, this color conceit continues to influence the "racial" picture of the universe at the very end of the twentieth century.

Chapter 3

The cultural unconscious and collective differences

"Race" and racism—and inquiries into whiteness and blackness—have hardly been issues of central concern in psychoanalysis, psychiatry, and clinical psychology. The institutional racism of these therapeutic professions—however unintentional it may have been historically—has tended to relegate these issues to a peripheral position in both theory and practice. These issues have not so much been repressed as they have simply been ignored or neglected as serious concerns.

One explanation for this state of affairs is that the underrepresentation of blacks and members of other "minority groups" in these therapeutic professions has effectively marginalized these issues. Not only the collar but also the very skin of these professions has been white. For example, Polly Young-Eisendrath (1987) has noted the absence of African-Americans among Jungian analysts in America. I would add that there is a quite conspicuous underrepresentation of blacks not only among Jungian analysts but also among all other psychoanalysts, as well as among psychiatrists and clinical psychologists—and, apparently, little or no effective effort at affirmative action to rectify the situation.

Clinical social work has been more responsive to issues of "race" and racism. There is a much more equitable representation of "blacks" and members of other "minority groups" in clinical social work than in the other therapeutic professions. In addition, since clinical social work as a therapeutic profession adopts a psychosocial rather than an exclusively psychological perspective, it is more attentive to social issues like "race" and racism. Also, because "racial" discrimination tends historically to be a reliable indicator of relative economic deprivation and because the therapy that clinical social workers provide is a more affordable service than the therapy that psychoanalysts, psychiatrists, and clinical psychologists provide, the patients of clinical social workers tend disproportionately to be members of "minority groups."

Schools of social work in universities offer courses on "ethnocultural issues," "cultural sensitivity," "ethnic-minority concerns," and (without mincing words) "oppression of diverse populations." As admirable as these curricular efforts are, as valuable as they may be, they are not attempts to analyze but to "sensitize." They function primarily at the level of the conscious, rather than at the level of the unconscious. They tend to operate on the surface rather than at a depth. What we need in addition, I believe, and what psychoanalysis uniquely offers us is an opportunity to address issues of "race" and racism from the perspective of the unconscious.

One reason why these issues have historically not been a topic of much immediate concern specifically for psychoanalysis is that, for Freud, the unconscious was primarily if not exclusively a sexual unconscious. By now we know—and we should acknowledge explicitly—that there is far more to the unconscious than sex. As decisive as sex is in psychical reality (and who denies that fact?), it is not the only content of the unconscious— and other contents, such as "race," are no less serious than sex. In addition to the sexuality of the unconscious, there is what I call the "raciality" of the unconscious. (I should perhaps state emphatically that, by the "raciality" of the unconscious, I do not mean that there is a "racial" instinct, in the sense that some psychoanalysts assert a sexual instinct. Nor do I mean that different "races" have, by nature, different psyches. Such notions would be patently racist. I mean that for many people—and for many patients—"race" is an issue, an unconscious content, just as important as, or even more important than, sex.) The problem is not, however, simply that Freud and many psychoanalysts after him have tended to describe the unconscious in sexual terms. That particular problem is merely an aspect of a much more general theoretical and practical problem—and that is the reductive tendencies that psychoanalysis, both Freudian and Jungian, has exhibited historically.

REDUCTIVE TENDENCIES AND REALITY RESPONSES

The reductive tendencies to which Freudian analysis has been especially prone are the result of a quite specific theoretical and practical assumption. (By "Freudian analysis," I mean all of those schools of thought in the Freudian tradition, however much they may now differ from Freud. I wish not to vulgarize the Freudian tradition but merely to criticize both it and the Jungian tradition.) As the philosopher Paul Ricoeur says, Freudian analysis belongs to "the school of suspicion" (1970: 32). In Freudian analysis, everything is suspect; nothing is what it seems to be; everything is always something else. Historically, Freudian analysis has tended to assume that any manifest content is a derivative of a latent content. "Derivative" is the decisive term. The implication is that because manifest contents are derivative from these latent contents, they are reducible to them. The method of Freudian analysis is to identify derivatives and then ultimately to reduce them to unconscious motives. (For Freud, the unconscious motive is an instinctual—most often, a sexual—wish that is the expression of a drive in relation to an object.) In Freudian analysis, these derivatives are distortions, a result of repression or other defenses. In this sense, the manifest content is merely an apparent content; the latent content is the real content. The Freudian method privileges latent contents as basic, or phenomenal, and regards manifest contents as merely derivative, or epiphenomenal. At the extreme, the tendency in Freudian analysis is to assume that a dream that is apparently about "racial" conflict is not "really" about that at all. From this perspective, "racial" conflict is only an allusion—an indirect, defensive, distortive reference—to some other conflict (for instance, sexual conflict). The effect is to deny the specific reality of "race" as a content of the unconscious and to deflect attention from it as a serious issue for the dreamer.

Freudian analysis has also tended to be reductive in another respect. It has minimized the importance of cultural factors. Historically, it has tended to reduce cultural factors to instinctual factors, especially sexual factors. There have been exceptions to this rule, perhaps most notably Karen Horney, who quite properly criticized Freud for "disregard of cultural factors" and for "false generalizations" about ostensibly instinctual, or biological, factors (1937: 21). Although feminist Freudian analysts after Horney have emphasized cultural factors in the effort to address issues of sex, sexism, and gender, Freudian analysts have yet to apply such considerations systematically to issues of "race," racism, and ethnicity.

Jung criticizes Freudian analysis for reductive tendencies (especially the tendency to an exclusively sexual reduction) and proposes an additional, alternative perspective that he calls "constructive." He says that the constructive perspective *"analyzes*, but it does not reduce." It analyzes the psyche "into *typical* components." (These typical components are archetypes.) Then, however, Jung acknowledges that the constructive method is, after all, also reductive—at least in a certain sense. "If one can speak of reduction at all," Jung says, "it is simply reduction to general types, but not to some general principle arrived at inductively or deductively, such as 'sexuality' " (*CW* 3: 187, para. 413). That is, the constructive method reduces the psyche to typical components, and sexuality is only one among many such components, not a general principle to which all of the other types are reducible. In short, if Freudian analysis has tended to be sexually reductive, then Jungian analysis has tended to be archetypally reductive. From the constructive perspective, one typical component of the psyche would be sexuality, but there would also be many other, equally significant typical components (among them, I would add, "raciality").

This constructive perspective has also been reductive in another sense. Historically, Jungian analysis has tended to regard the typical components of the psyche as strictly archetypal, not stereotypical. That is, it has tended immediately to reduce the stereotypical to the archetypal, the cultural to the natural. If, as Jung says, "archetypes are simply the forms which the instincts assume" (*CW* 8: 157, para. 339), Jungian analysis, like Freudian analysis, has been instinctually reductive, although it has not been specifically sexually reductive. That is, Jung posits many instincts—and many archetypes—not just one. Although Jungian analysis has not emphasized personal factors to the exclusion of collective factors (as Freudian analysis has tended historically to do), it has, like Freudian analysis, minimized the importance of cultural factors. By no means are all collective factors natural, or archetypal. Many, if not most, collective factors are quite specifically cultural, or stereotypical.

The Jungian analyst Joseph L. Henderson has recently introduced the term "cultural unconscious." He situates the cultural unconscious topographically between what Jungian analysts call the collective unconscious and the personal unconscious. Henderson notes that much of "what Jung called personal was actually always culturally conditioned" (1990: 104). I would add that much of what Jung called collective was also culturally conditioned. Henderson, however, reserves the term "collective unconscious" for archetypal factors. In contrast, as I regard the cultural unconscious, it is an aspect of the collective unconscious, which comprises not only archetypal factors but also stereotypical factors—which include, of course, apparently "racial" factors (collective attitudes and behaviors that are really *ethnic* factors) that have prejudicial and discriminatory consequences.

In addition, Jungian analysis tends to assume that "racial" contents are not so much references to any external reality (such as the cultural reality of racism) as they are reflections of an internal reality. For example, Jungian analysis tends to regard blacks in dreams (especially in the dreams of whites) as images of the "shadow" and to reduce them to personifications of "dark," negative, or inferior, aspects of the dreamer, a self who unconsciously projects them onto an other. However valid this reductive method may be in many cases, the assumption is that, although such dreams are apparently about "racial" blackness, they are really about psychical "darkness." The effect, again, is to deny the reality of "race" as a content of the unconscious. (In another sense, the method does, of course, imply that the dreamers of such dreams are unconsciously racist to the extent that they defensively and invidiously project certain psychical inferiorities endemic to the self onto a "racial" other, who serves them as a convenient scapegoat.)

Fortunately, many contemporary analysts and therapists—Freudian, Jungian, and otherwise—are evidently not as reductive in practice as theory might indicate. In an international survey on responses to social and political material, Samuels (1993) discovered that many analysts and therapists address "racial" or ethnic material realistically. That is, they consider it a reality as real as any other and not merely an appearance, or a derivative of some other, more basic reality to which it is reducible. Many analysts and therapists always offer what Samuels calls "reality responses" to this material, or they sometimes combine reality responses with other responses—for example, responses that regard this social and political material as simultaneously "symbolic" of a non-social, non-political psychical reality. (Of course, some analysts and therapists who are purists never offer reality responses.) Ultimately, what the unconscious requires is a flexible, not a rigid, response, one that is a function of what specific patients happen to privilege as reality. For some patients, the unconscious issue will be strictly personal psychical relations, conflict, and identity; for others, it will be collective "racial" relations, conflict, and identity—or other equally vital social and political concerns.

JUNG, FREUD, ANTI-SEMITISM, AND COLLECTIVE PSYCHICAL DIFFERENCES

Historically, psychoanalysis has had a special interest in one variety of racism—and that is anti-Semitism. The sheer number of psychoanalysts—so many of whom happened to be Jews—on whom Hitler, the Nazis, and the Holocaust had a catastrophic impact more than suffices to explain the singularity of this concern. The topic of anti-Semitism, however, had originally become a controversial issue in psychoanalysis much earlier, two decades before Hitler, in the dispute between Freud and Jung. In 1914, in a historical account that served a polemical purpose, Freud criticized Jung for a radical divergence from psychoanalytic theory and practice. Initially, Freud said, Jung had impressed him in part because "he seemed ready to enter into a friendly relationship with me and for my sake to give up certain racial prejudices which he had previously permitted himself" (*SE* 14: 43). What is apparently a compliment is really an accusation: Jung had "seemed" (but, at least in the version of events that Freud promulgates, evidently had not been) ready to relinquish certain anti-Semitic biases. In the context of the controversy between Freud and Jung over the very definition of "psychoanalysis," Freud's remark is, of course, an *ad hominem* attack, an attempt to impugn Jung's integrity.

If that were all there were to it, anti-Semitism would hardly have assumed the importance that it has had in psychoanalysis. Jung, however, was capable of quite insensitive comments about ostensible psychical differences between Germans and Jews. In 1933, Jung wrote in an editorial in the journal of the International General Medical Society for Psychotherapy, of which he was president: "The differences which actually do exist between Germanic and Jewish psychology and which have long been known to every intelligent person are no longer to be glossed over, and this can only be beneficial to science." Simultaneously, he explicitly denied any anti-Semitic intent: "At the same time I should like to state expressly that this implies no depreciation of Semitic psychology, any more than it is a depreciation of the Chinese to speak of the peculiar psychology of the Oriental" (*CW* 10: 533–4, para. 1014).

The German chapter of the international society had been conformed to National Socialism, or "Nazified," pledged to *Mein Kampf*, and purged of all Jews. (Jung arranged for Jewish analysts and therapists in Germany to remain members of the international society. Later, he helped a number of Jewish analysts and therapists to escape the Nazis, and he tried, without success, to help Freud. An emissary of Jung traveled from Zurich to Vienna with five thousand dollars for Freud, but Freud rejected the money.) M.H. Göring, a cousin of Hermann Göring, had been designated leader, or "Führer," of the German chapter. This was hardly a propitious time for Jung, as president of the international society, to be asserting the existence of significant psychical differences between Germans and Jews. (I should emphasize that Jung was president of the international society, *not* the German chapter.) Jung protested that the interest in collective psychical differences was hardly a new topic for him. For example, as early as 1928, well before the accession of Hitler as chancellor of Germany, Jung had published this comment:

> Thus is it a quite unpardonable mistake to accept the conclusions of a Jewish psychology as generally valid. Nobody would dream of taking Chinese or Indian psychology as binding upon ourselves. The cheap accusation of anti-Semitism that has been levelled at me on the ground of this criticism is just about as intelligent as accusing me of an anti-Chinese prejudice.

There would be nothing intrinsically objectionable about such a proposition, if it were to attempt to explain collective psychical differences in terms of history, culture, and ethnicity. In this case, however, Jung appears to explain such differences in terms of "race" and evolution:

> No doubt, on an earlier and deeper level of psychic development, where it is still impossible to distinguish between an Aryan, Semitic, Hamitic, or Mongolian mentality, all human races have a common collective psyche. But with the beginning of racial differentiation essential differences are developed in the collective psyche as well.
>
> (*CW* 7: 152, para. 240, n. 8)

By apparently explaining collective psychical differences "racially" and evolutionarily, Jung commits a naturalistic fallacy. In spite of the fact that on other occasions he explains such differences historically, culturally, and ethnically, in this particular instance he confuses the issue.

The mere fact that Jung had addressed the issue of collective psychical differences prior to Hitler and the Nazis is no excuse for what in 1934 he defiantly admitted was a deliberately incautious assertion of "the difference between Jewish and 'Aryan-Germanic-Christian-European' psychology" (*CW* 10: 540, para. 1025). The assumption was, Jung said, that "my sole purpose was to blurt out my 'notorious' anti-Semitism." That he "might also have something good and appreciative to say" about Jewish psychology, in addition to anything critical that he might have to say, evidently never occurred to anyone, he complained. In discussing collective psychical differences, Jung insisted that he intended "no value-judgments," no imputation of inferiority or superiority (*CW* 10: 541–2, paras. 1030–1). By even mentioning the topic of collective psychical differences at that particular time, however, he inadvertently lent psychoanalytic credibility—which is to say, a certain "scientific" respectability—to the spurious notion that such differences are the result of "racial" differentiation.

Nor does it matter, under these circumstances, after Hitler and the Holocaust, that in 1908 Freud advised Karl Abraham that they were more immediately compatible intellectually "because of racial kinship" than Freud and Jung were. According to Freud, the fact that Jung was a Christian, not a Jew like Abraham, resulted in "great inner resistances." In Freud's opinion, Jung's connection with psychoanalysis was "the more valuable for that." Freud concluded: "I nearly said that it was only by his appearance on the scene that psycho-analysis escaped the danger of becoming a Jewish national affair" (Freud and Abraham 1965: 34). A Jewish national affair is not exactly a "Jewish science," but in this case it is Freud, not Jung, who asserts significant "racial" differences between Jews and Christians. Of course, the fact that Freud was no less capable than Jung of problematic projections on the basis of "race" does not exculpate or vindicate Jung.

A conference held in New York at the New School for Social Research in 1989 and co-sponsored by the C.G. Jung Foundation for Analytical Psychology, the Postgraduate Center for Mental Health, and the Union of American Hebrew Congregations, addressed the issue of Jungians, Freudians, and anti-Semitism. The book that resulted from that conference includes a compilation of important primary sources on the topic of psychoanalysis and anti-Semitism (Adams and Sherry 1991). Also in 1989, at the Eleventh International Congress for Analytical Psychology in Paris, Jungian analysts conducted a workshop on the issue (Bernstein *et al.* 1991). Events such as these are a necessary if not a sufficient condition for any possible conversation—let alone any conceivable reconciliation—between Jungians and Freudians who share an interest in eradicating any trace of racism in psychoanalysis.

The reason that I mention these matters is not to advocate the reunification of psychoanalysis as an institution and a discipline; nor is it to defend Jung against accusations of anti-Semitism; nor is it to label him a racist. I raise these issues because I believe that any serious effort to develop a multicultural psychoanalysis must acknowledge the total context in which Jung asserted the existence of significant psychical differences between Jews on the one hand and "Aryans," Germans, Christians, or Europeans on the other hand—and, unfortunately, that context includes elements of a "racial" (if not a racist) discourse, as Samuels (1993) has demonstrated. If we are effectively to address any significant psychical differences that may now exist collectively—say, between "whites" and "blacks"—without, that is, projecting fallacious "racial" notions from the self onto an other, then the example of Jung demands systematic scrutiny. What I propose is to scrutinize Jung on the issues of "race," racism, and ethnicity just as feminists have scrutinized Freud on the issues of sex, sexism, and gender.

THE COLLECTIVE DIMENSION: ARCHETYPES AND STEREOTYPES

The very idea of the collective as a dimension of the psyche seems to me, in this respect, a potentially invaluable contribution to psychoanalysis. "We have to distinguish between a personal unconscious and an *impersonal* or *transpersonal unconscious*," Jung says. "We speak of the latter also as the *collective unconscious*" (*CW* 7: 66, para. 103). Freud seems to repudiate the collective unconscious in no uncertain terms. "I do not think we gain anything," he says, "by introducing the concept of a 'collective' unconscious." Actually, however, Freud accepts the fact that the unconscious has a collective dimension. He merely considers the concept redundant. "The content of the unconscious, indeed, is in any case," he says, "a collective, universal property of mankind" (*SE* 23: 132).

According to Jung, the collective unconscious comprises archetypes. He contends that archetypes are "similar to the Kantian categories" (*CW* 10: 10, para. 14). Jung asserts that they are "*categories* analogous to the logical categories which are always and everywhere present as the basic postulates of reason," except, in the case of the collective unconscious, they are "categories of the *imagination*" (*CW* 11: 517–18, para. 845). Freud also acknowledges the existence of archetypes, although he calls them phylogenetic prototypes (*SE* 21: 17). In a Kantian allusion, he says that these prototypes, which he also calls phylogenetic schemata, are comparable to "the categories of philosophy." That is, the schemata "are concerned with the business of 'placing' the impressions derived from actual experience." Freud describes the circumstances under which a schema may exert a collective influence over individual experience. When experiences are not in strict conformity with a schema, he says, "they become remodelled in the imagination—a process which might very profitably be followed out in detail." He continues: "It is precisely such cases that are calculated to convince us of the independent existence of the schema. We are often able to see the schema triumphing over the experience of the individual" (*SE* 17: 119).

Historically, probably in large part because of the dispute between Freud and Jung, Freudian analysts have not done what Freud recommended—that is, they have not detailed the process by which collective prototypes, or schemata, exert a dominant influence over individual experiences. It is Jungian analysts who have emphasized archetypes and who have pursued and explored this process. There is no reason now, however, for psychoanalysts of every school of thought not to avail themselves of the concept of a collective dimension of the psyche. I believe that we need to redefine the "collective" to serve the purposes of a multicultural psychoanalysis.

Jung is not always consistent in how he defines the "collective unconscious." Sometimes he says that archetypes are images, as if they were quite specific contents. Sometimes, however, he says that archetypes are pure forms, or categories of the imagination, and, on that basis, distinguishes more precisely between archetypes and archetypal images. When he distinguishes archetypes from archetypal images, he says that the former are collective inheritances and the latter, personal acquisitions. Archetypes, Jung says, are inherited categories that "give definite form to contents that have already been acquired" through individual experience. That is, they do not determine the specific content of individual experience but constrain the form of it, "within certain categories" (*CW* 15: 81, para. 126). As sensible as the distinction is between archetypes and archetypal images, it nevertheless does not adequately address the fact that personal acquisitions through history, culture, and ethnicity also have a collective dimension. What Jung calls archetypes and what Freud calls prototypes, or schemata, are natural rather than cultural categories. They are categories of human nature, not human culture. Jung and Freud are neo-Kantians: it is as if they were both attempting to write a psychoanalytic critique of the pure imagination.

What we need, in addition, is a psychoanalytic critique of the historical, cultural, and ethnic imagination—one that would, as I have previously said, "emphasize cultural rather than natural categories (for example, ethnic rather than 'racial' categories)." That is, we need also to be neo-Diltheyians. "Addressing the issue in this manner," I have said, "is similar to what Wilhelm Dilthey was attempting when, instead of writing a critique of pure reason as Immanuel Kant had done, he proposed writing a critique of historical reason—by which he meant a critique of historical categories, or a critique of cultural categories" (Adams 1991: 253–4). Such a psychoanalytic critique would not, of course, be a critique of historical reason but a critique of the historical imagination. It would acknowledge that the categories of the imagination have a historical, cultural, and ethnic dimension.

There are two dimensions, not just one, to the collective: an archetypal (a natural—that is, a transhistorical, transcultural, transethnic) dimension and a stereotypical (a historical, cultural, ethnic) dimension. Both dimensions of the collective may also be either conscious or unconscious. There is a collective conscious as well as a collective unconscious—and both include stereotypes and stereotypical images as well as archetypes and archetypal images. From this perspective, what Henderson calls the cultural unconscious is one aspect of the collective unconscious—and there is also a cultural conscious.

When I say that the collective unconscious includes archetypal images, I do *not* mean that these images are inherited. All images are acquired through individual experience. Rather, I mean that not all images are acquired from culture; some—in fact, many—are acquired from nature—by which I mean, in this case, "environmental nature." Through individual experience, we acquire images from environmental nature and unconsciously categorize them in collective, archetypal, or typical ways. In addition, these images from environmental nature exhibit typical properties (intrinsic to these images) that participate in and contribute to this unconscious categorization. In the acquisition of archetypal images, there is a mutual, or reciprocal, influence between "human nature" (or the human psyche) and environmental nature. The properties of images from environmental nature do not determine the unconscious categorization, but they do constrain it. All other things being equal, individuals, by human nature, will tend to experience and unconsciously categorize the same image from environmental nature in a typical (an identical or at least very similar) way, in part because of the typical properties of the image.

In addition, both stereotypes and archetypes, as well as stereotypical images and archetypal images, may have either a negative or a positive value in psychical reality. We may stereotype or "archetype" persons and peoples not only consciously or unconsciously but also positively or negatively—as "good" or "bad" (types and images may be either honorific or defamatory). We may also, of course, stereotype or "archetype" them in a myriad of other ways that are much more evaluatively specific than the adjectives "good" and "bad" that psychoanalysts, especially those with an interest in object relations, so frequently employ. Those who adopt an object relations perspective need to articulate a terminology that would be much more adjectivally adequate to the varieties of psychical experience. The "exciting" and "rejecting" objects of W.R.D. Fairbairn (1990), for example, are more specific than simply "good" and "bad" objects, but we need many more such adjectives, and we need to employ them differentially rather than merely oppositionally.

This redefinition of the "collective" clarifies matters even as it complicates them. Rather than a topographical or an axial model of the psyche,
I prefer a radial model that includes the personal and collective, the
conscious and unconscious, the positive and negative, stereotypes and
stereotypical images, and archetypes and archetypal images.

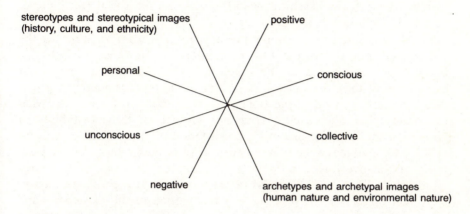

A radial model of the psyche

The advantage of the radial model is that it more accurately reflects the
complexities of psychical reality than does either a topographical or an
axial model. A radial model avoids the above–below, top–bottom opposition of a topographical model, as well as the up–down, left–right
opposition of an axial model. The radial model exemplifies how types
and images, the forms and contents of the psyche, may occur in any
number of possible combinations and permutations.

I do not believe that any mere model of the psyche will eliminate
archetypal or stereotypical projections. *Projective typification*, as I call it,
seems to me not just a defense but an irreducible, ineradicable fact of
psychical existence. In what I have called *the psychical construction
of reality*, the self continuously, projectively typifies the other. There is
not only an archetypal but also a stereotypical dimension to projective
typification. In this respect, I have argued that "the individual vision of
external reality is mediated—that is, *psychically constructed*—by schemata, categories, or 'types' (be they archetypes or stereotypes), which if
not naturally inherited, are so culturally ingrained in the unconscious that
they might as well be" (Adams 1991: 253). (Prominent among these are,
of course, "racial" prejudices—biases that through a process of *cultural
ingraining* prove especially difficult to modify.) To attempt to alter such
projective typifications, I believe that psychoanalysis needs to develop a

psychology of knowledge. Such a psychoanalytic epistemology would be comparable to the "sociology of knowledge" of Alfred Schutz (1962, 1964) and Peter L. Berger and Thomas Luckmann (1966). Berger and Luckmann speak specifically of "the social construction of reality." A psychology of knowledge would, however, afford a more comprehensive perspective on the construction of reality than a sociology of knowledge would. In short, the psychical would encompass the social (or, I prefer to say, the cultural) as a special case.

In one sense, the other simply presents too much information for the self immediately to process. Our perceptions of the other are selective because our experience of the other is partial. In another sense, our experience of the other may also, of course, be prejudgmental or prejudicial, the result of our projections onto the other. In this respect, what the philosopher Hans-Georg Gadamer says about the inevitability of "prejudgment" and the pejorative connotation of "prejudice" is relevant (1975: 240). We may type others because we prejudge them, either positively or negatively. I do not merely advocate the retraction of projective typifications. That solution seems to me too facile. It is no simple matter to retract them. What I propose is a recognition of the existence—and the peculiar persistence—of such projections. The unconscious purpose of projective typifications is evidently to diminish uncertainty—and attendant anxiety—in the encounter between self and other. Such projections are a simplification by which the self immediately and conveniently reduces the complexities of the other to apparently manageable, or controllable, proportions. What interests me most are the collective dimensions of projective typifications as they appear both unconsciously and consciously in the personal experience of the individual—and that is what this book is about.

THE MULTICULTURAL IMAGINATION AND THE FANTASY PRINCIPLE

In what I call *the multicultural imagination*, what matters is how the self imagines (and how the self might reimagine) the other. We need to go beyond the pleasure principle, the reality principle, and the repetition compulsion to what I call *the fantasy principle*. I do not, as Freud did, reduce fantasies to wishes. The motivation of a fantasy may be a wish, but it may also be hate, fear, anger, hurt, sorrow, spite, contempt, envy, jealousy, gratitude, respect, awe, reverence, joy, love—and all other imaginable emotions. Nor do I oppose fantasy to reality, as if the one were necessarily false and the other true. Reality is not given; it is constructed psychically in and through fantasy, both consciously and unconsciously. Nor do I romanticize fantasy, which can be either creative or destructive. As Jung says, "Developing fantasy means perfecting our humanity" (1977: 40).

In order to develop fantasy, we need to *analyze* it. Specifically, we need to analyze the "racial" fantasies of the self in relation to the other—and of the other in relation to the self. These include fantasies about whiteness and blackness; white supremacy and purity; black pride and power; white and black separatism; segregation and integration; sex, violence, and intelligence; difference, similarity, and identity; superiority and inferiority; Eurocentrism and Afrocentrism; Europe and Africa—and perhaps most importantly, the "civilized" and the "primitive."

Although Freud wanted psychoanalysis to be a multicultural project— witness the determination to repudiate the notion of a "Jewish science" and the effort to extend psychoanalysis from Vienna to Zurich, to other countries, to other cultures—it was Jung who really broadened the cultural base of psychoanalysis (however inadequate the attempt may appear to us now, when we so ardently espouse multiculturalism as a morally proper, ideologically exemplary, socially responsible, and politically correct ideal). Jung laid the foundations for, or pointed the way toward, a multicultural psychoanalysis.

Whereas Freud's interests were primarily in the Jewish and Greek traditions—for example, those imposing symbolic figures of Moses and Oedipus (although I might also mention that amazing collection of Egyptian and other antiquities as evidence of more extensive interests)— Jung's interests were in the Christian, Greek, Indian, Chinese, American (including Native-American and African-American), African, and many other traditions. Freud traveled outside Europe only one time, to America in 1909, when he and Jung delivered lectures and received honorary doctorates at Clark University. Jung traveled outside Europe many times—to America (including "Native America," that is, Taos Pueblo), to India, to the Middle East, and twice to Africa: the first time in 1920 to North Africa and the second time in 1925–6 to Central Africa, or "Black" Africa.

As "civilized" Europeans, both Freud and Jung had an interest in "primitive" psychology. Freud analyzed totems and taboos, Jung analyzed mystical participations and collective representations. Jung not only traveled more extensively than Freud did but also wrote more inclusively on the topic of primitive psychology. Like Freud, Jung was a universalist, who believed that there is a fundamental unity to the human psyche, independent of time and place—and, I would emphasize, independent of "race." According to Jung, at bottom, we are all archetypally identical, typically human. Jung also believed, however, that there is a diversity to the psyche—that we are not only archetypally the same but also historically, culturally, and ethnically different. History, culture, and ethnicity are circumstances that condition human nature and differentiate us.

In spite of the ambiguities in what Jung says about collective psychical differences, I believe that the interest that he evinces in the issue provides us (and by "us," I mean both post-Freudians and post-Jungians) with an opportunity to develop an authentic multicultural psychoanalysis. Jung says some problematic things about collective psychical differences, but he also says some truly astute, even prescient things. A liberal construction of Jung would generously regard him as a psychoanalyst who—in emphasizing difference—anticipated the keen contemporary concern with multicultural issues. For example, Samuels portrays Jung as a precursor of those who currently profess an interest in the topic of cultural differences. Samuels says of Jung that "we should recognize that, alongside the unfortunate excursions into racial typology, we can also discern the seeds of a surprisingly modern and constructive attitude to race and ethnicity." He notes that, in contrast to various problematic or even reprehensible remarks about "race," Jung also frequently repudiated "a Eurocentric, judgmental approach to other cultures" and demonstrated both "respect for and interest in" cultural differences (1993: 309). This seems to me both an accurate description and an equitable evaluation of the paradoxes of Jung.

Chapter 4

Going black, going primitive, going instinctive

I now wish to present for consideration some associations: black–primitive–instinctive. These are associations that exist, I contend even now, in the psyches of whites of European origin. By the nineteenth century, at the climax of colonialism and imperialism, and well into the twentieth century, these associations were widespread and commonplace. Associations may be of two kinds. They may be based on contiguity, or they may be based on similarity. In this case, the associations black–primitive–instinctive are based on a perceived—or, more accurately, a projected—similarity.

"Primitive" is a controversial word. Although the cultural anthropologist Stanley Diamond notes that it has no "pejorative significance" etymologically, it does have a negative connotation historically. Colonialists and imperialists have employed the word to promote an invidious distinction. If, as Diamond says, it implies "a relative sense of origins," then why not "original" rather than "primitive?" Rather than "abandoning the word, as is periodically suggested, hedging it with quotes, prefacing it with the inexplicit irony of 'so-called' or replacing it with limited and misleading expressions" that are euphemistically inadequate, Diamond recommends that we "define it further and so help to reach agreement on what *primitive* means" (1974: 125). Some have attempted to do just that (although in ways that Diamond would consider unacceptable). For example, C.R. Hallpike (1979) has combined cultural anthropology and developmental, cognitive psychology in an effort to define "primitive thought." I continue to employ the word "primitive" (often within quotation marks to emphasize that it is, indeed, "so-called") not because there *are* primitives but simply because colonialists, imperialists, and psychoanalysts like Jung and Freud have said that there were.

"Going black" is, in origin, a British expression. An equivalent expression is "going primitive" (or "going native"). In the colonialist, imperialist context, to go black was to revert—or, in psychoanalytic terms, to regress—to an earlier and lower state. That is, the expression "going black" has both temporal and spatial connotations. To go black is to "go back"—in time and space. This reversion is a regression not, as Ernst Kris says, "in the service of the ego" (1952: 177) but, rather, in the service of the id, or instinct. To go black is to "go instinctive." It is to return to a before and a beneath, to a state or a stage that the civilized white European, whether British or not, has presumably superseded.

Freud contends that civilization is a defensive compromise that entails the renunciation of instinct in exchange for a promise of security. According to Freud, this is a process that inevitably produces discontent. To be civilized is, by definition, to be discontented. Freud expresses wonder at the assertion "that what we call our civilization is largely responsible for our misery, and that we should be much happier if we gave it up and returned to primitive conditions." In an effort to explain "this strange attitude of hostility to civilization," he relates it to "contact with primitive peoples and races." He attributes it to a first impression that was evidently a misperception by Europeans of what primitives are really like: "In consequence of insufficient observation and a mistaken view of their manners and customs, they appeared to Europeans to be leading a simple, happy life with few wants, a life such as was unattainable by their visitors with their superior civilization" (*SE* 21: 86–7). Freud's happy primitive is a version of Rousseau's noble savage. The civilized white European in contact with the primitive encounters an other that is, to the romantic or nostalgic self, the very epitome of the instinctive. Under these circumstances, the discontented, civilized white European may feel tempted (and also feel threatened) by the prospect of "going black." (At the extreme, such an individual may even feel that to go black, to go primitive, or to go instinctive would be to "go insane.")

The associations black–primitive–instinctive constitute a series of ideologized, theorized, or fantasized analogies. The black, the primitive, and the instinctive are alleged to be analogous. They are signifiers of an underlying something, a shared meaning, a signified. What is this signified? The common denominator by which the "black," the "primitive," and the "instinctive" are divisible is a psyche that is presumed to be not merely different from but qualitatively inferior to the European psyche—which is "white," "civilized," and "rational." That is, implicit in these associations are the oppositions black–white, primitive–civilized, instinctive–rational and, most important of all, inferior–superior.

The philosopher Paul Roubiczek contends that humans naturally think oppositionally. To define any concept is necessarily to oppose it to another concept. Roubiczek asserts a principle of inseparability: that we cannot, for example, think "bright" (or "light") without simultaneously thinking "dark," without opposing the one to the other. However many degrees of "brightness" (or "lightness") and "darkness" there may be, they are still oppositionally inseparable. The construction of "scales of degrees which seem to exclude the opposites," Roubiczek says, is ultimately dependent on the opposites (1952: 11). Try as we may, the attempt "to suppress, to exclude or to overcome" these opposites never succeeds entirely. According to Roubiczek, the opposites continue to condition how we think—and also how we feel and how we act. If the opposites are ignored or neglected, the influence that is exercised on us by them is unabated and merely "unnoticed" (1952: 16). If we inevitably think in opposites, Roubiczek says, then all we can do is try to notice them and to develop a critical attitude toward them. He thus advocates the conscious application of opposites rather than an unconscious projection of them.

Just how "naturally" we think in opposites is a controversial question to which I do not believe Roubiczek provides a conclusive answer. I would note that just as there is no "opposite sex" (only different sexes), there is no "opposite race." We may, of course, arbitrarily oppose one sex or one "race" to another, but an arbitrary *opposition* does not mean that the sexes or "races" *are opposites*. Merely thinking in opposites does not make it so. Sexes and "races" may merely be different in some respects—and, even if they are, the differences may be insignificant. Thinking in opposites may not do justice—it may, in fact, do grave violence—to the varieties and complexities of experience. Oppositional thinking may require less effort—or, in terms of psychical entropy, less energy—but just because differential thinking (in relative degrees rather than absolute kinds) may be more difficult, the necessity of more strenuous psychical exertion hardly proves that the former is more "natural" than the latter. In short, difference does not inevitably entail opposition.

The associations black–primitive–instinctive and white–civilized–rational are not only oppositional. They are also judgmental. They entail a value judgment of inferiority–superiority. The European psyche is purported to have attained, both evolutionarily and developmentally, both phylogenetically and ontogenetically, qualitative superiority. The supposition is that the European psyche is higher and the non-European psyche lower on an evolutionary and developmental scale. From a psychoanalytic perspective, at the black-and-white extremes of the scale, at the bottom and the top of it, are the unconscious and conscious or the id and ego. This top–bottom hierarchy also implies that the self may either "look down on" or "look up to" the other. In the colorist hierarchy, "black" and "white" are considered the distinguishing features, the identifying markers, of unconsciousness and consciousness. "Black" is the signifier of the id, "white" the signifier of the ego. The Freudian analyst Octave Mannoni says that the savage, or the primitive, "is identified in the unconscious with a certain image of the instincts—of the *id*, in analytical terminology" (1964: 21). In this sense, an "id–egoized" opposition is a version of the "primitive–civilized" opposition.

The black, the primitive, and the instinctive are judged to have no ego, only an id—or such an unevolved, undeveloped ego that it hardly bears comparison with the white, civilized, rational European ego. For example, the psychologist Alfred Storch, an influential contemporary of Freud and Jung, states: "In primitive man the ego does not yet possess the definiteness of form which it attains in civilized man. It consists of separate heterogeneous components which have not yet united into a whole" (1924: 23). In effect, Storch pathologizes the primitive psyche. He compares it to the insane psyche of the schizophrenic, in which he observes "the destruction of the developed ego as a unit," "the acquired independence of the partial components," and "the loss of the boundaries between the ego and the external world" (1924: 24). According to Storch, the primitive and the schizophrenic are psychically comparable because neither of them possesses a unitary ego. In the primitive, the ego has not yet been developed; in the schizophrenic, it has been destroyed.

LÉVY-BRUHL: THE "PRIMITIVE" AND THE "CIVILIZED"

The ostensible differences between the primitive and the civilized, which I summarize from the works of Lucien Lévy-Bruhl, whose anthropology profoundly influenced Jung's psychology, as well as Storch's, may be schematized in two columns, as follows:

Primitive	*Civilized*
concrete percepts	abstract concepts
attachment to sense impressions	detachment from sense impressions
emotion (feeling)	intellect (thinking)
prelogical	logical
mystical	causal
collective	individual
law of participation	law of contradiction
subject–object unity	subject–object duality

Lévy-Bruhl was a French anthropologist. He was born in 1857 and died in 1939. (Lévy-Bruhl was almost an exact contemporary of Freud, who was born in 1856 and died in 1939. In contrast, Jung was born in 1875 and died in 1961.) The intent of Lévy-Bruhl's anthropology is evident in the titles of two of his books that have been translated into English: *How Natives Think* (originally published with a French title that can be translated literally as *Mental Functions in Inferior Societies*) and *Primitive Mentality*. Lévy-Bruhl described the primitive psyche as prelogical, mystical, and collective, in contrast to the civilized psyche, which he described as logical, causal, and individual. He asserted that the primitive psyche obeys the law of participation, whereas the civilized psyche obeys the law of contradiction. Lévy-Bruhl rejected the universalist theory of "the identity of a 'human mind' which, from the logical point of view, is always exactly the same at all times and in all places" (1910/1985: 18). He believed that, at least from what he called the logical point of view, there were two very different psyches: the one primitive, the other civilized.

Lévy-Bruhl poses the following question: "Why is it that primitive mentality shows such indifference to, one might almost say such dislike of, the discursive operations of thought, of reasoning and reflection, when to us they are the most natural and almost continuous occupations of the human mind?" The indifference or dislike is not due, he says, to "incapacity" or to "inaptitude." Nor is it "the result of profound intellectual torpor, of enervation and unconquerable weariness" (1921/1966: 29–30). In discussing primitives, Lévy-Bruhl dismisses "a number of different hypotheses, such as the feebleness and torpidity of their minds, their perplexity, childlike ignorance, stupidity, etc., none of which take the facts sufficiently into account" (1921/1966: 32). In fact, in rejecting the characterization of the primitive psyche "as a rudimentary form of our own," he repudiates the notion that it is "almost pathological"—that is, almost insane. To his credit, Lévy-Bruhl does not pathologize the primitive psyche, as Storch does. "On the contrary," he says, "it will appear to be normal under the conditions in which it is employed" (1921/1966: 33). What are these conditions?

According to Lévy-Bruhl, primitives are "prelogical," by which he insists that he does not mean that they are "antilogical" or "alogical"— that they are against logic or without it. How does he define the prelogical psyche of the primitive? "By designating it 'prelogical,' " he declares, "I merely wish to state that it does not bind itself down, as our thought does, to avoiding contradiction. It obeys the law of participation first and foremost" (1910/1985: 78). This is the law of *participation mystique*, or mystical participation. From the perspective of logic, the primitive psyche does not abide by the law of contradiction by which the civilized psyche judges a proposition valid or invalid. Perhaps it is not irrelevant in this respect to note that Freud says that the unconscious in dreams also disregards contradictions. " 'No,' " he says, "seems not to exist as far as dreams are concerned" (*SE* 4: 318). That is, the unconscious functions, as the primitive tends to do, by a "both–and" unity rather than an "either–or" duality.

In a sense, according to Lévy-Bruhl, the question of validity simply does not arise for the primitive—or at least is not a primary consideration. Lévy-Bruhl defines the law of participation as follows:

In other words, the opposition between the one and the many, the same and another, and so forth, does not impose upon this mentality the necessity of affirming one of the terms if the other be denied, or vice versa. This opposition is of but secondary interest. Sometimes it is perceived, and frequently, too, it is not. It often disappears entirely.
(1910/1985: 77)

By the law of contradiction, something (or someone) cannot simultaneously be both "A" and "Not-A." If "A" is affirmed, then "Not-A" must be denied, and vice versa. By the law of participation, however, primitives may "think" one thing and the opposite of that thing, they may even "be" one thing and the opposite of that thing, at one and the same time—without apparently feeling that they are contradicting themselves. In contrast to "us," "they" may be both subject and object simultaneously. Lévy-Bruhl says:

> Our perception is directed toward the apprehension of an objective reality, and this reality alone. It eliminates all that might be of merely subjective importance ... But with the primitives there is no such violent contrast as this. Their perception is oriented in another fashion, and in it that which we call objective reality is united and mingled with, and often regulated by, mystic, imperceptible elements which we nowadays characterize as subjective.
>
> (1910/1985: 59)

The primitive psyche is "subjectivistic," the civilized psyche "objectivistic."

As primitives, according to Lévy-Bruhl, do not obey the law of contradiction, neither do they experience subject–object duality. In a sense, the primitive is not an individual. Rather, it is the collective that influences the primitive through representations. Lévy-Bruhl says that the *représentations collectives*, or "collective representations," of the social group dominate the primitive. These collective representations are inculcated in the primitive psyche by various means, including myths and rituals. Because the primitive does not consistently and continuously experience subject–object duality, these collective representations, Lévy-Bruhl says, "are not always, strictly speaking, representations." He continues:

> What we are accustomed to understand by representation, even direct and intuitive, implies duality in unity. The object is presented to the subject as in a certain sense distinct from himself; except in states such as ecstasy, that is, border states in which representation so called disappears, since the fusion between subject and object has become complete.
>
> (1910/1985: 362)

It is only by studying the primitive that we can discover the laws of these collective representations, Lévy-Bruhl maintains. "Collective representations have their own laws," he says, "and these (at any rate in dealing with primitives) cannot be discovered by studying the 'adult,' civilized, white man" (1910/1985: 13–14).

In a sense, the primitive does not think. Lévy-Bruhl contends that the "impressions" of the primitive "have only a far-off resemblance to ideas

or concepts." These impressions "are felt and lived, rather than thought."
Lévy-Bruhl elaborates:

> Neither their content nor their connections are strictly submitted to
> the law of contradiction. Consequently neither the personal ego, nor
> the social group, nor the surrounding world, both seen and unseen,
> appears to be yet "definite" in the collective representations, as they
> seem to be as soon as our conceptual thought tries to grasp them.
>
> (1921/1966): 447)

Whatever may be gained by civilized thinking, in the process something
is lost—or destroyed—in primitive feeling and living. The adult, civilized,
white man, who thinks ideas or concepts rather than feels and lives
impressions, "therefore despoils them"—that is, the collective representations—"of what there is in them that is elementally concrete, emotional
and vital" (1921/1966: 447).

The structural anthropologist Claude Lévi-Strauss criticizes Lévy-Bruhl
for indulging in spurious oppositional thinking. Lévi-Strauss prefers
" 'prior' rather than 'primitive' " (1966: 16), as if the primitive is simply
earlier and the civilized later. He rebukes Lévy-Bruhl for perpetrating a
"false antinomy between logical and prelogical mentality." According to
Lévi-Strauss, this is an untenable dichotomy. "The savage mind," he says,
"is logical in the same sense and the same fashion as ours." Lévi-Strauss
maintains that, "contrary to Lévy-Bruhl's opinion, its thought proceeds
through understanding, not affectivity, with the aid of distinctions and
oppositions, not by confusion and participation" (1966: 268). It is not
oppositional thinking as such that Lévi-Strauss condemns—he contends
that the human mind, whether savage or not, thinks oppositionally. Lévi-
Strauss believes that it is by means of oppositions that we structure
experience. In this respect, he utilizes information theory and compares
the mind to a computer that calculates by means of binary oppositions.

If Lévy-Bruhl dichotomizes the primitive and the civilized on the basis
of a prelogical mentality, Lévi-Strauss also, however, contrasts the primitive and the civilized not only in terms of a certain temporality (the
earlier–later, before–after opposition) but also on the basis of a "savage"
mind. He imagines the primitive–civilized opposition as a "raw–cooked"
opposition. However inadequate Lévy-Bruhl's dichotomous distinction
between the civilized and the primitive may seem from Lévi-Strauss's
perspective, it is nevertheless not merely a simplistic value judgment.
Lévy-Bruhl does not judge the civilized as unequivocally more valuable
than the primitive. Although in entitling one of his books *Mental Functions in Inferior Societies*, he implies that his own society is superior, he
does not regard the civilized as unambiguously positive and the primitive
negative. The traits that Lévy-Bruhl associates with the primitive may be
earlier but they are not necessarily lower or lesser than those that he

associates with the civilized. It is, in fact, the civilized that, he says, "despoils" the primitive of what is concretely, emotionally, and vitally distinctive about it.

Lévy-Bruhl is also not without his critics among psychologists. For example, Kurt Goldstein, in a discussion of the concept of "primitivity," explicitly rejects the equation of the primitive with the prelogical. Goldstein concludes that, whether primitive or civilized, "man always lives in two spheres of experience: the sphere in which the subject and object are experienced as separate and only secondarily related, and another one in which he experiences oneness with the world" (1969: 8). He argues that the people "living in 'primitive' societies may not have an inferior mentality but that they possess, like all human beings, the concrete–abstract unity of the human mental capacity" (1969: 13). Goldstein is, however, like Lévy-Bruhl in at least one important respect— he does not pathologize the primitive. The behavior of primitives, he declares, *"is not like the behavior of our patients"* (1969: 15).

Whorf also criticizes, from a linguistic perspective, the notion of a prelogical, primitive mentality. Ironically, he cites Jung in order to prob- lematize the opinion of both Lévy-Bruhl and Jung that the primitive cannot think—or does not think as the civilized does. Whorf says that "one of the clearest characterizations of thinking is that of Carl Jung." Among the four functions of thinking, feeling, sensation, and intuition that Jung describes, Whorf regards thinking as "the function which is to a large extent linguistic" (1956: 66). It is language, Whorf suggests, that affords evidence of sophistication of thought in primitives. He proposes to apply linguistics to analyze "the differences, real or assumed," between the civilized and the primitive. He wonders whether, as the notion of mystical participation employed by Lévy-Bruhl seems to imply, the civili- zed and the primitive have different mentalities "apart from the differ- ences between their cultures." (He also questions whether Freud's and Jung's equation of the primitive with the infantile has any analytic value.) Perhaps the civilized mentality is simply reflective of the linguistic simi- larity of Western culture, in contrast not to a primitive mentality but to "many diverse types of mentality" that are reflective of the linguistic diversity of non-Western cultures. This, Whorf says, is "one of the great psychological world-questions" to which linguistics may eventually pro- vide an answer. Whorf does not immediately reject the notion of a primitive mentality. He argues that if it does exist, it is, at least in some respects, not inferior but superior:

We are accustomed to think of such a mentality as is implied by PARTICIPATION MYSTIQUE as less of a thinking mentality, as less rational, than ours. Yet many American Indian and African languages abound in finely wrought, beautifully logical discriminations about causation, action, result, dynamic or energic quality, directness of experience, etc., all matters of the function of thinking, indeed the quintessence of the rational. In this respect they far out-distance the European languages.

(1956: 80)

Many primitive cultures, "far from being sub-rational, may show the human mind functioning on a higher and more complex plane of rationality than among civilized men." Even if these cultures were, in some sense, less rational, that would not necessarily mean that they were less civilized. "We do not know," Whorf concludes, "that civilization is synonymous with rationality" (1956: 81).

JUNG IN NORTH AFRICA

Wandlungen und Symbole der Libido, the book that marked Jung's theoretical divergence from Freud, was originally published in 1912 (translated into English in 1916 as *Psychology of the Unconscious, CW* B). It was then extensively revised in 1952 (retranslated into English in 1956 as *Symbols of Transformation, CW* 5). Although there are references to Lévy-Bruhl in *Symbols of Transformation*, there are no references to him in *Psychology of the Unconscious*. There are, however, numerous references to Lévy-Bruhl in Jung's works published after 1912. When did Jung first read any of Lévy-Bruhl's works? From 1905 until 1913, Jung was a lecturer in psychiatry at the University of Zurich. In his autobiography *Memories, Dreams, Reflections*, Jung states that the three principal subjects that he lectured on were psychopathology, psychoanalysis, and—significantly—"the psychology of primitives" (1963: 117). Sometime after 1912, if not before, Jung apparently read Lévy-Bruhl's *How Natives Think* (or *Mental Functions in Inferior Societies*), which was originally published in 1910. In an interview with Ximena de Angulo, Jung says that "he had known Lévy-Bruhl personally." At some point, Jung had entertained Lévy-Bruhl as a "house guest in Kusnacht" (De Angulo 1977: 214).

It is not difficult to appreciate what attracted Jung to Lévy-Bruhl. Like Lévy-Bruhl, Jung had an interest in the collective dimension of the psyche—what Jung eventually called the collective unconscious. He explicitly equates his "archetypes" (or, perhaps more accurately, his "archetypal images") with Lévy-Bruhl's "collective representations." Jung also attempts to demonstrate, through the amplification of ethnographic parallels, that the myths and rituals of the primitive are comparable to the fantasies of the insane. The references to Lévy-Bruhl in Jung's *Collected Works* emphasize the psychological function of collective representations and participation mystique. In short, just as Sir James G. Frazer's writings provided anthropological justification for Freud's psychological hypotheses, so did Lévy-Bruhl's for Jung's.

This "psychoanthropology" provides a context for Jung's trips to Africa. Jung traveled to Africa twice, once to North Africa in 1920, when he was 45, and then again to Central Africa in 1925–6, when he was 50. The trips were an occasion for Jung to "go primitive," to obtain direct experience of primitive psychology, and to ponder the issue of self and other. In a discussion of what it was like for Europeans like Jung to have "gone primitive," the cultural critic Marianna Torgovnick says that anthropologists, "especially when influenced by Freud, collaborated with other aspects of our culture in perpetuating an image of the primitive that is still with us, and still immensely powerful and seductive" (1990: 3). Freud is not the only psychoanalyst whom Torgovnick mentions as a primitivist-modernist. Although she refers to Jung's "journey" to Africa, as if she is under the misimpression that he traveled there only once, she notes that his experiences in Africa had an enormous impact on his theoretical formulations: "When Jung formulated his theories of the human psyche, he did so with his journey to Africa behind him; this was, for men of his generation, the equivalent of the European Grand Tour. To Jung as to many other moderns, Africa is the quintessential locus of the primitive" (1990: 11).

In North Africa, Jung traveled first to Algiers, then along the Mediterranean coast and into the Sahara desert. "At last," he says, "I was where I had longed to be": in a non-European culture, with "a different race" and "a different historical tradition and philosophy." Jung had yearned to be in a position that would enable him to reflect psychologically on the European self from the perspective of a non-European other. His trip to North Africa afforded him that opportunity. "I had often wished," he says, "to be able for once to see the European from outside, his image reflected back at him by an altogether foreign milieu." North Africa was a mirror for Jung's own psychological self-reflection. In experiencing the Arab culture of North Africa, Jung "learned to see to some extent with different eyes and to know the white man outside his own environment" (1963: 238– 9).

One of Jung's first observations was about the pace of life. North Africans, Jung says, were living in "twilight consciousness," a dream, as it were, from which Europeans threatened rudely to awaken them. In this respect, Jung's own pocket watch was for him "the symbol of the European's accelerated tempo." In contrast to the North African, who lived in "that duration which is still the closest thing to eternity," the European lived by "time and its synonym, progress," which had "irrevocably taken something from him." That something of which the European had been forever deprived was a sense of eternity, of duration. Whereas technology—"steamships, railroads, airplanes, and rockets"—speeded up the European, moved him forward, the deeper Jung traveled into North Africa, "the more time slowed down for me" and even "threatened to move backward" (1963: 240).

Another of Jung's observations was about feelings. The North Africans, Jung remarked, "live from their affects and have their being in emotions." They feel, he contends, but they do not reflect, or think, as Europeans do. In the North African "the ego has almost no autonomy." In contrast, the European, who possesses a more or less autonomous ego, has gained the ability to will and to intend. In the process, however, the European has, again, lost something. That something, in this case, is a certain existential vitality. "What we lack," Jung laments, "is intensity of life" (1963: 242).

A DREAM: HAVING ONE'S HEAD PUSHED UNDER WATER

Before returning to Europe from North Africa, Jung had a dream that he says "summed up the whole experience." He recounts the dream as follows:

> I dreamt that I was in an Arab city, and as in most such cities there was a citadel, a casbah. The city was situated in a broad plain, and had a wall all around it. The shape of the wall was square, and there were four gates.
>
> The casbah in the interior of the city was surrounded by a wide moat (which is not the way it really is in Arab countries). I stood before a wooden bridge leading over the water to a dark, horseshoe-shaped portal, which was open. Eager to see the citadel from the inside also, I stepped out on the bridge. When I was about halfway across it, a handsome, dark Arab of aristocratic, almost royal bearing came toward me from the gate. I knew that this youth in the white burnoose was the resident prince of the citadel. When he came up to me, he attacked me and tried to knock me down. We wrestled. In the struggle we crashed against the railing; it gave way and both of us fell into the moat, where he tried to push my head under water to drown me. No, I thought, this is going too far. And in my turn I pushed his head under water. I did so although I felt great admiration for him; but I did not want to let myself be killed. I had no intention of killing him; I wanted only to make him unconscious and incapable of fighting.
>
> Then the scene of the dream changed, and he was with me in a large vaulted octagonal room in the center of the citadel. The room was all white, very plain and beautiful. Along the light-colored marble walls stood low divans, and before me on the floor lay an open book with black letters written in magnificent calligraphy on milky-white parch-

ment. It was not Arabic script; rather, it looked to me like the Uigurian script of West Turkestan, which was familiar to me from the Manichaean fragments from Turfan. I did not know the contents, but nevertheless I had the feeling that this was "my book," that I had written it. The young prince with whom I had just been wrestling sat to the right of me on the floor. I explained to him that now that I had overcome him he must read the book. But he resisted. I placed my arm around his shoulders and forced him, with a sort of paternal kindness and patience, to read the book. I knew that this was absolutely essential, and at last he yielded.

(1963: 242–3)

Jung's dream is an encounter not only between Europe and Africa but also between Europe and "Arabia," between West and East, between Occident and Orient. As the cultural critic Edward W. Said says, the Orient was virtually "a European invention." To the European, the Orient was "a place of romance, exotic beings, haunting memories and landscapes, remarkable experiences" (1978: 1). In this sense, Jung's Arabic dream is the very epitome of what Said calls "Orientalist discourse" (1978: 6). It is a hegemonic projection of the European collective unconscious onto what Said calls an arbitrary "imaginative geography" (1978: 54).

As Jung interprets the dream, the Arab prince is "a messenger or emissary of the self." By the "self," Jung does not mean what we ordinarily mean when we use the word—and as I consistently use the word in this book—simply to refer to an individual as distinct from others. Nor is it synonymous with what "self psychologists" like Heinz Kohut mean by the word. Jungians often capitalize the word as "Self" to distinguish it from ordinary usage. As Jung defines the "self," it sometimes refers only to the totality of the personality, or the psyche, inclusive of both the conscious and the unconscious, but sometimes also to an entity with intelligence (knowledge or wisdom), intentionality, and agency not only different from but also superior to the ego. Whether in sometimes positing such an entity Jung commits the fallacy of hypostatizing a metapsychological—or even a metaphysical—assertion is, for me at least, a very serious question. To the extent that the "self" resembles "god," some Jungians not only reify but also tend to deify this ostensible entity. Jung interprets the dream by reference to the Bible. Jung's wrestling the prince is like Jacob's wrestling the angel. Just as the angel was "a messenger of God who wished to kill men because he did not know them," so the prince was a messenger or emissary of the self who wished to kill Jung because he did not know him. "Therefore," Jung concludes, "he first came forward as my enemy; however, I held my own against him." When the prince next came forward, "he sat at my feet," Jung says, "and had to learn to understand my thoughts, or rather, learn to know man" (1963: 243–4).

Thus the civilized, European ego of Jung has to wrestle with and win over a primitive, North African, or Arabic, representative of the self. "Obviously, my encounter with Arab culture had struck me with overwhelming force," Jung says. "The emotional nature of these unreflective people who are so much closer to life than we are exerts a strong suggestive influence upon those historical layers in ourselves which we have just overcome and left behind, or which we think we have overcome." According to Jung, the primitive is like a child, the civilized like an adult. Jung asserts that "a characteristic of childhood is that, thanks to its naïveté and unconsciousness, it sketches a more complete picture of the self, of the whole man in his pure individuality, than adulthood." As a result, "the sight of a child or a primitive will arouse certain longings in adult, civilized persons." These longings, Jung says, "relate to the unfulfilled desires and needs of those parts of the personality which have been blotted out" in the service of the persona, the mask that the ego wears in order to adapt to the demands of society (1963: 244). Freud also compares the primitive to the child: "The essential point, however, is that we attribute the same emotional attitudes to these primitive men that we are able to establish by analytic investigation in the primitives of the present day—in our children" (*SE* 23: 81–2). (This comparison persists in the terminology of contemporary psychoanalysts who call the most immoderate emotional attitudes of patients "primitive," on the assumption that such attitudes are developmentally immature, or "childish.") The historian of ideas George Boas notes that "the cultural primitivist" (of whom both Freud and Jung are representatives) designated "a new exemplar" of the primitive in the "Child"—as well as in the "Irrational," the "Neurotic," and the "Collective Unconscious" (1990: 8).

Jung says that he traveled to North Africa "to find a psychic observation post outside the sphere of the European." He wanted to experience a non-European, a non-Eurocentric, a non-ethnocentric psychological point of view, or frame of reference. "I unconsciously wanted to find that part of my personality," he remarks, "which had become invisible under the influence and the pressure of being European." When Jung wrestles the Arab prince, he confronts—and subdues—the "primitive" part of his own, European psyche. "This part," he says, "stands in unconscious opposition to myself, and indeed I attempt to suppress it." That part of himself tries to drown him—kill him by pushing his head (a symbol of the ego) under water (a symbol of the unconscious). That is, when Jung goes to North Africa, he gets in "over his head" or "out of his depth" and in the process almost drowns. The submersion is an image of the subliminal, the subconscious. To be under water is, topographically, to be under the conscious—to be unconscious. In the dream, Jung fights for his psychical life with a part of his own personality: "In keeping with its nature, it wishes to make me unconscious (force me under water) so as to kill me; but my aim is, through insight, to make it more conscious, so that we can find a common modus vivendi" (1963: 244). In this life-and-death struggle, Jung does not try to kill that part of himself—he merely tries to keep it from killing him, from rendering his ego utterly unconscious.

THE WATERS OF THE UNCONSCIOUS

"Water," Jung says, "is the commonest symbol for the unconscious" (*CW* 9,1: 18). In a discussion of the dreams of white South Africans, the Jungian analyst Lee Zahner-Roloff mentions the ambivalent European attitude toward going black—or, as he calls it, "turning black." He states: "Whatever the African continent has meant to the Western European, the relationship has been one of love and hate, entailing for the European a fear of 'turning black'—an inelegant phrase that bespeaks Europe's historical attraction/aversion to Africa." He then relates the dream of a white South African:

> *I am standing at a "whites only" beach. A black wave comes and threatens to swamp me. It was like a flood. But the water withdrew and it was calm again. I felt impending doom, and then a sense of relief.*
> (1990: 25)

Zahner-Roloff maintains that this dream requires no interpretation—the meaning seems obvious to him: it is a menacing image of going black. He does say, however, that the dream has a public and collective as well as a private and personal dimension. "When this dream was shared publicly," he reports, "there was a sense of mutual experience, that the unspeakable fear known by all whites was expressed through the subjectivity of one person" (1990: 25–6). It is a dream that resonates collectively in the unconscious of many white South Africans. The dream is similar to Jung's underwater dream. In both dreams, the waters of the unconscious threaten to overwhelm, or drown, the dreamer. In the dream of the white South African, land is an image of the ego, water of the unconscious (the id for Freud, the shadow for Jung). In this respect, the white beach–black wave opposition, an especially apt image of apartheid, is the liminal state of "racial" (and psychical) segregation, a boundary between white and black, conscious and unconscious, ego and id (or shadow). Separate and unequal facilities imply separate and unequal realities: "whites only," "blacks only."

It is Freud who says, "Where id was, there ego shall be" (*SE* 22: 80), and imagines psychoanalysis as a drainage project to reclaim land from the waters of the unconscious. (There is evidently no psychical distance, in this respect, between the Zuyder Zee and the Cape of Good Hope.) The Freudian analyst Cornelius Castoriadis insists that the land reclamation project should not be interpreted as "the elimination or the absorption of the unconscious" (1987: 102). According to Castoriadis, the waters of the unconscious are the waters of the imagination. To eliminate the unconscious, Castoriadis says, would be to eliminate the imagination:

> How can we conceive of a subject that would have entirely "absorbed" the imaginative function, how could we dry up this spring in the depths of ourselves from which flow both alienating phantasies and free creation truer than truth, unreal deliria and surreal poems, this eternally new beginning and ground of all things, without which nothing would have a ground, how can we eliminate what is at the base of, or in any case what is inextricably bound up with what makes us human beings—our symbolic function, which presupposes our capacity to see and to think in a thing something which it is not?
>
> (1987: 103–4)

Castoriadis regards the land reclamation project as "unrealistic, utopian and wrong." In contrast to the ego psychology of Freud, Castoriadis says, "Where ego is, id must also appear." He notes that one of the primary objectives of psychoanalysis is to facilitate the emergence of contents, or images, from the unconscious. What Castoriadis calls the "radical imagination" is radical precisely because, in the etymological sense, it "is rooted in the unconscious." The radical imagination "has to come out, which does not mean that all the products of the radical imagination are 'good', but they have to come out" (Gordon 1991: 489). Whether a sea (as with Freud) or a spring (as with Castoriadis), the unconscious (or imagination) is metaphorically the "wet," and the ego is the "dry"—and it is an anti-psychoanalytic, anti-"psychoecological" act to attempt to dehydrate the psyche.

Like Castoriadis, Hillman advocates a psychology of the imagination— an imaginal psychology rather than an ego psychology. As Hillman interprets water, it signifies death—that is, the death of the ego. (In contrast, land signifies the death of imagination.) In dreams, Hillman says, the ego "fears drowning in torrents, whirlpools, tidal waves." Psychoanalysts ("have they such dry souls?" Hillman asks) frequently interpret such dreams to signify that "the dreamer is in danger of being overwhelmed by the unconscious in an emotional psychosis, flooded with fantasies—no ground, no standpoint" (1979: 152–3). The Jungian analysts Edward C. Whitmont and Sylvia Brinton Perera provide an example of the "dry" interpretation that Hillman criticizes. They interpret the image of a "tidal wave" in a dream as a portent of "an imminent psychotic episode" (1989: 107). Similarly, both Jung and Zahner-Roloff interpret metaphorically "wet" dreams as a mortal threat of being submerged or inundated by the waters of the unconscious.

INTEGRATION OF THE SHADOW

The *modus vivendi* that Jung attempts and ultimately accomplishes when he interprets his dream of drowning is an integration of the unconscious and the ego. In this respect, although the prince is not a black African, he is a dark African, an Arab. "The Arab's dusky complexion," Jung says, "marks him as a 'shadow,' but not the personal shadow, rather an ethnic one associated not with my persona but with the totality of my personality, that is, with the self." The prince is a transpersonal, or archetypal, shadow, an image from the collective unconscious. According to Jung, in the psyche of the rational, civilized white European the vitally primitive, unconscious part of the personality is often symbolized by a black or dark image—a shadow that is cast by the ego. "The predominantly rationalistic European finds much that is human alien to him," Jung contends, "and he prides himself on this without realizing that his rationality is won at the expense of his vitality, and that the primitive part of his personality is consequently condemned to a more or less underground existence" (1963: 244–5).

Jung does not explicitly interpret the image of the book, although he does say that it is his book, that he has written it. Jung, of course, wrote many books during his life—and they were all psychology books, books about the psyche. If this book is his book, it is perhaps a book about his own psyche, or psychical life. Curiously, although it is an open book—as one may say that one's life is an open book—and although the script is familiar, Jung does not know the contents of his own book. He may have written the book, but apparently he has yet to read it—or interpret it. If in dreams the unknown is the unconscious, then Jung is evidently unconscious of what he has written in the book of life, his autobiography. In a white room with light walls, Jung paternally, perhaps paternalistically, forces the dark Arab prince to read a book with white pages, as if the shadow must learn about the ego—just as the ego must learn about the shadow—in order for integration of the opposites to occur through insight.

Jung interprets the dream as a victorious, triumphal effort at integration of the opposites—the civilized and the primitive, time and eternity, thinking and feeling, the rational and the vital, the conscious and the unconscious, the ego and the shadow—all in the service of individuation. Under the suggestive influence of North Africa, however, he experiences the dream as a homicidal threat:

> First of all there was the danger that my European consciousness would
> be overwhelmed by an unexpectedly violent assault of the unconscious
> psyche. Consciously, I was not a bit aware of any such situation; on
> the contrary, I could not help feeling superior because I was reminded
> at every step of my Europeanism. That was unavoidable; my being
> European gave me a certain perspective on these people who were so

differently constituted from myself, and utterly marked me off from them. But I was not prepared for the existence of unconscious forces within myself which would take the part of these strangers with such intensity, so that a violent conflict ensued. The dream expressed this conflict in the symbol of an attempted murder.

Jung asserts that there was something within himself—a primitive part of his own European psyche—that unconsciously identified with the North African psyche. Although he did not realize it at the time, he concludes, in retrospect, that he was in jeopardy of being completely overwhelmed by the experience. "I was not to recognize the real nature of this disturbance until some years later," he says, "when I stayed in tropical Africa." (Jung is referring to his trip to Central Africa in 1925–6.) It is in reference to his trip to North Africa that Jung first mentions the possibility of going black. He states: "It had been, in fact, the first hint of 'going black under the skin,' a spiritual peril which threatens the uprooted European in Africa to an extent not fully appreciated" (1963: 245).

For Jung, the primitive North Africans, or Arabs, evoke in the civilized European "an archetypal memory of an all too well known prehistoric past which apparently we have entirely forgotten." (The civilized is, in this sense, a forgetting—or a repressing—of the primitive.) In encountering the primitive, Jung says, "We are remembering a potentiality of life which has been overgrown by civilization, but which in certain places is still existent." For Jung, Africa is that place *par excellence*. To relive that past in the present, uncritically, would be to regress—to go back, to go barbaric, and, as it were, to go black. "If we were to relive it naively, it would constitute a relapse into barbarism," Jung contends. "Therefore we prefer to forget it." Rather than forget or relive the past, Jung recommends that we remember it in the present. If the contrast between the primitive and the civilized should "appear to us again in the form of a conflict"—as it does in Jung's dream of wrestling the Arab prince, which he interprets as the shadow of the self—"then we should keep it in our consciousness and test the two possibilities against each other—the life we live and the one we have forgotten." Such a confrontation, Jung suggests, is not merely symptomatic: it serves a psychical purpose. Because initially the purpose may seem incomprehensible, Jung recommends patience. It is imperative, he says, to "content ourselves for the time being with noting the phenomenon and hoping that the future, or further investigation, will reveal the significance of this clash with the shadow of the self." In this respect, in regard to his dream of wrestling with the Arab prince, Jung confesses ignorance: "I did not at the time have any glimmer of the nature of this archetypal experience." The experience did, however, provoke in him "the liveliest wish to go to Africa again at the next opportunity" (1963: 246).

Chapter 5

Jung in "Black" Africa

Five years later, Jung's wish was fulfilled. This time he traveled to Central Africa—or "Black" Africa. He was accompanied by Godwin Baynes, a British Jungian analyst, and George Beckwith, an American friend and game hunter. On the trip, they met Ruth Bailey, a young British woman (who, many years later, in Jung's old age, after his wife's death, became his housekeeper in Zurich). The four of them traveled together. Jung and Baynes filmed the trip with a 16-millimeter camera. Stephen Segaller and Merrill Berger describe the black-and-white footage as follows:

> In the flickering monochrome images of the Jung–Baynes home movies, the expedition is seen to trek through the bush and into the highlands, with vignettes of tribal life interspersed through the film. At one point, in a cave apparently occupied by a family and its goats, Dr Jung is seen to be prodding and tickling a wide-eyed African boy of three or four years old; at another, he applauds as two boys re-enact the incident in which the expedition cook was almost attacked by a hyena in his tent. Seemingly as comfortable in his colonial role of expedition leader (seen distributing wages to the bearers at a folding card-table) as he would be in his Zurich study, Jung regarded the African visit as enjoyable and informative.
>
> (1989: 53)

The film, of course, captures only a part, not the whole, of the trip, which was certainly "informative" but by no means always "enjoyable" for Jung.

Segaller (1989) includes clips from the film in a recent videotape documentary about Jung. In the first scene, Jung and his party are walking across a bridge over a river, the bearers following. Then they come toward the camera, the bearers carrying baskets and boxes, and on the left an African man, a government soldier, marching in a European uniform, his rifle on his shoulder, his sword in his hand. In pith helmet, khakis, with walking stick and rifle, Jung approaches with his party through a stand of bamboo. Next, six African women are carrying amphorae on their heads. Then Jung is walking out from behind a tree into a scene of children, with bowls on the ground. In another scene, two young African men are sitting on the ground, one of them smoking a cigarette and someone else standing with a rifle. Then Jung, pipe in his mouth, is going through a box or crate, the lid up, inspecting tins. There is a group of seven girls, one with a pot on her head, then a crowd of children. Next, Jung is sitting with an African man with a coffee tin in his hand. There is a scene of African girls, water bearers. Several African men, dressed in their finest, pose in a group. Then a number of African men are seated in the foreground, while others, including Europeans, are standing and strolling in the background. A group of men, including the *laibon*, or medicine man, are all sitting on the ground, except for Jung the psychoanalyst, who sits in a chair. There is a scene of Africans moving around, one flinging a cloak or shawl over his shoulder. Next, Jung is seated on a chair under a straw roof, out of the sun, at a folding table, wearing his pith helmet, apparently handing out money to a line of African men. The government soldier in European uniform maintains order, while someone else pushes the people along. There is a scene of music and dancing, one African man playing a stringed instrument, and Jung smoking a pipe in the shade and getting up. Then African men are in a circle, dancing up and down. Jung directs two young African men in a game of make-believe, the one man pretending, evidently like a hyena, to sneak up on and surprise the other man, who is lying on the ground and pretending to be sleeping. There are Masai with their cattle. Next, Jung is walking with Ruth Bailey, he with his rifle, she with her walking stick. Finally, Jung and others emerge from the jungle. Jung comes around from under a tree, waving what appears to be a handful of vegetation.

Jung's trip to Central Africa was for him a journey into what Joseph Conrad called "the heart of darkness." In the novel by that name, the civilized–primitive opposition is for Conrad a light–dark, day–night, enlightened–benighted, clear–cloudy opposition. Once upon a time, not so long ago, Marlow suggests, England was Africa. "I was thinking," he says, "of very old times, when the Romans came here, nineteen hundred years ago—the other day." When the civilized Romans invaded the primitive English (which was, in historical terms, just the other day), the experience was "like a flash of lightning in the clouds." (In this analogy, Romans are to English as Europeans are to Africans.) The bolt of civilization struck and, for an instant, starkly illuminated the sky. Since then, civilization has been a flickering of light in the dark, a mere glimmering of as yet indeterminate duration. "We live," Marlow says, "in the flicker—may it last as long as the old earth keeps rolling! But darkness was here yesterday" (1899/1971: 5). According to Marlow, the Romans did not colonize the English—they merely conquered them:

They were no colonists; their administration was merely a squeeze, and nothing more, I suspect. They were conquerors, and for that you want only brute force—nothing to boast of, when you have it, since your strength is just an accident arising from the weakness of others. They grabbed what they could get for the sake of what was to be got. It was just robbery with violence, aggravated murder on a great scale, and men going at it blind—as is very proper for those who tackle a darkness. The conquest of the earth, which pretty much means the taking it away from those who have a different complexion or slightly flatter noses than ourselves, is not a pretty thing when you look into it too much. What redeems it is the idea only. An idea at the back of it; not a sentimental pretence but an idea; and an unselfish belief in the idea—something you can set up, and bow down before, and offer a sacrifice to . . .

(1899/1971: 6–7)

In this rationalization for civilization—or the crime of empire—ideology is redemptive only to the extent that it is a form of idolatry for which one is willing, unselfishly, to sacrifice oneself.

Conrad, of course, is the novelist who develops a character, Kurtz, who epitomizes the associations "going black," "going primitive," "going instinctive," and "going insane." It is words, the "common, everyday words," that Kurtz speaks that are symptomatic of a pathological unconscious. "They had behind them, to my mind," Marlow says, "the terrific suggestiveness of words heard in dreams, or phrases spoken in nightmares" (1899/1971: 67). Kurtz had not lost his mind—he was perfectly lucid in conversation—but he had lost his soul. In the solitude of the jungle, away from civilization, Kurtz's soul "had looked within itself, and, by Heavens! I tell you," Marlow exclaims, "it had gone mad" (1899/1971: 68).

For the colonialist, imperialist white European, Africa was the "dark continent." For Freud, "the sexual life of adult women" was also a dark continent (*SE* 20: 212). Jung says that on a visit to the Wembley Exhibition in London in 1925 he "was deeply impressed by the excellent survey of the tribes under British rule, and resolved to take a trip to tropical Africa in the near future" (1963: 253). Jung traveled to Kenya and Uganda and trekked to Mount Elgon. When he returned to Europe, he promised to ponder the psychical impact of the trip on himself personally—"how Africa affects oneself." While traveling in Africa, he had been too busy to pause and reflect. "I had no time to think," he said. "But I am going to" (1973: 22).

SEDUCTION AND PANIC ATTACKS

The second mention that Jung makes of going black occurs in his account of the 1925–6 trip. He describes three Elgonyi women, the expedition's "water bearers, a woman and her two half-grown daughters, who were naked except for a belt of cowries." It is an exotic-erotic portrait—"local color" in the full sense of the term:

They were chocolate-brown and strikingly pretty, with fine slim figures and an aristocratic leisureliness about their movements. It was a pleasure for me each morning to hear the soft *cling-clang* of their iron ankle rings as they came up from the brook, and soon afterward to see their swaying gait as they emerged from the tall yellow elephant grass, balancing the amphorae of water on their heads. They were adorned with ankle rings, brass bracelets and necklaces, earrings of copper or wood in the shape of small spools. Their lower lips were pierced with either a bone or iron nail. They had very good manners, and always greeted us with shy, charming smiles.

(1963: 261)

Jung looked at the women, but he did not talk to them:

With a single exception . . . I never spoke to a native woman, this being what was expected of me. As in Southern Europe, men speak to men, women to women. Anything else signifies love-making. The white who goes in for this not only forfeits his authority, but runs the serious risk of "going black." I observed several highly instructive examples of this. Quite often I heard the natives pass judgment upon a certain white: "He is a bad man." When I asked why, the reply was invariably, "He sleeps with our women."

(1963: 261–2)

Jung, whom Freud accused of desexualizing psychoanalytic theory by redefining "libido," refers to going black in a seductive description of African women. The equation is as follows: even so much as to speak to African women—naked, pretty, slim, swaying, shy, charming African women—is to make love to them, which is to run the risk of going black. The risk for the white European man—and for Jung—is that he may be seduced by the African woman into making love, going black, and, in the process, forfeiting authority.

After leaving Mount Elgon, Jung traveled to the Sudan, where he says "we had a very exciting experience." He met the chief of a local tribe, among whom were, he says, "the blackest Negroes I had ever seen." He describes what I call his panic attack as follows:

When the chief proposed that he give a *n'goma* (dance) in the evening, I assented gladly. I hoped that the frolic would bring their better nature to the fore. Night had fallen and we were all longing for sleep when we heard drums and horn blasts. Soon some sixty men appeared, martially equipped with flashing lances, clubs, and swords. They were followed at some distance by the women and children; even the infants were present, carried on their mothers' backs. This was obviously to be a grand social occasion. In spite of the heat, which still hovered around ninety-three degrees, a big fire was kindled, and women and children formed a circle around it. The men formed an outer ring around them, as I had once observed a nervous herd of wild elephants do. I did not know whether I ought to feel pleased or anxious about this mass display. I looked around for our boys and the government soldiers—they had vanished completely from the camp! As a gesture of good will, I distributed cigarettes, matches, and safety pins. The men's chorus began to sing, vigorous, bellicose melodies, not unharmonious, and at the same time began to swing their legs. The women and children tripped around the fire; the men danced toward it, waving their weapons, then drew back again, and then advanced anew, amid savage singing, drumming, and trumpeting.

It was a wild and stirring scene, bathed in the glow of the fire and magical moonlight. My English friend and I sprang to our feet and mingled with the dancers. I swung my rhinoceros whip, the only weapon I had, and danced with them. By their beaming faces I could see that they approved of our taking part. Their zeal redoubled; the whole company stamped, sang, shouted, sweating profusely. Gradually the rhythm of the dance and drumming accelerated.

In dances such as these, accompanied by such music, the natives easily fall into a virtual state of possession. That was the case now. As eleven o'clock approached, their excitement began to get out of bounds, and suddenly the whole affair took on a highly curious aspect. The dancers were being transformed into a wild horde, and I became worried about how it would end. I signed to the chief that it was time to stop, and that he and his people ought to go to sleep. But he kept wanting "just another one."

I remembered that a countryman of mine, one of the Sarasin cousins, on an exploratory expedition in Celebes had been struck by a stray spear in the course of such a *n'goma*. And so, disregarding the chief's pleas, I called the people together, distributed cigarettes, and then made the gesture of sleeping. Then I swung my rhinoceros whip threateningly, but at the same time laughing, and for lack of any better language I swore at them loudly in Swiss German that this was enough, and they must go home to bed and sleep now. It was apparent to the people that I was to some extent pretending my anger, but that seems to have struck just the right note. General laughter arose; capering, they scattered in all directions and vanished into the night. For a long time we heard their jovial howls and drumming in the distance. At last silence fell, and we dropped into the sleep of exhaustion.

(1963: 270–2)

Many things might be said about this passage and about what it reveals about Jung's and white Europeans' conscious or unconscious experience of black Africans—or their projections onto that experience. I believe that it is obvious that Jung suffered a panic attack, and that this was more than mere anxiety over whether he might end up being struck by a stray spear.

In another context, Jung describes a fear, "a panic, which is typical of the collective unconscious." He compares this panic to "the bush fear, a particular kind of fear which seizes you when you are alone in the bush." It is a fear of "going astray in the bush—the most terrible thing you can imagine, people go mad in no time—or you may develop the symptom of feeling yourself looked at on all sides, of eyes everywhere looking at you, eyes that you do not see." According to Jung, he himself suffered such a panic attack: "Once, in the bush in Africa, I kept turning around in a small circle for half an hour so that my back would not be turned to the eyes which I felt were watching me." Although Jung says that the eyes were actually there, "doubtless, the eyes of a leopard perhaps," he never actually spotted the spots of the leopard, not to mention the eyes (1984: 75). This account of bush panic obviously has all of the elements of a paranoid delusion. Evidently, one can go mad momentarily, or experience temporary insanity, not only when one is together with a tribe of black Africans at a *n'goma* but also when one is alone in the bush. In both instances, the collective unconscious threatens to seize, or possess, Jung.

Jung is not the only white European who ever panicked. In a work of autobiographical fiction, the French novelist Marie Cardinal describes a similar experience:

My first anxiety attack occurred during a Louis Armstrong concert. I was nineteen or twenty. Armstrong was going to improvise with his trumpet, to build a whole composition in which each note would be important and would contain within itself the essence of the whole. I was not disappointed: the atmosphere warmed up very fast. The scaffolding and flying buttresses of the jazz instruments supported Armstrong's trumpet, creating spaces which were adequate enough for it to climb higher, establish itself, and take off again. The sounds of the trumpet sometimes piled up together, fusing a new musical base, a sort of matrix which gave birth to one precise, unique note, tracing a sound whose path was almost painful, so absolutely necessary had its equilibrium and duration become; it tore at the nerves of those who followed it.

My heart began to accelerate, becoming more important than the music, shaking the bars of my rib cage, compressing my lungs so the air could no longer enter them. Gripped by panic at the idea of dying there in the middle of spasms, stomping feet, and the crowd howling, I ran into the street like someone possessed.

(1983: 39)

The novelist Toni Morrison cites this passage in a discussion of whiteness and the literary imagination. She wonders what there was in the jazz that Armstrong played that night to drive "this sensitive young girl hyperventilating into the street" (1992: vii). Evidently, not only dancing to a *n'goma* in Africa but also listening to African-American music in Europe is enough to induce a panic attack. Just as Jung fears that he might be wounded or killed by a stray spear, Cardinal fears that she might become possessed by the other and die.

A DREAM: HAVING ONE'S HAIR KINKED

After describing the scene of the *n'goma*, Jung recounts a dream. This is the third time that he refers to the risk of going black. Jung says:

During the entire trip my dreams stubbornly followed the tactic of ignoring Africa. They drew exclusively upon scenes from home, and thus seemed to say that they considered—if it is permissible to personify the unconscious processes to this extent—the African journey not as something real, but rather as a symptomatic or symbolic act. Even the most impressive events of the trip were rigorously excluded from my dreams. Only once during the entire expedition did I dream of a Negro. His face appeared curiously familiar to me, but I had to reflect a long time before I could determine where I had met him before. Finally it came to me: he had been my barber in Chattanooga, Tennessee! An American Negro. In the dream he was holding a tremendous, red-hot curling iron to my head, intending to make my hair kinky—that is, to give me Negro hair. I could already feel the painful heat, and awoke with a sense of terror.

I took this dream as a warning from the unconscious; it was saying that the primitive was a danger to me. At that time I was obviously all too close to "going black." . . . In order to represent a Negro threatening me, my unconscious had invoked a twelve-year-old memory of my Negro barber in America, just in time to avoid any reminder of the present.

(1963: 272–3)

If, as Jung says, the image of the African-American barber in Chattanooga, Tennessee, was an invocation of a twelve-year-old memory, it would apparently be a reference to an event that occurred in either 1913 or 1914, since Jung traveled to Central Africa in 1925–6. William McGuire, however, suggests that the memory actually dates from 1910. Jung traveled to America in that year in order to analyze Medill McCormick, a great-nephew of Harold Fowler McCormick, the inventor of the mechanical harvester, a grandson of Joseph Medill, publisher of the *Chicago Tribune*, and a member of one of the wealthiest families in America. After graduation from Yale University, Medill McCormick had assumed the position of manager and assistant editor-in-chief of the newspaper. Under the stress of that job, excessive indulgence in alcohol, and the influence of a dominant mother, he suffered a nervous breakdown in 1908. He traveled to Zurich to seek analysis from Jung for what was evidently a bipolar disorder. After two months in Europe, he returned to America. In 1910, he suffered a relapse. According to McGuire, McCormick traveled to Tennessee, where, in a manic state, he imagined that "he was fighting the Civil War battles of Chickamauga and Missionary Ridge near Chattanooga—retracing them with a relief map, on horseback, at the rate of twenty-five miles a day" (1995: 307). Evidently, it was while conducting an emergency analysis of a patient who wanted to refight the Civil War that Jung received a haircut from an African-American barber.

The dream of the African-American barber with a red-hot curling iron is a nightmare that terrified Jung. As Jung interprets the dream, Africa (as the unconscious) posed a threat to his ego. In effect, Jung felt that he was in danger of going black, going primitive, going instinctive, going insane: losing his ego—which was tantamount to becoming possessed, to succumbing to the law of participation and to subject–object unity. Jung epitomizes what Torgovnick calls the identity crisis of Western civilization. "What is clear now," Torgovnick says, "is that the West's fascination with the primitive has to do with its own crises of identity, with its own need to clearly demarcate subject and object even while flirting with other ways of experiencing the universe" (1990: 157).

Jung had other dreams during his trip, but they were all, without exception, not African dreams but European dreams, which dealt exclusively with "personal problems." From this, he concluded that his dreams were indicating that "my European personality must under all circumstances be preserved intact." Very like Torgovnick, Roger Brooke says, "It would seem that the 'European personality' that was so threatened has to do with the specifically European constitution of identity" (1991: 60). Jung gradually realized that the entire trip had been a journey not only into the interior of Africa but also into the interior of himself. In traveling to Central Africa, he had had an ulterior, unconscious motive:

To my astonishment, the suspicion dawned on me that I had undertaken my African adventure with the secret purpose of escaping from

Europe and its complex of problems, even at the risk of remaining in Africa, as so many before me had done, and as so many were doing at this very time. The trip revealed itself as less an investigation of primitive psychology ("Bugishu Psychological Expedition," B.P.E., black letters on the chop boxes!) than a probing into the rather embarrassing question: What is going to happen to Jung the psychologist in the wilds of Africa? This was a question I had constantly sought to evade, in spite of my intellectual intention to study the European's reaction to primitive conditions. It became clear to me that this study had been not so much an objective scientific project as an intensely personal one, and that any attempt to go deeper into it touched every possible sore spot in my own psychology. I had to admit to myself that it was scarcely the Wembley Exhibition which had begotten my decision to travel, but rather the fact that the atmosphere had become too highly charged for me in Europe.

(1963: 273)

We now know what happened to Jung the psychologist in the wilds of Africa: he decided to stay white rather than go black. He epitomizes the fear of the white European that to go black is to go primitive, to go instinctive, which is to go insane, which is to lose his ego—and, Jung says, to forfeit his authority. Rather than become a Kurtz, Jung—or his ego—cracks his whip and shouts a curse in order to disperse the primitives and stop their dance, their trance, his panic attack.

The dominant image in Jung's nightmare is Jung's hair—his straight hair, which the African-American barber with the red-hot curling iron would turn into kinky hair. The question is, what does hair signify unconsciously to Jung? The psychologist Charles Berg presents a Freudian interpretation of hair. According to him, the unconscious significance of hair is sexual. As evidence, he cites the associations of dreamers who regard hair, especially erect hair, as a phallus, or symbolic penis, and hair loss as a symbolic castration. It is at "the genital level," he contends, that hair has unconscious significance (1951: 39). Berg would presumably interpret Jung's dream as symbolizing castration anxiety. The analyst Medard Boss offers an existentialist interpretation of hair. Although he acknowledges that hair may have an association with sexuality, he maintains that such an association is only a special case of the more general human experience of physicality, or embodiment. He says that hair signifies "the 'bodyhood' or the 'bodying' of human existence" and hair loss the deterioration or annihilation of vitality (1977: 158). In all probability, Boss would interpret Jung's dream as exemplifying existential anxiety.

JUNG ON DREAM INTERPRETATION

Jung made five important methodological contributions to dream interpretation. These include: (1) phenomenological–metaphorical interpretation, (2) amplificatory interpretation, (3) compensatory interpretation, (4) subjective interpretation, and (5) prospective interpretation. A Jungian interpretation of Jung's nightmare should properly comprise an application of all five methods.

First, in contrast to Freud, who maintains that the images in a dream are not what they seem to be, that there is a distinction between manifest appearance and latent reality, Jung insists that the images really are what they apparently are. To the extent that Jung consistently adheres to this position, he tends to be a phenomenologist, or an essentialist. That is, he asks what the essence of any image is. He attends to the specific phenomenal attributes, qualities, or properties of the image. He asks what an image essentially is, both in general (collectively) and in particular (personally). What is decisive in an interpretation is what the dreamer regards as the essence of the image. What matters is the psychical reality of the dreamer, not the attributes, qualities, or properties of an object in external reality. Attributes are, in this sense, attributions. What is crucial is what the dreamer attributes to the phenomenon. The phenomenological method that Jung employs is a variety not of metaphysical essentialism but of what Douglas Medin and Andrew Ortony call "psychological essentialism." As Medin and Ortony define psychological essentialism, it is "not the view that *things* have essences, but rather the view that people's *representations* of things might reflect such a belief (erroneous as it may be)" (1989: 183). What the dreamer, correctly or incorrectly, believes the essence of an image to be is the criterion of interpretation. Ultimately, Jung is not, however, strictly and exclusively a phenomenologist. It would be more accurate to say that he is a phenomenologist–metaphorist. He does not just ask what an image is, phenomenologically. He also asks what it means, metaphorically. He asks what an image is like, psychically, to the dreamer.

Second, whereas Freud emphasizes association to images, Jung also recommends amplification of them. Amplification is an intertextual, comparative–contrastive method of interpretation. To amplify an image is to compare it to (and to contrast it with) the same or similar images in dreams, myths, and other texts. (The same or a similar image may, of course, have a different significance in different texts—and the differences may be more important than the similarities.)

Third, in contrast to Freud, who interprets dreams retrospectively, Jung also interprets them prospectively. Whereas for Freud an image in the dream has a cause in the past, for Jung an image also has a purpose in the future (a purpose that is not always and only a wish). Freud's method of interpretation is basically archaeological, Jung's teleological. According to Jung, there is not only a past tense but also a future tense—an anticipatory dimension—to the unconscious.

Fourth, Jung interprets dreams not only on the objective level but also on the subjective level. ("Objective" and "subjective" are not, in this sense, synonymous with "true" and "false." An objective interpretation is an interpersonal interpretation in terms of an object—or an object relation. A subjective interpretation is an intrapsychic interpretation in terms of the subject.) For Freud, images in dreams are references, or allusions, to objects in external reality. According to Jung, they are also reflections, or correlatives, of the internal reality of the subject. That is, the images are not so much residual representations of objects, derivative from external reality, as they are spontaneous presentations, autonomous personifications, or figurations of the subject, constitutive of internal reality. The images are fundamentally reflexive, rather than referential. From this perspective, the images primarily present, personify, or figure aspects of the internal reality of the subject, the dreamer, and only secondarily represent objects in external reality.

Fifth, Jung interprets dreams as compensations. The unconscious is the unknown—which includes the repressed, the ignored, the neglected, and whatever else is excluded from consideration for whatever reason. In dreams, the unconscious compensates the partial, prejudicial, defective conceits of the ego. That is, according to Jung, dreams offer alternative perspectives on the defensive, egocentric attitudes of the dreamer.

A REINTERPRETATION OF THE RED-HOT CURLING IRON DREAM

Jung interprets his nightmare as a warning from the unconscious. This is not, however, the only conclusion that Jung might have reached, nor the only interpretation that he could have made of his dream. In fact, it is an ego-defensive interpretation. Applying Jung's five methods of interpretation to the dream, how might we reinterpret Jung's nightmare?

From a phenomenological perspective, hair is hair. It is what it is—and not something else, for example, a phallus, or symbolic penis. From a metaphorical perspective, what is hair like? In a seminar, Jung asks one of the participants what hair means and receives the reply, "Thoughts." Jung responds by applying a combination of the phenomenological–metaphorical and amplificatory methods of interpretation to the image of hair:

> Yes. It very often stands for thoughts, by virtue of the fact that in primitive psychology hair is mana, the irradiation or emanation of mana from the head. Therefore to cut the hair deprives the man of his strength. Samson lost his strength when his hair was cut by Delilah.

The analyst is often represented as a barber in dreams because he washes people's heads. That is a proverbial expression with us, when we scold somebody, we say: "*Ich habe ihm den Kopf gewaschen*" (I washed his head). Then combing the hair means straightening out thoughts, cleaning or putting the hair in order is a symbol for putting the mind in order. In primitive psychology, also the hair is magical; to obtain the hair of a person is to have that person's mana.

(1976 2: 336)

Jung amplifies the image of hair by recourse to primitive psychology and the myth of Samson and Delilah. Mana is elemental, natural power present in an object or person—in this case, in hair on the head. Applying the phenomenological–metaphorical method of interpretation, Jung contends that hair is a metaphor for thoughts (potentially powerful thoughts) because, like hair, thoughts emerge from the head, or mind—and, by extension, that cutting may be a metaphor for depriving, that washing may be a metaphor for scolding, and that combing may be a metaphor for straightening.

In Jung's nightmare, the threat is not that Jung's white skin will turn black but that his straight hair will turn kinky. That the risk of going black is represented by the image of hair on the head, rather than skin on the body, is a symbolic indication that the danger is mental, or psychical. In another context, Jung applies the phenomenological–metaphorical method of interpretation and notes that not infrequently in women's dreams "the analyst is represented as a hairdresser (because he 'fixes' the head)" (*CW* 13: 347). Metaphorically, dressing hair is like fixing thoughts. In Jung's dream, however, the situation is reversed. It is not Jung, the analyst, who is the barber. Jung is the person having *his* hair, *his* head, fixed, or kinked. Jung is in the position of the patient. Hair, like thoughts, emerges from the head, and in this case for Jung's hair to turn kinky implies that his thoughts could turn kinky, or go black.

Applying Jung's compensatory method to his nightmare results in a very different—and a more properly Jungian—interpretation from the one he proposes. In his dream, Jung is not having his hair cut, although that is one of the things that a barber does. Nor is he having his hair washed. He is most definitely not having his hair combed, his thoughts straightened. He is having his hair kinked, his thoughts *unstraightened*. It apparently never occurs to the white European Jung (or, if it does occur to him, he resists the implication) that he is, as we say in slang, too "straight": that perhaps he should become "kinky." Perhaps in Jung's dream the unconscious is attempting to compensate his ego's too civilized white European attitude. From a compensatory perspective, perhaps the dream is not *warning* Jung *not* to go black—or to think black—but *inviting*, *encouraging*, or *challenging* him to do so.

David Shapiro has said to me that surely I must mean not that the dream tempts Jung to go black but that *"he* is tempted to go black" (1993, 12 April). On this cautionary note, he expresses a concern that I have committed a fallacy—that I have reified, or hypostatized, the unconscious, as if it were an entity capable of agency. Shapiro quite correctly observes that I attribute autonomy to the dream—and to the unconscious. I do believe that Jung is tempted to go black, but he is tempted to do so *by the unconscious, by the dream*. In a sense, the dreamer dreams the dream, but in another, very real sense, it dreams him—and, in this case, tempts him. I do, however, also regard Jung as an example of what Shapiro calls "rigid character" (1965, 1981, 1989). Jung exhibits characterological rigidity in that he proposes an ego-defensive interpretation of the dream and does not, in this case, entertain the distinct possibility of a compensatory function for the unconscious.

STRAIGHT VERSUS CROOKED: NORM AND DEVIATION

Phenomenologically, what is the essence of "straight?" What is "straight-*ness*?" Semiotically, the signifier "straight" is defined in opposition to other signifiers—that is, in opposition to what is *not* straight. The "straight" has significance in relation to the "unstraight." In terms of the physical phenomenon of hair, for example, the unstraight may be the kinky, but it may also be the curly or the wavy. In terms of other physical phenomena, the unstraight may be the crooked or the curved. For instance, the "semantic differential" that Charles E. Osgood and colleagues developed to measure meaning includes both the opposition "straight–crooked" (1957: 40) and the opposition "straight–curved" (1957: 52). In fact, in the instructions to the instrument, the opposition "straight-–crooked" is the word-pair that Osgood selects to exemplify the semantic differential procedure:

> Each item you see will be composed of two pairs of words. Your job is to encircle the world in the second pair which goes best with the capitalized word in the first pair.

STRAIGHT–crooked   noble–bestial

(1957: 40)

(It is perhaps not irrelevant to note that in the library copy that I happened to consult a previous reader had circled in ink the word "noble.")

In comparing primitives to schizophrenics, Storch also discusses the straight–curved or straight–crooked opposition. He cites examples from the research of the developmental psychologist Heinz Werner. Storch notes that "a war cry of the New Zealanders" includes "a reference to the curved rudder of the enemy." The curved rudder alludes, he says, "to the treacherous character of the enemy." Evidently, only a friend has a straight rudder, or a loyal character. Being curved or "being crooked" has both a physical and a psychical significance. Storch also mentions another example that Werner cites from the research of Emil Kraepelin on dream language: "The straight director, a crooked writer." In ordinary language, this expression means "He writes otherwise than one would expect" (1924: 13). In both of these examples, the straight has a positive value, the curved or crooked, a negative value. The examples are included in Werner's influential study of mental development, where Storch's "curved" and "crooked" are translated as "twisted" and "bent" (1957: 162).

For G. Stanley Hall, the psychologist who invited Freud and Jung to America in 1909 to deliver lectures and to receive honorary doctorates at Clark University, black skin and kinky—or "crooked"—hair are physical proofs of psychical differences. In a discussion of what he calls "the negro question," Hall asserts a direct relation between surface and depth:

> In history no two races, taken as a whole, differ so much in their traits, both physical and psychic, as the Caucasian and the African. The color of the skin and the crookedness of the hair are only the outward signs of many far deeper differences, including cranial and thoracic capacity, proportions of body, nervous system, glands and secretions, vita sexualis, food, temperament, disposition, character, longevity, instincts, customs, emotional traits, and diseases. All these differences, as they are coming to be better understood, are seen to be so great as to qualify if not imperil every inference from one race to another, whether theoretical or practical, so that what is true and good for one is often false and bad for the other.
>
> (1905: 97)

Hall dichotomizes the white and the black, the straight and the crooked. On that basis, he then declares that it is difficult if not impossible to infer that "Caucasians" and "Africans" are similar or identical in any significant respect. "Crookedness" signifies to Hall that blacks are essentially, not just incidentally, different from whites. Although Hall does not equate black and crooked with false and bad, white and straight with true and good, he does commit a fallacy. He erroneously assumes that surface realities are not merely superficial appearances but profound indications of depth realities and then deduces, illogically, that outward, physical traits like skin and hair are conclusive evidences of inward, psychical traits.

From a psychoanalytic perspective, physical (or material) reality is the medium of expression for psychical (or mental) reality. This is also the case from a transcendentalist perspective. For instance, Ralph Waldo Emerson says: "Every word which is used to express a moral or intellectual fact, if traced to its roots, is found to be borrowed from some material appearance." That is, every signifier that is used to express a psychical reality, if pursued to its source, is discovered to be derived from a physical reality. The very first example that Emerson cites in support of this proposition pertains to physical straightness. "*Right*," he says, "originally means *straight*; *wrong* means twisted. As a psychical reality, or as a moral or intellectual fact, being "right" (as in the sense of "correct," 'true," or "proper"), if followed to its origin, is ascertained to be appropriated from the physical reality, or the material appearance, of being "straight." In this sense, the literal significance of a physical reality serves as the basis for the metaphorical significance of a psychical reality. According to Emerson, it is not only words but also things, or physical phenomena, that have psychical, or metaphorical, significance. For example, just as what is straight may be an expression for what is right, Emerson notes that light and dark are expressions for "knowledge and ignorance" (1836/ 1971 1: 18). (The possibilities for racist applications of this light–dark, knowledge– ignorance opposition are, I would emphasize, considerable in white–black relations.) Emerson contends that "there is nothing lucky or capricious in these analogies"—that is, there is nothing arbitrary in them. "These," he says, "are not the dreams of a few poets, here and there, but man is an analogist, and studies relations in all objects" (1836/ 1971 1: 19).

Whether these poetic–analogical significances are natural and necessary (as all transcendentalists maintain), or whether they are cultural and contingent (as some semioticians insist), they are nevertheless the basis for the constitution or construction of a certain psychical reality. Osgood poses the question whether such significances are culturally relative or universal. He wonders whether they are "entirely dependent upon culture" or whether "it is possible that they present even more fundamental determinants operating in the human species." In an attempt to provide an answer, he analyzes responses from "five widely separated primitive cultures." The generality of certain significances is, he says, "quite striking." The example that he cites is the light–dark (or white–black) dichotomy. *Good*, he says, is "almost always *up* and *light* (*white*)," and *bad* is "*down* and *dark* (*black*)." In this respect, Osgood mentions a "prevalent myth" that relates "how the gods helped the original man" to ascend from the depth of the "dark" underworld to the surface of the "light" world (1957: 23).

The straight tends to function as a norm, and departures from it tend to function as deviations. The straight is "normal," and the unstraight, "deviant." In current slang, straight means "conventional, respectable, socially acceptable." It also means "heterosexual" or "not practicing sexual perversions." It means "not using or under influence of drugs, sober, abstinent." In contrast, a kink means a "mental twist," an "odd or fantastic notion," a "crochet, whim." It also means, more recently, a "state of madness," an "instance of, the practice of, or suffering resulting from sexual abnormality." A kink also means a "Black person," a "Negro," a "criminal," a "sexually abnormal person" (*Oxford English Dictionary*). The denotations and connotations of "straight" are more or less positive, those of "kinky," more or less negative. To be kinky is to be unconventional, unrespectable, socially unacceptable, homosexual, sexually perverse, unsober, odd, fantastic, crochety, whimsical, mad, black, and criminal.

That a number of these significances of "straight" and "kinky" are relatively recent, contemporary American slang expressions that were, in the strict sense, unavailable to the Swiss Jung in 1925–6 does not mean that they are irrelevant in the context of the trip to Central Africa. Cumulatively, the significances indicate a historical trend. It is no accident that physical straightness and kinkiness have served as a convenient metaphor for psychical normality and deviance. Implicit in, intrinsic to, the straight and the kinky is the capacity for metaphorical extension, for a projection onto a variety of phenomena—and, of course, straightness and kinkiness potentially entail a vast array of additional metaphorical applications. That is, the abstract concepts of "normality" and "deviance" are incipient in the concrete images of the "straight" and the "kinky." In Jung's dream of the red-hot curling iron, his unconscious availed itself of this tacit, metaphorical potentiality. In a discussion of marriage, adultery, and prostitution, Jung says: "If things cannot go straight they will have to go crooked" (*CW* 10: 121, para. 248). I would add that even (or perhaps especially) when things such as white European egos are straight, they may need to go crooked.

INITIATION AS TRANSFORMATION: THE INNER BARBER

If Jung had been less defensive—if he had been true to his own compensatory method—then he would have welcomed, rather than resisted, a "kinky," or deviant, interpretation of his dream. In his nightmare, Jung is not in the position of the psychoanalyst (the barber) but in the position of the patient. The implication is that Jung could use an African or African-American analyst, a medicine man, a *laibon*, to fix his head, to change his mind. Interpreted in this manner, the dream could be regarded as an initiation—in which the red-hot curling iron is applied to Jung's thoughts.

In a discussion of rituals of initiation, Mircea Eliade describes what he calls the "symbolism of magical heat" (1958: 85). According to Eliade, medicine men or shamans often endure an ordeal by heating—or by burning (they may, for example, Eliade says, "touch red-hot iron")—in order to experience a transformation from the profane to the sacred. Eliade asserts that "we are in the presence of a fundamental magico-religious experience, which is universally documented on the archaic levels of culture: access to sacrality is manifested, among other things, by a prodigious increase in heat." What is symbolized by this process is that "the human condition has been abolished" (1958: 86).

That is, a lower state has been heated up and burned away—killed off, as it were—in order for a higher state to be entered into: "The respective initiations, though following different paths, pursue the same end—to make the novice die to the human condition and to resuscitate him to a new, a transhuman existence." In this respect, "becoming heated" is symbolic—or, Eliade says, symptomatic—of a metaphorical "death to the human condition" and a metaphorical birth, or rebirth, to a divine condition. "He who obtains magical heat," Eliade declares, "vividly demonstrates that he belongs to a superhuman world" (1958: 87). In Jung's nightmare of the red-hot curling iron, his ego feels that it cannot stand the heat, the pain, of the initiatory process. (I would emphasize that the potential transformation is not intrinsically a threat, a risk, a danger. It is the ego—or the bias of the ego—that experiences it as such.)

Jung does not apply either his subjective method or his prospective method of interpretation to his nightmare. He interprets the image of the barber objectively and retrospectively. He reduces the image to a residual reference to an object in external reality, a cause in the past. The image, he says, is of his African-American barber in Chattanooga, Tennessee. Jung regards the image as a memory. In contrast, a subjective and prospective interpretation would regard the image of the barber as a fantasy, a spontaneous, autonomous reflection of the internal reality of the subject, with a purpose in the future. Such an interpretation would ask what the image of the barber reflects about the psychical reality of Jung—and what anticipatory, or purposive, function the image might serve.

From this perspective, the image would be a personification of an aspect of Jung. It would be a figuration of the "inner barber" rather than a representation of any "outer barber." One aspect of Jung (the barber) applies the red-hot curling iron to another aspect of Jung (the ego). If, according to Jung, hair is often a metaphor for thoughts and a barber is often a metaphor for the psychoanalyst, then evidently one aspect of Jung (an "instinctive," "primitive," "black" aspect) believes that another aspect (the "rational," "civilized," "white" aspect) needs to be analyzed—needs to be unstraightened, needs to be kinked, needs to be rethought. In terms of his own theory of psychological types, Jung categorizes himself as a thinking rather than a feeling type. Thinking is his superior, conscious function, feeling his inferior, unconscious function. The barber-psychoanalyst in Jung's dream applies a red-hot curling iron to Jung's head, to his hair, to his thoughts. Heat is often a metaphor for feelings. The image of the red-hot curling iron would seem to suggest that it is only through unconscious feelings that Jung's conscious thoughts can be transformed—his ego compensated, his mind changed.

Chapter 6

Hair: kinky, straight, bald

Historically, kinky or straight hair is, of course, not only a white man's but also a black man's (and a black woman's) issue. The opposition is not just "kinky–straight" but "kinky–*straightened*." It is not only whites who may "go black," or "go kinky," but also blacks who may "go white," or "go straight." Malcolm X describes the first time that he had his hair "processed," or "conked." ("Conked" is a pronunciation of "conged"— from "Congo," as in the hair processing preparation "congolene.") He purchased lye, eggs, and potatoes, and his friend Shorty prepared the congolene to apply to his head:

> A jelly-like, starchy-looking glop resulted from the lye and potatoes, and Shorty broke in two eggs, stirring real fast—his own conk and dark face bent down close. The congolene turned pale-yellowish. "Feel the jar," Shorty said. I cupped my hand against the outside, and snatched it away. "Damn right, it's hot, that's the lye," he said. "So you know it's going to burn when I comb it in—it burns *bad*. But the longer you can stand it, the straighter the hair.
>
> (1965: 54)

Malcolm X says, "The congolene just felt warm when Shorty started combing it in. But then my head caught fire." All the heat and pain were, however, well worth it, or so he felt at the time:

> My first view in the mirror blotted out the hurting. I'd seen some pretty conks, but when it's the first time, on your *own* head, the transformation, after the lifetime of kinks, is staggering.
>
> The mirror reflected Shorty behind me. We both were grinning and sweating. And on top of my head was this thick, smooth sheen of shining red hair—real red—as straight as any white man's.
>
> How ridiculous I was! Stupid enough to stand there simply lost in admiration of my hair now looking "white," reflected in the mirror in Shorty's room. I vowed that I'd never again be without a conk, and I never was for many years.

This was my first really big step toward self-degradation: when I endured all of that pain, literally burning my flesh with lye, in order to cook my hair until it was limp, to have it look like a white man's hair. I had joined that multitude of Negro men and women in America who are brainwashed into believing that the black people are "inferior"—and white people "superior"—that they will even violate and mutilate their God-created bodies to try to look "pretty" by white standards.

(1965: 55)

In this instance, the mirror serves as a device for self-degradation, not for self-reflection.

Malcolm X describes his unconsciousness, or false consciousness, his self-degrading desire—in looking up to whites who look down on blacks—to "look white," to "go white." (In this respect, I might also mention Michael Jackson's admission that he has had plastic surgery, including a "nose job," and his denial of suspicions that he has deliberately gone white by cosmetically bleaching his skin. Jackson has recently said that his "whiteness" is the result of treatments for the skin condition vitiligo.) Malcolm X criticizes both black men who wear conks and black women who wear wigs—"green and pink and purple and red and platinum-blonde wigs"—in an effort to look like white men and women. "It makes you wonder," he remarks, "if the Negro has completely lost his sense of identity, lost touch with himself" (1965: 56).

Hair-straightening is a conspicuous image in Spike Lee's film *Malcolm X*. The film (Lee, S. 1993) differs significantly from the screenplay (Baldwin, Perl, and Lee 1992), but in both versions the first scene (in which Lee exercises a certain cinematic license) depicts Malcolm X's very first conk. The movie opens with Shorty getting up from a shoeshine stand and striding over to a barber shop. A boy accompanies him, carrying a paper bag and a cloth sack, containing the ingredients. Shorty then slices potatoes, cracks eggs, and mixes them with Red Devil lye. "Little" (the future Malcolm X's "slave name") appears from a back room. A number of older men tease him. "There he is," one says. "Hey, fixing to get that first conk laid on—hey, Homeboy? It'll be hot like hell!" Another one says, "Don't be scared, son. You ain't got nothing to worry about. You're in the hands of an expert! My hair was just like yours..." He slowly removes his hat and reveals his gray, balding head. "And look what he did for me." As Shorty applies the concoction, he warns Little that it will burn his scalp. He says, "Hold on." Little replies, "I'm holding, but it's heating." Shorty says, "Gotta make it straight." Little's head gets so hot that he cannot stand it. When he tries to stand up, the men try to hold him down. He rushes to the sink and washes the congolene out of his hair. Feeling his hair through a towel, he says, "I can tell it's laying down." Then he looks in the mirror. "Ooh-ooh!" he exclaims—and laughs. With a smile of satisfaction, he asks, "Looks white, don't it?" The men congratulate him: "All right! All root! All reet!" They give him skin all around.

A later scene shows Shorty conking Little's hair again. This time, however, something goes excruciatingly wrong. When Little goes to the sink to wash his hair, there is no water. He turns the taps, but nothing— not a drip, not a drop—comes out of the faucets. Finally, in desperation, he dunks his head in the toilet—an image, evidently, of just how low he is willing to go in an effort to go white. Not until he converts to the Nation of Islam and becomes "Malcolm X" does he stop conking his hair and trying to look white.

CRISES OF "RACIAL" IDENTITY

Malcolm X is not, of course, the only African-American who has resorted to extreme measures in a desperate effort to look white. In an account of the identity crises that can result from "transracial" adoptions, Sonia L. Nazario provides another, especially poignant example. She describes Nathan Hatton, whom she identifies as a 22-year-old freshman at Eastern Michigan University. Nazario reports: "Nathan was only a few years old when he began trying to look white, spending hours in the bathroom plastering down his hair. He would get down on all fours and drag his head on the living-room carpet, straining to straighten the kinks." According to Nazario, Nathan is now proud of his "transracial" adoption and his white parents. She quotes him as saying, "I don't care what other people say so much any more. I'll lose my mind if I worry about it" (1990, 12 September: A, 8).

The jazz musician and composer Charles Mingus recounts in his auto-biography how as a child he also styled his hair in an attempt to be accepted by people of one color or another. Mingus describes how older boys designated him the "underdog" because he was "a kind of mongrel, lighter than some but not light enough to belong to the almost-white elite and not dark enough to belong with the beautiful elegant blacks." For Mingus, ambivalence toward hair style was a function of the ambiguity of skin color. Writing about himself in the third person, Mingus says, "There really was no skin color exactly like his. So he changed from burning his hair with his mother's hot-comb hair straightener to wetting it to make it kink up for the real beautiful natural dignified wiry and woolly look." It was all, however, to no avail: "Nobody accepted him, kinks or no." A complexion neither light nor dark, neither white nor black, but "yellow" was simply fraternally unacceptable. "The black hate in the air for Whitey was turned on him, a schitt-coloured halfass yella phony," Mingus says. "Others could hiply call each other *black son of a bitch* or *nappy-headed nigger* but they took no 'brother' schitt from him" (1971: 65).

It was not so much "who" Mingus was as "what" he was that gave him pause for psychological reflection:

> Whenever he looked in the mirror and asked "What am I?" he thought he could see a number of strains—Indian, African, Mexican, Asian and a certain amount of white from a source his father had boasted of. He wanted to be one or the other, but he was a little of everything, wholly nothing, of no race, country, flag or friend.

The result was a defiant, everything-and-nothing attitude toward the issue of identity: "So finally Charles gassed his hair straight and ran around with the other mongrels, the few Japanese, Mexicans, Jews and Greeks" who attended high school with him. Even that solution presented a problem, however, for they spoke other languages and could exclude him whenever they wanted to. "All he wanted," he exclaims in frustration, "was to be accepted somewhere and he still wasn't, so fuck it!" Beneath the underdog, Mingus cultivated another identity that privileged psychical reality over physical reality:

> He became something else. He fell in love with himself. "Fuck all you pathetic prejudiced cocksuckers," he thought. "I dig minds, inside and out. No race, no color, no sex. Don't show me no kind of skin 'cause I can see right through to the hate in your little undeveloped souls."
>
> (1971: 66)

Psychoanalysts, of course, diagnose self-love as narcissism, which may be either pathological or healthy. For Charles Mingus, self-love was an assertion of self-acceptance, whether he was acceptable to the "other," to anyone else, or not. For him, digging minds rather than bodies—rather than skin—was developing soul.

Nathan Hatton and Charles Mingus exemplify the difficulties of what Erikson calls "identity confusion" or "identity diffusion" (1968: 212). They both suffer a crisis of "racial" identity (Helms 1990; Harris, Blue, and Griffith 1995). Although it is developmentally normal for an adolescent like Mingus (and perhaps even a child like Hatton) to have an identity crisis (to have anxiety about skin condition and hair style), in the case of African-Americans "race" complicates the issue. For example, bell hooks describes a visit with friends who have a daughter at an age when self-image and such physical factors as skin and hair are such sensitive psychical concerns:

> Their little girl is just reaching that stage of preadolescent life where we become obsessed with our image, with how we look and how others see us. Her skin is dark. Her hair chemically straightened. Not only is

she fundamentally convinced that straightened hair is more beautiful than curly, kinky, natural hair, she believes that lighter skin makes one more worthy, more valuable in the eyes of others. Despite her parents' effort to raise their children in an affirming black context, she has internalized white supremacist values and aesthetics, a way of looking and seeing the world that negates her value.

This negation, this negativity, is neither novel nor exceptional. It is a pervasive, collective phenomenon. "Of course this is not a new story," hooks notes. "I could say the same for my nieces, nephews, and millions of black children here in the States" (1992: 3).

HAIR IN CONTEMPORARY AFRICAN-AMERICAN CULTURE

In contemporary African-American culture, hair is a subject of considerable importance. For blacks who demand an education in racism, it is a special interest. Not all whites are sympathetic. For example, David Sacks, when he was a junior at Stanford University and editor-in-chief of the *Stanford Review*, disparaged a popular new course: "Black Hair as Culture and History." At the time, students, faculty, and administrators at Stanford University were discussing the merits of revising the undergraduate curriculum, which had traditionally emphasized the "Great Books" of Western civilization. The controversy was over whether to develop a more inclusive, multicultural curriculum. Although "Black Hair" was not, strictly speaking, part of the debate, Sacks cites the course as a symptom of "politically correct" conformism and a decline in academic standards.

If Kennell Jackson, the professor who taught the course, were not so earnest, Sacks says, "one might mistake the class for a parody of multiculturalism." Sacks continues, in a satirical, if not sarcastic, tone:

> The syllabus, handed out on the first day of class, includes such lectures as "The Rise of the Afro" and "Fade-O-Rama, Braiding and Dreadlocks." According to this course outline, local hair stylists will visit for a week of discussions. Enrolled students will view the 1960s musical "Hair," read Willie L. Morrow's "400 Years Without a Comb" and Dylan Jones's "Haircults," and study the lyrics of Michael Jackson's hit pop single "Man in the Mirror."

Sacks derides the effort to "teach students that the Afro represents 1960s rebelliousness and that straightening one's hair is a symbol of cultural subordination." This is not, he says, an intellectual endeavor that encourages individual inquiry but a psychological exercise that "promotes group therapy." According to Sacks, "Black Hair" is not a serious course for African-American students who want—and need—to learn about racism from a cultural and historical perspective. It is a frivolous, trendy course in which they will only "struggle with the dilemma over whether to straighten one's hair or to remain 'natural.'" Sacks concludes: "One wonders how Martin Luther King Jr would have reacted to the implication that one of the most important things a black student can think about is his hair" (1992, 29 July: A, 10).

However King might have felt, other African-Americans—like Spike Lee—do apparently feel that hair is a significant, not a trivial, subject. Lee's film *School Daze*, which is a commentary on colorism among blacks who themselves maintain a racist light–dark opposition, includes a song-and-dance number, "Straight and Nappy," written by his father, Bill Lee. Two groups of African-American college coeds, one with straight hair and light skin (the "Wannabees," those who want to be, or want to look, white), the other with nappy hair and dark skin (the "Jigaboos," or "Jigs"), confront each other in a dormitory hall, where Lee has them exchange insults about hair:

Jane: Pickaninny.
Doris: Barbie Doll.
Rachel: High Yella Heffer.
Dina: Tarbaby!
Vivian: Wanna be White!
Kim: Jigaboo!
               (Lee, S. 1988: 221)

The scene then shifts to the red, orange, yellow, and green neon glow of the "Madame Re-Res Beauty Salon," where the two groups continue the confrontation, singing and dancing:

Chorus: Talkin' 'bout how good and bad hair
                whether you are dark or fair
                go on and swear
                see if I care
                good and bad hair.
                      . . .
Wannabees: Don't you wish you had hair like this
                then the boys would give you a kiss
                'bout nothin' but bliss
                then you gonna see what you missed
Jigs: If a fly should land on your head
                then I'm sure he'd break all his legs
                'cause you got so much grease up there
                tell me, dear, is that a weave you wear
                      . . .
Wannabees: Bad hair is only good for one thing

	if you get a lick, back it'll spring
	caint cha, don't cha hair stand on high
	caint cha comb it and don't you try
Jigs:	Don't you know my hair is so strong
	it can break the teeth out of a comb
	I don't have to put up at night
	what you have to keep out of sight
	. . .
Wannabees:	Your hair ain't no longer than [finger snap]
	so you'll never fling it all back
	and you 'fraid to walk in the rain
	oh, what a shame, who's to blame
Jigs:	Don't you ever worry 'bout that
	'cause I don't mind being BLACK
	go on with your mixed-up head
	I ain't gonna never be 'fraid
Wannabees:	Well you got nappy hair
Jigs:	Nappy is all right with me
Wannabees:	My hair is straight you see
Jigs:	But your soul's crooked as can be.
	. . .

(Lee, B. 1988: 154–6)

The Wannabees and Jigaboos "dis" (demonstrate disrespect for) each other with colorist caricatures over the extent to which light and dark are synonymous with good and bad among African-Americans. Lee lets the Jigaboos have the last word. They insist that psychical reality is more important than any physical reality—which is, after all, only an appearance. One's hair may be straight, but one's soul may be crooked.

Kathy Russell, Midge Wilson, and Ronald Hall discuss what they call the "color complex" (they employ the word "complex" in the psychoanalytic sense). The color complex includes a "hair complex." Russell, Wilson, and Hall describe the entrepreneurial efforts of Madam C.J. Walker, an African-American woman who invented, patented, manufactured, and marketed a variety of health and beauty items—among them, products to straighten hair. According to Walker, a secret formula had been revealed to her by an old man in a vision. She claimed that the ingredients included substances from Africa. Walker also redesigned a European hot comb specifically for African-American women. Russell, Wilson, and Hall note that "in 1910 the *Guinness Book of World Records* identified Madam Walker as the first self-made millionairess in history." Walker maintained that the secret formula and hot comb were for the sole purpose of beautiful, healthy hair—not straight hair. The word "straightener" was never to be used, she insisted, by the African-American women who sold the products door-to-door (1992: 44–5).

Magazines such as *Ebony* and *EM* (*Ebony Man*), written and published specifically for blacks, regularly contain a number of advertisements for hair products. For example, among the items advertised in *Ebony* (1993 April) are "Revlon Creme of Nature Creme Relaxer and No Lye Creme Relaxer System," "Right On Curl," "John Paul Mitchell Systems Super Strengthener," described as "a post-processing salon treatment," which "ensures that your hair remains its absolute healthiest through straightening, coloring, or perming," and "African Pride Shampoo and Conditioner" with "One Step Ancient African Formula." (Also advertised is "Vantex Skin Bleaching Creme.") Among the products advertised in *EM* (1993 April) are "Duke Ultimate Strength Texturizing Kit" (for "better, easier wave control"), "Duke Curl Activator and Instant Spray Moisturizer" (to "bring your hair ALIVE with a natural wave pattern and sheen") "Duke Wave and Curl Texturizer" (which "turns on the attraction by turning up the energy for today's straighter styles"). In these advertisements, the kinky is the natural state of African-American hair—and it is implicitly tense and dead. Once it is straightened, or processed, it is relaxed and enlivened. The natural–processed, tense–relaxed, dead–enlivened oppositions are thus additional variations on the theme of the kinky–straightened opposition.

BALDNESS AS THE ZERO DEGREE OF HAIR

Also included in *EM* is an article written by an anonymous author who enumerates four categories of hairstyles: "the corporate look, peer group style, professional group (hair stylists), and the artistic style (musicians, artists, etc.)." A hair stylist identified as an advanced training instructor is quoted as saying: "Each group will wear the hairstyle differently to symbolize something." Even lack of hair, even the bald head, can be a bold fashion statement. "Being bald," the advanced training instructor says, "is appealing to women" (1993 April: 58).

One decade may celebrate, as in the musical *Hair*, a variety of styles, as long as they are long, not short, while another decade may glorify the bald or shaved head. For example, Richard Sandomir notes that the National Basketball Association playoffs "will be a nightly tribute to the shaved head." According to Sandomir, "the hairless head is the style du sport" for both Michael Jordan of the Chicago Bulls and Charles Barkley of the Phoenix Suns—as well as for many other African-American players. The shaved head, he says, is "the ultimate anti-coif and a brash statement of rebellion against a hair-obsessed society." It is a decisive, defiant, existential gesture: "The shaved head says you have chosen this look, this style, this way of life; that you recognize the psychic, physical or even material value of full baldness; that you favor it over a full head or fringe of hair." The benefits of the shaved head are innumerable:

> Bald men with a fringe of hair are told by the shaved heads that they don't know the tonsorial epiphanies of lopping it all off, for theirs is a proactive superbaldness. They talk about how freely their shaved heads flout society's hair conventions. How women ask to touch their smooth and bare expanses of scalp. How it brings inner peace, especially to men who've falsified their naked pates with bad and noticeable toupees. How it creates a kind of agelessness where no one knows if you're balding or turning gray or white. How it makes others think more boldly, more fearfully about you.

Sandomir, who wrote the book *Bald Like Me*, emphasizes that the shaved head is "a symbol of male sexuality" (1991, 5 May: C, 1 and 12).

John Howard Griffin, who wrote the book *Black Like Me*, also mentions the sexual symbolism of the shaved head. Griffin, a white man, who, in order to "pass" for a black man, ingested vitiligo medication, endured ultraviolet exposure, and dyed his skin, also shaved his head. After the transformation, the first African-American with whom Griffin had a conversation remarked on the sex appeal of his shaved head:

> He grinned at me and said: "Man, you really got your top shaved, didn't you?"
> "Yeah, doesn't it look all right?"
> "Man, it's slick. Makes you look real good." He said he understood the gals were really going for bald-headed men. "They say that's a sure sign of being high-sexed." I let him think I'd shaved my head for that reason.
> (1960: 14)

The contrast in symbolic significance between the shaved head and the unconked head could not be more extreme, as Griffin discovers in conversation with another African-American, who, like Spike Lee, deplores the racist divisions that exist even among African-Americans:

> "Until we as a race can learn to rise together, we'll never get anywhere. That's our trouble. We work against one another instead of together. Now you take dark Negroes like you, Mr Griffin, and me," he went on. "We're old Uncle Toms to our people, no matter how much education and morals we've got. No, you have to be almost a mulatto, have your hair conked and all slicked out and look like a Valentino. Then the Negro will look up to you. You've got *class*. Isn't that a pitiful hero-type?"
> (1960: 34)

Later, in order to avoid violence, Griffin has to suffer in silence the racist abuse of a white boy who calls him "*Mr. No-Hair, Baldy, Shithead*" (1960: 38). (A shaved black head may, of course, have a very different meaning from a shaved white head—as a new generation of racists, or "skinheads," have subsequently demonstrated.)

In *Funnyhouse of a Negro*, the playwright Adrienne Kennedy employs the image of baldness to dramatize the disastrous effects of racism on a black woman, Sarah. Sarah has a desperate, pathological desire to be lighter, whiter, than she already is, "to become a more pallid Negro than I am now." She wants to go white: to write on white pages, eat at a white table, associate exclusively with white friends. Although both her mother and father were black, her mother had straight hair and light skin, while her father had kinky hair and dark skin. Sarah has kinky hair and yellow skin. "In appearance I am good-looking in a boring way; no glaring Negroid features, medium nose, medium mouth and pale yellow skin," she says. "My one defect is that I have a head of frizzy hair, unmistakably Negro kinky hair" (1988: 6).

Several other characters appear in the play—among them, Queen Victoria, the Duchess of Hapsburg, Patrice Lumumba, and Jesus. Sarah has gone insane because of the "racial" conflict that she suffers in psychical reality, and these characters are evidently dramatizations of multiple personalities, or dissociative identities—what Kennedy calls "alter egos or selves" (1987: 96). In the play, all of these characters go bald. So does Sarah: "She is suffering so till her hair has fallen out" (1988: 8). It is as if Sarah unconsciously tries to somatize a solution to the problem of "racial" conflict. Baldness is a symptom, a compromise formation, by which she attempts, once and for all, to nullify the oppositions kinky–straight, black–white. Finally, however, it is suicide, not somatization, that is, for Sarah, the ultimate response to racism.

For Kennedy, baldness is fallenness, a most unfortunate fall from a state of grace into a state of "race." In the "racial" funnyhouse, the fallout is not just of hair but of love. Just as our hair may fall out, we may fall out of love, as Sarah's mother falls out of love with her father, falls out of love with blackness. The loss of hair is, in this sense, a metaphor of the loss of love. It is precisely when Sarah's mother falls out of love with her father that her father rapes her mother and conceives Sarah. Falling out of love is falling into hate.

In dramatizing white–black, love–hate conflict, Kennedy employs a beautiful–ugly opposition. She emphasizes self-reflection in the mirror of racism. The scene is a funnyhouse-funhouse: a combination of an asylum (in which all of the characters are "funny" in the sense of "insane") and a sideshow house of mirrors (in which images of the self are not accurate reflections but grotesque distortions). As in the fairy tale "Snow White" (to which Kennedy repetitively alludes), the question for Sarah is,

"Mirror, mirror, on the wall, who is the fairest one of all?" In the mirror of racism, her mother was the lightest, or whitest, one of all, while her father was the darkest, or blackest, one of all. Sarah is "in between" (1988: 11), the yellowest one of all. When Sarah looks in the mirror, she sees a self-image that is not "fair" (or white) but "unfair" in both senses of the word—not only black (or yellow) but also unjust. The fairy tale is an unfair tale that does not do justice to Sarah. It is as if the image of Snow White is a constant presence, an incongruent imposition, when Sarah looks in the mirror. To the extent that the fairy tale serves as the very epitome of a European, or Eurocentric, aesthetic to which Sarah aspires but can never attain, it distorts her own self-image, her own self-reflection, and unfairly condemns her to a futile pursuit of whiteness—to insanity and, finally, to suicide.

Kennedy saw the Walt Disney movie *Snow White* when she was 8 years old. "I thought after seeing this movie," she says, "that somehow in some way we were all sleeping and had to be awakened before we could really live" (1987: 18). Kennedy wondered why the stepmother wanted to kill Snow White. "To be the 'fairest' in the kingdom," she concluded, "must be very important" (1987: 20).

In *The Colored Museum*, the playwright George C. Wolfe, artistic director and producer of the New York Shakespeare Festival, employs the image of baldness to satirize the kinky–straight opposition. In the play, he includes a scene that he entitles "Hairpiece." On a vanity are two wigs, "an Afro wig circa 1968 and a long, flowing wig," both on wig stands. An African-American woman enters the scene. Her head is wrapped in a towel. The woman removes the towel, revealing "a totally bald head." She begins applying makeup to her face. At that, Janine, the stand with the Afro wig, opens her eyes and then, staring at the bald woman in disbelief, wakes up LaWanda, the stand with the long, flowing wig. Laughing, Janine says: "Just look at the poor thing, trying to paint some life onto that face of hers. You'd think by now she'd realize it's the hair. It's all about the hair." LaWanda responds: "What hair! She ain't got no hair! She done fried, dyed, de-chemicalized her shit to death." Janine adds: "And all that's left is that buck-naked scalp of hers, sittin' up there apologizin' for being odd-shaped and ugly." In unison, the two wig stands exclaim: "The bitch is bald!" They then express approval that the bald woman is about to break up with a man whom LaWanda describes as a "fool" and Janine describes as a "political quick-change artist." Janine continues: "Every time the nigga went and changed his ideology, she went and changed her hair to fit the occasion" (1992: 18). For some African-Americans, Wolfe implies, hair and ideology have both been fashion statements, the one opportunistically changing with the other.

The bald woman is to meet the man for lunch in order to break up with him. She will wear one hairpiece or the other, the Afro wig or the long, flowing wig. An argument breaks out between Janine and LaWanda over which one of them—that is, which one of the wigs—the bald woman should wear. Janine turns to the bald woman and says of LaWanda: "Now set her straight and tell her you're wearing me." LaWanda counters, pun intended: "She's the one that needs to be set straight, so go on and tell her you're wearing me." The bald woman has not yet decided which wig to wear. Janine, the stand with the Afro wig, shouts:

> What do you mean, you ain't made up your mind! After all that fool has put you through, you gonna need all the attitude you can get, and there is nothing like attitude and a healthy head of kinks to make his shit shrivel like it should!
>
> That's right! When you wearin' me, you lettin' him know he ain't gonna get no sweet-talkin' comb through your love without some serious resistance. No-no! The kink of my head is like the kink of your heart, and neither is about to be hot-pressed into surrender.

LaWanda, the stand with the long, flowing wig, replies: "That shit is so tired. The last time attitude worked on anybody was 1968. Janine, girl, you need to get over it and get on with it" (1992: 20). The argument between Janine and LaWanda gets so furious that the bald woman finally takes matters into her own hands. At the end of the scene, or so it says in the stage directions that Wolfe provides, "*The* WOMAN *screams and pulls the two wigs off the wig stands as the lights go to black on three bald heads*" (1992: 21).

The bald head is an example of what the semiotician Roland Barthes calls the "zero degree." According to Barthes, the absence of something (in this case, hair) is itself significant, is itself a signifier. Barthes states that "the zero degree testifies to the power held by any system of signs, of creating meaning 'out of nothing' " (1968: 77). Thus having no hair, having nothing on the head, may be especially meaningful—not in spite of the absence but because of it. As Una Chaudhuri (1994) has remarked to me, it is arguable that in the kinky–straightened opposition, "natural" hair is the zero degree of "cultural" hair. In this sense, kinky would be the "raw" state of hair, and straightened would be the "cooked," or processed, state. It seems to me, however, that baldness is the *most* zero degree of hair—if such a superlative be permissible—because hairlessness is the ultimate state of nothingness. Baldness, not natural hair, is an absolute zero degree because it is a nothing that implies the creation of potentially infinite meanings.

TECHNOLOGY: MAKING ONESELF OVER IN ANY IMAGE ONE CHOOSES

Hair is one of the most easily alterable physical appurtenances. It is easier to change one's hair style than to change, say, one's skin color, one's nose, one's lips, or other parts of one's body, although through technology, including cosmetics, contraptions and devices, or surgery, all of those things are now possible, too. Through technology, one may now have a total "makeover," either temporary or permanent. One may make oneself over in any image one chooses. The aesthetic dimension of what is considered, collectively, at a particular time and place, either beautiful or ugly is, in a sense, the least of it. Thoughts, the ideas in ideology, are reflected in the multiplicity of stylistic, or symbolic, statements that people make with their hair. Hair may symbolize not only thoughts but also attitudes. The communicative possibilities of hair are, if not infinite, at least vastly diverse. They are by no means reducible to the simplistic opposition kinky–straight. In this respect, baldness as the zero degree of hair functions as a sign of the ability of anyone and everyone freely—which is to say, arbitrarily—to alter his or her appearance, to adopt any style, to make any statement, personal or political.

Raymond Firth notes that on one level hair is simply a physical (or natural) phenomenon but that on another level it is a psychical (or cultural) phenomenon with immense symbolic value. According to physical anthropologists, hair is a biological fact that is "a true racial character." From that perspective, variations in the length, form, texture, and color of hair are functions of "race." However, for Firth, who is a cultural anthropologist, hair may also serve the purposes of "social action" and "social differentiation" (1973: 262–3).

Firth discusses male and female hair, short and long hair, hair loss, wigs, and hair "statements," including the "Afro":

A more recent kind of statement, indicating not a personal relationship so much as a personal commitment, has been the wearing of "Afro" hair styles by black American women. Appearing in the mid-1960s as a manifestation of black pride, with its suggestion of African, not American origins and independence, the "Afro" became a symbol of ethnic identity and as such a political statement. So it could be observed that a young woman student arriving from the south at a northern university might soon abandon her straightened, wavy hair style for the frizzled, heightened style which affirmed her solidarity with other blacks on the campus. Now that black identity has been made much more clear and some political advance made, it seems, the "dramatic spherical cloud" of the Afro is less commonly worn. The reasons also include the pressures to change any fashion, and the fact that the Afro demanded special treatment in combing and conditioning which could not only be more costly than some other styles but also could affect the quality of the hair. Yet it has been pointed out that the Afro has been important in helping to free black women from the problems of dealing with kinky hair in a straight-haired society, and stimulate them to adopt a wider variety of bold hair styles. In this context it is revealing to read what E. A. Hoebel wrote at an earlier period: "A definitely New World symbolism has arisen among American Coloreds in the matter of hair form. The passion for hair-straightening and kink-removing compounds among American Coloreds reflects an identification of non-kinky hair with social status among whites" (1966, 283; cf. *Time Magazine*, 25 November 1971). How faded and distorted does this opinion now seem, however accurate it may then have looked!

(1973: 273–4)

The variety of hair styles is everywhere evident in the post-kinked, post-conked, cornrowed, dreadlocked diversity of personal and political, private and public statements that African-Americans now proudly make with their hair. I would add that as recently as 1992 I witnessed on the street in New York City a young African-American man cruelly ridiculing an older African-American man for continuing to wear an Afro. As late as 1994, Michel Marriott reports, a new generation of African-Americans suddenly developed a certain nostalgia for the Afro: "Sharnteek Whitmore, 27, a barber who has been cutting hair for 11 years, said that lately, almost a quarter of his customers at the S & B Barber Shop on Malcolm X Boulevard in Harlem ask for Afros" (1994, 26 June: 1 [Style], 33).

Ever on the alert to detect and defeat efforts at integration, racists have apparently realized what transformative possibilities are implicit in technology. An especially egregious example is the arrest of Jonathan Preston Haynes, a neo-Nazi white supremacist, in the murder of Martin Sullivan, a plastic surgeon from Chicago. Haynes confessed to killing both Sullivan and a hairdresser in San Francisco in 1987. In court, the Associated Press reports, he angrily denounced people for "diluting the Aryan beauty" by using various technologies, including hair dyes and contact lenses: "I condemn bleach-blond hair and tinted blue eyes. I condemn fake Aryan beauty brought about by plastic surgery. You fought World War II against Aryan beauty. Stop feeding off Aryan beauty like a herd of locusts in a wheat field" (1993, 11 August: A, 11).

Although I have no sympathy for Haynes, I do have an interest in what motivates him, as well as what motivates the people who so enrage him. He is evidently so angry because technology enables us to commit what he considers to be an "unnatural act." What appears perverse to him is the possibility of deception. What if a black woman—with hair bleached blond, eyes tinted blue, and body surgically plasticized—deceived him, so that he believed that she was a white woman? What if technology enabled her to "pass" for white? What so disturbs Haynes, what plagues him like locusts in wheat, is that technology subverts what he regards as the natural order of things, so that he can no longer confidently identify the other as such.

From a psychoanalytic (in contrast to a racist) perspective, what is important is *why* one styles oneself in a certain way. For example, is the motive conscious or unconscious? Is the style an identification with a collective trend, or is it the articulation of a personal desire? Straightening hair from a sense of "racial" inferiority is utterly different from straightening it from a sense of what I would call equal stylistic opportunity. Why should blacks have to look "natural" any more than whites do? Why should they have to explain, justify—or excuse—any style?

What we are currently witnessing is a proliferation of hair styles among both blacks and whites. No longer do blacks necessarily style their hair in an effort to look white, and whites now often style their hair in an effort to look black, which, to them, suddenly seems more stylish. The self, whether black or white, adopts, adapts—appropriates—the look of the other. Not only that, but also many blacks and whites are now availing themselves of the opportunity to style themselves in ways that exist nowhere in nature. What "race" does one belong to if one has blue, green, pink, or purple hair?

CIVILIZATION, PROGRESS, CUMULATIVE HISTORY, AND CHANCE

Lévi-Strauss suggests that what makes racism so difficult to ameliorate is the association of white skin and straight hair with the apparent progress of white civilization. Mere argumentation, he says, will hardly suffice to persuade whites that they are not superior to blacks, unless we effectively address the civilized–primitive opposition:

> It would be useless to argue the man in the street out of attaching an intellectual and moral significance to the fact of having a black or white skin, straight or frizzy hair, unless we had an answer to another question which, as experience proves he will immediately ask: if there are not innate racial aptitudes, how can we explain the fact that the white man's civilization has made the tremendous advances with which we are all familiar while the civilizations of the coloured peoples have lagged behind, some of them having come only half way along the road, and others being still thousands or tens of thousands of years behind the times. We cannot therefore claim to have formulated a convincing denial of the inequality of the human *races*, so long as we fail to consider the problem of the inequality—or diversity—of human *cultures*, which is in fact—however unjustifiably—closely associated with it in the public mind.

> (1952: 6–7)

The answer to the question of innate "racial" aptitudes, Lévi-Strauss says, is a cultural—or historical—rather than a natural one. The problem is that "anything which does not conform to the standard of the society in which the individual lives is denied the name of culture and relegated to the realm of nature" (1952: 11).

Progressivism employs the metaphor of the road of civilization, with white peoples marching ahead and black peoples struggling and straggling behind. According to Lévi-Strauss, unilinear progressivism is "*false evolutionism*," in which human societies, "both in the past and in far distant lands, are treated as *phases* or *stages* in a single line of development, starting from the same point and leading to the same end" (1952: 13). This version of events is a variety of cultural Darwinism, which equates the civilized–primitive opposition with an evolved–unevolved opposition. "We might, of course, say that human societies have made a varying use of their past time," Lévi-Strauss remarks, "and that some have even wasted it; that some were dashing on while others were loitering along the road." For such a metaphor to make sense, however, it would have to be a strictly historical (or cultural) road, not a "racial" (or natural) one. In this respect, Lévi-Strauss offers for consideration an alternative opposition: cumulative–noncumulative. There would be "two types of history," two types of human societies: one that historically develops an internal, innovative capacity to acquire knowledge cumulatively, another that does not—at least not so dynamically. From this perspective, progressive human societies would be those "in which discoveries and inventions are accumulated to build up great civilizations." To Lévi-Strauss, such a historical formulation appears "far more flexible and capable of differentiation" than any "racial" one (1952: 19).

Ultimately, Lévi-Strauss proposes another metaphor: civilization is a game of chance. He says that "a more accurate metaphor would be that of a gambler who has staked his money on several dice and, at each throw, sees them scatter over the cloth, giving a different score each time." For the gambler, it all depends on a random, seven-come-eleven toss of the dice. "What he wins on one," Lévi-Strauss says, "he is always liable to lose on another, and it is only occasionally that history is 'cumulative', that is to say, that the scores add up to a lucky combination" (1952: 22). It is simply by historical chance—or luck—that certain human societies, rather than others, have made progress. According to Lévi-Strauss there is no innate "racial" aptitude for civilization, among the signs of which are white skin and straight hair, for the history of civilization is just a crap shoot in which some peoples have merely happened to be luckier than others.

Chapter 7

Jung on "race" and the unconscious

To hear Jung tell it, he owes a great theoretical debt to African-Americans. In 1912, with the permission of William Alanson White, Jung analyzed fifteen African-American patients at St Elizabeths Hospital in Washington, DC, the largest psychiatric institution in America. It was these African-American patients who provided the evidence that Jung needed to formulate a truly universal—that is, a typically human—rather than a "racial" theory of the collective unconscious. The contents of the collective unconscious, Jung says, belong not "to any particular mind or person" but "to *mankind in general*." He continues:

> When I first came across such contents I wondered very much whether they might not be due to heredity, and I thought that they might be explained by racial inheritance. In order to settle the question I went to the United States and studied the dreams of pure-blooded Negroes, and I was able to satisfy myself that these images have nothing to do with so-called blood or racial inheritance, nor are they personally acquired by the individual. They belong to mankind in general, and therefore they are of a *collective* nature.
>
> (*CW* 18: 37, para. 79)

African-Americans thus prove to Jung that what he calls the collective unconscious is not a hereditary, "racial" unconscious. "Race," or blood, Jung concludes, is irrelevant.

Just how "pure-blooded" the African-Americans that Jung analyzed really were is, of course, problematic because of the history of miscegenation in America, especially under slavery. On the assumption, however, that the fifteen patients had only black and no white blood, Jung conducted research that was an effort to accumulate empirical evidence for or against any "racial" hypothesis about the collective unconscious. This research, which was not scientific by any statistical criterion, was at least suggestive enough to convince Jung that, collectively, there is only a "human" unconscious.

Psychoanalysis is not merely of European origin; it is also, more specifically, of Greek origin. Historically, it is Greek myth—in particular the Oedipus myth—that has had, through Freud, a decisive impact on psychoanalytic theory. According to Freud, the Oedipus myth—in the form of the Oedipus complex—remains a vital experience in contemporary psychical reality. Jung describes the shock that accompanies the recognition that this ancient myth is also a modern complex. The realization that the "incest fantasy" is at the origin of the Oedipus myth is a profoundly impressive discovery. In the archaeology of the unconscious, Jung says, it is comparable to the spectacle in "a modern city street" of "an ancient relic"—an artifact that provides us with an opportunity to acknowledge "the higher continuity of history." It demonstrates that the forms of existence in the present are only "slightly different" from those in the past, when "similar passions moved mankind." It disabuses us of the notion that there are any significant differences between ancient and modern psyches. As we moderns strive to appreciate "the infinite variability of the individual psyche" around us, "we suddenly catch a glimpse of the simplicity and grandeur of the Oedipus tragedy, that perennial highlight of the Greek theatre." A narrow perception instantaneously expands into a broad vision, which "has about it something of a revelation." As a result, "the gulf that separates our age from antiquity is bridged over, and we realize with astonishment that Oedipus is still alive for us." The Oedipus myth "teaches us that there is an identity of fundamental human conflicts which is independent of time and place." We moderns relinquish "the vain illusion that we are *different*, i.e., morally better, than the ancients." We discern that "an indissoluble link binds us to the men of antiquity." The modern self thus achieves both "sympathy" for and "intellectual comprehension" of the ancient other. We descend into the underworld of the unconscious, and in "subterranean passages of our own psyches we grasp the living meaning of classical civilization." Simultaneously, "we establish a firm foothold outside our own culture from which alone it is possible to gain an objective understanding of its foundations." In effect, we learn just how universal—just how typically human, or archetypal—the psyche is. "That at least is the hope we draw," Jung says, "from the rediscovery of the immortality of the Oedipus problem" (*CW* 5: 3–5, para. 1).

According to Jung, it is not only white Europeans—or white Americans—but also African-Americans who are, at least unconsciously, Greeks. As evidence that we moderns are all psychically the same as the Greeks, or the ancients, Jung cites the dream of an African-American patient at St Elizabeths Hospital. The dominant image in the dream is not of Oedipus but of Ixion, who was crucified not on a cross, like Christ, but on a wheel:

A Negro told me a dream in which occurred the figure of a man

crucified on a wheel. I will not mention the whole dream because it
does not matter. It contained of course its personal meaning as well
as allusions to impersonal ideas, but I picked out only that one motif.
He was a very uneducated Negro from the South and not particularly
intelligent. It would have been most probable, given the well-known
religious character of the Negroes, that he should dream of a man
crucified on a *cross*. The cross would have been a personal acquisition.
But it is rather improbable that he should dream of the man crucified
on a *wheel*. That is a very uncommon image. Of course I cannot prove
to you that by some curious chance the Negro had not seen a picture
or heard something of the sort and then dreamt about it; but if he had
not had any model for this idea it would be an *archetypal image*,
because the crucifixion on the wheel is a *mythological motif*.

(*CW* 18: 38–9, para. 81)

The dream of the African-American man is evidence, Jung says, not of a
personal, "Christian" unconscious but of a collective, "Greek" unconscious:

> In the dream of the Negro, the man on the wheel is a repetition of
> the Greek mythological motif of Ixion, who, on account of his offence
> against men and gods, was fastened by Zeus upon an incessantly
> turning wheel. I give you this example of a mythological motif in a
> dream merely in order to convey to you an idea of the collective
> unconscious. One single example is of course no conclusive proof.
> But one cannot very well assume that this Negro had studied Greek
> mythology, and it is improbable that he had seen any representation
> of Greek mythological figures. Furthermore, figures of Ixion are pretty
> rare.

(*CW* 18: 40, para. 82)

In this "psychomythology," the image of Ixion is, as it were, "all Greek"
to the African-American dreamer. Jung declares, in no uncertain terms:
"Insane Negroes, very black Negroes, whom I have analysed in the United
States, had Greek myths in their dreams—Ixion on the wheel, for instance.
It is only illusion to think they are far apart; the Negro has the same
kind of unconscious as the one that produced those symbols in Greece
or anywhere else." Archetypal images are the result not of a diffusionist
tendency but of an "autochthonous" aptitude, an intrinsic psychical disposition spontaneously to generate images that are typically human (1984:
71–2). African-Americans demonstrate that the collective unconscious is
capable—independent, as Jung says, of time and place (and, I would
emphasize, independent of "race")—of producing archetypal images. It
is not the psyche as a whole but only a part of it that Jung regards as
universal in implication. Thus he contrasts the "homogeneity" of the

unconscious with the "heterogeneity" of the conscious (*CW* 6: 491–2, para. 851). (Theoretical consistency, however, would seem to demand that it is the collective unconscious that is homogeneous and both the personal unconscious and the conscious that are heterogeneous.)

DIFFERENT CONTENTS BUT THE SAME FORMS

Jung argues that if a modern African-American dream contains exactly the same image as an ancient Greek myth (for example, the crucifixion of a man, like Ixion, on a wheel), then the image is evidence of a collective, typically human, unconscious. In this instance, Jung states that the images in the African-American patients at St Elizabeths Hospital were neither "racial" inheritances nor, I would emphasize, personal acqui-sitions. Evidently, he regards them as human inheritances. In this instance, he seems to espouse the unconscious inheritance of images. Such a notion, however, is inconsistent with the distinction between archetypes as forms and archetypal images as contents. When Jung distinguishes archetypes from archetypal images, he says explicitly that only the forms, or catego-ries of the imagination, are collectively inherited. The specific contents, or images, are never collectively inherited but always personally acquired through individual experience. What makes an image archetypal is not that it is collectively inherited. What makes it archetypal is that, although it is personally acquired through individual experience, it is collectively informed, or categorized, in a typically human way. It is not the sameness of specific contents, or images, that proves the existence of the collective unconscious but rather the sameness of forms. When Jung is most precise (and most cogent), he defines the "collective unconscious" as a purely formal, categorical unconscious—not as what I would call a *contentual* unconscious. Archetypes are constants, and archetypal images are vari-ables. What is independent of time and place is the abstract form, not the concrete content. The forms are psychological themes (or, as Jung says, mythological motifs) on which the contents are quite specific vari-ations.

In an allusion to Jung, Jacques Lacan says that "interpretation is based on no assumption of divine archetypes, but on the fact that the uncon-scious is structured in the most radical way like a language" (1977: 234). If the unconscious is, indeed, structured like a language, that deep, syntactical structure is, according to Jung, the grammar of an archetypal *lingua franca*—or perhaps a *lingua africana*, a "Swahili" with a duration of several millennia. "The main features of human life have remained the same for five or six thousand years or more, for an interminably long period," Jung says. "Primitive tribes are moved by the same emotions as we are." He contends that "the fundamental conceptions of life and the world are the same." Whether primitive or civilized, "our unconscious speaks a language which is most international." It is not only the dreams of African-Americans but also the dreams of Africans that confirm to Jung the existence of the collective unconscious:

> I analysed dreams of Somali Negroes as if they were people of Zurich, with the exception of certain differences of languages and images. Where the primitives dream of crocodiles, pythons, buffaloes, and rhinoceroses, we dream of being run over by trains and automobiles. Both have the same voice, really; our modern cities sound like a primeval forest. What we express by the banker the Somali expresses by the python. The surface language is different yet the underlying facts are just the same. That is why we can make historical parallels.
>
> (1984: 70)

Apparently, it is not only psychoanalysis that is interminable (as Freud says) but also the collective unconscious. As different as the contents—the languages and images—may be on the surface (between the animals of Africa and the machines of Europe), at a depth the forms are the same.

In this instance, Jung does not argue that a Somali and a Swiss would have to dream exactly the same image in order to prove the existence of the collective unconscious. Quite to the contrary, he explicitly states that even radically different images would still constitute evidence of the collective unconscious, if, I would emphasize, those images served the same psychical purpose, or emotional and conceptual function. From the perspective of archetypes, whether we are squeezed psychically by a python or a banker is incidental. What is essential is the typically human, psychical experience of being "squeezed." Of course, the banker may squeeze a Swiss for profit, and the python may squeeze the Somali for some other reason, but the banker and the python are both images of what I would call, in this case, the archetype of "constriction." I do not mean to suggest, however, that only the form (constriction), not the specific content (either banker or python), is relevant. That the image is a banker and not a python may be a very significant difference in the psychical reality of the dreamer.

To establish the existence of the collective unconscious, African-American dreams need not duplicate the particular content, or images, of Greek myths. All that is necessary is for Somali dreams to parallel the general form of Swiss dreams. In short, there is no unconscious inheritance of images. Images are not collectively inherited but are personally acquired by individuals in different situations, or circumstances—in different places, at different times. The acquisition of images is strictly situational, or circumstantial, dependent on what is available to the individual locally. If the locale is Africa, some images will differ from what they would be if the locale were Europe. If an image is unavailable locally, the individual will not—indeed, cannot—dream it. (This does not imply that images are necessarily facsimiles of objects in external reality. The imagination does not just categorize, or inform, images. Often, it also transforms images in what Freud tends to call distortive ways or in what Jung tends to call creative ways. The individual personally acquires all images but, in the process, imaginatively adapts some objects from external reality in such a way that the image in psychical reality is significantly different from the object.)

Although all images are personal acquisitions, the experience of the individual in this respect is not idiosyncratic. The individual does not exist in isolation from history, culture, and environment. The images available to the individual at a specific time, in a specific place, are also available to other individuals at that same time, in that same place. A common historical, cultural, and environmental context provides an array of images of which individuals avail themselves. Individuals at the same time and in the same place will tend to dream the same images because they tend to have the same history, culture, and environment. That is, images—whether unconscious or conscious—have a collective dimension that Jung does not adequately acknowledge. Individuals experience life and the world in typical ways not only because they share a "human nature" but also because they share a history, culture, and environment with other individuals.

DIFFERENCES IN BEHAVIOR, INFLUENCES ON CHARACTER

Not only do Africans or African-Americans provide Jung with evidence for a typically human, rather than a "racial" collective unconscious, they also serve him as evidence of the social construction of insanity:

> To be crazy is a relative conception. For instance, when a Negro behaves in a certain way we say, "Oh well, he's only a Negro," but if a white man behaves in the same way we say, "That man is crazy," because a white man cannot behave like that. A Negro is expected to do such things but a white man does not do them. To be "crazy" is a social concept.
>
> (*CW* 18: 35, para. 72)

Jung does not pathologize behavioral differences, nor does he "racialize" them. He relativizes them. He argues that what appears sane or insane depends on the social context, on a set of social expectations. A white man who "behaves black" in white society may be called "crazy," while a black man who "behaves white" in black society may be called "crazy." According to Jung, attitudes toward behavioral differences between whites and blacks are a function of culture. For a white to go black—or to "behave black"—is not to go insane, although other whites may think or feel that the individual has "gone crazy." From the perspective of cultural relativism, the deviation of individuals, whether white or black, from the behavioral norms of the group to which they apparently belong "racially" is not an indication of insanity but simply a departure from a certain set of social expectations. In spite of what Jung says, he does not believe that insanity is merely a social construction. He did, after all, serve at the Burgholzli Hospital in Zurich under Eugen Bleuler, who introduced the term "schizophrenia," and he himself wrote a book on what psychiatrists then called "dementia praecox." Jung is only observing, in this instance, that craziness may be equated socially with blackness (or whiteness) in the case of radically nonconformist behavior. Presumably, the more difference between the behavioral styles of "racial" groups, the more probable the ascription of insanity to any individual who, consciously or unconsciously, adopts the style of the other.

In commenting on the character of white Americans, Jung remarks on "the great influence of the Negro, a psychological influence naturally, not due to the mixing of blood." From the perspective of a white European, he contends that white Americans have been unconsciously influenced by African-Americans in styles of laughter, walk, music, dance, religion, naïveté, vivacity, talk, and mass sociability. He remarks on how difficult it is "to decide how much of all this is due to symbiosis with the Negro," but on the whole, "taken all in all, the wide influence of the Negro on the general character of the people is unmistakable" (CW 10: 46–7, para. 96).

In an anecdote replete with "racial" caricatures, Jung comments on the style of American laughter. He identifies with an African-American youth as a "brother" who was most certainly not a typical Yankee. On a trip to America, Jung was "the guest of a pretty stiff and solemn New England family of a rather terrifying respectability." The family had no sense of humor; they could laugh at nothing, including themselves. "It felt," Jung says with a certain irony, "almost like home. (There are very conservative and highly respectable folk in Switzerland, too. We might even better the American record in this respect.)" The white family employed several black servants as waiters. Jung describes the scene as follows:

I felt at first as if I were eating lunch in a circus and I found myself diffidently scrutinizing the dishes, looking for the imprint of those black fingers. A solemnity brooded over the meal for which I could see no reason, but I supposed it was the solemnity or serenity of great virtue or something like that which vibrated through the room. At all events nobody laughed. Everyone was just too nice and too polite. Eventually I could stand it no longer, and I began to crack jokes for better or worse. These were greeted with condescending smiles. But I could not arouse that hearty and generous American laugh which I love and admire.

In a last, desperate attempt to provoke laughter from the white family, Jung tried "some Chinese on them" (perhaps a "racial" or ethnic joke):

> So I came to my last story, really a good one—and no sooner had I finished than right behind my chair an enormous avalanche of laughter broke loose. It was the Negro servant, and it was the real American laughter, that grand, unrestrained, unsophisticated laughter revealing rows of teeth, tongue, palate, everything, just a trifle exaggerated perhaps and certainly less than sixteen years old. How I loved that African brother.

Jung does not say what effect the incident had on decorum at the table. He acknowledges that the anecdote is "a rather foolish story," but for him it is nevertheless indicative of just how humorless, just how witless, white Americans would be without the influence of African-Americans (*CW* 10: 503–4, paras. 950–1).

According to Jung, white Americans may suddenly "go black"—or, as the case may be, "go yellow." He says that "then you get these interesting stories of decent young girls eloping with Chinamen or with Negroes, because in the American that primitive layer, which with us is a bit difficult, with them is decidedly disagreeable, as it is much lower down." This phenomenon, Jung contends, is identical with " 'going black' or 'going native' in Africa" (*CW* 18: 148, para. 341).

HERO-MOTIF AND VICTIM-MOTIF

Jung notes that in the dreams of white Americans images of African-Americans inevitably "play no small role as an expression of the inferior side of their personality." In contrast to white Europeans, who egocentrically (or egotistically) think highly of themselves and unconsciously project their own inferior aspects onto "the lower classes," white Americans project their inferior aspects onto "races" that they consider "lower" than themselves. Jung implies that the white–black, master–slave opposition is the image that historically conditions this projection of high–low values, while a white–red, pioneer–warrior opposition conditions the projection onto Native-Americans. The African-American serves, in this sense, as an ignoble savage, the Native-American as a noble savage. Jung thus romanticizes Native-Americans, as many white Americans do. This romantic notion ignores, neglects, or represses the entire, sordid history of broken treaties, forced removal to reservations, and attempted genocide. White Americans may have enslaved African-Americans, but they tried to exterminate Native-Americans. For some white Americans, the

Indian may have been a hero, but for others, the Indian was only a villain. To ascertain the unconscious influence of Native-Americans on white Americans, Jung interprets dreams. The interpretation of dreams for this purpose requires patience. Jung says that "as the great majority of dreams, especially those in the early stages of analysis, are superficial, it was only in the course of very thorough and deep analyses that I came upon symbols relating to the Indian." If the white American unconsciously selects the "Negro" to express the inferiority of the victim-motif, to express the superiority of the "hero-motif" the white American "chooses the Indian as its symbol." (Presumably it is active resistance to aggression that earns for Native-Americans a certain respect that white Americans refuse to accord African-Americans. As former warriors, Native-Americans are heroes; as former slaves, African-Americans are merely victims in the collective unconscious of white Americans.) In this respect, Jung mentions that the red man, or Native-American, is profiled on money minted in America. It is significant, he remarks, that "certain coins of the Union bear an Indian head." If the Indian-head penny and nickel have now been replaced by the Lincoln-head penny and the Jefferson-head nickel, the image of the Native-American in the collective unconscious of white Americans once had a value that was not only monetary but also psychical. "This is a tribute to the once-hated Indian, but it also testifies to the fact that the American hero-motif chooses the Indian as an ideal figure," Jung says. "It would certainly never occur to any American administration to place the head of Cetewayo or any other Negro hero on their coins" (*CW* 10: 47, para. 99).

Cetewayo—or, alternatively, "Cetshwayo"—was, after Shaka, the last great king of the Zulus. In 1879, the British invaded Zululand. At the end of the war, they deposed Cetshwayo and exiled him to Capetown. In 1882, they shipped him from the Cape Colony to England, where he met Queen Victoria. She gave him a photograph of her royal highness. He posed, in native costume, for a portrait. In 1883, the British divided into three parts the Zululand that they had conquered. They allotted Cetshwayo one of the parts to rule. He died in 1884. If Americans have yet to place the head of a black man or woman on a coin, they have at least placed such heads on stamps. The recent "Black Heritage" commemorative postal issue includes such African-American heroes as Benjamin Banneker, Frederick Douglass, Sojourner Truth, Booker T. Washington, W.E.B. Du Bois, James Weldon Johnson, A. Philip Randolph, Harriet Tubman, Ida B. Wells, George Washington Carver, Matthew Henson, Duke Ellington, Jesse Owens, Jackie Robinson, and Martin Luther King, Jr.

According to Jung, the image of the Native-American in the unconscious of the white American is an image of fantastically heroic proportions. "The hero," Jung says, "is always the embodiment of man's highest and most powerful aspiration, or of what this aspiration ought ideally to be and what he would most gladly realize." In this respect, "what kind of fantasy constitutes the hero-motif" is of decisive significance. "In the American hero-fantasy," he contends, "the Indian's character plays a leading role." As an example, Jung mentions the difference between sports in America and Europe. Americans, who are superior in performance to Europeans, are trained athletically, he says, as if they were being initiated ritualistically. Not only in sports but also in other endeavors the Native- American signifies to the white American a number of positive values: "His extraordinary concentration on a particular goal, his tenacity of purpose, his unflinching endurance of the greatest hardships—in all this the legendary virtues of the Indian find fullest expression" (*CW* 10: 47–8, para. 100).

In directly addressing Americans, Jung explicitly associates the hero with the primitive—that is, with the Native-American:

> It is inevitable that the heroic attitude should be coupled with a sort of primitivity, because it has always been the ideal of a somewhat sporty, primitive society. And this is where the real historical spirit of the Red Man enters the game. Look at your sports! They are the toughest, the most reckless, and the most efficient in the world. The idea of mere play has almost entirely disappeared, while in other parts of the world the idea of play still prevails rather than that of professional sport.
>
> (*CW* 10: 513, para. 977).

In contrast to the amateur sport of Europeans, the professional sport of Americans is not play but work. In America, where (in spite of protests from Native-Americans) teams retain such mascot names as "Indians," "Redskins," "Warriors," and "Braves"—and where, in a recent World Series, a certain gesture, or "chop," by fans with a foam-rubber souvenir in the shape of a tomahawk provoked accusations of racism (Anderson 1991, 13 October: 8, 1; Lipsyte 1991, 18 October: B, 10; Giago 1994, 13 March: 8, 9)—sport is serious (and profitable) business. Perhaps it is not irrelevant to wonder how Jung would interpret the success (if not the dominance) of contemporary African-Americans in such sports as track and field, baseball, football, and basketball—to say nothing of boxing.

THE "INDIANIZATION" OF WHITE AMERICANS

According to Jung, white Americans "go red" not only behaviorally but also physically, or anatomically. He asserts that, "in America, the skull and pelvis measurements of all the European races begin to indianize themselves in the second generation of immigrants." (Jung does not say whether he also believes that the African "races" begin to indianize themselves, although logical consistency would seem to require such a conclusion.) This process, he contends, is a function of "the mystery of the American earth" (CW 10: 13, para. 18). That is, it is environment, rather than "race," or blood, that accounts for this "indianization" of white Americans. "The admixture of Indian blood is increasingly small," Jung says, "so it plays no role." It is the land of America that forms "the 'Yankee' type," which "is so similar to the Indian type" (CW 10: 45–6, para. 94).

Jung waxes anecdotal about the influence of Native-Americans on white Americans. On his first visit to America, in 1909, Jung witnessed hundreds of workers leaving a factory in Buffalo, New York. To an American accompanying him he remarked: "I really had no idea there was such an amazing amount of Indian blood in your people." In response, the American wagered that there was "not one drop of it in this whole crowd." For Jung, the Native-American "racial" influence was physiognomically obvious. "But don't you see their faces?" he inquired quizzically. "They are more Indian than European." The American, however, informed Jung that most of the workers were probably Irish-Americans, Scottish-Americans, and German-Americans. "Subsequently," Jung says, "I learned to see how ridiculous my hypothesis had been." Citing the American anthropologist Franz Boas (who, Jung noted, was not without critics), he nevertheless continued to maintain that there are "measurable anatomical changes in many American immigrants, changes which are already noticeable in the second generation" (CW 10: 502–3, para. 948).

There are curious environmental (rather than "racial") factors in America, Jung contends, that subtly influence the immigrant from Europe. "The foreign country," he says, "somehow gets under the skin of those born in it." Mysteriously, as they stand on the very land of America, as they breathe in the very atmosphere of America, they rapidly evolve, as it were, into Indians. "There is an x and a y in the air and in the soil of a country," Jung says, "which slowly permeate and assimilate him to the type of the aboriginal inhabitant, even to the point of remodelling his physical features" (CW 10: 510, para. 968). (I should perhaps emphasize that, in terms of Darwinian evolutionary theory, environmental factors can, of course, have no such immediate Lamarckian influence.) Jung declares that "the spirit of the Indian gets at the American from within and without"—with the result that "there is often an astonishing likeness in the cast of the American face to that of the Red Indian" (CW 10: 510–11, para. 970).

In comparison with white Americans, white Europeans are "pale faces" indeed. "The old European inheritance," Jung says, "looks rather pale beside these vigorous primitive influences." The influence of Native-Americans on white Americans is psychical as well as physical. Not only in the physiognomy but also in the architecture of America, he asserts, there is visible evidence of the unconscious impact of Native-Americans on the Yankee type. "Have you ever compared the skyline of New York or any great American city with that of a pueblo like Taos?" Jung asks. "And did you see how the houses pile up to towers towards the centre? Without conscious imitation the American unconsciously fills out the spectral outline of the Red Man's mind and temperament" (*CW* 10: 514, para. 978). As a psychoanalyst, Jung privileges unconscious influence over conscious imitation. Like the Native-American, the white American unconsciously scrapes the sky.

"JES GREW": UNCONSCIOUS INFLUENCE AS INFECTION OR CONTAGION

In contrast to going black in America, going black in Africa tends to be a total experience. White Europeans in Africa, Jung says, desperately defy the tendency to go black, futile as the effort may be. He notes that "you observe a violent resistance in the white man against the primitive or exotic country in which he lives." White Europeans who settle in Africa "either hate that country or they just love it." Whatever the case, "they *nolens volens* begin to get assimilated by the soil and they develop a very curious mentality." Hate it or love it, Africa exerts an ineluctable influence on white Europeans, as if the earth were quicksand. "It is just as if the unconscious part of their psyche was sinking down into the peculiar phenomenon of 'going black.'" Africa—or the primitive—is, ultimately, an irresistible force by which "these people get lured away unconsciously from their civilized sphere" (1973 1: 380–1). As Jung says, "No one can shield himself from this unconscious influence." He continues:

> Even today the European, however highly developed, cannot live with impunity among the Negroes in Africa; their psychology gets into him unnoticed and unconsciously he becomes a Negro. There is no fighting against it. In Africa there is a well-known technical expression for this: "going black."
>
> (*CW* 10: 121, para. 249)

Jung, a white European, did not live among "Negroes" in Africa but only traveled with and among them. He noticed the psychology of black Africans getting into him, and he fought against it. He resisted the impulse and did not go black.

Jung says that the influence of African-Americans on white Americans is infectious. African-Americans do not just affect white Americans; they infect them:

> This infection by the primitive can, of course, be observed just as well

in other countries, though not to the same degree and in this form. In Africa, for example, the white man is a diminishing minority and must therefore protect himself from the Negro by observing the most rigorous social forms, otherwise he risks "going black." If he succumbs to the primitive influence he is lost. But in America the Negro, just because he is in a minority, is not a degenerative influence, but rather one which, peculiar though it is, cannot be termed unfavourable— unless one happens to have a jazz phobia.

(*CW* 10: 47, para. 97)

However curious the influence of African-Americans on white Americans may seem, it is innocuous (and, if one enjoys jazz, perhaps even regenerative), at least in comparison with the influence of black Africans on white Africans.

Jung hypothesizes that "the peculiarities of the American temperament" are due in large part to the pervasive presence of the African-American, "that most striking and suggestive figure." America is a "piebald" nation in which whites and blacks live together in close proximity. The influence that African-Americans exert on the unconscious of white Americans Jung calls a contagion: "What is more contagious than to live side by side with a rather primitive people? Go to Africa and see what happens. When it is so obvious that you stumble over it, you call it 'going black' " (*CW* 10: 507, paras. 961–2).

Africans and African-Americans share the caricature of "natural rhythm," which also influences white Americans. Jung remarks: "The rhythm of jazz is the same as the *n'goma*, the African dance. You can dance the Central African *n'goma* with all its jumping and rocking, its swinging shoulders and hips, to American jazz. American music is most obviously pervaded by the African rhythm" (*CW* 10: 508, para. 964). White Americans can afford to dance to jazz, whereas white Africans— or white Europeans like Jung—participate in a *n'goma* only at great risk, the least serious consequence of which is apparently a panic attack.

If there is a "Negro problem," Jung says, it is a problem that whites make for blacks—and, inadvertently, for themselves. Whites may affect blacks, but blacks infect whites mimetically, unconsciously:

The white man is a most terrific problem to the Negro, and whenever you affect somebody so profoundly, then in a mysterious way, something comes back from him to yourself. The Negro by his mere presence is a source of temperamental and mimetic infection, which the European can't help noticing just as much as he sees the hopeless gap between the American and the African Negro. Racial infection is a most serious mental and moral problem where the primitive outnumbers the white man. America has this problem only in a relative degree, because the whites far outnumber the coloured. Apparently he can assimilate the primitive influence with little risk to himself. What would happen if there were a considerable increase in the coloured population is another matter.

I am quite convinced that some American peculiarities can be traced back directly to the coloured man, while others result from a compensatory defence against his laxity. But they remain externals leaving the inner quick of the American character untouched, which is not the case where "going black" is concerned.

(*CW* 10: 509, paras. 966–7)

According to Jung, it is a question of being outnumbered, of being overwhelmed. He suggests that the influence of African-Americans on white Americans is mostly external, or behavioral, rather than internal, or psychical. White Americans may "behave black," but, unlike white Africans, they do not run such a great risk of "going black"—that is, "thinking black" and "feeling black." Because they are in the majority, white Americans can afford relative behavioral assimilation, which is very different from absolute psychical identification. If there is laxity in blacks, there is rigidity in whites. Staying white rather than going black is a defensive compensation against a relaxation of the ego. Just as Jung defended himself from the risk of going black, defended himself against the fear of losing his white, European ego on his trip to Africa, he suggests that white Africans must do the same since black Africans comprise the vast majority of the population. In contrast, white Americans have less to risk, less to fear, merely because the demographics of the United States are different.

Jung does discuss influences that are not so innocuous, when the issue is not jazz but savagery and slavery. The examples that he mentions are South Africa and the American South. Jung employs a master–savage, master–slave opposition in an attempt to explain the dynamics of the colonialist, imperialist project. In the civilized–primitive hierarchy, the master occupies a higher position, the savage or slave, a lower position. In terms similar to those that Conrad employs, Jung says in reference to America that "the conquerors always drop toward the level of the conquered, for it is much easier to go down ten feet than to climb up one." The civilized is, in this sense, a small step on a slippery slope either up from or down to the primitive. "The whole effort toward human development is to push us up that one foot, and if we let go any of the things which we have gained by civilization, we slip quickly." As an example, Jung cites the experience of the Dutch in South Africa. They were, he says, "at the time of their colonizing a developed and civilized people," but they "dropped to a much lower level because of their contact with the savage races." They became brutalized, or primitivized, in the effort at mastery. Jung elaborates:

The savage inhabitants of a country have to be mastered. In the attempt to master, brutality rises in the master. He must be ruthless. He must sacrifice everything soft and fine for the sake of mastering savages. Their influence is very great; the more surely they are dominated, the more savage the master must become. The slave has the greatest influence of all, because he is kept close to the one who rules him.

Like the Dutch who settled in South Africa, the white Europeans who settled in America had pretensions to being, quite literally, a "master race." Jung addresses white Americans as follows: "You, today, are influenced by the Negro race, which not so long ago had to call you master." The influence, he says, is not so great in the American North as it is in the American South, "where I find what they call sentiment and chivalry and romance to be the covering of cruelty." White Americans in the South are physically brutal because they themselves are psychically brutish. "Southerners treat one another very courteously," Jung says, "but they treat the Negro as they would treat their own unconscious if they knew what was in it." They unconsciously project their own savagery onto African-Americans. "When I see a man in a savage rage with something outside himself," Jung concludes, "I know that he is, in reality, wanting to be savage toward his own unconscious self" (1977: 15–16). The white Southerner and the Afrikaner thus "outprimitive" the primitive, the black who serves them as an all too convenient excuse for the projection of what Jung was eventually to call the "shadow."

Although the equation of "influence" with "infection" or "contagion" is problematic, it is also perhaps instructive, nonetheless. If we were to take these words literally, it would be easy for us, from a position of superiority, immediately to condemn this language as nothing but a variety of racism that equates "white" with "healthy" and "black" with "unhealthy." (Significantly, Jung does not say that the influence of Native-Americans on white Americans is an infection, or contagion.) Would it not be more sensible, more sensitive, to use an apparently neutral word like "suggestion" (we might then speak of the self as *suggestible* and the other as *suggestive*)? Jung is, of course, employing the language of disease, what Susan Sontag (1978) calls "illness as metaphor." He was not only a psychoanalyst but also a medical doctor, a psychiatrist. According to Jung, going totally black (or white) is to experience blackness (or whiteness) as illness, or sickness. The white European who has gone black and the black African or African-American who has gone white have "gone psychopathological."

The metaphor of disease emphasizes that the other is infectious, or contagious, to the self—not just "influential." One "catches" color (blackness or whiteness). One contracts it like a disease when the self contacts the other. In these terms, color—or what it implies behaviorally and psychologically—is, like a disease, transmissible or communicable, and no one, black or white, is immune from its effects. What are we to make of Freud's own comparison of psychoanalysis to a disease? According to Lacan, Freud said to Jung, on arriving in the United States in 1909, that they, the Europeans, were bringing the "plague" to the unwary, unconscious Americans (1977: 116). Are we ill with psychoanalysis, are we sick of it?

Calvin C. Hernton, who discusses sex and racism in America, says that some white women "first get the desire to have sexual intercourse with a Negro through a kind of contagion" (1965: 49). According to Hernton, it is not only sex but also culture that is contagious:

> One finds in the North, scattered here and there, a few white women—old and young—who have adopted every characteristic, real as well as stereotyped, of the American Negro, from patterns of speech down to the very style of walking. It is, to say the least, amazing to see this phenomenon—the *white-Negro woman*. She has that "gyrating gait," that bouncing of the shoulders as she talks, that slur in her voice, that earthy twirl in her pelvis when she dances, that Negro-like contempt of whites. She is thoroughly aware of every injustice committed against the Negro, she can sing along with Lead Belly, Ray Charles, Billie Holiday, Muddy Waters and Mahalia Jackson as well as any Negro. She knows who Nat Turner, Sojourner Truth, and Fred Douglass were. Her vocabulary is conspicuously incomprehensible to white people, for she can speak the "ethnic" language as well as any Negro, maybe better, and she has had the kind of organic intimacy with Negroes—men and women—that has made her know them as well as, if not far better than, they know themselves.
>
> (1965: 51–2)

To go black or to "go ethnic" in this sense is a parody or a travesty.

Contemporary post-colonialist critics like James Snead also employ the term "contagion." In particular, Snead cites the novel *Mumbo Jumbo* in which Ishmael Reed discusses the phenomenon of "Jes Grew," the contagion of black culture that, like Topsy in the novel *Uncle Tom's Cabin*, "jes' grew" and continues to spread, irresistibly, irrepressibly throughout white culture, which, like all cultures, is not immune to unconscious influence. One of the characters says of Jes Grew, "For some, it's a disease, a plague, but in fact it is an anti-plague" (1972: 33). For Reed, the contagion of Jes Grew is a black African antidote to the real disease, which is white European culture. If, as Snead says, contagion is "the dominant metaphor" for Jes Grew, the contagion is a "benevolent" one—and "all cultures, colors, and nationalities are subject to its 'pandemic.' " According to Snead, "Perhaps the most important aspect of cultural contagion is that by the time one is aware of it, it has *already happened*" (1990: 245). That is, as Jung says, cultural contagion is an unconscious influence of which we only become conscious after the fact, after the self has "caught" the color of the other.

MIMICRY, MOCKERY, MENACE

The transmissibility or communicability of behavior and psychology is one of the concerns of contemporary "cultural studies" (a considerable part of which is multicultural studies). The issue is mimesis: how the self imitates, or mimics, the other. The post-colonialist critic Homi Bhabha states that "mimicry emerges as one of the most elusive and effective strategies of colonial power and knowledge." It has, he asserts, the structure of "an *ironic* compromise." According to Bhabha, colonial mimicry is a desire to create an other who is "*a subject of a difference that is almost the same, but not quite*" (1984: 126). In the effort to create an other in the image of oneself, the desire is not for an other who is absolutely identical with the self but for one so very similar to the self and yet just different enough from the self to continue to be recognizable as an other. Bhabha contends that an ambivalent attitude conditions colonial mimicry and compromises it ironically. This is a state "between mimicry and mockery" (1984: 127). When the self colonizes an other, it tries to force the other to imitate, or mimic, the self—with, however, a crucial, residual difference. For example, Bhabha says that "to be Anglicized, is *emphatically* not to be English" (1984: 128). In the context of Africa, to be Europeanized is not to become European. The desire is to create not a European but, rather, a Europeanized African—a European *manque*. Because, however, the other mocks the self even as it mimics it, the other also menaces the self. The "menace" that the other poses is disruptive to the authority of the self (1984: 129). The other has a subversive effect, finally, on all of the efforts of the self to dominate the other.

In discussing the psychology of colonization, Mannoni says that the non-European accepts European civilization in part but rejects it as a whole. He speculates that "it is this attitude which gives Europeans the impression that the native is ready enough to mimic them but never succeeds in emulating them." Mannoni insists that the psyche of the non-European "is certainly not to be expressed as a fraction in which the numerator represents the proportion of Western civilization which he has already absorbed and the denominator the total amount we feel he ought to absorb." The extent to which the non-European has been "Europeanized," or colonized, "in reality depends on the way in which he, as he was, has reacted to ourselves as we are." Because the colonizer expects the colonized to become an exact duplicate, "a simple reflection," of himself, he cannot appreciate an emergent novelty. Mannoni notes that "we frequently fail to see that it is something entirely new, especially if we are expecting a slavish imitation." According to Mannoni, the colonized inevitably disappoints the unrealistic expectations of the colonizer. "It may well be," he says, "that it is just because we look for a too faithful copy that we tend to see the actual result as grotesque mimicry" (1964: 23).

Bhabha describes mimicry as a strategy. To him, it is a quite deliberate ploy, a colonial policy. In short, he emphasizes the conscious intent of the self in the attempt to colonize the other. Although he also notes that there is a certain irony to this conscious intent, since, inadvertently, it also has subversive effects (the result mocks and menaces the self), he does not discuss unconscious processes, as Jung does. Bhabha considers only one variety of imitation, in which the self consciously—and unidirectionally—coerces the other to mimic it. In contrast, Jung discusses another variety, in which the self not only consciously influences the other but is unconsciously influenced by it, in spite of itself. It is in this sense that he says that the influence is "infectious" or "contagious." (According to Jung, if, at the extreme, self and other identify with each other, become absolutely identical with each other, then the result is unhealthy. Presumably, the ambivalent, ironical similarity-with-a-difference that Bhabha describes is a comparatively healthy relation, however coercive it may be in one direction and however subversive it may be in the other direction.) As Jung describes this mutual influence, it is a bidirectional transmission or communication of behavior and psychology. Unconscious, unintentional mimicry works both ways: on the self as well as on the other. As the primitive is civilized, so the civilized is primitivized; as the African is Europeanized, so the European is Africanized; as the black is whitened, so the white is blackened—and much, perhaps most, of this process occurs unconsciously, unintentionally. White Europeans may go black, but black Africans may also go white.

According to Jung, like it or not, color—or all that it implies—gets under one's skin. The effect is unconscious—subcutaneous, subliminal, subconscious:

> You cannot live in Africa or any such country without having that country get under your skin. If you live with the yellow man you get yellow under the skin. You cannot prevent it, because somewhere you are the same as the Negro or the Chinese or whoever you live with, you are all just human beings. In the collective unconscious you are the same as a man of another race, you have the same archetypes, just as you have, like him, eyes, a heart, a liver, and so on. It does not matter that his skin is black. It matters to a certain extent, sure enough—he has probably a whole historical layer less than you. The different strata of the mind correspond to the history of the races.
>
> (CW 18: 46–7, para. 93)

The paradox is that it is not difference but sameness that induces us to go black, yellow, or any other color. One might even say that only apparently do we ever "go other." In fact, we really always only "go self," or "go human." Jung says that the other gets under the skin of the self because human beings, although different on the surface of the body are the same in the depths of the psyche, in the collective unconscious. Our psychical organs (the archetypes) are just as typically human as our physical organs.

Like Lévi-Strauss, Jung argues that if skin color matters at all, it matters not as a natural or "racial" phenomenon but as a strictly cultural or historical phenomenon. Ultimately, it is history, not "race" or skin color, that matters. If there is "psychogeological" stratification, it is not "racial" but historical. Any correspondence between the stratification of psyches and the history of "races" is accidental. From the position of the white European, primitive peoples, by definition, have experienced certain stages of history but not others, which civilized peoples have experienced. This notion may be a historicist bias (which uncritically converts a putative difference into an opposition and then imposes a valuation that judges the civilized to be superior and the primitive to be inferior), but at least it is not a racist prejudice. From the perspective of what Jung calls the historical layers of the psyche, it is only by accident (Lévi-Strauss would say, by chance or lack of luck) that some cultures have not yet had the historical experience of some other cultures. Otherwise, we are all typically human, or archetypally identical. There is no natural, racial—or essential—difference between peoples, primitive or civilized. There are only cultural, historical, accidental differences, which are relative, not absolute. (Of course, as we know all too well, even accidents of history can have a tragic, even catastrophic effect.)

Chapter 8

The color complex

"Complex" is a term that Jung introduced into psychoanalytic discourse. A complex is an unconscious feeling-toned set of ideas. Beginning in 1902, Jung (*CW* 2) and colleagues at the Burgholzli Hospital conducted a series of word association experiments at the Psychiatric Clinic of the University of Zurich. Jung designed this research project to investigate unconscious complexes. He instructed participants in the experiments to react to a list of one hundred stimulus words with response words, or associations. He interpreted disturbances in reaction (for example, a conspicuous delay in the reply) as evidence of an unconscious complex. These psycholinguistic experiments confirmed empirically the existence of what Freud called "repression." In contrast to Freud, however, who emphasized sexual complexes, Jung demonstrated that individuals might have an unconscious complex on any issue about which they had an especially sensitive feeling-toned set of ideas. One might, for instance, have a "racial" complex (or, for that matter, a racist complex).

Although historically psychoanalysis has not evinced much interest in "race" in the white–black sense, no fewer than three articles on the topic appeared in the very first year of the very first psychoanalytic journal in America. One article was on the dreams of African-Americans, another was on schizophrenia (or dementia praecox) in African-Americans, and yet another was on the "color complex" of African-Americans.

In the third article, John E. Lind, a psychiatrist at the Government Hospital for the Insane in Washington, DC, presents case material in an effort to demonstrate that the basis of delusions among psychotic African-Americans is "a complex which is extremely common, one might almost say, universal, in the negro." This complex is a function of "the social subordination of the negro in the United States." Because color is "the most obvious racial distinction" between whites and blacks, Lind calls this complex the "color complex." According to Lind, the color complex is present also in African-Americans who are not psychotic. As evidence, he mentions "the somewhat primitive theological conception" among

African-Americans, who, he asserts, personify god and the angels as white. Lind acknowledges that there are exceptions:

> I have seen works of art for sale in stores catering to negro trade, representing scenes in Paradise, translations, etc., where the celestial figures were black, a startling, vivid black. The motives prompting such production, as well as those which might actuate their purchase and their acceptance as a faithful representation of the future state are probably a note of defiance, a protest against the orthodox color scheme of salvation.

As a rule, however, "the future blessed state according to their ideas is one in which they will display a spotless integument and the first ceremony in the ritual of their entrance to Heaven is the casting aside of the ebony husk" (1914: 404).

If this account of the religious aspects of the color complex in African-Americans seems merely the anachronistic, offensive opinion of a white psychiatrist, consider what Malcolm X says about the "Uncle Tom" type half a century later, in 1963, in an anti-integration speech that he delivered at the University of Michigan, evidently to a largely white, largely Christian audience:

> This type has blind faith—in your religion. He's not interested in any religion of his own. He believes in a white Jesus, white Mary, white angels, and he's trying to get to a white heaven. When you listen to him in his church singing, he sings a song, I think they call it, "Wash me white as snow." He wants to be—he wants to be turned white so he can go to heaven with a white man. It's not his fault; it's actually not his fault. But this is the state of his mind. This is the result of 400 years of brainwashing here in America. You have taken a man who is black on the outside and made him white on the inside. His brain is white as snow. His heart is white as snow.
>
> (1989: 31)

Like Lind, Malcolm X maintains that the mental state, or psychical reality, of certain African-Americans includes a white god (or white Jesus) and white angels. Studs Terkel also documents the differences among blacks over the correct color of religious images. He quotes one African-American who felt so strongly about the issue that he ejected from his house one of his close friends who had objected to the image of a white Jesus on his wall:

> He had a cup of coffee and he looked at the wall and say, "You mean to tell me you got a blond-head, blue-eyed Christ on your wall?" By ding, I thought, You so-and-so. Honest to goodness, I said, "I very seldom do this, but it's a good idea if you get out of my house. I don't

mind you being critical, but don't come in and tell me what I got to put over my walls."

(1992: 91)

Terkel interviews another African-American, however, who, like a fundamentalist, would appeal to the biblical text to resolve the controversy. "Take it to the Bible," she says. "They are always painting Christ with blond hair and blue eyes. Anybody know that if his mother was from Egypt, how would he have come out with blond hair and blue eyes?" (1992: 146).

Lind asserts that the dreams of African-Americans often fulfill repressed wishes "to be white." He also reports that word association experiments which he conducted with psychotic African-Americans "to such words as 'black, white, negro, skin, colored' " produced disturbances in reaction, and he speculates that the same would probably be true of "mentally normal negroes." According to Lind, the color complex in African-Americans is, in effect, a "blood complex":

> The acceptance of the superiority of the white race, or rather the general acquiescence in the desirability of Caucasian blood is further evidenced by the fact that mulattoes are prone to boast of the admixture of white blood, usually exaggerating this considerably in spite of the fairly obvious inference that such heredity is almost certainly tainted, to say the least. On the other hand, they never boast of the Ethiopian strain.

That is, the color complex is fundamentally an "inferiority complex." In this respect, Lind cites Alfred Adler, who contends that "the 'will to power' of Nietzsche" and "a sense of inferiority" explain many psychical difficulties:

> This sense of inferiority is concretely represented in the negro by his color and when he has failed to adapt himself to reality it is not surprising that he compensates himself by the creation of a new order of things: He makes himself white, his seeming dark hue is due to a disguise which he has adopted for one purpose or another, or it has been acquired accidentally. By the simple conversion of his outer skin into another color, he symbolizes his identification with the, to him, superior race, the white race. He is then on a par with the more favored beings and as such has adjusted himself with the world.

(1914: 405–6)

In an effort to describe the psyche of African-Americans, Lind thus combines Freudian fulfillments of wishes, Jungian disturbances of reactions in relation to unconscious complexes, and Adlerian compensations of inferiority.

For African-Americans, "reality" is a social construction by white Americans. As Lind says, African-Americans occupy a socially subordinate position that white Americans have constructed on the basis of a "racial" distinction, the difference in skin color. The inferiority complex of African-Americans is, in this sense, a reflection of inferior status. The psychical reality of African-Americans is thus a function of social reality. African-Americans might simply accept this social reality, this inferior status, but many do not. Instead, they reject it. They fail to adapt, as it were, and construct an alternative, psychical reality (in some cases, a delusional, psychotic reality) in which, as if in a dream, they fulfill a wish to be white—that is, to be equal to whites (or superior to blacks). What is, in Freudian terms, a wish-fulfillment is, in Adlerian terms, an inferiority-compensation.

Lind presents cases of psychotic African-Americans who either believe that they are already white or who intend to become white. One patient who "claims that he is a white man" but cannot "explain why he is not the same color as other white men" exhibits "the palms of his hands which are very light colored as is usual with his race, and says that shows what his real color ought to be." Another patient maintains that "dye in the water in which he washed changed his color." When Lind asks another patient why he compulsively "spends hours of every day washing his face and hands," the man answers, " 'Get paint off.' " One patient observes "silver on the roof" and declares that he is going to "take a bath in that and turn white." A patient who says that she is really white insists that "the present color of her skin has been caused by eating dark-colored food." Another patient says that "someone has put the color of dyed animals on her" (1914: 406–8).

Lind discusses in detail the case of an African-American patient who believed that he "was not a negro, but painted black." He was convicted of murder and incarcerated in Leavenworth Penitentiary in 1907. In 1912, he was transferred to the psychiatric ward. A week later, he announced that " 'he has a secret paint which he can use that will turn him white.' " Later in 1912, he was committed to the Government Hospital for the Insane. In letters to the warden and prison physician, he wrote, " 'I left some oil in a can in the storeroom that will take this paint off.' " According-ing to the patient, the black paint was a disguise that he had adopted "in order that he might mingle freely with the negroes to carry out certain business and political projects." Almost every morning he requested "a half pound of Epsom salts with which to bleach himself, again some fish-oil which may remove the paint, etc." In another letter, he implored the hospital physician not to " 'ignore the fact that I has this paint own [sic: on] myself.' " If the physician " 'did not tess [sic: test] it for me,' " he would have to remain in the hospital for a long time, although he acknowledged that a hospital is perhaps " 'not a place to tess such a thing as a disguise.' " The patient stated that at the time that he committed the murder "he had on the black paint." He had "had himself painted black because the colored people had him tangled up in certain laws he had made, so he wore the paint for a disguise." In addition, he said that "he was doing some work for Lincoln and didn't want people to recognize him" (1914: 408–11)

Lind imagines the patient as he was just prior to the murder. The image is a conventional racist caricature of the African-American. According to Lind, the man must have been "a fairly typical negro, loving the physical excitements of life, as his race does, the warm sunshine, the catchy music, the alcoholic glow, the vivid color, the one hundred and one things which make existence happy for the negro in the summer time." Then, suddenly, in a fight over a woman at a picnic, he killed another man. Eventually, as a compensation for the intolerable reality of a life sentence, he devised an alternative, psychical reality—a delusional, psychotic reality: "he is not the negro imprisoned for murder, because he is a white man disguised as a negro." This delusional, psychotic reality is a color complex (a superiority complex that compensates an inferiority complex), in which the patient "symbolizes superiority by the color white." Thus the patient maintains that "the whole thing is a case of mistaken identity." As a result of "some mischance he has been confused with another man of the same name, a poor Washington negro, who has committed a murder" (1914: 412–14). If he could only remove the black paint that disguises his true identity as a white man, he could prove his innocence.

LIND AND JUNG: A COMPARISON

It is not only black patients but also white psychiatrists like Lind who may have a color complex. In another article in which he discusses phylogenetic elements in psychotic African-Americans, Lind defines the "Negro" as an individual whose "father was a slave" and whose "grandfather was a cannibal." This is "black" humor indeed. Lind says of the African-American that it is "necessary first to identify him in some measure with the native African." If African-Americans and Africans are not identical, they are much more similar than different. Lind confesses that he has "always found a difficulty here in the current conception that the present-day African has reached levels only slightly inferior to the white race." He discounts the very notion as sheer ignorance from inexperience:

This theory is held most extensively in regions where the Negro is infrequent and by persons having to do only occasionally with individuals of this race and then only with selected specimens. It will not be found accepted among the intelligent inhabitants of the so-called "black belt" precisely because they are able to observe large aggregations of the race. The Negro, studied judiciously by those who are competent, appears to be at a much lower cultural level than the Caucasian.

Any semblance of parity between blacks and whites is merely a deceptive appearance, the result of slavish, or apish, imitation by the "Negro":

> It is true that with his talent for mimicry, recalling to us in some measure our jungle cousins, he is able to present a remarkably exact, albeit superficial representation of the white man. But no one who has associated with Negroes is willing to believe that this strange resemblance extends much below the surface. It would be strange indeed if a race as low in the social scale as the Negro is in his native land could inherit by a half-century of juxtaposition all those group ideals which were acquired by the Caucasian in several thousand years of evolution with all the advantages of climate in his favor.
>
> (1917: 303)

Lind believes that both Africans and African-Americans are vastly inferior to whites. I wonder what response words Lind himself would have associated to the stimulus words "black," "white," "negro," "skin," "colored." Would he, too, have evinced certain disturbances of reaction? What color complex, what feeling-toned set of ideas about "race," unconsciously influenced Lind?

Although Lind purports to describe phylogenetic elements, he fallaciously conflates natural (or "racial") elements with cultural (or ethnic) elements. A "cultural level" or a "social scale" proves nothing phylogenetically. Both Lind and Jung analyzed insane "Negroes" in Washington, DC, in the first decade of the twentieth century. The conclusions that they reached, however, were radically different. Lind argues that blacks are phylogenetically, naturally, or "racially" inferior to whites. Jung argues that blacks are typically human, archetypally the same as whites. According to Jung, if blacks are, in any sense, significantly different from and "inferior" to whites, they are so only historically or culturally. "Blood" is important to Lind; to Jung it is utterly inconsequential.

When Jung returned to Switzerland from America after analyzing the fifteen insane "Negroes" at St Elizabeths Hospital in Washington, DC, in 1912, he reported on the experience in terms very similar to those that Lind employed. Jung describes the adaptation of the African-American to the influence of the white American as an idealization: "For him the white man is pictured as an ideal: in his religion Christ is always a white man. He himself would like to be white or to have white children; conversely, he is persecuted by white men." Jung says that in the dreams of African-Americans "the wish or the task of the Negro to adapt himself to the white man appears very frequently" (*CW* 18: 552, para. 1285). The implication is that in America, where whites and blacks are not merely different but socially unequal, the one superior and the other inferior, where "racial" persecution is not a paranoid delusion but a pervasive social reality, African-Americans tend, consciously or unconsciously, to "go white"—to adapt to, or identify with, the persecutor in order to survive the victimization that they suffer.

Jung also discusses the color complex. He says that blacks have a white complex and that whites have a "Negro" complex, or black complex. Addressing white Americans, Jung says:

> Just as the coloured man lives in your cities and even within your houses, so also he lives under your skin, subconsciously. Naturally it works both ways. Just as every Jew has a Christ complex, so every Negro has a white complex and every American a Negro complex. As a rule the coloured man would give anything to change his skin, and the white man hates to admit that he has been touched by the black.
>
> (*CW* 10: 508, para. 963)

(Should we also add, for good measure, that every Christian has a Moses complex?) Jung is saying that every "racial" or ethnic group has a feeling-toned set of ideas about other "racial" or ethnic groups. Historically, in white–black relations, these unconscious complexes have been colorist. Skin color has been the physical difference that whites have arbitrarily and conventionally employed to indicate ostensible psychical differences. Blacks do not merely want to change skin, or change color, nor do they merely touch the skin of whites; they also get under, live under, the skin of whites. That is, they get under, live under, the conscious of whites as a quite specific color complex. A white who hates to admit that he has been touched by a black is "touchy." In this sense, "getting under one's skin' is an expression that describes a certain irritation that we may experience when someone else affects us. It suggests that when we go either black or white, we may get irritated by the experience. (We may, of course, be stimulated or "touched" emotionally in other ways as well.)

Both Lind and Jung remark on the religious notions of African-Americans. Lind says that blacks (except for certain defiant protestations) always imagine god and the angels to be white; Jung says that blacks always imagine Christ to be white. In commenting on the expansion of Christianity and the conversion of various peoples, however, Jung says that over the centuries the religion "turned into something its founder might well have wondered at had he lived to see it." Jung implies that black worship of a white god would probably have perplexed and vexed even Christ. He says that "the Christianity of Negroes and other dark-skinned converts is certainly an occasion for historical reflections" (*CW* 9,1: 14, para. 25).

If black Americans have a white complex that includes a white Christ, white Americans also have a black complex that, Jung suggests, may eventually include a black Christ. "Don't forget that from the Jews, the most despised people of antiquity, living in the most despicable corner of Palestine or Galilee, came the redeemer of Rome," Jung says. "Why should not our redeemer be a Negro? It would be logical and psychologically correct" (1984: 706). African-Americans, of course, have already been crucified—or lynched—by white Americans on a tree that, as the song says, bears strange fruit. Jung implies that it would be an ironically apt archetypal compensation if the redemption of whites were to occur through the Second Coming of Christ as a black savior, or messiah.

WHITES AND CIVIL RIGHTS

The Jungian analysts Rivkah Scharf Kluger and H. Yehezkel Kluger recount a dream that includes just such an image. The dreamer, a woman who is presumably white, encounters a black Christ in the company of a black woman:

> I kept moving along. I came to a church on the right side as a man and a woman walked out the door and passed in front of me. And I saw that the man was Christ. He was black-skinned, as was the woman with him.

> (1984: 167)

According to the Klugers, who interpret this dream as an integration of a light–dark opposition, the black-skinned Christ is an other-sided, unconscious compensation for the one-sided attitude of the white-skinned ego of the dreamer. The Klugers also cite a dream that situates the dreamer, another white woman, in the middle of a violent "racial" conflict between whites and blacks:

> She and her family arose before dawn to see the Easter sunrise and the Second Coming of Christ. As the day grew light, they discovered to their horror that it was not the sun but the flames of burning crosses carried by the Ku Klux Klan which appeared over the horizon. As the army of white-robed Klansmen approached from the east, an army of blacks approached from the west, and the battle was soon raging about her. She was attacked by the one side for being a "nigger-lover" and by the other side because she was white.

As the Klugers interpret this dream, it exemplifies "a serious split between good and evil, white and black," not only in the collective unconscious but also in the personal unconscious. Apparently, the question is, who is really religious, who is really Christian? "Many people think of blacks as fervently religious," the Klugers remark, "and the Klansmen, as witness their crosses, purport to be Christian too." On the collective level, the dream depicts the "racial" polarization that exists between whites and blacks in America. The extremism of the Klansmen, who take the name of Christ in vain, burn the cross of crucifixion, and perpetrate a perverse parody of Christianity and the Second Coming, provokes an equal and opposite reaction from African-Americans. The consequence of white supremacy is a war between the "races." On the personal level, the dream indicates that the dreamer has little or no peace of mind. In the image of "racial" conflict, the dream metaphorically portrays a psychical split. According to the Klugers, the dreamer is, on the conscious level, a perhaps too proudly devout Christian. Through the dream, the unconscious compensates the one-sided, too-good, self-righteously religious attitude of the ego. The compensatory alternative that it presents for consideration by the ego is a two-sided, good-and-evil image. The Klugers suggest that the dreamer must consciously integrate these extremes, reconcile the white–black, good–evil, east–west oppositions, in order to obtain true peace of mind. Otherwise, the conflict may continue unconsciously and eventually "erupt violently" (1984: 166–7).

What most interests me about the dream, however, is the love–hate opposition and the fact that the dreamer has evidently gone black. She is, as the dream says, a "nigger-lover" (and, by implication, a Klan-hater). Although she is, herself, a white, she evidently empathizes with—in fact, sympathizes with—blacks. On the surface, in physical reality, she is white, but at a depth, in psychical reality, she is black. She has a white body, or skin, but in the dream she has a black identity, or soul. She has identified with the black cause in the struggle against racism. If she is one-sided, as the Klugers say, she is on the side of the blacks. In this sense, the dream is perhaps less a compensation for a certain self-righteous religious attitude, as some Jungians might suppose, than it is an apocalyptic revelation of the psychical difficulty intrinsic to taking sides. In the struggle against racism, a white woman who is a true Christian (in opposition to the false Christians in the Ku Klux Klan) has to take the moral and ethical side—has to go black. The dream implies that this is a difficult and uncomfortable but very righteous position (in the sense of civil rights), in the very middle of "racial" conflict.

The Jungian analyst Edward F. Edinger also interprets a dream in which "race" is the dominant issue. Like the Klugers, Edinger offers a compensatory interpretation. He says that "dreams that emphasize blackness usually occur when the conscious ego is one-sidedly identified with the light." By the "light," Edinger means the "right"—that is, a self-righteous attitude. He describes the dreamer as "a white man who was very active in the black civil rights movement." Edinger recounts the dream as follows:

I am in Hades and trying repeatedly to escape without success. There is some sort of wild sexual orgy. Everyone is covered with black tar.

According to Edinger, the dream is an unconscious compensation, an implicit criticism, of the ego of the dreamer. "This patient," Edinger says, "had exteriorized his personal need to accept blackness by engaging in social action to force society to accept blacks." The words "need" and "force," it seems to me, indicate a certain bias on the part of Edinger. It is as if the dreamer had no will in the matter and could only coerce (rather than persuade) other whites to accept blacks as equals. Edinger suggests that an inappropriately egocentric obsession with "race" obliged the dreamer unconsciously to compel other whites to agree with him. In this case at least, social action is, for Edinger, apparently nothing more than a form of "acting out." In this respect, I wonder what those blacks and whites who conducted sit-ins at lunch counters in the American South would say. Edinger asserts that the dreamer acted "very self-righteously by projecting the shadow on all who did not agree with him." In support of this interpretation, Edinger mentions (but does not interpret) other dreams by the same dreamer. "Although in his conscious life he was involved in demonstrations to overcome discrimination," Edinger says, "he had dreams that he was in black restaurants that discriminated against whites" (1985: 150).

The interpretation that Edinger proposes seems to me quite problematic (if not socially and politically reactionary). The location of the dream is Hades, the underworld, an archetypal metaphor for the unconscious, from which the ego again and again tries defensively to ascend—but to no avail. Egocentrism is evidently a form of escapism. The scene in the underworld, or unconscious, is one of orgiastic sexuality. For Jungians, sex in a dream does not always have a literal significance but often has a metaphorical significance: "eros" as the capacity to relate. In this context, the dream presents the ego with an opportunity to relate to others in the most intimate way imaginable.

In this dream, to be related to others in the unconscious is to be covered with tar—which is another image of going black. (There may also be an implicit pun in the dream: "Tartarus" is the section of Hades reserved for the punishment of the wicked.) "Race" is a "touchy" subject, and, phenomenologically, tar is a sticky substance—as Joel Chandler Harris (1955) emphasizes in the "Tar-Baby" tale of Uncle Remus. To be "sexually" and "racially" related is evidently to be "tarred," to be "stuck," as Brer Rabbit was by Brer Fox. To be actively involved in the civil rights movement is to be inextricably related to the other—to be, in the unconscious, other-sidedly identified with the dark. Evidently, a white cannot be committed to blacks without being "blackened" in the process. Finally, in regard to the dreams of black restaurants that discriminate against whites, discrimination does not always imply bigotry; it may also imply differentiation. In this case, for example, discriminating may mean differentiating the white self and the black other from the white other, reserving the right to refuse service or food to racists—that is, metaphorically to "serve" or "feed" (or nourish) racism. Social and political action may be a means to an end, which is individuation.

A "TOUCHY" SUBJECT

In reference to the question of touching the skin of the other, I would note that in addition to the literal meaning of being touched, there are two other, metaphorical meanings. Being "touched" means being moved by an experience. It also means being slightly mentally unbalanced. For the self to be touched by the other can mean to be affected emotionally or to become somewhat crazy. Tactile sensitivity, at the level of epidermal pigmentation, has psychical connotations and implications.

The most intimate level of touching is, of course, the sexual level, as the whole sordid history of laws against miscegenation amply demonstrates. Jung, who had his own "color complex," was capable, in this respect, of the most appalling remarks about mixing the white and black "races" sexually. He declares that "there is a danger in the mixture of the races, against which our instinct always sets up a resistance." Jung projects his own bias against "interracial" procreation onto the rest of us, as if we were all instinctively revolted by the very idea. "Sometimes," he says, "one thinks it is snobbish prejudice, but it is an instinctive prejudice." In this context, the concept of "instinct" signifies to Jung the immutability of a separatist disposition in human nature. From this perspective, sexual intercourse between the "races" appears to be an "unnatural act." Not only that, but it is also a relatively sterile act. It is a "fact," he contends, that "if distant races are mixed, the fertility is very low, as one sees with the white man and the negro." According to Jung, if sexual intercourse occurs, "a negro woman very rarely conceives from a white man." In addition, the consequence of miscegenation—"a mulatto"—will in all probability be a person of "bad character." Jung compares humans to animals and—implicitly—whites to horses and blacks to donkeys, and, in doing so, he appeals to insidious genetic notions. Sexual intercourse between horses and donkeys produces "mules," he notes, which "have peculiar, vicious qualities and are not fertile." If mules (which, in this spurious analogy, are comparable to mulattoes) do happen to conceive, "they have abortions." In another, even more bizarre comparison between humans and animals, Jung says that "it is the same with butterflies." (Perhaps it is not irrelevant in this respect to note that the butterfly is a traditional symbol of the psyche. The metamorphosis of the butterfly symbolizes the transmigration of the soul—or, as Jungians say, the transformation of the psyche.) Jung mentions experiments with butterflies of the same species from north and south of the Mediterranean (that is, "European" butterflies and "African" butterflies). He says that "they can't propagate, they don't really mix." Then he resorts to a cliche: "So with a great effort, you can bring oil and water together for a while: you can make a sort of foam, an emulsion, but then it separates again." When oil and water do mix (that is, when black and white mix), they do so only apparently—and only temporarily: then they "naturally" separate. If the result is not infertility, it is insanity. Miscegenation is a cause of "racial" psychopathology, "the cause of many cases of insanity." Between different "races" there is no effective sexual adhesion. "A great difference of race," Jung asserts, "nearly always causes a certain fragile, sensitive disposition because the units are not well glued together—that is at least a way of expressing these very difficult problems of psychopathology" (1988: 643–4).

According to Jung, different "races" may touch, but if they do so sexually, they do not mix. Although elsewhere he maintains that archetypally the only "race" is the "human race," that the collective unconscious is not a function, for example, of blood, and that what are apparently "racial" differences are really only historical differences, here he insists that psychology (or psychopathology) is a function of biology— a function, for instance, of semen. When Jung indulges in biological reductionism, he engages in psychological racism. Farhad Dalal has argued that Jung was a racist in the white–black sense (not just personally but theoretically and practically) and that therefore contemporary Jungian analysis has a "racist core" (1988: 263). I believe that it would be more correct to say that there were "two" Jungs: one who sometimes categorized people in terms of a "biology" and another who sometimes categorized them in terms of a "history." This does not mean, of course, that the appeal to ostensible historical differences is necessarily accurate or adequate. The notion that some people have at least one more "historical layer" than some other people is a European, Eurocentric, ethnocentric version of events—a "progressivist" account that is self-serving rather than "other-serving." Is Jungian theory and practice intrinsically and ineluctably racist? Are contemporary Jungians (or post-Jungians) racists? Some Jungians (as well as some Freudians) may, of course, be racists, but it seems to me that Jungians are under no duress to accept uncritically everything that Jung may have said on the topic of "race." They *are* under a scientific and ethical obligation to scrutinize and revise Jungian theory and practice when experience and evidence contradict it. To be a "Jungian" does not mean to be "Jung," any more than to be a "Freudian" means to be "Freud." Analysts who idealize Freud and Jung, who idolize them as gods or worship them as heroes, as if analysis were nothing more than a personality cult, perform a grave disservice.

Whereas, for Freud, the ego is fundamentally a "body ego" (*SE* 19: 27), for the Freudian analyst Didier Anzieu, it is a "skin ego." Anzieu does not mention skin color. He discusses skin as the surface that bounds the ego. In this sense, the skin is the ego boundary *par excellence*. The skin, Anzieu says, is a container and retainer, both physically and psychically, it is "the interface which marks the boundary with the outside and keeps that outside out," and it is "a site and a primary means of communicating with others, of establishing signifying relations" (1989: 40). When we add the dimension of skin color to this definition of the skin ego, we complicate matters. What is contained or retained inside the skin ego may be obtained by the other. Conversely, the outside that has been kept out may become the inside that has been let in—or forced in. Finally, communication or signification by means of the skin ego— or, in this case, by skin color—may be positive or negative or any other value on the continuum between the two extremes of "good" and "bad." Is it any wonder, then, that "touching," in every sense of the word, and "getting under the skin" are, for the ego, such sensitive issues?

UNTOUCHABILITY AND TOUCHABILITY

It is not only "getting under one's skin" but also "getting on one's skin" that is a special concern, or obsession, of racists. The psychohistorian Joel Kovel employs the clean–dirty opposition to explain the aversion that white Americans have had historically to touching black Americans. White Americans have had a cleanliness-is-next-to-godliness image of themselves. From this perspective, the self is always at risk of becoming unclean and ungodly when it comes in contact with the other. The difference between the white self and the black other is dirt and the devil. In this sense, Kovel says, African-Americans have been comparable to "untouchables" (1970: 81). The fear of going black is a fear of "getting dirty." Kovel contends that among peoples who have had to endure racist projections, "none have suffered the appellation of filthiness so much as Negroes, and this peculiar fate has had something to do with the natural melanotic pigmentation of their skin" (1970: 82). Nature (in this case, black skin) has served as a convenient projective test for culture. White Americans have projected their own racist psychical reality onto a readily available external reality, the black skin of African-Americans. Kovel cites a news magazine survey of "racial" attitudes at the time of the civil rights movement. The article quotes white Americans who have a phobic aversion to coming in contact with the black skin of African-Americans. One person says: "It's the idea of rubbing up against them. It won't rub off but it doesn't feel right either." Another person says, "I don't like to touch them. It just makes me squeamish. I know I shouldn't be that way but it still bothers me." In the context of untouchability, blackness is essentially dirtiness. "The nuclear experience of the aversive racist," Kovel asserts, "is a sense of disgust about the body of the black person based upon a very primitive fantasy: that it contains an essence—dirt" (1970: 83–4). Kovel equates dirt symbolically with shit. This is an excremental vision of racism that situates the essential content not only on the inside of the body, at a depth, but also on the outside of the body, on the surface—on the skin. In touching the other—in rubbing up against the black skin of the other—dirt or shit may rub off on the clean white skin of the self. Kovel notes that the oppositional, hierarchical logic of racism "is radically split along lines of goodness and badness" (1970: 132). In this defensive splitting, the relevant oppositions are white–black, clean–dirty, mind–body, and good–bad. It apparently never occurs to white Americans that they have a dirty mind, or ego, that fears and loathes black skin and unconsciously projects onto the bodies of African-Americans what most disgusts them about themselves.

"Touching" is an emotional issue in a dream that Bosnak interprets. Bosnak, who identifies the dreamer as "a stiff white professor in his middle years" (1988: 39), narrates the dream as follows:

> I'm walking through a run-down black neighborhood. I'm right by the bridge that will take me to the white neighborhood. I don't feel completely at ease, although I'm not frightened. I stop near a tall young black man. He is hanging on the jungle gym in a playground. The bars are really too low for him, but he keeps his feet off the ground by swinging his legs around in a counterclockwise motion. His feet touch me. I move back. But the farther back I move, the farther he swings out. He keeps on touching me. I walk calmly away. He comes after me. I get angry at him and curse him out. I tell him that he has to leave me alone. He stays back but still throws a stone at me when I'm on the bridge. He doesn't hit me.

The dreamer, Bosnak says, initially reacted to the dream with "pride that he didn't run away from the young man but rather defended himself." The feeling-tone of the white man's ego is defensive toward the black man's efforts to touch him. The dreamer characterizes the young black man as "very limber." In spite of what the dream says about not being frightened, Bosnak says that it becomes evident "how much the dreamer fears the black man." Apparently, however, "the young man wants to come in contact with him"—that is, in contact with the ego. Bosnak notes that the black man "keeps trying to touch the I-figure." The result is annoyance and rage: "This irritates the professor immeasurably, and he gets angry" (1988: 40).

Bosnak then recounts the process of dream interpretation, which in this case involves active imagination—an example of what Mary Watkins (1986) calls "imaginal dialogues"—and a willing suspension of prejudice:

At this point I ask the dreamer to describe the whole dream environment precisely. I also ask him what the young man looks like now. Then I ask the professor not to be so aggressive toward the man this time around. Now it comes out that the black man has no malicious intentions. What is frightening the dreamer is his own prejudice regarding blacks. This specific black man appears to be different from the way he is in the dreamer's prejudiced view. In dreams, just as in daily life, we frequently react to the figures we encounter from the standpoint of all kinds of prejudices. When reliving a dream, it can be useful to suspend this prejudice and let the dream figure speak for himself. I suggested to the professor that instead of the tirade he aimed at the young man, he should ask what he wants from the dreamer, why he keeps touching him. The dreamer does this. The young man answers immediately, spontaneously, "Don't be so uptight, man! Hang loose!" The black man starts to laugh. "Relax, man, relax. Don't be so tense."

In the imaginal dialogue that the dreamer conducts, the characterological flexibility of the black man, as distinct from the characterological rigidity of the white man, becomes obvious. Bosnak observes that "present in the image" of the black man is the trait of looseness, in contrast to the stiffness of the white man: "He is a relaxed figure with whom the terribly tense professor has little affinity." Active imagination enables the dreamer to develop a waking (rather than merely a sleeping, dreaming) relation with the black man. "It is now possible for the professor to consult the young black man from time to time when he feels particularly tense," Bosnak remarks. "At such moments, he can evoke the black neighborhood and have a further conversation with the young man" (1988: 40–1).

This is a qualitatively different relation from the one that the dreamer had in the dream. "In the dream," Bosnak emphasizes, "habitual consciousness remained ultimately untouched by the relaxed young man ('He doesn't hit me')." The advantage of active imagination is that it circumvents the defensive ego. Active imagination, Bosnak observes, "does not let itself be carried away by the resistances that the stiff professor (the figure with whom the "I" identifies) has toward the relaxed man who hangs loose." Bosnak concludes: "Thus, the active imagination can establish contact between the dreamer and relaxation. This diminishes his identification with what makes him into a stressed-out, up-tight person" (1988: 41–2).

This dream demonstrates just how "touchy" a subject "race" is. In the dream, the black man tries desperately to reach out and touch the white man (he swings out and finally hits out)—but the dreamer defensively avoids contact, remains untouchable. The dreamer, who lives in a white neighborhood, crosses over a bridge (an image of liminality between the conscious and the unconscious) into the black neighborhood. The scene of the dream is where the white man confronts the run-down (or as Bosnak says, the stressed-out). The dreamer has evidently repressed, or ghettoized, that aspect of himself. The dreamer does not feel afraid, but he feels uneasy—an image of just how difficult it is for him to relax. The scene includes, significantly, an African (or African-American) apparatus—a jungle gym. (In this respect, the playground is implicitly in opposition to the workplace, the university where the dreamer is a professor.) From a Jungian perspective, the dream compensates a number of partial, prejudicial—and, in this case, racist—conceits of an up-tight, too-academic ego.

There is one important "racial" image that Bosnak and the dreamer do not interpret. I mean the image of hanging—which in African and African-American history evokes the image of lynching. As Jung says, "The Americans are certainly a very humane nation, or at least imagine they are, but this does not prevent so-and-so many Negroes from being lynched every year" (1973 1: 447). Just how many African-Americans were lynched by white Americans from the 1890s through the 1940s was recorded by the Tuskegee Institute and the *Chicago Tribune*—in the last decade of the nineteenth century, 1,111; in the first five decades, respectively, of the twentieth century: 791, 561, 281, 120, and 32 (Davis 1991). In the dream, there is no noose around the black man's neck—he is not dangling from a rope—but he is swinging, feet off the ground. African-Americans do, of course, "swing" in other, more positive senses of the word, but there is touchy, negative, grim, deadly unconscious wit ("black," or gallows, humor) in this image as well.

SHADOW AND SOUL

Emil Gutheil says that it is the black skin of African-Americans that makes them so symbolically evocative to white Americans. "In the United States," he remarks, "the 'Negro' appears in dreams of white people as a symbol of repressed desires, or as a symbol of white, but otherwise tabooed persons" (1951: 191). Although Gutheil is a Freudian analyst, he is also sensibly eclectic. He explicitly equates this repression or taboo with the Jungian concept of the shadow. He observes that white Americans associate the black skin of African-Americans with such concepts as "death," "the devil," "another race," "the different," and "the (sexually) abnormal" (1951: 191–2). Gutheil notes that "(in connection with the symbolism of the shadow) in the dreams of whites, the 'colored' person often represents the uncanny, the unknown, the thing that is different in itself." From these representations, Gutheil concludes that the "anti-Negro spirit" expresses "the mysterious part of our own psyche"—the aspect of themselves that white Americans fear. "Because we do not comprehend it directly," he says, "we are afraid of it." White racists "are talking about their own id drives," which they unconsciously project onto African-Americans (1951: 193). Gutheil continues:

> What is outside of us can be attacked and destroyed, while forces which we harbor internally cannot be dealt with effectively. Therefore, people who suffer from this type of anxiety create an external object, a target; they attack it and, in so doing, have the satisfaction of having attacked the "cause" of their own discomfort. They believe that their cause is just. However, such a projection is always futile; it can lead only to repetitive patterns, since it is operating on a purely symbolic level. It does not offer real solutions. It is this, among other things, that makes a person who is sick with prejudice inclined to consider the object of his attack as abnormally sensual, criminal, and cunning.

African-Americans, by virtue of the black skin that visibly distinguishes them from white Americans, serve as a convenient objective correlative—an object relation that is, in effect, not so much an object representation as an object misrepresentation, because it is really a self-representation. "What I have said of racial prejudice applies to all forms of xenophobia," Gutheil says. "The fear of the foreigner is the fear of the foreign in ourselves" (1951: 193–4). The psychoanalytic proposition that Gutheil asserts in an effort to interpret white racism against African-Americans is only a special (although a particularly egregious) case in a more general theory of alienation. The alien is the other within the self—that "inner other" from which the self is most alienated, that stranger from which the self is most estranged.

Hillman describes how in dreams, down in the deep, dark underworld of the unconscious, the soul dwells with depression and death. For Hillman, it is the ego, not the soul, that anxiously experiences depression and death as negative. In order for the ego to develop soul, it must descend into the underworld, where it can be deepened and darkened by becoming depressed—where it can die metaphorically. For Hillman, depression and death are, in this sense, positive terms. It is in this context that he discusses images of blacks in the dreams of whites. He proposes a psychological rather than a sociological interpretation of these images. "It is a Jungian convention," he says, "to take these blacks as shadows, a convention to which there can be no objection." Hillman does, however, take exception to the tendency to reduce such images to "potentials of vitality (sexuality, fertility, aggressivity, strength, emotionality)." He also notes that "the content of the black shadow has been further determined by sociological overtones." The burden of sociological projections by whites onto blacks is an unbearable darkness of being. Hillman elaborates:

> Personal associations to blacks in the culture affect the interpretation

of the image. The black shadow today supposedly brings spontaneity, revolution, warmth, or music—or frightening criminality. In other eras, black figures in whites' dreams might have been loyalty, or apelikeness, or lethargy, servility, and stupidity, or been translated into superb force and wholeness . . . Blacks have had to carry every sort of sociological shadow, from true religion and faithfulness, to cowardice and evil. The sociological vogues all have forgotten that The Black Man is also Thanatos.

(1979: 144–5)

By Thanatos, Hillman does not mean literal death. He means the metaphorical death that black figures rising, or returning, from the unconscious (or, as he puts it, the underworld—a night of the living dead, where shadows are shades) pose in dreams to the ego.

Hillman regards black figures emerging from the unconscious as "returning ghosts from the repressed netherworld—not merely from the repressed ghetto." In this ghastly aspect, blacks haunt the dreams—and the egos—of anxious whites. "But anxiety," Hillman observes, "as we have known ever since Freud, signals the return of the repressed, and the repressed nowadays, goodness knows, is certainly not sexuality, not criminality, not brutality—all those things we say that black figures 'represent.' " According to Hillman, black figures are not representations of objects from external, social reality; they are presentations of imaginal essences from internal, psychical reality: "They present death; the repressed is death. And death dignifies them" (1979: 145). In the dreams of whites, it is not death instinct, or death drive, but death anxiety that is signified by blacks—who, in the process, are dignified by it. Hillman concludes:

Following this through then, black persons in dreams would no longer have to carry the sociological shadow of primitivity (for the developmental fantasy of the ego), vitality (for the ego's heroic strength), or inferiority (for the ego's moral or political fantasy). In other words, we would move away from a pseudo negro-psychology to a genuine shadow-psychology, an attempt to restore to the black figures "the idea of a subtle essence."

(1979: 146)

From this perspective, black figures in dreams are shadowy, shady characters indeed, who in their essential subtlety imaginally epitomize a metaphorical death of the white ego.

It is not, however, only a shadow psychology that Hillman advocates in contrast to an ego psychology. He also recommends a soul psychology, a depth psychology that is a dark psychology. Hillman recounts how he moved from Zurich to Dallas, to a black neighborhood:

Dallas is open in ways that are shut tight in Zurich. Of course, sitting here in Europe it's hard to see the virtue of this kind of city; of course, it looks psychopathic. But there is a slowness there, and a warmth—for instance, we live in a black section, old-fashioned, with wonderful talk. Everything happens on the porches, out in the street: phoning, music, visiting, shouting. Plenty of depression, too. And there is courtesy there and that way of joking and that way of walking in the heat. I get all kinds of images from my neighbors, all kinds of feelings. You know it was from the blacks that we got the word "soul" back into our language. So there's a good reason I like living in Dallas.

(1983: 128)

Hillman (who finally does, in spite of himself, wax sociological) implies that, in contrast to blacks, whites are fast, cold, new, silent. For whites, everything presumably happens not on the outside (the porch or the street) but inside (the house). Whites have an ego, anxious about depression and death, but evidently they have no soul—and no sense of humor—as blacks do. For Hillman, the white ego has to die metaphorically—has to be depressed, deepened, and darkened—not in order to be reborn but in order to be ensouled. In this sense, it is not just modern man in general (as Jung says) but modern white man in particular who is in search of a soul.

Hillman maintains that in order for whites to find the soul that they have lost, they must "range widely." Going beyond the narrowly restrictive confines of themselves, or their egos, however, does not entail going beyond Western civilization. Hillman says, "I have not gone East, gone primitive, gone animal, or gone into the future or on my own private inner voyage." What Hillman calls "re-visioning" is not the mere sightseeing of a tourist in the there and then of the non-Western other. It is a working-through by a seeing-through of the Western ego. Hillman advocates looking into "the geographical, historical, and religious limits of our Western tradition, which issues forth here and now into the amazing soul questions of today" (1975: xvi).

ALLIANCE OR MEDIATION

To the extent that psychoanalysis has produced a "theory" of "race," color, and the unconscious, it has tended to emphasize racist "id" or "shadow" projections by whites onto blacks. As the "other," blacks have served whites as scapegoats, correlatives of desires (or drives) and inferiorities incompatible with a certain notion of the "self." Most (although not all) of the projections have been negative: dirty, deadly, devilish, abnormally sexual, criminal, lethargic, servile, stupid, cowardly, and evil. If whites have a color complex, or a "black" complex, it comprises these projections, among others. These projections, of course, are potentialities intrinsic to whites as well as blacks. The white ego, however, defensively excludes these capacities from consideration.

The white supremacy of this ego is a white "purity" that it phobically attempts to preserve. As Gutheil says, negrophobia is a variety of xeno-phobia; or, in the examples that Kovel provides, merely to touch the untouchable black other is to defile the pristine white self. This purity is a rigidity that whites unconsciously and uncritically (or consciously and hypocritically) maintain in opposition to the ostensible laxity of blacks. The white ego is a white ethic of discipline, restraint, control. I do not mean that whites are, in actuality, more disciplined, restrained, and controlled than blacks. What I mean is that in order to sustain this ethic as an ideal the white self requires a black other: if the black other did not exist, the white self would have to invent it. Racism or colorism is such an intractable problem because the very persistence of the white ego is dependent on the maintenance of a color complex that enables whites to define the "self" in opposition to an "other." In this sense, blacks function as an effigy of all those "primitive" capacities that whites believe they have relinquished in an effort to become "civilized." For blacks to be undisciplined, unrestrained, uncontrolled (as whites tend to presume them to be) is to be unrepressed—that is, liberated from the defensive strictures of the ego. Whites detest blacks precisely because they typify, projectively, what whites covet, which is an indulgence in attitudes and behaviors that whites purport to have renounced. In this respect, "loose" blacks are both a rebuke and an allure to "stiff" whites, as in the dream that Bosnak interprets.

Hillman especially interests me because he argues that the white self requires a black other not in order to perpetuate a defensive ego but in order to subvert it—or at least to revise or "re-vision" it. Although when he says that, for whites, blacks epitomize death, he may seem simply to reiterate a reactionary, racist caricature, Hillman selects death, I believe, because it is rhetorically so extreme, so hyperbolic. The image of the deadly black (in contrast to the images of dirty, devilish, abnormally sexual, lethargic, servile, stupid, cowardly, or evil blacks) is the ultimate anxiety, for it entails the utter demise of the white ego. For Jung, the ego has to "die" in order to be reborn; for Hillman, the white ego has to "die"—be "blackened" (or "go black")—in order to be ensouled. The souls of black folk are, in this sense, the shadows of white folk, for whom the only hope for the self is to be depressed, deepened, darkened through an encounter with an "external other" that conveniently personifies the "internal other," a white inferiority complex that the white ego excludes from consideration and relegates to the unconscious.

Hillman does not offer any comparable commentary on the black ego. For example, he does not ponder what purpose white figures in blacks' dreams have served. If blacks have been burdened by the projections of whites, what sociological or psychological shadow has been carried by whites in the unconscious of blacks? What has the black self rejected and then projected onto the white other? Perhaps the reason that Hillman does not pose these questions or attempt to provide answers to them is that the two cases are not symmetrical. Blacks may be Thanatos to whites, but whites, it seems obvious to me, are not Eros to blacks. Even if the black ego might need to be "whitened" (or "go white") in some sense, to be whitened would not be to be "enlivened" (in contrast to the white ego, which needs to be blackened, or "deadened"). Nor does Hillman address the issue of a black inferiority complex. If whites have external-ized their own internal inferiorities, projected them *onto* blacks as an external other, then have they also projected their own inferiorities *into* blacks? Has projective typification been, at least sometimes, a variety of projective identification? Psychoanalysts define "projective identification" as a process by which the self projects unconscious contents into an other in an effort to induce that other to identify with those contents so that the self can then control and manipulate the other. Historically, have at least some blacks unconsciously identified with inferiorities that whites, from a position of social, political, and economic supremacy, have pro-jected into them in order to dominate and exploit them? Is the recent insistence on "Black Pride," "Black Beauty," and "Black Power" a com-pensatory reaction against a previous sense of inferiority that racist whites insidiously inculcated in blacks? What is the color complex, or the "white complex," of contemporary blacks?

At least Kovel, Bosnak, Gutheil, and Hillman do not presume to speak *for* blacks; they speak *to* whites. I agree with Samuels when he says of analysts that it is "an abuse of our authority when we define the typical psychology of this or that group." It follows logically, he says, that "we should consider expressly allying ourselves with marginal and so-called minority groups" (1991: 199). This recommendation seems to me a *non sequitur*. By an "alliance" Samuels seems to mean not merely a thera-peutic but an explicitly political alliance in which the analyst would unite in solidarity with the patient—and I consider this an unanalytic position. Samuels is much more persuasive when he describes the analyst as a mediator of difference rather than an ally in politics. In this respect, he quite properly insists that "differences not be defined or predefined" by the analyst. In fact, he says that differences cannot be defined in advance, precisely because "they are terra incognito," yet to be explored with the patient in the therapeutic dialogue:

> The analyst is not an authority or teacher who has a priori knowledge of the psychological implications of the patient's ethnic and cultural background. Rather he or she is a mediator who enables the patient

to experience and express his or her *own* difference. The one thing analysts are good at is getting people to talk about what they implicitly know but have not yet consciously expressed.

(1991: 200)

Psychoanalysis is, in this sense, an experiential, expressive therapy that affords patients an opportunity to speak for themselves and to define for themselves how they may or may not be significantly different from others, ethnically or culturally. If psychoanalysis is a "talking cure," it is also a "listening cure"—and if analysts have those "ears to hear" (*SE* 7: 77) that Freud says are requisite to effective analysis, then they will need to be attentive, in a nonpresumptuous way, to any ethnic or cultural differences that patients may deem relevant. Only in this way, it seems to me, will analysts (and perhaps especially white analysts) ever be in any position to appreciate the psychical realities of black patients or the souls of black folk.

Chapter 9

The mirror of identity

Sir Laurens van der Post, a white South African by birth, a vocal opponent of apartheid, author of many books about Africa (including an account of the virtual extinction of the Bushmen), and a close friend of Jung for many years, recounts how he and Jung discussed Africa when they met for the very first time. He told Jung that he had just written a book about Africa and had used as an epigraph a quotation from Sir Thomas Browne: "We carry with us the wonders we seek without us: there is all Africa and her prodigies in us" (1975: 50). For van der Post, as for Jung, Africa is not only a physical reality but also a psychical reality, prodigious in implication. In this sense, the literal Africa serves as a provocative correlative of the metaphorical "dark continent" in the white unconscious, in the geography of the white imagination. In conversation with van der Post, Jung addresses the ambivalent desire and fear that Africa has historically induced in whites:

> He generalized at length from his own experience in this regard that night, impressing on me how it inevitably provoked in the white man a great temptation to revert to an utterly uncontemporary version of himself, all the more powerful and difficult to resist because in most cases it was unconscious. As a result the resistance of the white man in Africa to "go black," or "native," as he put it, produced so powerful an undertone in his spirit that it brought tensions which were almost unendurable and caused him either to succumb utterly and become a pale, effete version of the primitive or to reject and hate the dark man who had served to evoke it. The farther from his own instinctive self, the greater the temptation and the greater the fall, or the more intense the rejection in the European we call prejudice and hatred.

According to van der Post, there was, for Jung, an alternative to either primitivism or racism: "The task of modern man was not to go primitive the African way but to discover and confront and live out his own first and primitive self in a truly twentieth-century way" (1975: 51).

PRIMITIVE, NATURAL, INSTINCTIVE, HEALTHY

In what was originally a lecture to the Jung Institute and the Analytical Psychological Club of Zurich in 1954, van der Post also discusses "going black." (Jung himself was present for the occasion.) Van der Post explicitly repudiates any notion that whites are superior and blacks inferior. Europeans and Africans are simply different—and van der Post declares that he honors the differences. In emphasizing difference, he poses the issue of "race" in terms congenial to contemporary multi-culturalists. Although he rejects the superior–inferior valuation, van der Post does, however, employ the primitive–civilized opposition—but only, he says, for lack of better words:

> To my black and coloured countrymen who may read this book I would like to explain my use of the words "primitive" and "civilized" man. I use these words only because I know no others to denote the general difference which undeniably exists between indigenous and European man in Africa. I am, however, fully conscious of their limitations and relativity. They are not intended to convey a feeling of superiority. I do not think of the European as a being superior to the black man. I think of both as being different and of the differences as honourable differences equal before God. The more I know of "primitive" man in Africa the more I respect him and the more I realize how much and how profoundly we must learn from him. I believe our need of him is as great as his is of us. I see us as two halves designed by life to make a whole. . . . Nor am I unaware, when I speak of "primitive" man, that there are thousands of black people in Africa who are as "civilized" as any of us. Like me and many others of my white countrymen, those thousands are the permanently de-tribalized children of Africa. I know from my own experience how terrible is their frustration and how great their anguish of spirit and mind.
>
> (1955: 24–6)

We might, of course, wonder why another word that van der Post employs—"indigenous"—might not be preferable to "primitive." There are also other alternatives, such as the word "primordial," which Jungians use in other contexts—or the words "prime," "primary," or "primal," all of which may have the positive value of first in priority or first in importance. According to Mannoni, to be euphemistic is an exercise in futility. He says that he uses "the word 'primitive'—always between inverted commas—because the alternatives, such as 'isolated', 'unevolved', 'archaic', 'stationary', and 'backward' are in fact no better." He suggests that to substitute another word for "primitive" merely represses the concept—and, as Freud says, the repressed always returns as a symptom. Mannoni maintains that "the idea of primitivism is still there, though veiled and hidden, and this concealment simply increases the chances of error" (1964: 22). Better not to mince words, he insists, than to pretend that the concept does not exist.

Van der Post does use another word as a synonym for "primitive." The black man, he says, is the "natural" man—in contrast not only to the "cultural" man (the opposition that Lévi-Strauss and other structural anthropologists employ)—but also to the "synthetic" (in the pejorative sense of "artificial") white man (1955: 208). Van der Post, who invokes the *participation mystique* of Lévy-Bruhl, maintains that the white man in Africa is an unbearable, projective burden for the black man:

> We have talked all through this century of the white man's burden in Africa, yet what fatal irony there is in the phrase. Would it not be more accurate at the moment to talk of the black man's burden? I refer of course to this burden of terrible unconscious projection which modern European man thrusts upon the natural African who, by reason of his primitive instinctual life and "participation almost mystical" in his natural environment, is such a suitable container for it. Yet it is this very projection, outcome of the insidious civil war raging in the innermost being of modern man, which prevents the white man from ever seeing the black man as he really is. The white man can see in the black man only those aspects which confirm and justify his own projection and enable it to pass itself off as an outward and genuinely objective condition—which it is not. The results for both parties, of course, are deplorable. Since the European possesses physical power, this dreadful confusion compels him to create a form of society wherein the black man is condemned to play only that part which the increasingly exacting projection of the white man demands of him.
>
> (1955: 71–2)

According to van der Post, the European does not accurately perceive the African but projects onto him unconscious aspects of himself. These aspects are parts of his personality that are in conflict with his ego. They are the primitive parts of himself that he has rejected as incompatible with his civilized self-image. As a result, the white self's vision of the black other's reality is mediated—obscured and obstructed—by a variety of prejudicial and discriminatory projections.

In discussing Europe and Africa, Jung also employs the nature–culture opposition. He suggests that the civilized white European has projected his own pathology, or insanity, onto the primitive black African. According to Jung, to be civilized is not merely to be discontented, as Freud says, but, at the very worst, to be deranged. Jung identifies the Europeans as "only a tiny fraction of humanity," inhabiting not so much a real continent as that "peninsula of Asia which juts out into the Atlantic Ocean." He remarks on the audacity of these peoples, who, "calling themselves 'cultured,' " set themselves so far apart from the primitive. Europeans consider themselves civilized, he says, merely "because they lack all contact with nature." From the perspective of Central Africa, he says, "it would certainly look as if this fraction had projected its own unconscious mental derangements upon nations still possessed of healthy instincts" (*CW* 7: 204–5, para. 326).

Mannoni accepts but qualifies the account that Jung provides of projection. He says that Jung may well be correct to regard "errors of perception in colonial matters" as the consequence of "the projection on to the object of some defect which is properly attributable to the subject." Even if, as Jung maintains, Europeans endow natural or instinctive peoples with traits that do not properly belong to them, "the projection is not quite as he describes it." To equate instinct with health, as Jung apparently does, is merely to promote "a form of primitivism." There are "two opposite forms" of primitivism: "on the one hand there are those who, like Jung, think that this youthfulness of the instincts represents health and normality, and on the other those who see it as barbarousness and brutality" (1964: 198). In this respect, Lévi-Strauss maintains that it is when whites themselves are attitudinally barbaric that they define the other as a barbarian. "By refusing to consider as human those who seem to us to be the most 'savage' or 'barbarous' of their representatives, we merely adopt one of their own characteristic attitudes," he says. "The barbarian is, first and foremost, the man who believes in barbarism" (1952: 12).

In discussing the attribution of either the healthy or the barbaric to the primitive, Mannoni contends that "these are more or less the two opposite attitudes men take of Nature, though there is no objective justification for either." Whichever attitude is adopted, "the choice is decided for each man by the attitude he spontaneously adopts towards his own nature, or rather towards that confused picture he has in his imagination of his own instincts, of his own *id*." In this sense, Nature with a capital "N" is merely a reflection of "human nature"—or of the vague and equivocal fantasy that the individual has of it. "The Jungian attitude," Mannoni asserts, "is in effect a search for a lost innocence." He thus accuses Jung of a certain romantic nostalgia for the instinctive or the natural. According to Mannoni, Jung is a Crusoe with a Friday or a Prospero with a Caliban or Ariel. "What we project on to the colonial inhabitant, in fact, is not our 'mental derangement,' " Mannoni says, "but our most elementary and deeply-hidden fears and desires, the primal Good and Evil, not as a philosopher might see them, but rather as they might appear to a child in a dream, or as Shakespeare and Daniel Defoe saw them" (1964: 198).

Mannoni cautions Jungians (like van der Post) not to regard the natural as wholly positive—it is, at least partly, negative. This admonition seems to me salutary advice, although Jung is very often much more ambivalent about the instinctive than Mannoni apparently imagines. Jung frequently emphasizes just how ambiguous it is, just how barbaric and brutal it may be, especially when we repress it and then project it, or cast it like a shadow, onto the other. It is true that Jung and van der Post sometimes seem to indulge in a primitivism that is perhaps too sentimental, but many other times Jung, like Freud, quite properly repudiates any notion that the natural or instinctive is, purely and simply, synonymous with the healthy.

SELF-IMAGE, SELF-REFLECTION, SELF-RECOGNITION

Rather than unconscious projection, van der Post advocates conscious reflection, as Jung does when he says that he traveled to Africa in order to see his own white European self-image reflected back at him, objectively, from outside. Van der Post deliberately inverts the conventional racist image of black Africans as a different or lower species—as subhumans, especially as simians. White Europeans are like baboons, he says, looking in a glass darkly:

> Modern man with his grievous and crippling realization of having lost the sense of his own beginnings, with his agonizing feeling of great and growing estrangement from nature, finds that life holds up Africa like a magic mirror miraculously preserved before his darkening eyes. In this great glass of time the inmost reflection of his ancient, timeless spirit stares out at him, and he can, could he but realize it, discover there his despised and rejected natural self, recognizing before it is too late the full horror of his stubborn rejection of it.
>
> There is a memory that has lived with me all my life from childhood in Africa which gives living illustration of this point. As children we used to take our mirrors, stand them on the ground in front of our tame baboons and then watch the creatures as for the first time they saw their own faces reflected back at them. It was amusing because the baboons could not realize that what they were looking at in the mirror was a reflection of themselves. The mechanism of reflection was quite beyond their comprehension and they could not accept the ugly, grimacing, increasingly irritable features staring back at them as their own. The only explanation of what they saw in the mirror was that there was another baboon in front of them, so they promptly looked for the stranger beast. They tried to touch its face, but felt only the glass against their purple fingers. They looked again and again behind the mirror, but the elusive creature could not be found. The only solution in the end was to pick up the mirror and smash it to pieces on the ground in their rage.

This I believe is a profound image of what happens in life and in Africa today. People and countries are mirrors to one another. They are, of course, also themselves just as the mirror is itself and not what it reflects, but they rarely recognize themselves; mostly they see what is hidden within themselves reflected in one another. The capacity to differentiate reflector and reflection in the many-dimensional realm of the living spirit and being of man is still primitive and relatively undeveloped in all of us, and future ages, no doubt, will laugh at us for this as we laughed at the baboon. I believe that the greatest of all the mirrors of our age is Africa. We all, East and West and bewildered twentieth-century man, stare into it as if hypnotized, but, like the baboons, we do not see and recognize in it the reflection of our own hidden selves. Nevertheless, the interest of the world is compelled by events in Africa because, unconsciously, the world apprehends that Africa may hold the secret of its own lost and hidden being. Without this miraculously preserved Africa, without this land and its unbroken allegiance to the original charter and meaning of life, this timely reflection might not be possible. Let us pray therefore that we all realize that it is also ourselves we are looking at in Africa and not destroy this precious magic mirror in our rage—as so many vanished civilizations before us have destroyed theirs to their own undoing.

(1955: 81–3)

Rather than smash the mirror in an act of iconoclastic anger, van der Post recommends that white Europeans learn, before it is too late, what baboons cannot learn: to reflect self-consciously, self-critically, on their own self-image in the mirror of Africa.

Van der Post's fable of baboons is remarkably similar to Wolfgang Kohler's observations of chimpanzees. Kohler notes that different kinds of animals, "monkeys, dogs, cats, and even birds, when faced by their own reflections in a mirror, react—even if only momentarily—as though a real individual of the same species stood before them." Kohler describes in detail the reactions of the chimpanzee Rana:

She gazed long and intently into the mirror, looked up and down, put it to her face and licked it once, stared into it again, and suddenly her free hand rose and grasped—as though at a body behind the mirror. But as she grasped emptiness she dropped the mirror sideways in her astonishment. Then she lifted it again, stared fixedly at the other ape, and again was misled into grasping into empty space. She became impatient and struck out violently behind the mirror; finding this, too, in vain, she "lay in wait", after the manner of chimpanzees when they watch (with the most aloof and harmless expression in the world) whether anyone outside their cage will touch the bars in a heedless moment. She held the mirror still in one hand, drew back the other arm as far as possible behind her back, gazed with an air of indifference at the other animal, then suddenly made a pounce at him with her free hand. However, both she and the rest soon became used to this side of the affair, and concentrated all their interest on the image; this interest did not decrease—as in the case of other species enumerated above—but remained so strong that the playing with reflecting surfaces became one of the most popular and permanent of their "fashions". Soon they dispensed with the human implement; having once had their attention drawn to it, they mirrored themselves in anything at all available for the purpose: in bright pieces of tin, in polished potsherds, in tiny glass splinters, for which their hands provided the background, and, above all, in pools of water.

(1927: 317–18)

It is not only Jungians like van der Post but also Freudians—and more particularly Lacanians—who have an interest in the capacity for psychical reflection. Lacan (1977), who mentions Kohler, argues that we form an ego, or self-image, through a process of psychical reflection that inevitably implies *méconnaissance*, or "misrecognition." According to Lacan, the image in the mirror of identity is an illusory, narcissistic, virtual reality, simultaneously an imaginary fascination with and alienation from the self.

Unlike Lacan, however, van der Post affirms the possibility of authentic human self-reflection that entails a recognition (rather than misrecognition) of the racist projections of white Europeans onto black Africans. If there is a "mirror stage" to racism in Africa, van der Post suggests, through the fable of baboons, that white Europeans, with self-reflective effort, can supersede that stage. To reflect psychically, we do not need a literal mirror in external reality. Jung defines "reflection" as "an act whereby we stop, call something to mind, form a picture, and take up a relation to and come to terms with what we have seen." He says that it is "an act of *becoming conscious*" (*CW* 11: 158, para. 235n.). To be self-reflective is, in this sense, to become self-conscious, self-critical.

According to Mannoni, self-reflection is so difficult because it entails self-doubt. This does not mean, however, that it is impossible. When the white self encounters the black other, Mannoni says, "the face of the 'savage' or the 'black man,' rouses in us at first this anxious hesitation, and makes us doubt ourselves." Whites repress the fact that "we are frightened of the faces we have ourselves made terrifying." The face of the savage merely reflects the savagery, "this unpleasant thing stirring to life in ourselves," that whites project onto it. Whites would rather attribute it "to something evil in the black man before us or to some quality inherent in his race or tribe," than to something inferior in themselves. "Naturally, once we begin to doubt ourselves when confronted with a human being of a type so different from our own, all kinds of things begin to happen," Mannoni says. "Sometimes, before this highly revealing mirror, the white man comes to see himself as he really is, which is what happened to Robert Louis Stevenson and perhaps to Rimbaud." These exceptions to the rule, however, are few and far between. Not everyone has the capacity for such self-reflection, such self-recognition. Mannoni observes that "very few men are capable, when they are at length obliged to acknowledge the existence of other people, of recognizing in them-selves what they never suspected was there, without an outburst of fear, hatred, or harshness they had directed towards an aspect of themselves which in very truth they had wanted to ignore." In addressing "this internal threat," whites have two alternatives—ignorance of it or reconcili-ation with it. Reflecting on themselves provides whites with an oppor-tunity to reconcile with the other, with that aspect of themselves that they prefer not to acknowledge (1964: 199). Mannoni offers further reflections on self and other in the mirror of identity. He suggests that whites are afraid of an unconscious aspect of themselves:

> We can explore the retinas of our own eyes by looking at a piece of white paper; if we look at a black man we shall perhaps find out something about our own unconscious—not that the white man's image of the black man tells us anything about his own inner self, though it indicates that part of him which he has not been able to accept: it reveals his secret self, not as he is, but rather as he fears he may be. The negro, then, is the white man's fear of himself.

> (1964: 200)

When whites look in the mirror, they see neither the other nor the self as they really are; they see only what the self fears that it may be, or become (if, as Jung says, it goes black). According to Mannoni, the only thing that whites have to fear is fear of themselves.

WHITENESS AS CONSCIOUSNESS, BLACKNESS AS UNCONSCIOUSNESS

Just as Spike Lee criticizes African-Americans who privilege external reality over internal reality (although one may have straight hair, one may have a crooked soul)—in contrast to G. Stanley Hall, who considers external reality to be a direct indication of internal reality (outward crookedness is evidence of inward crookedness)—van der Post condemns the white fallacy of literalizing an external, physical reality (in this case, skin color) as the sign of an internal, psychical reality: blackness on the outside as an indication of blackness on the inside. "You confuse two levels of reality," van der Post says. "You assume that because the black African has a black skin that he has a 'black being' and vice versa with the European." On the contrary, he insists, "the colour of a man's skin is not the colour of his being." Referring to white South Africans who apparently lack a capacity for metaphor, van der Post remarks:

> One of the more sinister symptoms of the pathological state of mind of my own people is that today they seem to have become incapable of this simple but vital differentiation in regard to their black countrymen. They are, therefore, quite terrified of "going black" themselves. I suggest that the blackness which they fear is not the colour of the African skin without but rather the nature of their own inner darkness. Could they but separate, emotionally, these two dimensions in "colour" and realize that the tide of "colour," the blackness which threatens their civilization, is largely within themselves, I am certain that colour prejudice would quickly lose its point and all the illusory defensive values attached to it disappear.
>
> (1955: 128)

As van der Post deliteralizes blackness, he (like Jung) pathologizes the civilized, not the primitive.

Although Jung describes in some detail how he and other white Europeans experience the prospect of "going black," he never once considers how black Africans experience the prospect of "going white." Van der Post suggests that, in Africa, just as whites are afraid of going black, blacks—and whites—are afraid of going white:

> I suspect that among many black Africans there is an instinctive fear of "going white" in the inner sense and that this fear plays its part in the problem we are discussing. I believe that this fear of "going white" exists at a certain level in all of us. It is the fear that man has of becoming more conscious, of becoming more aware of himself, of detaching himself from the herd and assuming greater responsibility for himself and his actions. For greater consciousness is not attained without effort, pain, and added responsibility and is maintained only by a continuous struggle. If this fear exists in modern civilized man, as I believe it does, it is even more active in primitive communities.
>
> (1955: 128–9)

Van der Post seems to equate "whiteness" with consciousness and individual identity—and "blackness" with unconsciousness and collective identity. (Why, I should wonder, would anyone "color-code" consciousness and unconsciousness at all? If one means "becoming conscious" or "becoming unconscious," why not just say so, without any colorist codification, as in "going white" or "going black?")

In fact, during the question-and-answer session following the original lecture in Zurich, a member of the audience remarked that van der Post appeared "to equate the black man not only with our dark selves but with our unconscious and with unconsciousness." The inevitable conclusion, the questioner noted, seemed to be that "the black man must be incapable of conscious or rational thought." In response, van der Post attempted to dissociate himself from any such implication:

> You know your question is a rather remarkable illustration of how deep down this confusion of the image reflected in the mirror with the mirror itself goes into all of us. For that I fear is at the root of the difficulty behind your question. Of course I do not equate the black man with our own or any other state of unconsciousness. In so far as I talk of the primitive man's unconscious I do so relatively. I do not mean that he has no consciousness and is incapable of rational thought. That would be both nonsense and an untruth; some of the most conscious individuals and finest natural intelligences I have encountered in my life have been among black countrymen of mine. So when I speak of the unconsciousness of primitive man I speak in a generality to which there are many striking exceptions already, but I have to do so. I do so because unsatisfactory as it may be I do not know of a better way of describing the difference which undoubtedly exists between indigenous and European societies in Africa. But it is a difference only of degree and it is this difference which makes the black man so readily a symbol for the white man of what is unconscious in himself. I repeat a symbol, because you see I do not equate the black man, as you put it, with the white man's unconscious. I merely suggest that his extra degree of unconsciousness and his more natural and organic behaviour make him a living mirror in which the white man sees reflected his own rejected and abhorred unconscious natural self. Like the baboon, the white man is incapable of differentiating between the mirror and his own reflection in the mirror. In the process he is burdening the black man with a despised and hidden aspect of himself. But that does not prevent the black man, like the mirror, from having a shape, a being and validity all his own. That shape, I cannot emphasize enough, does not exclude consciousness. On the contrary, because consciousness in it has not yet been separated from its deep and vital instinctive roots, as it increasingly is in the European in Africa, it has access to great power and is blessed with the promise of profound increase.
>
> (1955: 136–8)

Although van der Post concedes the inadequacy of any generalization about the unconscious of the black African in contrast to the conscious of the white European, although he admits exceptions to the rule, although he relativizes the putative psychical difference between Africans and Europeans as one of degree rather than one of kind, although he emphasizes the natural and the organic in contrast to the synthetic and the artificial, although he compares the European to a baboon incapable

of differentiation between projection and reflection, although he acknowledges the existence of rationally capable, naturally intelligent, instinctively conscious Africans, he nevertheless does quantify the white
European as more conscious, the black African as less conscious.

In spite of himself, van der Post tends to equate whiteness with consciousness and blackness with unconsciousness. For instance, he advocates
"the increase of Western civilization and its preservation in Africa
because I believe most profoundly in the increase of consciousness."
Whatever style of existence white Europeans "achieve in Africa must be
by the hard way of a deeper and expanding awareness of ourselves, our
being and the meaning of life," he says, "rather than by a recession into
the unconscious state from which mankind has so slowly and painfully
risen." By implication, black Africans are that portion of mankind who
have yet to rise into a conscious state. Van der Post does criticize the
consciousness of white Europeans as "fanatically narrow." As a result, he
says, it has "incurred tremendous instinctive enmities by its bigoted rejec-
tion and obstinate refusal to recognize other forces and values in the
nature of man." As valuable as "reason and intellect" are, white European
consciousness is also presumptuous. It is uncooperative and dominant in
relation to "other valid aspects of the spirit of man." Evidently, white
European consciousness is not so civilized after all. According to van der
Post, in becoming civilized, it has lost instinct and now must regain it:

> I believe that no matter what solution we arrive at in Africa must be
> preceded by an enormous expansion of the awareness of modern man
> in Africa, an expansion that will allow all the rich instinctive values
> which play so great a part in the life of the black man round us also
> to play a legitimate role in our own lives inevitably expressing itself in
> a liberalization of our own institutions and a broadening of the
> relationships between its human constituent members. In that sense I
> believe most profoundly in the preservation of white civilization in
> Africa.
>
> (1955: 192–3)

Van der Post is a liberal humanist, a psychological and political optimist
who eschews a tragic vision of reality that considers instinct irretrievable.
However problematic the equation of whiteness with consciousness and
blackness with unconsciousness is, at least van der Post does not (as some
psychoanalysts have tended to do) exclusively assign a positive value to
consciousness and a negative value to unconsciousness.

I would also add, with cautionary emphasis, that "consciousness" and
"unconsciousness" are not entities but only concepts, or theoretical constructs. Such a conceptualization has its advantages but also its limitations.
Concepts are simplifications. They are never entirely adequate to the
complexities of the phenomena that they purport to comprehend. In

addition, the concepts "conscious" and "unconscious" arbitrarily dichoto-
mize the psyche. The conscious–unconscious opposition implies a difference in kind rather than a difference in degree, when in actuality
consciousness and unconsciousness are only theoretical extremes on an
experiential continuum. Consciousness and unconsciousness are not
absolute but relative. They do not constitute a diametrical opposition.
Just as there is no such thing as "racial" purity, there is no pure consciousness or unconsciousness. There is only "more or less" consciousness
or unconsciousness. There are also, I would emphasize, many different
definitions of "unconsciousness" (Child *et al.* 1928/1966; Miller 1942;
Whyte 1960; Ellenberger 1970; Klein 1977; Bowers and Meichenbaum
1984). To suggest that white Europeans have egos and are conscious,
while black Africans have ids (or only unevolved or undeveloped egos)
and are unconscious, is to employ oppositional rather than differential
logic. That there may be differences, even profound differences, between
the psyches of the so-called civilized and the so-called primitive does not
necessarily mean that these differences are oppositions. Dichotomizing
experience is "splitting," which, ironically enough, psychoanalysts consider a "primitive" defense.

IDENTITY POLITICS: THE "OREO," "X," AND "WHITE NEGRO"

Just as the white European has a fear of going black (of becoming
unconscious), the black African—as well as the white European (van der
Post says "all of us")—has a fear of going white (of becoming conscious).
If there is a fear of going white, perhaps there is a reason for it. If to
become unconscious is to lose ego, then to become conscious is to gain
ego. From the perspective of the white European, it may at first seem
inconceivable that there could be anything to fear in gaining ego—but
the white European's perspective is, of course, the white European ego's
perspective, and this "I" is, by definition, egocentric. This "I" presumes
not only that it personifies "reason" in relation to the "reality principle"
but also that it constitutes the totality of the psyche, and, as both Freud
and Jung have demonstrated conclusively, this is by no means the case.
The ego is only a part, not the whole, of the psyche. Perhaps the real
question is why would we expect the unconscious *not* to experience the
conscious as a risk, a danger, a threat—to its very existence? Does not
unconsciousness experience consciousness as one more colonialist,
imperialist project?

Another way of putting it is: what do we stand to lose, if and when we
gain ego? Freud (who does have a tragic vision of reality) suggests that
what we lose when we gain ego and become civilized is instinct, or id.
(Similarly, van der Post says that white Europeans in Africa are increas-

ingly alienated from what is instinctively vital to them.) According to Freud, civilization demands the "renunciation of instinct." The method, he says, may be "by suppression, repression, or some other means" (*SE* 21: 97). It is losing id that makes civilized people discontented—and, I would add, perhaps it is this prospect that makes primitive people, as well as civilized people, justifiably afraid of gaining ego. In psychoanalytic theory, it would seem that whether a black African goes white, gains ego, and loses id, or whether a white European goes black, gains id, and loses ego, it all appears to be a zero-sum game, in which a gain on one side of the equation entails an equivalent loss on the other side. What seems problematic to me about this notion of the zero-sum game is that it regards the psyche as utterly unresilient and inelastic: there is no give-and-take, only gain-and-loss. In contrast, I posit a psychical resilience and elasticity that are, at least potentially, vastly expansive and inclusive. I do not believe that gaining id necessarily implies losing ego—or vice versa.

Van der Post argues that literal blackness or whiteness on the outside (on the surface of the skin) is no necessary indication of metaphorical "blackness" or "whiteness" on the inside (in the depths of the psyche). This seems to me a sympathetic but problematic proposition. In this respect, I would merely note that this is the very definition of what African-Americans refer to pejoratively as an "Oreo," the cookie that is black on the outside but white on the inside. An Oreo is an African-American who, to all appearances, looks black but who thinks, feels, and behaves white. The depreciation of the Oreo is, of course, another example of colorism. All colorism, whether by whites or by blacks, has the structure of a phobia, with its ambivalent attraction and aversion, desire and fear. In this case, going white and becoming an Oreo would be experienced as losing instinct, losing id, losing "racial" identity—or, in African-American vernacular, losing soul.

I would emphasize that these terms—"id," "identity," and "soul"—have significantly different meanings and are again an example of concepts that are only more or less adequate to the complexities of the psyche. The various nuances of id, identity, and soul are, it seems to me, irreducibly important. In this respect, one might reflect on the fact that African-Americans have been typically associated with both "body" (especially in the sexual sense of "id") and "soul" (or feeling), while white Americans have been typically associated with "mind" (or thinking). This logic has opposed the embodied soul to the disembodied mind—to the satisfaction, I might add, of neither blacks nor whites. Eldridge Cleaver addresses this white–black, mind–body opposition in terms of a number of projective typifications. He says that "the separation of the black and white people in America along the color line had the effect, in terms of social imagery, of separating the Mind from the Body." Cleaver identifies, along sexual lines, four stereotypical images that result from this split: "the oppressor whites usurping sovereignty by monopolizing the Mind, abdicating the Body and becoming bodiless Omnipotent Administrators and Ultrafeminines; and the oppressed blacks, divested of sovereignty and therefore of Mind, manifesting the Body and becoming mindless Supermasculine Menials and Black Amazons" (1968: 192).

Lena Williams discusses the ambiguities and ambivalences of the contemporary quest for black identity. "The ever-changing black experience in America is being assessed with a new intensity," she reports. "Skin color, how you talk, more specifically what you say and how you live your life are examples of the tests being used to determine what it means to be black in the 1990's." Blackness, in this sense, is not just how one looks but how one thinks, feels, and behaves. Williams says: "Some blacks measure blackness by standards that border on the arbitrary and capricious. Black youths, for example, are sometimes accused by their peers of 'acting white' simply because they study hard, go to the library or use standard English." She quotes one man who says of the Anita Hill–Clarence Thomas hearings: " 'I saw a black woman and a white man in black skin' " (1991, 30 November: 1, 1 and 26). From this perspective, one of America's Supreme Court justices is pejoratively an Oreo, a black man who has gone white and, in the process, lost his identity, or his soul.

Salim Muwakkil, an African-American journalist whom Terkel interviews, objects to the tendency of some blacks to criticize other blacks for going white, or "acting white." Such blacks, he says, perpetuate a victim identity that he calls the "internal nigger," the unconscious image of a black inferiority complex:

> I do think that black people overemphasize the "victimization" theory. If you are accomplished, can cope, and operate with success in the mainstream community, you are acting white. That's the perception in certain parts of the black community. A kind of anti-intellectualism. There's a reluctance to engage in competition because some black people fear that those rumors of inferiority may be true. So rather than expose the myth, they hang back. I don't want to let society off the hook, but that "internal nigger" has to be confronted by black people.
>
> (1992: 169)

Muwakkil aspires to a black identity that would be a "success identity," or "intellectual identity," one that blacks would not immediately and fallaciously equate with a white identity.

What would Malcolm X think of all the whites who in the 1990s, with Spike Lee, wear "X" caps? Is the cap on the head, like the hair on the head, a symbol of an effort by whites to go black, to think black, to feel black, to behave black? In a report on the trademarking of the "X" logo and the marketing of "X" products, Phil Patton says: " 'X' can denote experimentation, danger, poison, obscenity and the drug ecstasy. It is also the signature of a person who cannot write his or her name. But right now 'X' marks the mystery of Malcolm X—what his legacy is, what he could have been." Patton notes that the "X" appears on a variety of items: "caps and shirts, refrigerator magnets and trading cards, pins and air fresheners." He cites an estimate that sales of "X" merchandise could total $100 million in one year. "The irony is that Malcolm X, like many other members of the Nation of Islam and other blacks in the 60's, assumed the letter—now held to represent his identity—as an expression of a lack of identity," Patton says. "It replaced his legal last name, Little, as a place holder for an African name that was lost to history and slavery" (1992, 8 November: 9, 1 and 10). Paradoxically, in identifying with the "X" of a lost identity, not only blacks but also whites of "generation X" have gained identity. Perhaps in addition to the "X" cap, we need a new cookie, with vanilla on the outside and chocolate on the inside, to describe this identification by whites.

Whites do not suddenly identify with blacks in the 1990s. What Norman Mailer calls the "white Negro" appears on the American scene in the 1950s and, in an effort to be "hip" rather than "square," identifies with the stereotypical ethos of the "Negro," who serves as a convenient excuse to indulge in deviations from a repressive white moral norm. (In this sense, the white hip-hopster who appreciates rap in the 1990s is simply a contemporary version of the white hipster who enjoys jazz in the 1950s). Mailer, too, employs the civilized–primitive opposition (as well as the mind–body opposition). He says that "the Negro (all exceptions admitted) could rarely afford the sophisticated inhibitions of civilization, and so he kept for his survival the art of the primitive." Mailer describes the "Negro" in sensational terms: "he lived in the enormous present, he subsisted for his Saturday night kicks, relinquishing the pleasures of the mind for the more obligatory pleasures of the body, and in his music he gave voice to the character and quality of his existence, to his rage and the infinite variations of joy, lust, languor, growl, pinch, scream, and despair of his orgasm" (1957: 279). The "Negro," Mailer concludes, is a psychopath, at least in the psychical reality of whites, for whom blacks epitomize "perversion, promiscuity, pimpery, drug addiction, rape, razor-slash, bottle-break, what-have-you" (1957: 285). To some whites, to those who aspire to be "white Negroes," the attraction of an identification with the other is the appeal of "the liberation of the self from the Super-Ego of society" (1957: 290), from the strictures of conventional white morality, from the inhibitions of the white conscience. In short, whites who imitate the style of the "Negro" do so in an attempt to obtain at least momentary relief from repression. If in the past whites have relegated blacks to a position of actual inferiority, in the future "it is probable," Mailer says, "that if the Negro can win his equality, he will possess a potential superiority." As much as whites apparently desire a vicarious experience of putative black inferiority, they so fear the prospect of black superiority that this fear has become the very "underground" (that is, the unconscious) basis of politics in America. True "racial" equality would, Mailer speculates, radically alter "the psychology, the sexuality, and the moral imagination" of all whites (1957: 291). The description that Mailer provides of the "Negro" is replete with the rhetorical extravagance for which he is famous—or notorious. Even as he caricatures blacks in terms that a racist might employ—as more sexual and more violent than whites—he romanticizes them as potentially morally superior to whites. In this sense, the "white Negro" is for Mailer both a pale imitation of the black and the harbinger of a revolution in morality. The identity of the white who identifies with the black—that is, the white who thinks, feels, and behaves as if he were a black—is, for Mailer, an emergent, subversive intimation of a fundamental transvaluation of white moral (and political) values.

Who, exactly, is black? That is the question that the sociologist F. James Davis poses. In American history, a "black" has been any person with even a trace, however minute the fraction, of African ancestry. The American legal and social systems have defined "blackness" by adopting "the 'one-drop rule,' meaning that a single drop of 'black blood' makes a person a black" (1991: 5). This criterion is unique to African-Americans. The one-drop rule applies to no other "racial" group in America. Although it is estimated that 75 to over 90 per cent of African-Americans have some white ancestry, by the one-drop rule 100 per cent of them are categorized, oppositionally, as "blacks." The irony, Davis says, is that the one-drop rule that was forcibly imposed on African-Americans has been actively embraced by many of them in the name of "racial" identity, ethnic unity, or "minority group" solidarity. There has been a tendency to criticize or even ostracize those who deny "blackness" and betray the "race." Skin color and other ostensibly significant physical differences between whites and blacks thus provide a collective identity that, consciously and unconsciously, influences individual identity. Although, as Davis demonstrates, "blackness" is a legal and social construction—and not a true "racial" distinction—it functions, in effect, as a putatively natural, rather than a cultural, category. What is significant, however, is not that African-Americans "are" black in some literal sense but that they identify themselves as "black." As Davis says:

We have seen that it is the way people think, feel, and believe, not how they look, that makes them members of the black ethnic community. Along the entire color continuum, in response to common experiences that include systematic discrimination by whites, nearly all persons with some black ancestry have internalized the black identity.
(1991: 179)

In this respect, black identity is a conflation of a physical, natural, or "racial" reality with a psychical, cultural, or ethnic reality. Nothing is either "black" or "white," but thinking, feeling, believing—and, I would add, behaving—makes it so.

What is so remarkable is that both whites and blacks continue to color-code ethnic (or cultural) differences, in spite of the fact that "racial" (or natural) differences are obviously so insignificant. The avid contemporary interest in "identity politics" is, in this sense, only the most recent variation on a certain theme: the reduction of identity to a function of some collective factor such as class—or, in this case, "race." This is, of course, a simplistic account of identity formation. Black separatists and white supremacists are merely the most extreme proponents of a "racial" identity politics. Many others, more moderate, both black and white, also color-code differences in an effort to establish or maintain a sense of identity. The expression "going black" is a historical artifact of racist projections by whites, just as the one-drop rule is. Although the expression and the rule are patently anachronistic, they nevertheless remain obstinately operative. They evidently serve some unconscious psychological (if illogical) purpose. An individual identity distinct from collective factors such as "race" is evidently a difficult (although not impossible) ideal with relatively indifferent appeal. It seems that for many whites and blacks the solidarity of "race" is preferable to the solitude of individuation. Actually, at least as Jung defines "individuation," it is only apparently a solitary project. He states that individuation entails a simultaneous differentiation from and relation to collective norms—neither an identification with them nor an opposition to and isolation from them (*CW* 6). Individuation, or truly authentic individual identity, requires a critical evaluation of collective factors—and, I would add, an appreciation of ethnic differences as incomparably more significant than any "racial" differences.

Chapter 10

Frantz Fanon and Alice Walker on humanism and universalism

In contemporary discourse, "post-" is the prefix of choice. There are post-structuralists, post-modernists, post-Freudians, and post-Jungians. Are there also post-racists? I have expressed a preference for a "non-racial" rather than an anti-racist psychical reality, because I believe that a merely adversarial position tends to perpetuate "racial" categorizations and the white–black opposition. It seems to me that ultimately we need not so much to go against racism as to go beyond "race": to a psychical reality that is neither color-hypersensitive nor color-blind but properly color-attentive, perhaps even quite color-imaginative. We would notice differences in skin color; individually, we might (for whatever strictly personal reasons, aesthetic or otherwise) prefer some skin colors over others, but we would not "racialize" skin colors—that is, fallaciously endow them with "racial" values. Some have declared the end of ideology and the end of history; others have proclaimed the end of humanism (if not the end of humanity). Could there be an end to racism, and, if so, what would succeed it, what would supersede it? It seems to me that it could only be a variety of humanism—or universalism—neither naive nor facile but critical.

Are there universals? Geertz notes that the question of universalism, or the *consensus gentium*, is a contentious issue. He criticizes those who posit the existence of universals, "underlying necessities"—sociological, psychological, and ultimately biological factors that ostensibly constitute the common denominator of humanity (1973: 42). One of the individuals whom Terkel interviews on the issue of "race" in America says:

> I believe in my bones that the things that separate us make up one percent of who we are, that ninety-nine percent of our lives are similar. The same planet supports us. We have the same environment. You have two arms and legs and I have the same. We have given over so much over the years to that one percent, complexion, it's a travesty. I think it's one of the great tragedies of our species.

> (1992: 218)

As different as we may be historically, culturally, and ethnically, we are also, as Jung says, archetypally the same, typically human. It is not only "whites" like Jung who affirm a humanist position. Others who employ psychoanalysis to problematize racism also envisage a humanism that would effectively render "race" irrelevant. Among them are "blacks" like Frantz Fanon and Alice Walker. Fanon in the 1950s and Walker in the 1990s "psychoanalyze" the situation in an effort to humanize and universalize self and other. Fanon is a revolutionary who applies Freudian, Adlerian, and Jungian analysis, Sartrian existentialism, and Marxian ideology to criticize colonialism, imperialism, and racism. Walker is a human rights activist who employs Jungian analysis and feminism to criticize sexism and racism. For Fanon, the issue is the superiority–inferiority valuation; for Walker, it is the Eurocentric–Afrocentric opposition (as well as the male–female opposition). The issues and the means are different for Fanon and Walker, but the ends are similar: they both present a vision of humanism and universalism beyond racism.

FANON AND THE INFERIORITY COMPLEX

What Fanon offers is not so much a theory as a manifesto about the psychical actualities and potentialities of black existence. Jones reports that Freud once said to Marie Bonaparte: "The great question that has never been answered and which I have not yet been able to answer, despite my thirty years of research into the feminine soul, is 'What does a woman want?' " (1955 2: 421). Fanon poses similar questions: "What does a man want?" and "What does the black man want?" He replies that the black man is "not a man" but always "a black man," and what the black man wants is to become a white man (as Freud suggests that what a woman wants is to become a man). What Fanon proposes is "the liberation of the man of color from himself." Fanon says of the white man: "The man who adores the Negro is as 'sick' as the man who abominates him." Similarly, he says that the black man who loves the white man and "who wants to turn his race white" is as psychopathological as the black man who hates the white man (1967: 8). The decisive issue is neither adoration nor abomination but self-liberation, which is beyond both love and hate.

For Fanon, pigmentation is apparently destiny: "However painful it may be for me to accept this conclusion, I am obliged to state it: For the black man there is only one destiny. And it is white" (1967: 10). What he means is that the prevalent conditions of racism, which consigns the man with black skin to inferior status, destine him to wear white masks. If the black man has "an inferiority complex," Fanon says, it is not only economic but also psychological: the consequence of "the internalization—or, better, the epidermalization—of this inferiority" (1967: 11). In this one sense only is pigmentation destiny. Fanon declares: "I believe that the fact of the juxtaposition of the white and black races has created a massive psychoexistential complex. I hope by analyzing it to destroy it" (1967: 12). The psychoanalytic allusion, of course, is to Alfred Adler (1916), who argues that individuals often develop a sense of organic inferiority (in this case, the ostensibly inferior organ is the skin of the black man) for which they compensate—or, it may be, overcompensate.

Like Fanon, Mannoni also discusses the relation between "race" and inferiority. "The celebrated inferiority complex of the coloured peoples, which is so often invoked to explain certain traits of their behaviour, is no different from the inferiority complex pure and simple as described by Adler," Mannoni says. "It springs from a physical difference taken to be a drawback—namely, the colour of the skin." According to Mannoni, a difference must be "perceptible" in order for it to result in a complex. Even then, such a difference becomes a sign of inferiority only under certain disadvantageous demographic circumstances. Mannoni says that "an inferiority complex connected with the colour of the skin is found only among those who form a minority within a group of another colour" (1964: 39). I would say that there may be an inferiority complex even among people who are in the majority if the minority is in power socially, politically, and economically.

Fanon notes that "racial" relations include the possibility of sexual relations between both black women and white men and black men and white women. The inferiority complex that afflicts blacks prevents—or at least severely problematizes—any possibility of genuine love. Fanon wonders "to what extent authentic love will remain unattainable before one has purged oneself of that feeling of inferiority or that Adlerian exaltation, that overcompensation," that is apparently indicative of what Fanon calls "the black *Weltanschauung*" (1967: 42). In this respect, Fanon cites the autobiography of a black woman. Whether the white man she loves is beautiful or ugly is irrelevant to her. All that matters, she says, is that he is blond-haired, blue-eyed, and light-skinned. Fanon quotes a passage in which she recounts an anecdote. At the age of five, she emptied an inkwell over the head of a white boy. "This," Fanon remarks, "was her own way of turning whites into blacks." The effort, she realized, was merely an exercise in futility. She resolved, henceforth, that "if she could no longer try to blacken, to negrify the world, she was going to try, in her own body and in her own mind, to bleach it" (1967: 45). She would launder clothes until they were clean, white. Then she discovered that her grandmother, from Canada, had been a white woman. With that knowledge, she concluded that she could never love a black man—only a white man from France, with blond hair, blue eyes, and light skin.

Fanon confesses that, as a black man, he, too, wants to love a white woman—or, rather, wants her to love him, to love him as she would love a white man, as if he were a white man. The love of a white woman would, in effect, make him a white man—or make him feel like a white man. From this perspective, the white woman appears to be a precious possession. "I marry white culture, white beauty, white whiteness," Fanon says. "When my restless hands caress those white breasts, they grasp civilization and dignity and make them mine" (1967: 63).

A Freudian analyst would emphasize "sex" in this account of the difficulties, if not impossibilities, of authentic love between blacks and whites. An Adlerian analyst would emphasize "power." According to Jung, the Freudian and Adlerian perspectives are complementary. He acknowledges that "there are thousands of people who have a Freudian psychology and thousands who have an Adlerian psychology" (*CW* 18: 127, para. 278). In this specific case, however, as Fanon describes it, sex is merely a means to an end, which is power. Just as, according to Adler, there may be, in women, a "masculine protest" (1916: 100) against an inferior social position, there may be, in blacks, a "white protest" against an inferior social position.

In Freudian terminology, the "masculine protest" is simply "penis envy" (*SE* 14: 92). What Freud calls penis envy is, however, more accurately "phallus envy," for it is not the real penis but the phallus, or symbolic penis—and all that it implies (or as Lacan would say, all that it "signifies")—that is the decisive issue. As Robert S. Steele describes the penis, it is merely "the male organ of copulation," which includes in mammals "three columns of erectile tissue." Steele says that the penis is, "as a material object, prosaic" (1982: 336). Psychically, however, rather than physically (or materially), the penis is poetic—at least when it functions symbolically as the phallus. According to Lacan, the phallus is neither "a phantasy" nor "an object" and "even less the organ, penis or clitoris, that it symbolizes," but "a signifier" (1977: 285).

Not only Lacan and Lacanians but also Jung and Jungians refuse to reduce the phallus to the penis. "The phallus," Jung says, "is not just a sign that indicates the penis; it is a 'symbol' because it has so many other meanings" (*CW* 10: 337, para. 637n.). Jung maintains that the phallus is symbolic of power, or potency, and he repudiates the notion that it is reducible to "the *membrum virile* and nothing more" (*CW* 16: 157, para. 340). Similarly, Hillman declares: "The Freudian error lies not so much in the importance given to sexuality; more grave is the delusion that sexuality is actual sexuality only, that phallus is always only penis" (1972: 63).

For a Lacanian analyst, the phallus, or symbolic penis, signifies *jouissance*, or "enjoyment." For an Adlerian analyst, it would presumably signify *puissance*, or "empowerment." Although Juliet Mitchell is no Adlerian, as a feminist she apparently appreciates this symbolic equation. "No phallus," she says, "no power" (1974: 96). Like Lacan, whom Mitchell cites, she states: "The phallus is not identical with the penis, for it is what it signifies that is important" (1974: 396)—and one of the things that the phallus may signify is power.

From an Adlerian perspective, what induces some blacks to compensate with a "white protest" are the inequalities of power between whites and blacks. (From a Freudian perspective, this "white protest" would evidently be "color envy.") In a social situation where some people with one skin color happen to be powerful and other people with another skin color happen to be powerless, "whiteness" signifies power—or, as Fanon says, "civilization and dignity."

Fanon, of course, was writing about the inferiority complex of blacks in the 1950s, before the civil rights movement—not to mention the "Black Power" movement of the 1960s. Although the civil rights movement and the Black Power movement were protest movements, they were not a "white protest" but a quite definite "black protest." The motivation of these movements was not only equal opportunity, in both a legal and an economic sense, but also equal status, in a psychological sense. If these movements were a compensation for an inferior status, they were not, in any sense, an identification with what it was to be "white" but, rather, an affirmation of what it was to be "black." If blacks in the civil rights movement and the Black Power movement had a complex, it was not an inferiority complex but an "equality complex."

THE COLLECTIVE UNCONSCIOUS AS A CULTURAL UNCONSCIOUS

Whatever Freud (*SE* 22) and Jung (*CW* 8) may have said about the relation between psychoanalysis and *Weltanschauung*, Fanon proposes applying psychoanalytic theory to the black worldview. He says that "one should investigate the extent to which the conclusions of Freud or of Adler can be applied to the effort to understand the man of color's view of the world" (1967: 141). Fanon appropriates from Freud the concept of the trauma. He insists that even minimal contact with whites traumatizes blacks. In addition to Adler's "inferiority complex" and Freud's "trauma," Jung's "collective unconscious" provides a theoretical point of departure for Fanon's critical conclusions. (In this sense, Fanon is that rarity, a true pluralist, or integrationist, who eschews the unnecessarily divisive theoretical disputes to which psychoanalysis has been so susceptible historically. For Fanon, the Freudian, Adlerian, and Jungian perspectives are all properly psychoanalytic.) "Unless we make use of that frightening postulate—which so destroys our balance—offered by Jung, the *collective unconscious*," Fanon says, "we can understand absolutely nothing" (1967: 144–5). He contends that many blacks who have never actually encountered any whites—and therefore have never suffered any "real" trauma—

have nevertheless internalized unconsciously the collective values of whites. Fanon maintains that "Freud and Adler and even the cosmic Jung did not think of the Negro in all their investigations" (1967: 151). This assertion is more or less true of Freud and Adler but not of Jung, who thought about blacks—and theorized about them—to a quite considerable extent.

From a Freudian perspective, the white self tends to define the black other exclusively in terms of sexual potency. As a result, blacks are "phobogenic"; the mere presence of blacks induces a phobia in whites. Fanon says that whites who are "Negrophobic" have fantasies of assaultive, perverse sex with blacks: heterosexual rape fantasies in the case of white women, homosexual fellatio fantasies in the case of white men (1967: 154–5). "In relation to the Negro," he remarks, "everything takes place on the genital level." Whites fantasize that blacks "copulate at all times and in all places" (1967: 157). The white man, who idealizes "an infinite virility," considers the black man "a penis symbol" (1967: 159)— the phallus. Whereas the anti-Semite associates money with the Jew, the racist associates sex with the black. Whereas the Jew is killed or sterilized, the black is castrated: "The penis, the symbol of manhood, is annihilated, which is to say that it is denied" (1967: 162). Whites also fantasize about the size of the erect black penis. Thus Fanon quotes a Frenchman, a white man, who writes: "Four Negroes with their penises exposed would fill a cathedral. They would be unable to leave the building until their erections had subsided; and in such close quarters that would not be a simple matter" (1967: 169). Fanon comments:

> When one reads this passage a dozen times and lets oneself go—that is, when one abandons oneself to the movement of its images—one is no longer aware of the Negro but only of a penis. He is turned into a penis. He *is* a penis. It is easy to imagine what such descriptions can stimulate in a young girl in Lyon. Horror? Lust? Not indifference, in any case. Now, what is the truth?
>
> (1967: 169–70)

According to Fanon, the truth is that the average penis length of Africans is the same as that of Europeans, but, he adds, "these are facts that persuade no one" (1967: 170). The psychical reality of penis envy prevails over any external, or physical, reality. As with Clarence Thomas and "Long Dong Silver" (Berke 1991, 12 October: 1, 9), when whites measure blacks, the inches are merely in the pornographic imagination. Bob Herbert reports that "a crackpot professor" has even attempted to make a racist virtue of the notion that whites have smaller penises than blacks: to be less well endowed is to have "heightened intelligence" (1996, 12 February: A, 15).

From a Jungian perspective, the black man symbolizes to the white man not only sexuality in particular but also negative instinctuality in general. It is Jung, Fanon says, rather than Freud or Adler, who addresses this issue:

> Continuing to take stock of reality, endeavoring to ascertain the instant of symbolic crystallization, I very naturally found myself on the threshold of Jungian psychology. European civilization is characterized by the presence, at the heart of what Jung calls the collective unconscious, of an archetype: an expression of the bad instincts, of the darkness inherent in every ego, or the uncivilized savage, the Negro who slumbers in every white man. And Jung claims to have found in uncivilized peoples the same psychic structure that his diagram portrays. Personally, I think that Jung has deceived himself.
>
> (1967: 187)

Fanon is alluding, of course, to the shadow, which Jung defines as the inferior aspect of the psyche. According to Jung, the inferiority of the self is repressed and then projected (or cast like a shadow) onto the other.

Fanon criticizes the concept of the "collective unconscious," at least as Jung apparently defines it. "Jung," he asserts, "locates the collective unconscious in the inherited cerebral matter." It is true that Jung posits archetypes, or inherited forms, and occasionally situates them in the brain. Contrary to what Fanon apparently believes, however, Jung insists that the archetypal images, the specific contents of the collective unconscious, are not inherited but are acquired through the experience of the individual. Fanon argues that "the collective unconscious, without our having to fall back on the genes, is purely and simply the sum of prejudices, myths, collective attitudes of a given group." He accuses Jung of having confused "instinct" (what is inherited) and "habit" (what is acquired). In criticizing Jung, Fanon redefines the concept of the "collective unconscious" as a cultural rather than a natural unconscious. According to Fanon, Jung asserts that the archetypes are inherited in "the cerebral structure." From this perspective, "the myths and archetypes are permanent engrams of the race." Fanon, who disputes this contention, says: "I hope I have shown that nothing of the sort is the case and that in fact the collective unconscious is cultural, which means acquired." (I would say that the collective unconscious is *partly* cultural.) Although I do not believe that Fanon adequately appreciates the distinction that Jung proposes between archetypes as inherited forms and archetypal images as acquired contents, he quite correctly emphasizes that Jung does not sufficiently address the extent to which the contents of the collective unconscious are *acquired by the individual through culture* (Fanon says that racist contents of the collective unconscious are *imposed* on the black individual by white culture). What Fanon adds to the psychoanalysis of racism is the *cultural context*.

It is through contact with whites that blacks acquire, or assimilate, the collective values of the other; they do not inherit them. A black man, Fanon says, "who has lived in France and breathed and eaten the myths and prejudices of racist Europe, and assimilated the collective unconscious of that Europe, will be able, if he stands outside himself, to express only his hatred of the Negro" (1967: 188). If some blacks hate themselves, it is because whites hate an inferior aspect of themselves and repress and project it onto blacks. In contact with whites, blacks then internalize this shadow from the collective unconscious of whites. (The assumption is that a pristine black collective unconscious that had never been in contact with the white collective unconscious would not symbolize inferiority in the same way.)

THE SYMBOLISM OF EVIL AND THE IMPOSITION OF A CULTURE

Ricoeur (1967), who discusses "the symbolism of evil," says that in the Western, Judeo-Christian tradition evil is symbolized by what is considered to be unclean. "*In Europe*," Fanon says, "*the black man is the symbol of Evil.*" To whites, blacks symbolize virtually every variety of inferiority:

> The torturer is the black man, Satan is black, one talks of shadows, when one is dirty one is black—whether one is thinking of physical dirtiness or of moral dirtiness. It would be astonishing, if the trouble were taken to bring them all together, to see the vast number of expressions that make the black man the equivalent of sin. In Europe, whether concretely or symbolically, the black man stands for the bad side of the character. As long as one cannot understand this, one is doomed to talk in circles about the "black problem." Blackness, darkness, shadow, shades, blacken someone's reputation.

In short, Fanon says: "The archetype of the lowest values is represented by the Negro" (1967: 189).

From the perspective that Fanon adopts on psychoanalysis, or depth psychology, white men are hollow men. "In the remotest depth of the European unconscious," Fanon says, "an inordinately black hollow has been made." This inner, psychical space contains white immorality and shame: what Fanon calls the uncivilized self. Fanon asserts that "as every man climbs up toward whiteness and light, the European has tried to repudiate this uncivilized self, which has attempted to defend itself." The primary defense of whites has been projection, or transference: "When European civilization came into contact with the black world, with those savage peoples, everyone agreed: Those Negroes were the principle of evil." Fanon delineates the process by which whites project, or transfer, evil onto blacks:

Jung consistently identifies the foreign with the obscure, with the tendency to evil: He is perfectly right. This mechanism of projection—or, if one prefers, transference—has been described by classic psychoanalysis. In the degree to which I find in myself something unheard-of, something reprehensible, only one solution remains for me: to get rid of it, to ascribe its origin to someone else.

Thus whites defensively attribute to blacks, to others who are conveniently on the outside, what is inside themselves. "In Europe the Negro has one function: that of symbolizing the lower emotions, the baser inclinations, the dark side of the soul," Fanon says. "In the collective unconscious of *homo occidentalis*, the Negro—or, if one prefers, the color black—symbolizes evil, sin, wretchedness, death, war, famine." As the white man (or Western man) externalizes the internal, he imputes all of these symbolic values to the black man, who then, in turn, internalizes them. It is in this respect that Fanon criticizes the collective unconscious as "the unreflected imposition of a culture" (1967: 190–1).

If whites collectively impose this cultural unconscious on blacks, then it should come as no surprise, Fanon says, that blacks have "the same fantasies" as Europeans. (I would say that, historically, *some* blacks have had *some* of the same fantasies as Europeans.) The reason is simply that the black "partakes of the same collective unconscious as the European." It is therefore perfectly expectable, or predictable, for the black "to be anti-Negro," for, in the cultural context of racism, the black "has taken over all the archetypes belonging to the European." If once the black man was the slave of the white man, he is now "the slave of this cultural imposition." To the black man who has been imposed on by white culture and enslaved psychically by it, skin color literally pales to insignificance. "Color is nothing," Fanon notes, "I do not even notice it, I know only one thing, which is the purity of my conscience and the whiteness of my soul." According to Fanon, this "my-skin-may-be-black-but-my-soul-is-white" attitude (which is exactly the same as van der Post's "black-skin-but-white-being" attitude) is a pallidly pathetic and ultimately ineffectual assertion of the value of psychical reality over physical reality. In a group of white intellectuals, he says, a black man "will insist that attention be paid not to the color of his skin but to the force of his intellect" (1967: 191–3). Try as the black man may to forget that he has a black skin and to assert that he has a white soul or intellect, the white man, however, will inevitably remind him that he has a certain epidermal pigmentation.

For Fanon, the fundamental dilemma is color. "There are two ways out of this conflict," he says. "Either I ask others to pay no attention to my skin, or else I want them to be aware of it." Fanon repudiates this conflictual, oppositional logic and the "hostile, inhuman" fantasies that perpetuate it. The alternative that he advocates is "to reach out for the universal" (1967: 197), the typically human. As a universalist and human-ist, Fanon simply refuses to consider the issue of racism from the perspective of *"either–or"* (1967: 203). Evidently, only a "both–and" position, one in which the white other would simultaneously both notice and disregard the skin color of the black self would effectively subvert the oppositional logic that sustains colorism. The universalist, humanist perspective would entail a recognition of physical differences but an indifference to them as any indication of significant psychical differences: what I call an "indifference to difference." As Fanon says, "My black skin is not the wrapping of specific values" (1967: 227).

WALKER AND AFROCENTRISM

Like Fanon, the novelist Alice Walker also rejects "either–or" oppositions, including the Afrocentric–Eurocentric opposition that is attractive to some contemporary African-Americans. Walker acknowledges the ambiguities of an exclusively Afrocentric position, one that accepts uncritically all things African merely because they happen to be from Africa. She is not a cultural relativist but a universalist and a humanist. What ultimately interests her is not "racial" values but "transracial," universal, human values. Like Fanon, she employs psychoanalysis to criticize the superficial notion that skin color wraps any specific values.

In *Possessing the Secret of Joy*, Walker condemns female circumcision—which in the case of clitoridectomy and infibulation is actually female castration—a practice that may be African but that is nonetheless inhuman. Walker and Pratiba Parmar (1993) have published a non-fiction book, *Warrior Marks*, and produced a documentary film by the same name about the practice. Female genital mutilation has recently been a topic of considerable controversy. A.M. Rosenthal, who commends Walker as an activist against female genital mutilation and who criticizes the practice as "the most widespread existing violation of human rights in the world," says that 80 million women are currently victims of the atrocity. He notes that, in men, the practice would be equivalent to "amputation or cutting of the penis and its surrounding tissues." Rosenthal describes the practice as follows:

> One form of mutilation is removal of the clitoris and labia minora. Infibulation, another form, is the removal of the external genitalia, the stitching up of the two sides of the vulva, sometimes with thorns, and the insertion of a sliver to keep only a small opening for the passage of urine and menstrual blood—all done without anesthetic while the child is held down.
>
> (1993, 12 November: A, 33)

Others, however, like Maynard H. Merwine, who does acknowledge that, from the perspective of Western liberalism and feminism, the practice is a violation of human rights, defend the practice "as an affirmation of the value of woman in traditional society" and "a joyous occasion" (1993, 24 November: A, 24). In opposing female genital mutilation, Walker recognizes the obvious effects of colonialism and imperialism, but she does not simply blame Europeans for every condition from which black Africans, especially women, suffer. Black Africans themselves, not only men but also women who actually perform clitoridectomies and infibulations on girls, are complicitly responsible for the inhuman suffering they perpetrate in desexing an entire sex.

Possessing the Secret of Joy is a psychoanalytic novel. The hero, Tashi-Evelyn ("Tashi" is her African name, "Evelyn" her Christian name) has three different psychoanalysts. It is through psychoanalysis that Tashi-Evelyn is able to appreciate the universal, typically human dimensions of experience. Walker is apparently much more sympathetic to Jungian analysis than to Freudian analysis. In the acknowledgements to *Possessing the Secret of Joy*, she expresses gratitude to Jung: "I thank Carl Jung for becoming so real in my own self-therapy (by reading) that I could imagine him as alive and active in Tashi's treatment. My gift to him" (1992: 285). The illustration on the cover of Walker's novel depicts what is described in the paperback edition (1993: copyright page) as "the hand of the author touching Carl Jung's alchemical or philosopher's stone, carved by Jung in 1950 and standing today in his garden in Bollingen, Switzerland."

The first psychoanalyst to whom Tashi-Evelyn goes is a Freudian, an imitation Freud. He is a "white witch doctor," who, like Freud smokes cigars and wears a beard. On his desk are "small stone and clay figures of African gods and goddesses from Egypt"; on his couch is "a tribal rug." This psychoanalyst asks questions to which Tashi-Evelyn has no answers. He sits in a chair behind her, "pen poised to at last capture on paper an African woman's psychosis for the greater glory of his profession." The sister of her husband Adam has brought her to the psychoanalyst: "Not to the father of psychoanalysis, for he has died, a tired, persecuted man. But to one of his sons, whose imitation of him—including dark hair and beard, Egyptian statuettes on his desk, the tribal-rug-covered couch and the cigar, which smells of bitterness—will perhaps cure me" (1992: 10–11).

Tashi-Evelyn experiences difficulty with the Freudian analyst, who asks her whether she knows why "Negro women" are regarded as "the most difficult of all people to be effectively analyzed." His question seems insensitive to her identity: "Since I was not a Negro woman I hesitated before hazarding an answer. I felt negated by the realization that even my psychiatrist could not see that I was African. That to him all black people were Negroes." His remarks also caricature her—and all blacks'—sexuality: "He'd been taken aback by the fact that I had only one child.

He thought this unusual for a colored woman, married or unmarried. Your people like lots of kids, he allowed." Tashi-Evelyn has no response to such ignorance: "But how could I talk to this stranger of my lost children. And of how they were lost? One was left speechless by all such a person couldn't know." Finally, the psychoanalyst breaks the silence by saying that Negro women "can never be analyzed effectively because they can never bring themselves to blame their mothers." The answer nonplusses Tashi-Evelyn. "Blame them for what?" she asks. "Blame them for anything," he says. Tashi-Evelyn's psyche explodes in associations to her mother and to her own birth, but she says nothing (1992: 18–19).

The Freudian analyst asks her about her dreams, and she tells him a lie—that she does not dream. "I do not dare tell him," she says, "about the dream I have every night that terrifies me." It is her husband, Adam, who recounts the recurrent nightmare to the psychoanalyst, as Tashi-Evelyn experiences it:

> There is a tower, she says. I think it is a tower. It is tall, but I am inside. I don't really ever know what it looks like from outside. It is cool at first, and as you descend lower and lower to where I'm kept, it becomes dank and cold, as well. It's dark. There is an endless repetitive sound that is like the faint scratch of a baby's fingernails on paper. And there are millions of things moving about me in the dark. I can not see them. And they've broken my wings! I see them lying crossed in a corner like discarded oars. Oh, and they're forcing something in one end of me, and from the other they are busy pulling something out. I am long and fat and the color of tobacco spit. Gross! And I can not move!

Tashi-Evelyn dreams that "they have imprisoned her and broken her wings." The psychoanalyst asks Adam who "they" are. Adam cannot say because he does not know (1992: 25–7).

JUNG AS THE WISE OLD MAN

The second psychoanalyst to whom Tashi-Evelyn goes is a fictional Jung. She travels with Adam to Zurich, where they stay with Jung in the tower that he built at Bollingen. Although Jung has retired from active practice as "doctor of the soul," he agrees to psychoanalyze Tashi-Evelyn "because I am an African woman and because my case was recommended to him by his niece, my husband's friend and lover, the Frenchwoman, Lisette." She has an instant affinity for Jung, whom Tashi-Evelyn and Adam call *Mzee*, "The Old Man." She describes him as follows:

> I liked The Old Man immediately. Liked his great, stooping height; the looseness of the ever-present tweed jacket that hung from his gaunt shoulders. Liked his rosy pink face and small blue eyes that looked at

one so piercingly it was difficult not to turn one's head to see what he was viewing through it. Liked, even, that he himself had at times a look of madness to match my own—though it was a benign look that seemed to observe a connection between whatever held his gaze and some grand, unimaginably spacious design, quite beyond one's compre- hension. In other words, he looked as if he would soon die. I found this comforting.

(1992: 49–50)

The fictional Jung is the very image of the "Wise Old Man," a personifi- cation of what Jung calls "the archetype of the spirit, who symbolizes the pre-existent meaning hidden in the chaos of life" (*CW* 9,1: 35, para. 74). Jung describes the psychical function of "the *archetype of the wise old man*, or *of meaning*" (*CW*, 9,1: 37, para. 79), as follows:

The old man always appears when the hero is in a hopeless and desperate situation from which only profound reflection or a lucky idea—in other words, a spiritual function or an endopsychic automa- tism of some kind—can extricate him. But since, for internal and external reasons, the hero cannot accomplish this himself, the knowl- edge needed to compensate this deficiency comes in the form of a personified thought, i.e., in the shape of this sagacious and helpful old man.

(*CW*, 9,1: 217–18, para. 401)

Tashi-Evelyn says that she is not afraid of Jung in part because she is not afraid of his house, by which she means his tower at Bollingen. He seems to be "an old African grandmother, metamorphosed somehow into a giant pinkfaced witchdoctor." Tashi-Evelyn sneaks up behind him and blows Jung's thin white hair, and he hugs her. She and Adam tell the old man that he is their last hope. He looks gravely at them and says: "No, that is not correct. You yourselves are your last hope" (1992: 52–3).

In the tower, Jung cooks meals of pancakes and sausages for Tashi- Evelyn and Adam. On warm days, he takes them sailing on Lake Zurich. In the evenings, he plays recordings of music from Africa and other non- European countries for them. He shows them black-and-white films from his travels, including his trips to Africa. One of the films includes a scene of "several small children lying in a row on the ground." Jung assumes that they are boys—and that he had interrupted an initiation, a rite of passage into manhood—but Tashi-Evelyn knows that they are girls. Into the frame a fighting cock suddenly struts, crowing, and Tashi-Evelyn faints. When she regains consciousness, she cannot bring herself to tell Jung and Adam that a picture, taken a quarter of a century ago, of a fighting cock has terrorized her into fainting. She lies and says that she has fainted from happiness. Jung is dubious, and the next day, when Tashi-

Evelyn begins to paint a series of "ever larger and more fearsome fighting cocks," he does not react with surprise (1992: 70–1).

Day after day, she continues to paint, until another image spontaneously emerges from her unconscious:

> And then one day, into the corner of my painting, there appeared, I drew, a foot. Sweating and shivering as I did so. Because I suddenly realized there was something, some small thing the foot was holding between its toes. It was for this small thing that the giant cock waited, crowing impatiently, extending its neck, ruffling its feathers, and strutting about.

Tashi-Evelyn now paints the fighting cock and the foot directly onto the wall of her bedroom, because only such a large surface can contain her active imagination. Jung asks: "Well, Evelyn, is it a man's foot or a woman's foot?" Tashi-Evelyn does not know, cannot answer. In response, she assumes "the classic pose of the deeply insane." Late that night, however, she suddenly realizes that it is the foot of a woman—not the foot of just any woman but the foot of M'Lissa, the *tsunga* who excised the clitoris of Tashi-Evelyn's older sister, Dura, a hemophiliac who bled to death from the initiation. The repressed returns to Tashi-Evelyn "as if a lid lifted off my brain." She recalls the childhood scene vividly:

> Underneath a tree, on the bare ground outside the hut, lay a dazed row of little girls, though to me they did not seem so little. They were all a few years older than me. Dura's age. Dura, however, was not among them; and I knew instinctively that it was Dura being held down and tortured inside the hut. Dura who made those inhuman shrieks that rent the air and chilled my heart.
>
> Abruptly, inside, there was silence. And then I saw M'Lissa shuffle out, dragging her lame leg, and at first I didn't realize she was carrying anything, for it was so insignificant and so unclean that she carried it not in her fingers but between her toes. A chicken—a hen, not a cock—was scratching futilely in the dirt between the hut and the tree where the other girls, their own ordeal over, lay. M'Lissa lifted her foot and flung this small object in the direction of the hen, and she, as if waiting for this moment, rushed toward M'Lissa's upturned foot, located the flung object in the air and then on the ground, and in one quick movement of beak and neck, gobbled it down.
>
> (1992: 71–3)

Finally, Tashi-Evelyn is able to tell Jung that she has remembered Dura's death, Dura's murder. She says that Dura "has been screaming in my ears since it happened," but Tashi-Evelyn "could not hear her." Jung replies, simply: "You didn't dare" (1992: 81–2).

Jung says that he has not been called *Mzee* since he traveled to Africa over twenty-five years ago. At the time, he had felt that the Africans were calling him "The Old Man" for some other reason than his age:

> Some quality of gravity or self-containment that they recognized. Perhaps I flatter myself, as whites do when blacks offer them a benign label for something characteristically theirs, but which they themselves have failed to acknowledge; deep in our hearts perhaps we expect only vilification; the name "devil," to say the least. It used to amaze me that wherever I lectured, anywhere in the world, the one sentence of mine which every person of color appreciated and rose to thank me for was "Europe is the mother of all evil," and yet they shook my European hand, smiled warmly into my eyes, and some of them actually patted me on the back.
>
> (1992: 83)

It is not only Tashi-Evelyn who is being healed but also Jung himself in his encounter with her and Adam:

> They, in their indescribable suffering, are bringing me home to something in myself. I am finding myself in them. A self I have often felt was only halfway at home on the European continent. In my European skin. An ancient self that thirsts for knowledge of the experiences of its ancient kin. Needs this knowledge, and the feelings that come with it, to be whole. A self that is horrified at what was done to Evelyn, but recognizes it as something that is also done to me. A truly universal self.
>
> (1992: 84)

From this perspective, the European and the African are not opposites but two parts, or halves, of the whole, the universal self. For the fictional Jung, to be healed is to be "wholed," to be psychically integrated.

Jung has only one other question that he wants to ask Tashi-Evelyn, and that is why she is not afraid of his tower at Bollingen and what she would say to a gift of a bag of clay, but he does not ask the question. Ultimately, Tashi-Evelyn has to ask herself the question about the tower and bag of clay—and answer it herself.

A DREAM: HAVING ONE'S WINGS BROKEN

Before Jung dies, he refers Tashi-Evelyn to another psychoanalyst, Raye, an African-American woman. At first, Tashi-Evelyn resents her: "Because she wasn't Mzee. Because she was black. Because she was a woman. Because she was whole." Eventually, however, Tashi-Evelyn begins to tell her about Africa, about the Olinka tribe to which she belongs, and about "Our Leader," who had led her people to independence. The leader had emphasized Afrocentric identity, eternal struggle against the oppression of blacks by whites, repossession of all African land, repatriation to Africa of all descendants of slaves, and "return to the purity of our own culture and traditions." The leader had insisted that "we must not neglect our ancient customs" (1992: 115)—among them, circumcision, or clitoridectomy and infibulation, the female initiation into womanhood. When she was young, Tashi-Evelyn had experienced orgasm by masturbation and, with Adam, by cunnilingus and intercourse, yet, in order to be accepted by the Olinka tribe, she had finally, willingly, given up that pleasure and yielded to genital mutilation, even though her own sister Dura had bled to death after her clitoris was excised.

Tashi-Evelyn and Raye eventually establish an effective psychoanalytic connection not because they both happen to be black women but because Raye is empathic, not only psychically but also physically. In an act of compassion, she suffers oral mutilation, or gum mutilation, in order to feel what it was like for Tashi-Evelyn to suffer genital mutilation. It disturbs Raye that what Tashi-Evelyn "must have endured during circumcision was a pain she could hardly imagine." In a surgical procedure analogous to clitoridectomy and infibulation, Raye has her gums clipped and scraped and then stitched by a dentist. The ordeal affords her "a faint idea" of the pain that Tashi-Evelyn has suffered. "I realized," Tashi-Evelyn reflects, "that though Raye had left Africa hundreds of years before in the persons of her ancestors and studied at the best of the white man's schools, she was intuitively practicing an ageless magic, the foundation of which was the ritualization, or the acting out, of empathy." Tashi-Evelyn now feels that she knows Raye because they have shared a similar experience. She feels grateful to Jung for having referred her to such an empathic psychoanalyst: "In my heart I thanked Mzee for her, for I believed she would be plucky enough to accompany me where he could not. And that she would" (1992: 130–2).

It is not a psychoanalyst—whether an imitation Freud, a fictional Jung, or an African-American woman—who successfully interprets Tashi-Evelyn's dream of being imprisoned in a tower and having one's wings broken. It is an anthropologist, Lisette and Adam's son Pierre, who tells Tashi-Evelyn that he knows "what the tower is, though not, perhaps, what it means" (1992: 160). Pierre reads to Tashi-Evelyn from a book about Africa by a French anthropologist who recounts an African creation myth. According to the myth, a father god created the mother earth, a goddess, a feminine body with an anthill for a sexual organ and a termite hill for a clitoris. The god desired intercourse with the goddess, but when he approached her, " 'the termite hill rose up, barring the passage and displaying its masculinity.' " Like a penis, the clitoris became erect and prevented intercourse, but the god was more powerful than the goddess and " 'cut down the termite hill, and had intercourse with the excised earth' " (1992: 169). What enables Pierre to interpret the collective and, for Tashi-Evelyn, the intimately personal significance of the creation myth is the identity that he possesses as a "racial," sexual, and cultural hybrid. Pierre is the new person, a complete blend, beyond white and black, beyond male and female:

> He seems a completely blended person and, as such, new. In him "black" has disappeared; so has "white." His eyes are a dark, lightfilled brown; his forehead is high and tan; his nose broad, a little flat. He has told me he likes men as well as he likes women, which seems only natural, he says, since he is the offspring of two sexes as well as of two races. No one is surprised he is biracial; why should anyone be surprised he is bisexual?
>
> (1992: 170)

As a hybrid, Pierre represents the possibilities of an identity beyond all oppositions.

Pierre interprets the creation myth as the origin of clitoridectomy. Man and woman were created psychically bisexual, with both a male soul and a female soul. The location of the man's female soul was in the prepuce; the location of the woman's male soul was in the clitoris. The man was circumcised in order "to rid him of his femininity"; the woman was circumcised, or excised, in order "to rid her of her masculinity." Pierre says that "men found it necessary to permanently lock people in the category of their obvious sex, even while recognizing sexual duality as a given of nature" (1992: 171–2).

Pierre projects slides onto a screen. The show includes an image of "a tall, rough, earthcolored column." It is a termite hill. "My bag of clay!" Tashi-Evelyn thinks. Pierre interprets the termite hill as the "dark tower" in Tashi-Evelyn's recurrent nightmare. Tashi-Evelyn is the termite queen "who loses her wings." In the dream, Tashi-Evelyn is lying in the termite hill "being stuffed with food at one end—a boring diet of mushrooms— and having your eggs, millions of them, constantly removed at the other." Tashi-Evelyn wonders how she could have known this in order to dream it, because no one told her. Raye suggests that it was told to her "in code somehow." She hypothesizes that "some coded, mythological reason" was given by the tribal elders to Tashi-Evelyn, who unconsciously knew this myth of pleasureless, desexed, insect reproduction and dreamed it (1992: 225–7). Tashi-Evelyn realizes that "there in her unconscious had remained the termite hill, and herself trapped deep inside it, heavy, wingless and inert, the Queen of the dark tower" (1992: 233–4). Like Fanon, who hopes to destroy for blacks the psychoexistential inferiority complex, Pierre dedicates his life "to destroying for other women—and their men— the terrors of the dark tower" (1992: 276).

TRANSFORMATION: DEATH AND REBIRTH

There is poetic license in this novel about a mythic Africa. The Olinka tribe is a figment of the novelistic imagination, as are such words as "tsunga," which Walker says may be "from an African language I used to know, now tossed up by my unconscious" (1992: 283). There is also a certain ironic justice to the novel: Jung travels to Africa twice in an effort to discover himself, to reflect objectively on his "civilized," European self from the perspective of the "primitive," African other; Walker travels, through the character of Tashi-Evelyn, to Africa, Europe, and America to discover herself, to define herself as a universalist and a humanist rather than an Afrocentrist. She reaches out her black hand to touch the alchemical or philosopher's stone that a white hand carved, and she is transformed psychically through the experience. Just as the fictional Jung wants to offer Tashi-Evelyn the gift of a bag of clay, Walker offers the real Jung a gift, a thank-you for the self-therapy she has received by reading him.

A psychoanalytic novel about female sexuality, about genital mutilation of women through clitoridectomy and infibulation, about circumcision of the penis and excision of the clitoris, about psychical bisexuality, about towers and bags of clay, about sexual organs as anthills and clitorises as termite hills, about pleasureless insect reproduction, might seem to require a Freudian emphasis. Is it not Freud who defines the unconscious in sexual terms—and Jung who desexualizes it? Walker, however, is a Jungian novelist, at least in *Possessing the Secret of Joy*. It is not through free association but through active imagination that Tashi-Evelyn, in watching Jung's films of Africa and painting the cock and foot on his wall, first begins to become conscious of the enormity of her experience as a desexed woman.

When Jung traveled to Africa in 1920 and again in 1925–6, he never imagined, of course, that an African-American woman would one day include him as a character in a novel. Jung did exist, but Walker also invents him. She not only reads Jung but also "writes" him for her own self-therapy. The fictional Jung serves her as a character who exemplifies a self who cannot discover himself unless he encounters the other, a self who is not whole until he integrates that part of himself, that half of himself, that is the other. To Walker, Jung represents the attempt to reconcile and perhaps transcend all oppositions: beyond white and black, beyond male and female, beyond Eurocentrism and Afrocentrism—beyond ethnocentrism and cultural relativism and toward universalism and humanism. In a sense, it is irrelevant whether Jung actually had the capacity to achieve this vision himself. It is the effort, the dedication of a life, as in the character of Pierre, the new person, the complete blend, with a pigmentation no longer either white or black, with an orientation no longer either male or female, that ultimately matters.

The final words of *Possessing the Secret of Joy*, below the signature of Tashi-Evelyn, are "Reborn, soon to be Deceased" (1992: 277). Even though Tashi-Evelyn is soon to experience a physical death, she has experienced a psychical rebirth. She has been reborn, or transformed symbolically, by becoming conscious of the significance of tower, bag of clay, cock, foot, anthill, termite hill, queen, and wings.

One of Jung's most important contributions to psychoanalysis is his concept of "symbols of transformation." In dreams, myths, and other products of the unconscious, certain images symbolize the possibility of transformative experience. These images often utilize the metaphor of death and rebirth to express the necessity for a change of attitude. In order for a new attitude to be "born," an old attitude must "die." Jung recounts an African myth and discusses death and rebirth as a symbol of transformation. "The birth of a new attitude," Jung says, "has a long historical background." In this respect, he mentions "a Negro myth which tells of a time when all were immortal and everyone could take his skin off." That is, to be immortal is to have the ability to take off one's skin and then put it back on. What one puts back on, I would emphasize, is the same old skin. Skin, in this sense, is a metaphor for the same old attitude. In contrast to mortals, who change and die, the immortals in the African myth never change, never die—and therefore never have the necessity to be reborn: until one day, that is. "One day," Jung says, "they were all bathing and an old woman lost her skin; she died, and that is how death came into the world" (1984: 90). That is also, I would add, how rebirth—the possibility (and the opportunity) to be reborn in a new and different skin—came into the world. The implication of the myth is that if an old attitude has to "die" before a new attitude can be "born," then, like the old woman, perhaps we all, black and white, need to bathe in the waters of the unconscious and lose our skins, in order to be transformed symbolically.

Chapter 11

The empathic self: going other, going different

Perhaps what we need is not only myth but also performance. In this respect, Anna Deavere Smith offers an impressive theatrical perspective on racism. In an article with a title that employs the "under the skin" metaphor, the theater critic John Lahr interviews Smith and reviews *Twilight: Los Angeles, 1992*, a performance about the "Rodney King incident," the case in which several white policemen severely beat a black man, whom they had arrested. The beating of King was videotaped and then televised in slow, blow-by-blow motion. When a first trial resulted in an acquittal of the policemen on charges of brutality, Los Angeles erupted in a riot of protest and vengeance. (A second trial eventually resulted in the conviction of two of the white policemen for violations of the civil rights of King.) Black men beat white men—among them, Reginald Denny. (Four black men also rescued Denny.) As with the beating of King, the beating of Denny was videotaped and televised.

In performance, Smith tries to get under the skin of the audience. Lahr reports that in a note to one of the dramaturges of *Twilight* she says that it is essential "that whites in the audience find points of identification." Smith does not mean only that whites must identify with blacks or other "people of color." In addition, she means that they must empathize, at least at some points, with themselves. ("Points of empathy *with themselves*," she emphasizes.) She does not want to produce "a situation where they merely empathize with those less fortunate than themselves." Smith wants to induce them to empathize with themselves—that is, with those who are more fortunate than others. She thus advocates a theater that addresses the politics of privilege: "My political problem is this: Privilege is often masked, hidden, guarded." In psychoanalytic terms, what is privileged is repressed. Privilege is unconscious. "This guarded, fortressed privilege," Smith says, is exactly what has led us to the catastrophe of non-dialogue in which we find ourselves." What Smith means is not "economic privilege" but the psychological privilege of a certain skin color. "I'm talking," she says, "about the basic *privilege* of white skin" (Lahr 1993, 28 June: 90).

To prepare *Twilight*, Smith audiotaped reactions of various individuals to the Rodney King incident, the riot, and the trials. The technology of the tape recorder enabled her to get under the skin of these individuals and to empathize with them. Lahr describes how Smith utilizes the tape recorder psychologically: "In rehearsal, with earphones on, she literally lets the characters take her over, playing back their words until images and gestures emerge from the rhythms." She derives bardic inspiration from Shakespeare. "As a student learning Shakespeare," she says, "I became fascinated with how the spoken word works in relationship to a person's psychology." Smith speaks the words of the persons whom she has audiotaped, mimics them, in an attempt to empathize with them. There is a collective as well as a personal aspect to the performance. "In Shakespeare," she notes, "the words held not just the psyche of the person but also the psyche of the time"—or a *Zeitgeist* (Lahr 1993, 28 June: 90).

Before Shakespeare, however, there was Smith's grandfather. "My grandfather," she says, "told me that if you say a word often enough, it becomes you." This remark evidently had a profound impact on Smith, who developed an interest in how the spoken word has "a spiritual power." She realized how language provides access to the other. The spoken word is a way "to know who somebody is, not from what they tell me, but from *how* they tell me." The effect is first physical, then psychical. Speaking the words of the other, Smith says, "will make an impression on my body and eventually on my psyche." She does not "understand" so much as "feel" the impression. In contrast to Jung and Cardinal, who describe their panic attacks at the prospect of "going black" as an impulsive, involuntary possession by the other, Smith describes her objective in "going other" as a voluntary, quite deliberate possession: "My goal would be to—these kinds of words are funny and probably, in print they sound even worse—become possessed, so to speak, of the person." Thus Smith defines "acting" as "becoming the other"— or being possessed of the other (Martin 1993: 51).

In Smith's very first acting class, the teacher required the students to select any fourteen lines of Shakespeare and say them "over and over again to see what happened." What happened to Smith was that she had "some kind of transcendental experience." She was "terrified, mystified" by the experience (but apparently not panicked, like Jung and Cardinal). In an effort to have the experience again, she "kept exploring what language was." In this exploration, she tried to formulate an explanation of the experience by recourse to the memory of what her grandfather had said. "I remembered what my grandfather told me because it's one of those experiences that is so peculiar you have to try to explain it to somebody," Smith says. "What happened to me? Was I crazy? What was it? It sounds really interesting but nobody can name it, so it's your quest"

(Martin 1993: 56). In acting, in speaking the words of the other, in becoming the other, in going other, had Smith temporarily gone insane? She had had, as she says, a transcendental experience—at least in the sense that she had transcended herself through the language of the other.

Smith entitled the performance *Twilight* after the nickname, or "tag," of Twilight Bey, who helped arrange a truce between gangs in Los Angeles. Bey chose the nickname to signify the psyche of the time in which he exists, what he calls the "limbo" between day and night, night and day, in reference to the truce that the gangs regarded as both "before your time" and "before its time" (Lahr 1993: 92). In the Christian tradition, "limbo" is an in-between, liminal place. The souls of individuals who are confined to limbo have not been condemned to hell. They are simply barred from heaven because they have not been baptized. In this sense, limbo is an intermediate or transitional space. As Smith quotes Bey, he defines "limbo" not religiously but psychologically:

> So sometimes I feel as though I'm stuck in limbo
> the way the sun is stuck between night and day
> in the twilight hours.
> Nighttime is like a lack of sun,
> but I don't affiliate darkness with anything negative.
> I affiliate darkness with what came first,
> because it was first,
> and relative to my complexion,
> I am a dark individual
> and with me being stuck in limbo
> I see the darkness as myself.
> And I see the light as the knowledge and the wisdom of the
>   world, and the understanding of others.
> And I know
> that in order for me to be a full human being
> I cannot dwell forever in darkness
> I cannot dwell forever in idea
> of identifying with those like me
> and understanding only me and mine.
>
> (1994: xxvi)

Psychically, Bey is in a twilight state between a metaphorical hell and heaven. In psychoanalytic terms, this place is a transitional space tantamount to what D.W. Winnicott calls "an intermediate area of experience" (1971: 13), or "potential space" (1971: 100)—a zone between subject and object, between internal and external, between me (or, as Bey says, "me and mine") and not-me. For the self, according to Bey, the way out of limbo is through empathy with the other.

This psychical limbo is a "racial" (or ethnic) boundary between white and black, light and dark. Smith acknowledges that, for artists, "boundaries of ethnicity" can produce "brilliant work." Such boundaries "provide safer places," supportive spaces. "In some cases," Smith says, "it's very exciting to work with like-minded people in similar fields of interest." (She also means, I believe, "like-colored" people.) "In other cases," she notes, "these boundaries have been crucial to the development of identity and the only conceivable response to a popular culture and a mainstream that denied the possibility of the development of identity." In addition to the benefits of boundaries, however, "the price we pay is that few of us can really look at the story of race in its complexity and its scope." There is an alternative, Smith suggests, to "racial" boundaries: "If we were able to move more frequently beyond these boundaries, we would develop multifaceted identities" (1994: xxv). In contrast to the unifaceted identity of "race" (or ethnicity), Smith advocates a multifaceted identity, a self that, through empathy, is able to experience what the other experiences.

A DREAM: HAVING ONE'S HEAD SHAVED AND OPERATED ON

As in psychoanalysis, sleeping, dreaming, and waking are important images for Smith. For example, when she interviews Reginald Denny about racism, he reacts, "I just want people to wake up." Racism, in this sense, is sleeping, or being unconscious. In order to become conscious, it is necessary to wake up—and to interpret dreams. Smith recounts one of her own dreams:

> *In her dream, Smith went into a hospital room, where she was alone with a Japanese man whose head was shaved and who had a perpendicular incision on the front of his forehead. She realized that the man didn't know what had happened to him and was terrified.*

In interpreting her dream, Smith associates it with Denny, who was also in a hospital room, with an injury to his head, and who did not know what had happened to him:

> "This is the place where I relate to Reginald Denny," she said of the dream. "It's a very terrifying place, to tell you the truth. It's a place that has to do—it's very, very deep—with coming into consciousness. Of the *terror* of coming into consciousness, whatever that consciousness is. So, for me, my point of connection with Denny is when he's in the hospital, not knowing who's there and having to put together why he's there." Smith's eyes shone suddenly with tears. Her voice cracked. "I guess that's what makes me so sad about America. I know we haven't yet come to consciousness. To me, there is something *very, very* dark and *very, very* disturbing about the inevitability of having to wake up

after this *horrible, horrible* accident, which is racism. The only way to
master this fear of coming into consciousness is by coming into the
consciousness of others, mimicking how other people did it, because
it's terrifying to come into my own."

(Lahr 1993: 94)

It is through "other-consciousness" that Smith attains "self-con-
sciousness."

In her dream, Smith, an African-American woman, visits a Japanese
man, a man of another "race." Why a Japanese man rather than a white
American man, rather than, say, Denny? Perhaps it is because of a
number of derogatory comments by Japanese about African-Americans
(and other "minority groups"). A remark about the relative intelligence
and literacy levels of Japanese and Americans was perhaps the most
offensive of these, because it was uttered by the then Prime Minister of
Japan. At a September 22, 1986, meeting of the Liberal Democratic Party,
Yashiro Nakasone invidiously contrasted Americans and Japanese on the
basis of the "racial" composition of the two countries. The implication
was that if America was as "racially" homogeneous and unicultural as
Japan—that is, if America was "pure" white—it would be as intelligent
and literate a country as Japan. According to Nakasone, it is minorities—
not only African-Americans but also Latin-Americans—who lower the
general intelligence and literacy level of Americans. "In America," Nakasone said, "because all those blacks, Puerto Ricans, and Mexicans are
included, they're far and away lower" (Treece 1986, 13 October: 66). Two
years later, in 1988, Michio Watanabe, another prominent member of the
Liberal Democratic Party, asserted that African-Americans are less fis-
cally responsible than Japanese. In Japan, he said, a family would commit
hari-kiri rather than remain in debt, but in America, "where credit cards
are much in use, a lot of blacks, and so on, think, 'We're bankrupt. We
don't have to pay anything starting tomorrow' " (Greenwald 1988, 15
August: 25). Like other African-Americans, Smith is surely well aware of
such instances of Japanese racism. In this respect, the Japanese man in
her dream may epitomize for Smith not only the "racial" other but also
the racist other—who, in coming to consciousness after an operation
on the forehead, also enables Smith herself, through empathy with the
other, to come to consciousness.

Jung asserts that the forehead is symbolically "the seat of the highest
form of consciousness" (1976 1: 67). The image of the forehead "indicates
the seat of thought, of supreme consciousness, and when anything happens
there it shows that it has to do with the process of individuation, because
supreme consciousness and individuation are identical." As Jung amplifies
the image, he observes that in Buddhism the forehead is a symbol of
transformation—of the possibility of a metaphorical rebirth: "The statues

of the Buddha, for instance, always have a certain sign on the forehead; it is the sign of the man with awakened consciousness, the man who is twice-born, who has undergone initiation" (1976 1: 75). To be "asleep" and to "wake up," to "die" and to be "born again," is to be transformed symbolically—to be initiated, or individuated. The sign on the forehead of the Japanese man is not just any sign. In this case, initiation, or individuation, involves an incision: a surgical procedure on the seat of thought, the seat of supreme consciousness.

Smith acknowledges that she is terrified, like the Japanese man—and like Denny—of waking up, of becoming conscious. The racist unconscious is, Smith says, deep and dark. Her dream implies that psychosurgery, rather than psychoanalysis, is necessary—but this need not be, in this case, a lobotomy. The incision in the forehead, through the skull, into the brain, may be a procedure to treat and cure the racism of the mind. Something is apparently wrong with the head of the Japanese man. He may be wrong-headed, or brain-damaged, but presumably he is not brain-dead (unless brain-death is a necessary metaphorical prelude to brain-rebirth). The head of the Japanese man is shaved. If, from a Jungian perspective, hair is often a metaphor for thoughts, the implication of hairlessness is thoughtlessness—another image of unconsciousness. It is also, however, an image of a possible transformation of consciousness. "Since olden times," Jung remarks, "shaving the head has been associated with consecration, that is, with spiritual transformation or initiation." The shaved head, he says, is another image of a metaphorical rebirth, for it evokes the image of "a new-born babe (neophyte, *quasimodogenitus*) with a hairless head." Jung, who had his own dream of an inner, African-American barber, states: "The custom of tonsure, which is derived from these primitive ideas, naturally presupposes the presence of a ritual barber" (*CW* 11: 228–9, para. 348). The implication is that the operation on the Japanese man is an initiation, or individuation, ritual.

THE UNCONSCIOUS AS CONCUSSION AND COMA

In contrast to van der Post, who equates becoming conscious with "going white," Smith equates becoming conscious with "going other," or empathizing with the other. The terror of becoming conscious is not, for Smith, a fear of losing id and gaining ego. It is the fear of realizing just how deep and dark racism—or what she calls the basic privilege of white skin (or perhaps, as with the Japanese man, the privilege of any other color than black skin)—really is. It is the fear of becoming conscious of what has happened to us, who is there in the hospital with us, and why we are there. From a phenomenological perspective, the hospital is an especially significant image. We are in the hospital because we are sick. The implication is that to be unconscious of racism is to be ill—in this case, mentally ill. To get well is to become conscious of racism. Essentially, we are hospitalized in order to be treated and cured. Like Denny, we have been injured, hurt, wounded by racism and need to be healed of it. The unconsciousness of racism is not the unconsciousness of sleep or dream but the unconsciousness of coma, or amnesia. To be in a coma is to be absolutely, not relatively, unconscious.

As the Associated Press reports the testimony of Denny in the trial of Damian Williams and Henry Watson, the two black men accused of attempting to murder him, the last thing that Denny remembered was turning to look when the right window of his truck was suddenly shattered. He did not remember "being pulled out of his big-rig gravel truck, being kicked and beaten or being hit over the head with a hammer." Nor did he remember "waking up six days later at Daniel Freeman Memorial Hospital without being able to see or talk" (1993, 26 August: A, 17). In this respect, the image of Denny in the hospital with a traumatic concussion serves us all as a drastic metaphor for just how extreme racism in America is. America is metaphorically comatose, or amnesiac, about racism.

Waking up from coma is qualitatively, radically different from waking up from sleep or dream. It is an abrupt transition that terrifies because it bewilders: we do not know who we are, what we are, where we are, why we are, or how we are. Personally and collectively, we are still stuck in the liminality of limbo, the zone that Smith calls twilight, between night and day, between black and white, between unconscious and conscious—which, in the image of the heads of the Japanese man and Denny, is perhaps, as Bey says, ahead of our time, ahead of its time. In *Twilight*, Smith implies that what we need is not a war between gangs in Los Angeles—or between "races" in America—but a truce, if not a peace.

Like psychoanalysis, which is a talking cure, Smith emphasizes language, the spoken word—but with a decisive difference. What is original with Smith is the performative dimension of the linguistic monologue. In order to empathize with the other, she embodies and enacts the other, bodies forth and acts out the other. She audiotapes the words that the other speaks and then, through monological mimicry, speaks those same words herself, verbatim. It is this physical, theatrical vocalization that renders authentic the psychical reality of the other. (The monological mimicry that Smith performs is different from the strategic, colonial mimicry that Bhabha discusses. It is also different from the unconscious influence, the contagious, or infectious, transmission or communication, that Jung describes between self and other.) Smith becomes conscious of the other at the very moment that she speaks the words of the other with such dramatic exactitude and precision. The result of this physicality and theatricality is an eloquently curative articulation of the unconscious racism that afflicts America. Through monologue Smith would establish a dialogue between self and other. This is the distinctive contribution of Smith to the prospects for an authentically multicultural psychoanalysis. In effect, Smith offers psychoanalysis a novel method that could serve it as a model of empathy with the "racial" (or even racist) other.

IDENTIFICATION, IMITATION, AND EMPATHY

In psychoanalysis, "empathy" is not, as with Smith, a synonym for "identification," although Freud does acknowledge that there is a relation between empathy and identification. In discussing "the problem of identification," Freud suspects that he encounters "the process which psychology calls 'empathy [*Einfuhlung*]' and which plays the largest part in our understanding of what is inherently foreign to our ego in other people." What most interests Freud are "the immediate emotional effects of identification." As a result, he does not discuss empathy, which he apparently considers a strictly "intellectual" aspect of identification (*SE* 18: 108). If he were to attempt a "more fundamental and comprehensive psychological analysis" of identification, he would have to address the issue of empathy. "A path," Freud says, "leads from identification by way of imitation to empathy, that is, to the comprehension of the mechanism by which we are enabled to take up any attitude at all towards another mental life" (*SE* 18: 110n.).

It is Kohut who has most insistently emphasized empathy in psychoanalysis. Kohut defines "empathy" in relation to the other. Empathy is the way "we think ourselves into his place." It is a process of "vicarious introspection" (1978: 207). Here, Kohut, like Freud, describes empathy as an intellectual process, not an emotional process by which we "feel" ourselves into the other's place. Elsewhere, however, Kohut describes it as "the capacity to think and feel oneself into the inner life of another person" (1984: 82). In this account of psychoanalytic epistemology, Kohut says that empathy is what enables us to know "what the inner life of man is, what we ourselves and what others think and feel" (1977: 306). Like Smith, Kohut notes that we may empathize not only with others but also with ourselves. Many analysts erroneously regard empathy merely as a way of feeling what the other is feeling. Kohut, however, maintains that it is also a way of thinking what the other is thinking. As Joseph D. Lichtenberg says, empathy has, simultaneously, both a cognitive and an affective dimension. Empathy enables us to know the other's "whole experiential state," the other's intellectual as well as emotional state (Lichtenberg 1984 2: 116).

It is easier, Kohut says, to empathize with people culturally similar to ourselves, more difficult but not impossible to empathize with people culturally different from ourselves:

Our psychological understanding is most easily achieved when we observe people of our own cultural background. Their movements, verbal behavior, desires, and sensitivities are similar to our own, and we are enabled to empathize with them on the basis of clues that may seem insignificant to people from a different background. Yet even when we observe people from a different background whose experience is unlike our own, we usually trust that we will be able to understand them psychologically through the discovery of some common experiences with which we can empathize.

(1978: 210)

Kohut does not say that it is a common nature (or "human nature") that enables the self to empathize with the other. (He simply does not address this issue. For example, he does not, as Jung does, suggest that the self "goes other" because "under the skin" self and other are archetypally the same, or typically human.) According to Kohut, what enables the self to empathize with the other, however culturally different the other may be, are "common experiences."

This account seems to me to beg an absolutely crucial question about the relation between self and other. Kohut says that we "trust" that we are able to empathize with an other who is culturally different (perhaps even radically different) from ourselves in spite of this difference, because of a commonality of experience. That is, he does not offer an explanation of how we might empathize with cultural difference, how we might think and feel ourselves into an other's place that might be very different from our own cultural place. In fact, Kohut contends that empathy is undependable when we encounter an other who is quite different from ourselves: "The reliability of our empathy, a major instrument of psychoanalytic observation, declines the more dissimilar the observed is to the observer" (1971: 37). Kohut seems to assume that the self just "is" either similar to or different from the other. I would emphasize that the self who is different from the other may "become" similar to the other.

If similarity is, indeed, the basis of empathy, then how does the self become similar to the other—or at least similar enough to be empathic with the other? The self may do so directly through experience (we may have a different experience than we have ever had, a similar or even the very same experience that the other has had), or the self may do so indirectly through the imitation of a different experience. Freud suggests that identification leads through imitation to empathy. When we identify with the other, we then begin to imitate the other—and finally to empathize with the other. What is absent from the account that Kohut provides of empathy is any description of the process of "imitation." In contrast to Kohut, who believes that we "think" and "feel" ourselves into the other's place by vicarious introspection, Smith evidently believes that we "act" ourselves into the other's place by imitation. That is, we achieve empathy performatively.

Although there is a historical connection between psychoanalysis and theater in the notion of "catharsis" as cure (not to mention the centrality of Sophocles' *Oedipus Rex* to Freud's theory and practice and the emphasis on hysterical, or histrionic, symptomatology), psychoanalysis is not an "acting cure." In fact, "acting" has tended to be equated pejoratively with "acting out." There are exceptions to this rule, perhaps most notably the "character analysis" of Wilhelm Reich, who emphasizes "the total behavior" of the patient. From this perspective, psychoanalytic material appropriately includes behavioral form as well as verbal content. How patients act is just as important as what they say. Reich asserts "that the behavior of the patient, his look, his manner of speech, facial expression, dress, handclasp, etc.," are factors of decisive significance (1949: 29). Other varieties of psychotherapy have, of course, adapted and applied theatrical techniques, often effectively. It is in the "gestalt therapy" of Frederick S. Perls that acting assumes quite special significance. Previously a Freudian analyst, Perls repudiates psychoanalysis (which he describes as an interpretative, intellectual technique) in no uncertain terms. According to Perls, interpretation is merely a variety of intellectualization. For example, rather than interpret a dream intellectually, he insists that the dreamer perform it theatrically, or "act it out" (1992: 69). Psychoanalysis, however, has remained, for the most part, a strictly verbal, nonperformative talking cure. For both Reich and Perls, if there has been an "actor," it has been the patient, not the analyst. The analyst has merely been an "audience."

Should analysts be (are they already), in any sense, performers? If, according to Freud, identification leads through imitation to empathy, to a comprehension in the other of what is radically different from the self, or "foreign" to the ego, then the implication would seem to be that analysts should be, if not performers, at least "imitators." I do not mean that they should do what Alice Walker has Raye, the African-American psychoanalyst, do when she deliberately suffers a gum mutilation that imitates the genital mutilation of Tashi-Evelyn, who describes this deed as "the ritualization, or the acting out, of empathy." Such extreme measures seem to me quite unnecessary—and problematic. Such a position would suggest that, in order to be effective, all analysts would have to experience the same or very similar traumas that patients have experienced. Smith, however, does not suffer a beating in order to empathize with Rodney King and Reginald Denny. She merely imitates how they say what they say about it—and then she shares that imitation, in performance, with an audience, who then empathize with it.

TRANSPOSITION, INTERPRETATION, QUOTATION, AND CURE

Although some philosophers and psychologists who discuss empathy describe it as a process of "projection" (they say that we project ourselves into the other), it would be more accurate to say, as Dilthey does, that empathy is a process of "transposition" (1976: 226). Transposition is the very opposite of projection in the psychoanalytic sense. Psychoanalytically, when we project ourselves onto (or into) the other, we impose ourselves, what and how we think and feel, on the other. In contrast, when we transpose ourselves empathically into the other, we expose ourselves to what and how the other thinks and feels. What Kohut calls the other's "place" is, in this respect, the other's "position." When we empathize with others, we do not usurp the position of the other, but we do occupy it in an effort to think and feel from that position as the other does. Dilthey says that empathy, or transposition, requires mental flexibility rather than rigidity. Like Smith, he cites Shakespeare and provides a theatrical, performative example in which an actor speaks words to an audience. "A flexible mind, following his words, facial expressions and movements," Dilthey says, "can now experience something which lies outside any possibility in its real life" (1976: 227). It may be impossible directly to experience what the other has experienced, but through empathy we may indirectly experience it. We may, as Dilthey says, "follow" the experience. Both Smith and Freud suggest that in order to follow it, we must, in some sense, imitate it, perform it, act it.

However valuable a service Kohut may have provided in emphasizing empathy, it does not seem to me that he has offered an adequate psychoanalytic account of it. Not only does he never discuss imitation, not only does he never describe the process by which we empathize with the different rather than the similar, but also he never adequately addresses what is absolutely unique to psychoanalysis: the distinction between the conscious and the unconscious. Psychoanalysts do not just think and feel themselves into the inner lives, or psychical realities, of other persons. They purport to think and feel themselves into the unconscious of other persons. The existence of the unconscious, as well as the psychoanalytic theory of the unconscious, thus radically complicates the function of empathy in psychoanalytic practice.

Patients enter analysis precisely because they do not know exactly what they think and how they feel—or why. Nor, of course, does the analyst know, although, as Lacan says, the analyst is "the subject who is supposed to know" (1978: 232). The analyst is supposed to know in both senses of the word "supposed." Analysts are supposed to know by virtue of the theoretical and practical knowledge that they possess, and they are supposed by the patient to know (there is a supposition on the part of the patient that analysts possess this knowledge). In the process of analysis, the patient is disabused of this supposition, for the knowledge that has been initially supposed is only eventually obtained in the therapeutic dialogue between self and other.

How does the analyst obtain a knowledge of the unconscious of the patient, and then how does the patient obtain that knowledge? The patient speaks a certain way, a characteristic way, and how he says what he says has unconscious implications. With what Theodor Reik (1949) calls a "third ear," analysts hear this "how" and "what"—but they also do something else, something more. As they listen, they silently formulate an interpretation, a psychoanalytic explication of the unconscious implications. They make explicit what is implicit, unconsciously so, in the speech of the patient. They may then offer this interpretation aloud to the patient. If they do so, the patient has an opportunity to accept it, reject it, or otherwise consider it. There are, of course, many other analytic interventions besides interpretations in the strict sense. In a certain sense, however, all interventions, even a verbatim quotation of the speech of the patient, are "interpretations," for no analyst ever quotes the entirety of what a patient says, exactly how the patient says it. Even the most apparently neutral, word-for-word quotation is a selection from the speech of the patient. The basis of this selectivity is some notion on the part of the analyst that those specific words are unconsciously significant and that the quotation of them will evoke in the patient that unconscious significance. In practice, the psychoanalytic theory of the unconscious mediates all interpretations, even all quotations, by the analyst.

If identification leads through imitation to empathy, then empathy leads through theory to interpretation—or to the unconscious. The patient speaks certain words to the analyst. The analyst, who identifies with the patient, not only hears these words with a "third ear" but also imitates them—that is, "speaks" these words, in silence, with what I would call a "second mouth." Then the analyst, with the aid of psychoanalytic theory, may selectively speak some of these words out loud to the patient, in a manner, perhaps a tone of voice, that demonstrates to the patient that the analyst has empathically comprehended what and how the patient thinks and feels unconsciously, so that the patient is then able empathically to know the unconscious implication. In this respect, both the patient and the analyst are, in turn, both actor and audience. The self performs for the other—and the other for the self.

Kohut provides an example of an empathic performance by an analyst. The analyst informed a patient about the cancellation of an appointment. At the next session, the patient was silent. Kohut says that the analyst, "in a warmly understanding tone of voice," interpreted the silence as an unconscious defense against extreme anger at the analyst (1984: 92). Kohut then mentions two other, alternative interpretations, which he regards as possibly equally valid. He asserts that *what* the analyst said is "of negligible importance" in comparison with *how* the analyst said it. The content of an interpretation may be wrong, he contends, but the interpretation may nevertheless still be right. What Kohut means is that the delivery of the interpretation demonstrates to the patient whether the analyst is empathic or not. He says that even if the analyst had merely said to the patient "you are deeply upset about the fact that one of your appointments was canceled," this utterance would have been an effective demonstration of empathy. (In this instance, the utterance is not a quotation but an interpretation. As the analyst interprets the silence of the patient, the cancellation of the appointment was, quite literally, a "disappointment.") Kohut does not say that the content of an interpretation is utterly irrelevant, but he does suggest that it is not decisive. According to Kohut, it is not the words that the analyst speaks but how the analyst speaks them that is crucial. He says that "the analyst could have spoken the same words" in such a manner that the patient would have continued to be silent. If the analyst "had failed to transmit her correct empathic perception of the patient's devastated state via her choice of words, the tone of her voice, and probably many other still poorly understood means of communication including bodily movements, subtle body odors, and the like," the patient would have remained taciturn and unresponsive (1984: 94).

It is not enough for the analyst merely to empathize with the patient. The analyst must also effectively demonstrate that empathy to the patient. There is thus a quite definite performative dimension to psychoanalysis. The analyst has to act empathic, not just think and feel or "be" empathic. (By "act" empathic, I do not mean that the analyst "pretends" to be empathic.) It seems to me that Kohut occasionally confuses the issue to the extent that he tends to conflate empathy with sympathy. In the example that he cites, he commends the analyst for a warm tone of voice. Although he does say that it is not enough for the analyst to be "warmhearted" (1984: 95), he seems, in this instance at least, to equate empathy with a demonstration of warmth toward the patient, or, I would say, sympathy for the patient. There is no necessary connection between warmth and empathy (although there may be between warmth and sympathy). The effective demonstration of empathy requires only that the analyst accurately act—that is, imitate (as Smith does in performance)—what and how the patient unconsciously thinks and feels.

Empathy is not a talent but a skill that an analyst develops and applies. It is not an aptitude or just an attitude. It is a method that an analyst may employ. Empathy, as such, Kohut emphasizes, is not curative. It is a necessary but not sufficient condition for a cure. According to Kohut, a cure occurs by analyzing defense, analyzing transference, and establishing "empathy between self and selfobject" (1984: 66)—or, as I would say, between self and other. Although Kohut discusses analyzing defense, analyzing transference, and establishing empathy in psychoanalysis as if they were in a sequential relation, with empathy the final term in a series, it seems to me that the capacity for empathy on the part of both analyst and patient is the prerequisite, the *sine qua non*, for an effective interpretation of defense and transference.

Empathy is of general importance in psychoanalysis, but it is also of quite particular importance when there is little or no common cultural experience between analyst and patient. When analyst and patient are "racially" or ethnically different, it is not enough for the self simply to be "sensitive" to the other. The self must be genuinely empathic with the other. In this case, empathy does not entail a denial of difference—by an appeal, for example, to a common "human nature." Rather, it requires an effort on the part of the analyst to obtain an experience of that "racial" or ethnic difference (and the unconscious implications of it) not through vicarious introspection but through a transpositional imitation of it and a performative demonstration to the patient. Because there is no necessary connection between "race" (or ostensibly significant physical differences such as skin color) and ethnicity, it is a potentially grave error for an analyst immediately to presume, for example, that a patient of a different color is culturally different—or psychically different—in any significant sense. Whether that is so remains to be seen and can only become known in the course of analysis, in the therapeutic dialogue between self and other. Appearances such as skin color can be grossly deceptive. To the extent that collective issues of "race" and racism have affected, perhaps even traumatized, individual patients, to the extent that "raciality" is an important unconscious concern of a patient, an analyst of a different "race" or color from the patient may need to make a special effort to be empathic, to know what and how the other is thinking and feeling.

Chapter 12

Case material, "race" material

I now wish to present some case material from four patients for whom "race," specifically in the white–black sense, was a significant concern. This is material that emerged in the course of the therapeutic dialogue. Although the material may have arisen, in part, as a result either of transference or of interaction between therapist and patient, I did not actively—consciously and deliberately—solicit the material. Although I happen to believe that "race" is a significant issue for more patients than therapists have historically appreciated, I do not believe that therapists should probe for such material from patients. I merely believe that therapists should attend to it and respond to it, seriously, if and when patients speak about it.

In this respect, therapeutic interviews differ radically from, for example, journalistic interviews. A journalist like Terkel (1992) may interview blacks and whites on what and how they think and feel about "race"— and the results may be valuable—but the process is very different from how a therapist "interviews" patients. Patients may disclose to the therapist information that they have never divulged to anyone else, even to those with whom they have had the most intimate relations. The confidence (in both senses of the word) that patients repose in the therapist is a trust that humbles every therapist. In addition, in contrast to a journalist, a therapist listens not only to what patients say but also for what they may mean unconsciously. Like any therapist with a psychoanalytic orientation, I observe the "basic rule," which is to invite (not require) the patient to say whatever comes to mind. For these four particular patients, "race" was one of many issues that came to mind. I would not say that it was the dominant issue for any of them, but it was for all of them an important issue. There was much more to these patients than I present. For me, they were not merely "cases," much less research projects. They were persons.

My intention is not to demonstrate a process of "cure" (much less of "individuation" in the Jungian sense). Nor is it to propose an original theory or to advocate a special technique. My aim is more modest. The presentation of this material will inevitably provide some indication of how I conduct therapy, but that is incidental to the primary purpose, which is to describe and document the "raciality" of the unconscious in four quite particular patients. Although I am a therapist with an interest in Jungian analysis, I am a pluralist who respects all of the schools of psychoanalytic thought. Each school affords a partial perspective on the psyche. None has a monopoly on the "truth" of the unconscious. If there is anything specifically "Jungian" about my presentation of material, it is that I emphasize the imagination: the "self-images" and "other-images" of these patients. What images do they employ? What fantasies do they compose? What psychical realities do they construct about "race"— especially about "self" and "other?" From this perspective, it is irrelevant whether a patient accurately remembers an *event* that actually occurred in external reality. What matters is how the patient continues to imagine an *experience* in psychical reality—and why. This capacity to imagine—and reimagine—experience is what I mean by the fantasy principle and, more specifically, the multicultural imagination. What interests me is the *imaginal* (not "imaginary," in the sense of "unreal") experience of the patient.

I do not offer myself as an example of how one ought to conduct therapy with patients for whom "race" is a significant issue. I intend to let these patients speak for themselves, as they spoke to me. Three of the patients happened to be "black"; one happened to be "white." What-ever the skin color happened to be, I did not assume that physical appearance had anything at all to do with the psychical reality of a particular patient or that "race" would become an issue between us. For me, there is a rule even more basic than the basic rule: assume nothing about what may be in the mind of the patient. In some cases, the therapist may be the first person of another "race" with whom the patient has ever had an opportunity to relate in a "non-racial," human way, not as a "type" but as a unique individual. In such cases, it is imperative for the therapist not unilaterally to "racialize" the therapy but simply to listen— and hear. If "race" happens to be a significant issue for patients, they will say so. Any assumption on the part of the therapist is a bias, and with patients who have experienced the trauma of "racial" prejudice, it is important for the therapist continuously to scrutinize any assumption, projection, countertransference, or interaction that may evoke or recapitu-late that traumatic experience.

Nor did I assume that when these particular patients spoke about "race" they were really speaking about—or alluding to—something else. I did not assume that "race" was merely a manifest content, a derivative of some other, more fundamental issue, a more "real" latent content. Nor did I assume that a concern with "race" as a collective social and political issue in adulthood was a derivative of some strictly personal psychical issue from childhood. A concern with "racial" conflict in adulthood may have very little, even nothing, to do with experiences of conflict in childhood. A patient may have had relatively nontraumatic experiences earlier in life and yet have had an extremely traumatic "racial" experience later in life. Finally, I did not take for granted that when these particular patients spoke about "race" they were really speaking only about them and me, either transferentially or interactionally. (I should perhaps note, with a certain caution, that the transferential or interactional assumption has, ironically, the same structure as a delusion of reference. Some therapists assume that many or most references by the patient to others are really nothing more than indirect references, or allusions, to the therapist. I do not share this indiscriminate assumption.)

Some therapists and patients believe that for therapy to be effective, the therapist and the patient should ideally be the same or at least very similar: for example, that female patients should work with female therapists or that black patients should work with black therapists. Whom the patient works with should, of course, always be the prerogative of the patient, and in certain cases it may make perfect sense for therapist and patient to be the same sex or same "race." As a clinical doctrine, however, this same-sex, same-'race" assumption is problematic on two counts. First, it is ultimately a sexist or racist assumption. There is no necessary connection between sex or "race" and the experiences of the patient and the therapist. Physical (anatomical or pigmentary) sameness is hardly a reliable indicator, or predictor, of psychical sameness. Second (and more importantly), if experiences of the other—encounters with (and perhaps conflicts with) the other—happen to be a significant issue for a patient, then a therapist with different experiences may enable the patient to address that issue even more effectively than a therapist with the same or similar experiences. Such a therapist must, however, be truly empathic, be able through imitation and transposition to know what and how the patient thinks and feels—and be able to demonstrate that to the patient.

Therapists who are general practitioners do already as a matter of course work with difference—with a variety of patients who have a variety of psychical realities. Such therapists work with patients of different sexes, "races" (or ethnicities), nationalities, ages, generations, sexual orientations, gender identifications, educations, occupations, social and economic classes, preferences, values, styles, and experiences. All of these factors converge in one, unique individual. The possibilities are virtually infinite. It is even arguable that if psychical differentiation (as well as psychical integration) is the therapeutic objective, then the more difference between therapist and patient, the better. Sameness between therapist and patient may be a defense against a decisive encounter with difference and against an opportunity for psychical differentiation. Therapy may be a success not in spite of difference but because of it.

As a result of racism, all blacks and all whites have color complexes—unconscious feeling-toned sets of ideas about skin color. There is indubitably a collective, stereotypical dimension to these color complexes. For example, a word association experiment that included "boy" would, in all probability, tend to elicit quite different reactions from whites and blacks, especially black men. To speak of *the* color complex of whites or *the* color complex of blacks, however, is to indulge in projective typification. There is not just one collective "white complex" about blacks or one collective "black complex" about whites. The collective, stereotypical dimension does exist. Such factors as history, culture, and ethnicity do influence—or inflect—individuals, but the experience of the individual is not reducible to these factors. The experience of the individual is not *sui generis*, but it is distinctive.

From a Jungian perspective, to the extent that individuals are unconsciously (and uncritically) identified with the collective dimension, they are undifferentiated. In such cases, a particular color complex of an individual would approximate the general color complex of a group. In this state of identification and undifferentiation, an individual mind would approximate what William McDougall calls "the group mind." According to McDougall, who does not so much as mention Jung, the group mind is synonymous with the collective psyche. He emphasizes that it does not mean "some mental entity that exists over and above all individuals comprised in the group and that might continue to exist though all the individual members ceased to exist" (1939: xiii). It is "not because minds have much in common with one another" that McDougall speaks of the group mind "but because the group as such is more than the sum of the individuals." The group mind is a whole that is more than the sum of the parts, and holistically the group mind "profoundly modifies the lives of the individuals" (1939: 12–13).

A Jungian perspective would acknowledge the existence and the influence of the group mind (or the collective psyche), but the purpose of therapy would be to enable the patient to disidentify and differentiate—and then to relate to the collective dimension in a conscious (and critical) way. The objective would be a relation other than identification between the personal dimension and the collective dimension. (Jungians seem to define "identification" more absolutely than Freudians do and to regard it more negatively. For Jungians, the patient should always be *related to* the other but never *identified with* the other.) I would emphasize, again, however, that the presentation of case material in this instance is not a demonstration of how I conduct therapy or how a Jungian might conduct it but a description and documentation of how four particular patients experienced—and imagined—the issue of "race" in the white–black sense.

THE CASE OF "WILLIAM"

"William" was a 41–year-old African-American. He was in recovery from many years of a heroin addiction and other substance abuse but was now HIV-positive. He had had a variety of therapeutic experience—from one-day-at-a-time, twelve-step "anonymous" programs to religious counselors whom he described as "spiritual advisors." He was exceptionally, eclectically knowledgeable about and autodidactically conversant with several different therapeutic traditions and persuasions. In particular, I recall one occasion when he had an extreme T-cell deficiency and I visited him at a hospital that predominantly serves African-Americans. He was on the AIDS ward. All of the other patients around him on the unit were, like him, black men. He had been reading a book, he said proudly, and then produced from the drawer of a table beside the bed *The Portable Jung* (Campbell 1971). William could expatiate as eloquently as any Jungian on the "inner this" and the "inner that"—including what I would call the "inner racist."

One of the symptoms that had afflicted William for many years, long before he became HIV-positive, was an allergy. One dermatologist had finally said to him, in exasperation, "You're just an allergic guy." William was allergic in more ways than one. I do not mean to suggest that the allergy was psychosomatic, although it may, of course, have been that, too. It was, however, much more than a literal, physical disease. For William, the allergy served a metaphorical, psychical purpose. It was both a symptom of a fundamental discomfort with life and world and a defense against what he experienced as toxic, even potentially fatal, external influences. He was, he said, allergic to the "environment," by which he meant, at least unconsciously, not only the natural and technological environment but also the social environment—including the "racial" environment. In short, William was not immune to the virus of racism and the post-traumatic effects of it.

To suppress the impulse to scratch an insufferable itch, William applied a topical prescription of a cortizone preparation. To me, a white man, this black man said: "It's awful not to be comfortable in your own skin." The unconscious metaphorical—that is, "racial"—implications of this image in the transference–countertransference context were obvious. I, too, suddenly felt uncomfortable in my own, white skin, acutely conscious of the difference between it and William's black skin. The skin "wept," he said, whenever he smiled—as if the epidermis were an eye and the exudation tears. Even when he was apparently happy, the skin—or what Anzieu calls the "skin ego" (1989)—was always sad. William had also received ultraviolet radiation for the condition. "They burned off my skin," he said. "I got darker than I ever was. I was raw. All my flesh would come off. I'd get up in the morning, and all my flesh would be on the bed."

In the next session, William repeated, "All my skin fell off." Then, as if it was important to him for me to imagine him as he once was, as lighter than he now appeared, he said, "I'm not this dark." A Freudian might regard this remark as a fantastic attempt to fulfill a wish to be white, or at least lighter, rather than an effort to be appropriately realistic. A Jungian might regard the entire process as alchemy in reverse—as a negative, regressive symbol of transformation, with the light darkened rather than the dark lightened (or, metaphorically, "enlightened"), with material burned raw rather than raw material cooked. Well before Lévi-Strauss, Jung employed the image of the raw and the cooked as a symbol of transformation: "The unconscious seizes upon the cooking procedure as a symbol of creation, transformation. Things go in raw and come out new, transformed" (1984: 332). To William, however, the experience was an image of perdition, an infernal, eternal damnation. He imagined it not as a transformative shedding of skin—a metaphorical rebirth, or what Jung calls "the motif of rejuvenation by casting the skin" (*CW* 5: 364, para. 569)—but as a torturous skinning alive: a "redeath." For protection from the ultraviolet radiation, he had worn goggles. When he had finally removed them, "I had rings around my eyes," he said, "like a raccoon." (Although he laughed as he described the image, I silently noted the history of "coon" as a racist epithet.) "All it did was burn me," he said. "I was in hell. *That* was a *depression*."

William distrusted and refused AZT. "That shit can kill you," he said. There was an alternative, he declared, that could completely reverse the virus and render him HIV-negative. It was Immunex. "It's coming from Kenya," he said, "from Africa." Although he was a Christian, not a Muslim, he could obtain it from "the Nation of Islam—you know, the Reverend Louis Farrakhan." William imagined a miracle: where Western medicine had failed, non-Western medicine would succeed. There would be an Afrocentric cure. Etiologically, race and racism had caused (or occasioned) the condition. Because William had been "tired of being different," he had developed a heroin addiction—and had eventually contracted the virus. Substance abuse had been "an escape from being black in America." This was not, I would emphasize, an excuse; it was conduct for which he now accepted responsibility.

As William imagined the situation historically, blacks had been enslaved by whites, but after they were emancipated, they were too undisciplined. It was all a matter of "character" and "integrity," he said. In critical terms that would have been theoretically congenial to Freud, William reduced the issue to one word: "pleasure." He elaborated: "I've seen what my people have done since they got out of chains. Pursuit of gratification. I have practiced delaying gratification. Walk away from it,

suffer through that shit. I made the hard choice. I am not a *hedonist*."
That is, where the pleasure principle was, there the reality principle
(which, by definition, entails delay of gratification) shall be. This was, of
course, an emphatic assertion of the ego against the id.

With a previous therapist—like me, a white man—William had had an
experience when suddenly "everything went black." He had blacked out.
When William regained consciousness, the therapist had said, "Get real,"
and—sarcastically, for effect—"Whitey *this*, whitey *that*. I'm white, and I
love you." Through this black-out, whitey-love experience, William
believed that he had finally gone beyond hate—and beyond black and
white: "I was a black man. I went through what's between us, transcended
that."

What was between us—between William and the previous therapist
and between William and me—was oppositional imagining rather than
differential imagining. For William, the reimagination of self and others
was tantamount to a transvaluation of conventional colorist values, a
deconstruction of arbitrary racist constructs. I do not mean to suggest
that William transcended, in any ultimate sense, all that is, as he said,
"between" blacks and whites. He remained, to a quite considerable
extent, in incredulous anguish over the issue. "I was never warned about
racist society," he said. "I was always told, 'Everybody's the same.' Damn,
why didn't anybody tell me, prepare me—so I wouldn't be so vulnerable,
so hurt?" Everyone, of course, is not the same. Everyone is different—but
neither is everyone, every black one and every white one, the opposite. As
I have said, just as there is no "opposite sex," there is no "opposite race"
or "opposite color." William may not have completely transcended these
spurious oppositions, but he did contemplate and appreciate a number of
new, emergent imaginative possibilities. The differential reimagining that
emerged in William would seem to pose the possibility of an authentic
alternative to the white–black opposition and superior–inferior valuation
that perpetuate white supremacy. The emergence of a tendency in William
to go "beyond" the racial opposition that existed historically "between"
us was an example of what Jung calls "the transcendent function" (*CW*
8), the regulative principle that results in a compensatory, complementary,
or corrective conjunction of the unconscious with the conscious in order
to redress the partial, prejudicial conceits of the ego. According to Jung
(*CW* 6), the transcendent function is a mediatory, dialectical process by
which a synthesis may emerge from oppositions, from thesis and anti-
thesis—in this case, from white and black.

THE CASE OF "JOE"

"Joe" was a 35-year-old African-American/Native-American. He had
aspirations as a painter and as a singer (as a child he had performed at

a famous theater in Harlem; now as an adult he performed at clubs in Greenwich Village on open-microphone nights). He believed that it was only a matter of time until he would become a celebrity.

Joe said that he would "like to go back to the days of the Indians." He wished that he could "share in the rituals of my ancestors." He was part-Cherokee, part-Apache, he said—Lakota or Cheyenne. He had another name besides Joe—a Native-American name: "Sunbeam." He described the qualities intrinsic to the image. "A sunbeam," he said, "helps things grow. It brightens the planet. It gives light and heat, warmth and color. The sun's a big ball of gas out there, but it has a lot of different properties that help you grow. Without it, you would freeze up. It could blow up the planet, if it went into a supernova. 'Sunbeam' means happiness, joyfulness. It means more than any other name I could find." For Joe, his name was a perfect, metaphorical expression of his identity, a sunny, beaming disposition: a self-image with many positive, radiant qualities (and at least one potentially negative, explosive quality). "The Indians," he said, "really knew how to use names." Jung says that libido, or psychical energy, "symbolizes itself in the sun or personifies itself in figures of heroes with solar attributes" (*CW* 5: 202, para. 297). In just this way, Joe considered himself the very personification of the sun, which served him as a symbol of the heroic qualities with which he identified or to which he aspired.

Joe was a "mixture"—what he called, with two hyphens, a "Native-African-American." He waxed indignant about the history of white–red relations. The whites "did enough to the Indians—they should leave them alone." According to Joe, the colonists "brought laws, rules, and regulations but no respect for the people who were here." The colonists "should have asked if they could move in here." They should have said, "It's your land. How about sharing it with us?" Instead, they "made peace treaties that they knew they weren't going to keep." Joe continued: "When they made the nation, they didn't even include the Natives in the nation. They just killed them. The Indians had a wonderful civilization. They killed only what they needed to survive." It was not only Native-Americans but also African-Americans who had suffered. "The white man," Joe said, "has done horrible things to Natives and Africans. It's not right to suppress a culture." The prevalent version of historical events was selective and partial to whites: "They don't tell the real story, only what they want to hear." At that point in the session, I intervened and asked Joe how he felt about the fact that he now had a therapist who was a white man. He replied: "I don't blame anyone now for what happened hundreds of years ago. I only hold it against the people who did it, only those people, only that particular group."

Although Joe assured me that he did not consider me personally culpable and complicit, the images by which he characterized whites historically quite possibly implied a certain attitude and an unconscious communication in the transference–countertransference context. Had I already done enough to Joe? Should I leave him alone? Had I no respect for him? Had I made a therapeutic alliance that I knew I was not going to keep? Would it be peace or war between him and me? Would I include him, or would I, in effect, kill him? Would I do horrible things to him, suppress him? Would I hear the real story that he wanted to tell, or would I, like other whites, only tell him an unreal story that I wanted to hear?

Joe said proudly, "I grew up in multicultural conditions." He considered it a privilege that he had acquired in the familial context a special appreciation of pluralism, of unity-in-diversity. A favorite avocation for Joe was science fiction, and he now applied that interest to the issue of racism. Joe said: "The view of earth from outer space is: 'What's the problem?' Space people who may be watching us from other parts of the galaxy may be thinking, 'OK, we'll use it against them, we'll use their divisions, their racial conflicts, against them.' Racism could be a tool for invasion if we keep it going long enough. If there really is intelligent life out there, it may not want us to unify, to become one planet." In this scenario, Joe imagined an extra-terrestrial perspective on racism. This was not a delusional fantasy but what I would call a hypothetical fantasy. Joe hypothesized that space people would wonder why earth people should consider race to be a problem at all. To any truly intelligent life, racism would seem absurd. If the space people happened to be not friends but enemies, invaders with a divide-and-conquer attitude, intent on war rather than peace, then the racial conflicts of earth people would serve a very convenient, instrumentalist strategic and tactical purpose. For Joe, a global defense of planetary unification was the only hope.

This futuristic fantasy is an example of what Jung calls the "motif of an extra-terrestrial invasion" (*CW* 10: 315, para. 600). According to Jung, the image is a variation on the archetypal theme of cosmic intrusion—an alien intervention comparable to divine or demonic intervention, for good or evil purposes, in human affairs. Jung analyzes the rumors, rampant in the 1950s, of flying saucers and concludes that these unidentified objects are a collective projection into outer space of unknown contents from inner space, from the psyche. "In the threatening situation of the world today," he says, "when people are beginning to see that everything is at stake, the projection-creating fantasy soars beyond the realm of earthly organizations and powers into the heavens, into interstellar space, where the rulers of human fate, the gods, once had their abode in the planets" (*CW* 10: 320, para. 610). This collective projection continues in the 1990s at the SETI Institute (the Search for Extra-Terrestrial Intelligence Institute), which employs radiotelescopes in an effort to discover evidence of the existence of "intelligent life elsewhere in the universe," on planets in orbit around a thousand stars similar to the sun (Wilford 1994, 25 January: C, 5).

What was distinctive about Joe was the psychically integrative—or "racially" integrationist—purpose that the projection served. It was inconceivable to him that space people could possibly be as unintelligent—as stupid or ignorant—as earth people, especially on the issue of "race." From an extra-terrestrial perspective, space people would be able to observe, from a distance, more objectively than earth people the "racial" situation, so divisive, so conflictual—and, if they were intent on invasion and conquest (or perhaps colonization), as whites had been historically, they would be in a position to do to all of us what some of us have already done to others of us.

THE CASE OF "BOB"

"Bob" was a 35-year-old white man, an artist. The issue that concerned him most was the effort to establish a relationship with what he called "the ideal woman," or "the perfect woman." He acknowledged that he had an idealistic, perfectionistic attitude in general, not only toward women in particular. Bob had no prior knowledge of the concept of the "anima," which Jung defines as the archetype of the unconscious feminine, which is personified in the psychical reality of a man and is then projected as an image onto a woman (or women) in external reality. Jung describes the projection by a man of "the feminine personification of the unconscious onto an anima figure, i.e., a real woman, to whom he is as much bound as he is in reality to the contents of the unconscious" (*CW* 10: 378, para. 714).

When Bob entered therapy, he had a girlfriend, Susan, with whom he had had a relationship for three years. Bob was ambivalent about the relationship because Susan was not the ideal, or perfect, woman. Although they shared professional and social interests, she was not the physical type he preferred. She had white skin, blonde hair, small breasts, thin lips, and blue eyes. According to Bob, she was very pretty in a conventional sense, enough so that many other men envied him. The problem, he said, was "the basic attraction level." He wanted to say to Susan: "I'm not sure that physically you're the woman I want to marry." He said to me, "I'd like someone darker." He had always wanted a woman of "another race, another color." The problem of physical attraction had another effect. It diminished the sexual pleasure that he experienced with Susan, although there were occasional exceptions to the rule. "I *actually*," he reported in one session, as if it were an extraordinary event, "enjoyed making love to her." In the next session, he announced that he had telephoned a date-line service. He hoped to meet a woman "different from me" and have an "interracial" relationship.

Before Bob met Susan, he had had a relationship for five years with a black woman, Linda. Physically, she had seemed the ideal, or perfect, dark woman. Psychically, however, Linda had not been what Bob had initially imagined her to be. He had imagined that if "I looked at the exterior, I wouldn't have to look any further." He had projected onto Linda a "racial" type. She was a black woman, and he had imagined that all black women were secure, assertive, aggressive, and morally superior to white women, because they had historically suffered, struggled, and succeeded against so much adversity. Because of this historical experience, black women like Linda now had "the moral right to ask for things." Bob had imagined that "because I was connected to her, I could do the same." The connection would enable him, too, to ask for things from a morally righteous position. In this projective typification, Bob imagined that a variety of positive, advantageous qualities would accrue, vicariously, to him if he were in a relationship with a black woman. He acknowledged that he had wanted Linda to "carry" him so that he would not have to "change." When Linda had not been secure, assertive, aggressive, and morally superior—when she was not the ideal, or perfect, dark woman— Bob had ended the relationship. "When I first asked her out," he said, "I had the feeling that she was *strong*, that she would help *me*, but it wasn't so—it was almost the direct opposite."

In one session, I asked Bob to draw a picture of the ideal, or perfect, woman. It took him approximately thirty minutes to draw the picture. He used a pencil, and would draw, erase, and redraw. "Each line I draw," he said, "I want to keep changing because I see"—and then he paused. I asked, "See what?" He replied, "I see so many more ways to make it more beautiful." In drawing only one image, he realized that there were "so many more images that are beautiful." He commented: "It's surprising to see how my hand can change the image with just a few strokes. It's changing every time I put a line to it. The more control I have, the more defined it becomes, but there are all these other possibilities." Then he said, laughing: "I feel sort of stupid. There are *thousands* of possibilities in this one sheet of paper." He remarked that the image was "a flat, two-dimensional representation of a person." The image "doesn't represent all of the qualities *in* a person or *in* a woman." He concluded: "It's a phenomenal task for me to go around with an image in my mind, trying to match it to a person. A person can change so much every day. I almost feel as if I've been limiting myself to this picture, this person, each day." The picture that he had drawn was an image of a woman, head to waist, nude, with black skin, black hair, large breasts, thick lips, and brown eyes—in quite obvious physical opposition to Susan. This was an exercise in "active multicultural imagination."

In the next session, Bob said, "I'd like to go out and meet more women." At that point, I asked him a question: If he could go "in" and develop a relationship with the "feminine" aspect (or aspects) of the psyche, would he still be so intent on the pursuit of women in external reality? "Probably not," he replied. The effect of the exercise in active imagination, Bob reported, was that he had "lost a certain happiness, or hope, in fitting the ideal image." He had realized that "there might not be a perfect image of a woman out there totally to fulfill my needs." He had concluded that "everything isn't really up to me." He was now "uncertain whether even my own self-image is 'real.' " I asked him, "How do you feel about that?" He replied: "Good but uneasy. I feel that I have no reference point to go by." If an other-image could change, perhaps a self-image could, too.

As Jung describes active imagination, it is the deliberate induction of fantasy. The activation of images requires the individual to accept uncritically and observe objectively what emerges, in fantasy, from the unconscious. The technique necessitates a relaxation of the ego in the service of the imagination. The individual focuses on an image, which may be a picture that he has drawn or is drawing. Jung says that "when you concentrate on a mental picture, it begins to stir, the image becomes enriched by details, it moves and develops" (CW 18: 172, para. 398). It is the plasticity of the image that dynamically expresses the unconscious in process. Active imagination is a projective technique that elicits material that facilitates reimagination. The changes that occur spontaneously in the image as the individual contemplates it relativize the ego, disillusion it. The ego realizes that it, too, is only an image, one self-image among many possible self- and other-images, which it does not, cannot, totally control.

Thus Bob gradually began to comprehend that the idealistic, perfectionistic ego was not in totalistic control of the situation. When the ego tried to exert control over the image of the dark woman, tried to delineate it, the ego experienced the stupidity of such an effort. It was as if the very paper on which Bob drew contained a virtual infinity of incipient, imaginative possibilities that he could now begin seriously, if uncertainly, to entertain. Bob began to appreciate that external reality is an appearance onto which individuals project images (among them, the anima) from psychical reality, that a projection is a two-dimensional event with physical length and breadth but none of the psychical depth of three-dimensional experience, that an actual image is only one among many possible images, that images are not static but dynamic, and that idealism, or perfectionism, is an illusion with no future.

THE CASE OF "BARBARA"

"Barbara" was a 33-year-old African-American. She had graduated from a prestigious college where she had earned a degree in an academic discipline that had been at odds with her own creative inclination. Her family had wanted her to be a successful businesswoman. Subsequently, she had worked in retail sales for a major department store. She had resigned that position because she hated the job. She had then taken a battery of vocational tests, including the Myers-Briggs Type Indicator, which Isabel Briggs Myers (1990) based on the theory of psychological types that Jung developed (*CW* 6). Barbara had discovered that she was an introvert. She described the ideal job as one in which she could say, "Leave me alone and let me work and I'll have lunch with you if I feel like it." She said that she was happy to know that introversion, from a Jungian perspective, was not necessarily an abnormal or psychopathological condition or a schizoid defense but merely a personality type, a natural orientation.

"Racial" identity was an issue for Barbara—but not because she wanted it to be. She did not make it an issue; others, both black and white, did. Music was one area of interest in which the issue assumed prominence. When she was 12 years old, she had discovered rock and roll. She had known "only two other black women in my life who liked rock and roll." Her best friend "had never met anyone else who liked it." To her black friends, rock and roll was "white" music. For Barbara, it was "an uncomfortable experience not to be able to relate that way" with her black friends. Then she mentioned the song "Do You Believe in Magic?" in which the Lovin' Spoonful sing the line "It's like telling a stranger about rock and roll." When she tried to tell her black friends about rock and roll, it was like talking to strangers. She was glad that African-American musicians like Vernon Reid, the lead guitarist of Living Colour, had recently founded the Black Rock Coalition (1991) to emphasize that rock and roll was not just "white" music by Elvis Presley or the Beatles but also "black" music by Little Richard, Chuck Berry, James Brown, Jimi Hendrix, and contemporary musicians.

At college, Barbara had worked in the campus record store. Although she loved rock and roll, white students would "come in to buy the records and look right through me," as if she did not even exist. At a graduation party where she was a black girl among many white students, she had wanted to dance to the rock and roll music. She was with some white boys who had said, "We need a girl for that"—as if she was not a girl but only a "black" girl. She had bought a Tears for Fears album, which had given her the idea that through Jungian therapy "crying would get rid of my fears."

To her black friends, Barbara was an "Oreo," black on the outside but white on the inside. To her, that characterization seemed "so untrue, so unfair." She had recently argued with a white friend about rock and roll. They had been listening to an old song by the Beatles, and the friend had made a disparaging remark. To me, Barbara said, "I hate the

Beatles—actually, I just don't get it." The friend had said that the Beatles are the foundation of rock and roll. Barbara had responded: "What the fuck are you talking about? Black people invented rock and roll." Her friend, she said to me, "thinks I like these things because they're white, not because I like them—and it pisses me off." Barbara compared the feeling to what she had felt when she read a magazine article that had said that O.J. Simpson "was trying to be white, that he had even tried to learn to play golf"—as if golf (like rock and roll) was an exclusively "white" activity. "You can't be just a god-damned individual," she said. One of the things she liked about herself, she said, was that "I can be color-blind in some situations—not in all, not in most, but in *some*." Her ability to be color-blind came "from not trying to be something I'm *not* but from appreciating something for what it *is*."

Barbara then burst out laughing. I said, "Tell me what's funny." She said, "I was looking for a black feminist Jungian." She thought that that might be a contradiction in terms. Now she was in therapy with a white man—and the problem was that most white men "don't get it." How could I be empathic? How could I know what and how she was thinking and feeling? "Most of you are so complacent," she said. "I don't mean *you*, but you know what I mean." I asked, "What are we complacent about?" She said: "You don't have to see things from another point of view. You don't have to, you don't try. If you're not trying, you're not listening—and you know how I feel about not being listened to." I asked, "What is the most important thing that you feel I have difficulty understanding about your point of view?" She said: "You haven't had that difficulty. Any time you're just being 'white,' I won't hold it back. I'll let you know."

It was not only white men but also black men who had difficulty understanding Barbara. When she revealed how intelligent she was, some black men called her an "uppity nigger" or an "uppity bitch." She said to me, "I can't help it if I'm smart, I didn't choose to be intelligent." Her intelligence was also an issue in the workplace, with whites. Blacks had advised her: "Don't let these white people see how smart you are. They'll be intimidated."

Barbara felt an attraction for a certain type of white man who she felt would not like her because "I'm black and therefore not his type." Although she loved the type, she also hated the type—"mostly for being white, because he wouldn't feel that way if he wasn't white." Why, I asked, was the type for which she felt this attraction white? "You got me," she said, "I'm cursed, I guess. I don't know. Ask my hormones. White people project onto black people, and I don't feel that I should have to waste my time fighting stereotypes." The type was capable of "only seeing what's on the outside." I said, "You wish that he could see what is on the inside." Yes, she said. "What would he see?" I asked.

"Himself," she replied. Barbara then described the type by reference to actors: "He looks like Ed Harris. Ed Harris has a bad haircut these days. Other than that, he's really cute. If William Hurt wasn't such a jerk, he'd probably be my type. That balding WASP look. I don't know—it does something to me." She was in a quandary: "Black people think I'm weird, and white people don't want me."

For Barbara, there was one specific experience that symbolized the dilemma. In college, she had been an officer in a black student organization. At one meeting, three non-black students had voted with the black students on some motion under consideration. Some of the black students had objected to the participation by non-black students. A faction of black students prepared an amendment that only African-Americans could be members of the organization. Barbara had been sympathetic to the non-black students, who she felt "had not been content to live with their own ignorance." She also felt that to exclude non-blacks was "wrong, period," because general student fees funded the organization. When white journalists attended and interrupted the next meeting, the issue became volatile. In the days after the meeting, Barbara had had an experience that became a "defining moment" for her. Walking down the hall of a campus building, she had heard a group of white students talking. When she turned the corner and the white students saw her, they abruptly stopped talking. The moment was a traumatic shock of recognition for Barbara. She suddenly realized that "the first thing people see in me is 'black.' " To me, Barbara said: "I have never recovered from that moment. Before that, I was an individual. I had been working my butt off to defeat that amendment, but it didn't matter. I wasn't *me*; I was one of *them*. It was 'them' or 'us.' " I asked, "You were too much of an individual for them?" Barbara replied: "No, I was too much of an Oreo. Some are born black; some have blackness thrust upon them. Blackness in America is a 'condition.' It's not just a feature. You turn a corner, and you get your feelings terribly hurt. It rocked my whole world. The ground was torn out from under my feet. I was shocked." I asked Barbara whether she felt that she was an Oreo. "Maybe I'm not an Oreo—I'm just me," she said. "Maybe I'm closer to an Oreo than a fudge cookie, but I'm me. After that moment, I could never be just me. I'd have to convince people to look past their prejudices first, not judge a book by its cover. It's such a pain in the ass."

At the time Barbara was in therapy with me, O.J. Simpson was on trial. Shortly after the acquittal, I had a conversation with an African-American therapist who wondered how many of his patients would mention the topic. Barbara was one of my patients who immediately broached the subject. The first words that she uttered were about the different reactions of whites and blacks to the verdict. "When the O.J. thing came down," she said, "a black friend of mine who works in the personnel department of a brokerage house told me that when she went into the ladies room after lunch, there was a cluster of white people who were talking. As soon as she entered the room, they quieted down. She said that she had never felt so isolated in her life. All day long, whites avoided eye contact with her." Barbara compared that incident with her own traumatic experience at college: "My friend already 'knew' that she was black. I hadn't known before. The point of that moment for me was that it was the first time in my life that I realized that when people saw me coming, they saw 'black.' My friend will recover—she's probably recovered already. I haven't. It was a temporary state for her. It's permanent for me." It was incredible to Barbara that the mass media had emphasized that "blacks and whites live in different worlds." Why was this news to anyone in America? I said to her, "You live between those worlds." She exclaimed, "Yes! I guess I'm doomed to be uncomfortable. I just wish I weren't so lonely. I feel as if I don't belong anywhere. I don't belong with black people, and I don't belong with white people—but *they* wouldn't want me anyway, if I did."

When Barbara had mentioned to her white boyfriend how uncomfortable she felt, he had said, "You don't pass the 'blackness' test." She had replied, "And God forbid that I should pass the 'whiteness' test." I asked Barbara what it would mean for her to pass the "blackness" test. "I would identify unconsciously with black people," she said, "but I don't, you know. A lot of blacks feel that they have to be twice as good as white people to 'make it.' They have a built-in inferiority complex, but I don't feel it. I don't feel that I have to prove to anyone that I'm just as good as a white person. I just know that I'm as good, and I don't give a shit whether white people know that I'm good enough." Similarly, Barbara said, to pass the "whiteness" test would mean that she unconsciously identified with whites. "I don't know about that," she said, "because I believe that I identify with the dominant culture, which just happens to be 'white.' I accept a lot of things that the dominant culture puts forth. Then, of course, as you know, I don't identify with the dominant culture in a lot of areas."

Barbara then denounced the practice of capitalizing the words "Black" and "White." She said that the practice "annoys the hell out of me" and remarked that "you only find that in black magazines." I asked what was so annoying to her about it. "I figure that it's unnecessary—superfluous," she said. "It's a small form of self-aggrandizement for black people, who then feel that they have to do it for white people too—so that we're clear about the categories." To categorize people oppositionally as either "black" or "white" was bad enough. To capitalize the categories was worse.

For Barbara, identity should be entirely a function of individuality. In internal reality, she experienced herself as an individual. That psychical reality, or self-image, was not, however, the only reality that she encountered. She also experienced—and suffered—the projective typifications, or other-images, that both whites and blacks imposed on her. To whites, she was physically "black"; to blacks, she was culturally "white." To neither whites nor blacks was she the individual that she experienced herself to be—but only an Oreo, one color on the outside, another color on the inside. She was a black woman who loved music that most whites and blacks stereotype as white music, who loved white men of a certain type and also hated them when they were unable to see that, on the inside, she looked just like themselves, and who had her feelings terribly hurt when others were unable to see through the external appearances of collective, "racial" identity to the internal reality of individual identity—to the unique Barbara who was able, at least sometimes, to be a color-blind individual in a color-hypersensitive, racist America. Barbara refused to accept the color biases—and color categories—of either whites or blacks. In spite of these prejudices, she maintained an identity as an individual, an intelligent and creative woman, struggling and striving to encounter others, "white" or "black," who, including a therapist, might be capable of an empathic, "non-racial," human relationship with her.

"RACIAL" OR ETHNIC ISSUES IN PSYCHOTHERAPY

What are we to conclude about the multicultural imagination and the "raciality" of the unconscious from the cases of William, Joe, Bob, and Barbara? It would be presumptuous to generalize too ambitiously from only four examples: two "blacks," one "red-black," and one "white"; three men, one woman; all adults in their thirties or forties. "Patients" do constitute a select group. I do not mean that they are necessarily any more "neurotic" than anyone else. I mean that individuals who decide to enter therapy are perhaps more amenable to a candid encounter with the other and are perhaps less resistant to change. The very decision to enter therapy indicates that these individuals are ready, at least to a certain extent, to enter, in all candor, a dialogue with an "external other," the therapist and, more importantly, with that "internal other," the unconscious. What do William, Joe, Bob, and Barbara exemplify? Are they representative, or typical? All four patients, in distinctive ways, strove to transcend, integrate, actively reimagine, or refuse to accept the categorical opposition between self and other, between white and black (and, in the case of Joe, between white and red). They all defied the racist, oppositional logic that has historically conditioned "racial" relations and that has, so far, prevented or postponed the emergence of an authentically multicultural imagination.

Recently, Samuels has spoken of a "plural" psyche and a "political" psyche (1989, 1993). I now speak of a "racial" psyche, in the sense that

I believe that "racial" issues are a ubiquitous theme, both personally and collectively, in the psyche of individuals of whatever color. From the results of an international survey that Samuels conducted to determine the frequency with which patients mention social and political themes, 34 of 129 British Freudian analysts, 36 of 59 British Jungian analysts, 36 of 108 American Freudian analysts, and 6 of 47 American Jungian analysts listed "racial" or ethnic issues as a theme. That is, one-third of these British and American analysts reported that "racial" or ethnic issues were a theme. As Samuels interpreted the survey, which included responses from a number of other countries besides Britain and America and from therapists as well as analysts, "racial" or ethnic issues was the sixth most frequent social and political theme, behind, in order, gender issues for women, economic issues, violence in society, national politics, and gender issues for men (1993: 223–4).

Overall, the results of the survey surprised and pleased Samuels, who had not anticipated that this many analysts and therapists were attentive to social and political themes. What concerned me—I could say, dismayed me—about the survey was, however, that only one-third of the British and American analysts (and only one-eighth of the American Jungians) listed "racial" or ethnic issues as a theme. I do not conclude from this that analysts and therapists should solicit such material from patients who do not spontaneously produce it, but I do believe that these statistics are an inaccurate reflection of the extent to which "race" (as well as ethnicity) is a serious issue for patients. The "raciality" of the unconscious is for some patients just as important an issue as any other. Unless and until analysts and therapists—and patients—begin to appreciate "racial" and ethnic themes as appropriate material for equal consideration with other themes, they will not adequately address the prospects for an authentically multicultural imagination as that possibility begins to emerge in other Williams, Joes, Bobs, and Barbaras—that is, in all of us.

Chapter 13

Color-change dreams and "racial" identity

Although Freud defines "psychoanalysis" as a therapy that analyzes "the facts of transference and of resistance" (*SE* 14: 16), he could, with equal justification, have defined it as a therapy that interprets dreams. For Freud, the dream is a *via regia*, "the royal road to a knowledge of the unconscious." The dream, he says, is "the securest foundation" of psychoanalysis (*SE* 11: 33). Jung, too, believes that the dream is "the direct expression" of the unconscious (*CW* 16: 140, para. 295). Freud says that every dream "has a meaning and a psychical value," and he considers the possibility that one dream might be the fulfillment of a wish; another, the fulfillment of a fear; another, a reflection; another, the reproduction of a memory (*SE* 4: 123). In the end, however, he asserts, quite emphatically, that every dream, without exception, "*is a (disguised) fulfilment of a (suppressed or repressed) wish*" (*SE* 4: 160). In contrast, Jung says that the theory "that dreams are merely the imaginary fulfilments of repressed wishes is hopelessly out of date." He acknowledges that some dreams do "represent wishes or fears," but he also contends that other dreams "contain ineluctable truths, philosophical pronouncements, illusions, wild fantasies, memories, plans, anticipations, irrational experiences, even telepathic visions, and heaven knows what besides" (*CW* 16: 147, para. 317). In spite of this apparently liberal perspective on dreams, Jung does propose a theory of interpretation virtually as unequivocal as the one that Freud proposes. Instead of a wish theory, he offers a "compensation theory" (*CW* 8: 253, para. 489). According to Jung, in many or most (if not all) dreams, the unconscious presents to the ego, which always has a partial, prejudicial, or even defective attitude, various alternative perspectives for consideration. If the ego is non-defensive enough, it is able to entertain seriously, in a self-reflective, self-critical way, whether it ought to adopt any of these perspectives.

Although Freud and Jung assume different interpretative positions with respect to dreams, they both privilege dreams as a special kind of material for the immediate access that they afford to the unconscious. I would only add that the "raciality" of the unconscious, like all other contents of the unconscious, is accessible through dreams. There are, of course, many kinds of "racial" identity dreams, but one kind that especially interests me is what I call the *color-change dream*, in which the dreamer or another figure in the dream changes color or "race."

For example, Fanon recounts a dream in which the dreamer, a black man, turns into a white man:

> *I had been walking for a long time, I was extremely exhausted, I had the impression that something was waiting for me, I climbed barricades and walls, I came into an empty hall, and from behind a door I heard noise. I hesitated before I went in, but finally I made up my mind and opened the door. In this second room there were white men, and I found that I too was white.*

(1967: 99)

Fanon does not provide any associations of the dreamer to the dream. He merely notes that the dreamer is a "friend" who "has had problems in his career." Although Fanon does not say so, presumably he interprets the lengthy walk, the extreme exhaustion, the climb up the barricades and walls, the hesitation and then the decision to open the closed door to the white men's room as the black man's extraordinary efforts to succeed in a career, in spite of all racist obstacles.

What Fanon does say, like Freud, is that "this dream fulfills an unconscious wish." Then, like Adler, he says that the dreamer "is suffering from an inferiority complex." According to Fanon, the dreamer feels that being black is inferior to being white, wishes that he were superior, or white, and fulfills that wish by going white in the dream. Fanon says that the dreamer is "in danger of disintegration." To prevent this result, Fanon proposes "to rid him of this unconscious desire." He advocates personal and collective action, in combination: "As a psychoanalyst, I should help my patient to become *conscious* of his unconscious and abandon his attempts at a hallucinatory whitening, but also to act in the direction of a change in the social structure" (1967: 99–100).

Fanon, of course, knows this particular patient as I do not—and cannot—know him. Perhaps this Freudian wish-fulfillment, Adlerian inferiority-compensation is an utterly accurate interpretation in every detail, and perhaps the personal and collective course of action is also a correct therapeutic recommendation. This interpretation, however, is also the product of certain Freudian and Adlerian assumptions, of theories that combine to determine, in practice, a quite specific—and not the only possible—interpretation. The dream does not say that the dreamer *wished* to be white. It says that he *found* that he was white. It is perfectly possible that the dreamer did not want to be white but only discovered that he was white—that is, realized that, after all his efforts to succeed in his career, he had gone white, in some sense.

I would emphasize "in some sense." From what Fanon reports, we cannot say with any certainty in exactly what sense that might have been in this case. We know, however, that, at least for some individuals, the experience of entering into or succeeding in careers (or other opportunities) from which whites have historically excluded blacks has been fraught with psychical conflict and ambivalence. In this dream, the ego finds, or discovers—that is, it becomes conscious of the fact—that the consequence of gaining entry to an exclusively white career is, in some sense, to become white. In this instance, perhaps "becoming white" is thinking, feeling, and behaving white—having conformed unconsciously to a style that the dreamer associates with whites and that he suddenly experiences as a loss of "racial" identity. If this were the case, then the objective of the analysis would be to explore all that the color-change may imply about "racial" styles (which might, of course, include a sense of inferiority) as an important factor in the identity of the dreamer.

RACIST WISH OR ADAPTIVE STRATEGY AND TACTICS

The anthropologist Robert A. LeVine also recounts a dream in which a black—a young African man, a Hausa from Nigeria—goes white:

> In my dream I found myself in an unknown city. A show was held in the arena of the city. The city was ruled by a beautiful young queen. I went to the arena myself and competed in some acrobatic events. I came first in walking on the hands, bull fighting, sword fighting, and shooting.
> After the show, every winner was called to receive his prize. When I came for mine, the people shouted that they didn't know me, I was a stranger from somewhere unknown to them and so I can't get anything.
> The queen, after hearing the complaints, asked me if I were a stranger and I answered yes. Hearing my answer, she asked two guards to take me to her palace for questioning. When the queen came to me in her place [sic: palace?], she was alone and asked me my name and what I wanted in her city. I answered her that I wanted employment there and that my name was Mouktar. She for a while looked at me curiously and then gave me a nice cold drink from a silver cup, after which I fell asleep. When I woke up [in the dream] I found myself dressed in richly decorated clothes with a golden crown on my head. Moreover, my color changed from black to white to suit the color of the people there. There were soldiers all around and on my right was the young queen. I was surprised how all this happened and I was about to ask the queen what all that was about when I was woken up. When I woke up I found myself wearing only my pajamas and my skin black as before.
>
> (1966: 53)

LeVine does not offer a psychoanalytic interpretation of this dream. Nor does he address the issue of the color-change from black to white. What interests him is what he calls "achievement imagery" in the dreams of black Africans. LeVine believes that the presence of such imagery indicates a motivation to achieve. Presumably, the reason that he includes this particular dream is that the dreamer competes successfully in a contest.

Raymond E. Rainville quotes this dream in a study of dreams at different stages of life, and he does propose a psychoanalytic interpretation. Like Fanon, he interprets the color-change as a wish-fulfillment. "It is revealing," Rainville says, "that a young man who grew up in an all-black society has the racist wish to be white" (1988: 178). To change color in a dream may be to fulfill a wish. What the dreamer explicitly wishes for in this dream, however, is not white skin but "employment." Although he has won a contest and has demonstrated various skills, he does not demand a prize from the queen. He wants work. It is precisely when he asks for a job that the queen offers him "a nice cold drink," a potion that puts him asleep, or renders him unconscious. When he wakes (or becomes conscious) in the dream, he is "dressed in richly decorated clothes with a golden crown on my head." When the queen makes him king, the dreamer reports that "my color changed from black to white to suit the color of the people there." Apparently, the queen and the other people are white. The dream does not say that the dreamer *wishes* that he were white. What it says is that he changes color in order to *suit* the people in this city. The dreamer assumes the coloration of the other to whom he has previously seemed a stranger. The motivation for the color-change is suitability. One might conclude that the dreamer is the sort of individual who, at least under certain circumstances, tends to suit others rather than suit himself.

The dreamer does not say what he thinks and how he feels about the color-change. The issue of suitability, however, suggests that, at least unconsciously, the dreamer is adaptive, that strategically and tactically he is the sort of individual who assumes the coloration of the other in order to suit the other, in order not to seem strange to the other. One might speculate that in order for blacks in a post-colonialist, post-imperialist Africa to achieve, to succeed in a culture effectively under the domination of whites, they cannot suit themselves but must suit others, must adapt themselves to the situation—if, for example, they want employment. Under such circumstances, becoming white in a dream may not be a racist wish or a wish literally to have white skin but may be—however much we may deplore the external, racist economic reality of the culture—a perfectly realistic adaptation to a less than ideal situation.

From such a perspective, white skin in the dream would be a metaphor that signifies all that whiteness implies culturally—and economically—for a Hausa in Nigeria. Evidently, no matter how competitive the dreamer is in acrobatic events—"walking on the hands, bull fighting, sword fighting, and shooting"—a demonstration of talent and skill is insufficient if the individual is a stranger. In addition, he must acknowledge that he is a stranger, state his name, and say what he wants. It is then that he receives a golden crown and white skin. From a Jungian perspective, these are symbols of the transformation that the ego of the dreamer has experienced in psychical reality. Such a transformation, such an adaptation, may seem merely an accommodationist capitulation to racism, pathologically compliant conformity to the other, and a loss or even a repudiation of black African identity. Alternatively, however, it may seem a quite pragmatic response of the ego to a deplorably racist external reality. (These interpretations are not necessarily mutually exclusive. They may be an example of overdetermination in the dream.)

Whatever the case may be, the color-change dreams that Fanon and Rainville interpret do not seem to me to be merely the fulfillment of a wish to have white skin. From a strictly Freudian perspective, the fact that one dreamer *found* himself to be white and one dreamer became white to *suit* the other by no means proves that they did not wish, quite literally, to be white. For Freudians, "found" and "suit" are merely a manifest content, a deceptive appearance, or distortive derivative, of a latent content, the motivation of which is a wish to become white. Such a reductive interpretation seems inadequate to me because it disregards the specificity of the images that the unconscious actually employs in the dream. Only through the specific images of the dream ("finding" and "suiting") do we arrive at an interpretation that is, in practice, more than a complacently rote application of a theory.

A Jungian perspective on these two color-change dreams might regard them as "persona" dreams. As Jungians define the "persona," it is the mask (as in what Fanon calls "black skin, white masks" in the book by that title) that individuals wear in an effort to adapt to the expectations or the demands of the culture in which they exist. As long as the ego is consciously related to the persona but is not unconsciously identified with it—that is, as long as individuals can, at will, put on the mask when the occasion requires but then take it off—they employ the persona effectively. Historically, blacks have demonstrated considerable ingenuity with a variety of personas that whites have projected onto them. I mean such caricatures as the "Sambo" stereotype. When blacks have not unconsciously identified with these stereotypes but instead have consciously related to them, they have often used them, in an opportunistic way, to take advantage of apparently impossible circumstances. In such cases, blacks have combined the persona with the archetypal image of the "trickster," who deliberately practices a certain deceit in order to manipulate the situation. An example would be the slave narratives in which blacks recount "puttin' on ole massa" (Osofsky 1969). In putting on a tricksterish persona, the black slave could "put on" the white master of the plantation.

The trickster, who Samuels says tends "to lie, to cheat, to steal," uses any means necessary. Samuels has recently argued that a tricksterish persona is often the only or the most effective strategy and tactic available to individuals or groups in an otherwise politically impossible situation. According to Samuels, the individual or group that adopts a tricksterish persona for political purposes does not reject "collective, cultural images" (1993: 96) but actively exploits such images in order to trick the oppressor. The "Sambo" stereotype would be an example of such a collective, cultural image that whites have historically projected onto blacks. The historian Stanley M. Elkins defines the "Sambo" type as "docile but irresponsible, loyal but lazy, humble but chronically given to lying and stealing" (1959: 82). Although Elkins says that the "Sambo" type is not "a universal type" (in Jungian terms, an archetype) but only "a plantation type" (1959: 87), he defines it in precisely the terms that Jungians define the "trickster."

The only issue would be whether blacks unconsciously identified with the "Sambo" type or whether they consciously related to it. To the extent that black slaves did not conflate the stereotype with the ego but used the stereotype opportunistically as a persona in order to deceive white masters, they were tricksters. The "Sambo" type is not, of course, in the strict sense, an example of a white mask on black skin. Rather, it is an example of a black mask on black skin. The "Sambo" type did not think, feel, behave, or "become" white. Black slaves did not become white masters but only behaved overtly in such a way as to deceive the oppressor even as they covertly retained and maintained a "black" identity. As black as the mask of the "Sambo" type may be, however, it is a mask that whites have imposed culturally on blacks. It is what Fanon calls a "cultural imposition." In that sense only has it been a "white" mask.

THE WHITE QUEEN: LEGEND AND HISTORY

Another Jungian perspective on the color-change dream that LeVine cites would emphasize the image of the white queen. The most famous fictional example of the white queen in Africa is the character that H. Rider Haggard presents in the novel *She* (1991). According to Cornelia Brunner (1986), "She" is an archetypal image of the anima, a personification and projection of the unconscious feminine aspect of the psyche in white European men. "The motif of the anima," Jung says, "is developed in its purest and most naive form in Rider Haggard" (*CW* 18: 545, para. 1280).

Van der Post says that "since the coming of European man in Africa he has been confronted with a legend that somewhere in the heart of Africa resides a great and beautiful white queen." The legend of the white queen, he asserts, "exercises the imaginations of some white men almost as much as those of the articulate black man." Van der Post notes that the white queen appears in "the work of Rider Haggard, who significantly enough was one of the first to stare unknowingly at the reflection of his own hidden self and that of the Europe of his day in the mirror of darkest Africa." Although we now "know Africa well enough to realize that no such queen exists and that probably no such queen has ever existed there," the legend of the white queen continues to appeal to the imagination. Van der Post attributes the persistence of the legend to a profound "need in the dreaming prophetic soul of man in Africa." (He does not say whether this is the soul of the white man in Africa or the soul of the black man in Africa. Presumably, he means both.) Van der Post suggests that "this feminine presence in the spirit of man" is, in the image of the white queen, a symbol of transformation. As the unconscious feminine emerges from "an immemorial neglect," it now begins to assume a position among "the conscious values of man." In the South Africa of the 1950s, however, van der Post says, "she is still so dangerously submerged that her existence is not even suspected" (1955: 171–3). There the feminine remains unconscious, utterly and collectively so—at least among white South Africans.

Van der Post maintains that the feminine presence "in the African soul was there long before the white man came to Africa and before the aboriginal of Africa even knew that white beings existed." As evidence, he mentions "a wonderful rock painting hundreds of miles from the sea in the wasteland of south-west Africa." One of the figures in the painting is a "white lady." Estimates of the age of the painting "vary from hundreds to some thousands of years, but in any case everybody is agreed that it was painted long before the coming of the white man in Africa" (1955: 173–4). Apparently, the reference is to a rock painting by the Bushmen in the Brandenberg Mountains in southwest Africa. The painting is "a hunting scene and the central figure is called the White Lady, though no more is known about it than the colour" (Parrinder 1967: 27). In spite of what van der Post says, not everyone agrees that the figure is even a lady. For example, Joseph Campbell says that "the now famous, more mysterious 'White Lady' " actually appears to be "a man—'a king,' they say" (1959: 383). If so, the "white lady" is hardly evidence of any legend of a white queen among black Africans before the arrival of white Europeans.

If there is no legend of a white queen among black Africans, there is, however, a history of such a queen, Mujaji of the Lovedu in the northeast Transvaal. "The character of this queen," Geoffrey Parrinder says, "and the nature of the country where she ruled, suggested a theme and provided a location for Rider Haggard which he realised in the famous romance called *She*." Parrinder observes that, like the fictional white queen "She," Mujaji "lived in seclusion and hence men believed in her wisdom and immortality." Mujaji was called " 'white-faced' " (1967: 118). Morton N. Cohen, who has conducted research into the possible sources of the white queen in *She*, describes Mujaji as "a fair-skinned woman with great magical powers, living in seclusion among her people." He says that she was famous "for her fair complexion and her immortality" (1960: 109). The anthropologists E. Jensen Krige and J.D. Krige also remark that "Mujaji was conceived to be immortal, inaccessible, mysterious." They note that it was "the fairness of her skin which captured the imagination of the early European pioneers." For white Europeans, "the fairness of her complexion easily became the subject of rumour and phantasy" (1943: 2). Apparently, there is no external evidence that Haggard used Mujaji as a historical source for the fictional white queen in *She*. From a Jungian perspective, however, Mujaji did not have to exist in order for Haggard to imagine a white queen in Africa. It would be perfectly predictable that white European men would personify and project their own unconscious feminine, or anima, onto Africa and fantasize the actual existence of a white queen.

Does the history of Mujaji, the white queen of the Lovedu, have anything at all to do with the dream of a young man of the Hausa? It is, of course, possible that such a young man might know that such a white queen had actually existed in Africa. Nigeria is, however, a considerable distance, approximately 2,000 miles, from the Transvaal. It seems to me improbable that the existence of Mujaji accounts for the presence of a white queen in the dream. In the dream, all of the people in the city— not just the queen—are evidently white, which is not the case with the Lovedu. It seems to me probable that the white queen in the dream of the young man is not an example of the transmission of an image by tradition, migration, or dispersion but an example of the autonomous capacity of the unconscious spontaneously to avail itself of the same or a very similar image at different times in different places, independent of direct cultural influence—and perhaps for very different psychical purposes.

What psychical purpose does the white queen serve for the dreamer? This particular dream is structurally similar to a fairy tale or folk tale. As Vladimir Propp (1968) describes the morphology of such tales, the dreamer is a "hero," and the white queen is a "tester" who interrogates him. When the dreamer responds satisfactorily, she offers him a "magical agent," the potion that induces sleep (unconsciousness) and produces a symbolic transformation (kingliness and whiteness). By this archetypal process, the dreamer is no longer a stranger or even a commoner but a white king, consort of the white queen.

Does the white queen in the imagination of white European men like Haggard have anything at all to do with the white queen in the dream

of a black African man? From a Jungian perspective, it would be usual
for a white man to personify and project the anima as a white woman.
This need not, however, always be so, as the case of my patient "Bob"
amply demonstrates. Bob was a white man with a black anima. For
Bob, the black woman was an idealistic, perfectionistic personification and
projection of the unconscious "feminine" aspect of his psyche. (Perhaps a
conventional Jungian would suggest that in such a case there is a shadow
aspect to the anima image, but, if so, in the case of Bob it was an
extremely, perhaps excessively, positive shadow.) Historically, there have
been a number of black animas—for example, the Shulamite woman who
in the Song of Songs says, "I am black but comely," and the Black Virgin
Mary (Begg 1985; Baring and Cashford 1991). Even the racist caricature
of the "Negro Mammy" is a black anima. The image of the black woman
has had a profound, unconscious impact on white men. Why should we
not expect the image of the white woman—in this case, a white queen—
to have an equally emphatic, an equally enigmatic, influence on a black
African man, especially one who struggles to survive and succeed in a
culture under the economic domination of whites?

WHITE EGO, BLACK ANIMA, BLACK SHADOW

In 1987, at Town Hall in New York City, I attended a screening of *The
Way of the Dream*, a documentary film series in which Marie-Louise von
Franz interprets a variety of dreams from a Jungian perspective. Frazer
Boa, the Jungian analyst who produced and directed the film series and
interviewed von Franz on camera as she interpreted the dreams, was
present at the screening I attended. During a segment entitled "Slaying
the Dragon," von Franz interprets a dream that, according to Boa, "*illus-
trates the tremendous power of the mother complex and the struggle
involved in a man freeing his anima from the black moods of the devouring
mother*" (1988: 157). The dreamer, a white man, is walking with a black
woman, apparently in Africa:

> *It was a hot summer's day and I was walking with a gorgeous black
> woman through rolling green country along the side of a jungle. We'd
> known each other for a long time and I called her my goddess. It was
> my pet name for her.*
> *Suddenly she stopped and said, "I have a problem." I didn't under-
> stand what she meant, but instead of telling me with words she pulled
> down the strap of her dress and bared her shoulder. Her black skin was
> peeling where it had been exposed to the sun and under the top skin,
> underneath the black, her skin was golden-white. She looked at me and
> said, "If I keep seeing you, it's going to happen all over my body. I've*

got to talk to my mother and get some advice from her about what to do."

We walked on and as we approached some farm implements two black guys suddenly came running out of the jungle screaming that they were going to take her back to their village.

I said, "Hell, I'd rather die than have that happen. You're not going to do that. You're not going to take her back."

We started to fight and when I woke I was winning and I knew I was going to win.

(1988: 158)

In the dream, the black woman is changing color—"going white" or "going golden-white."

Von Franz interprets the dream by recourse to the Jungian concept of the anima. She immediately mentions the black-but-beautiful Shulamite, who, she says, "is later transformed, according to medieval legend, into a white woman." When the Shulamite is finally married to Christ, she is "redeemed" by him "into becoming a white woman." Von Franz also cites the Queen of Sheba as "a black woman who was beloved of a white man," King Solomon. According to von Franz, "A white man meeting with a black woman and transforming her over time into a white woman has always fascinated Western mythology." In order to interpret the dream, von Franz employs alchemical amplification. "One of the recurring fantasies of the alchemists," she says, "was that the matter which they wanted to transform into gold was initially black. They compared it to a black woman who then takes off her skin or black garment and is transformed into pure gold" (1988: 159). The tacit, colorist assumption that motivates this Jungian interpretation of the dream is that the transformational color sequence in alchemy—from *nigredo* to *albedo*, that is, from black to white, or golden-white—is a universally applicable (rather than a culturally relative) color sequence, with color values from negative to positive.

The black woman in the dream is, von Franz says, the dreamer's "undeveloped," "relatively negative," "autoerotic," "narcissistic" anima, or unconscious feminine aspect of the male psyche. Von Franz interprets the color-change as a very positive symbol of transformation: "The peeling of the skin of the black female and the transformation into a white golden anima is the transformation of the loving capacities of a man, the transformation of his Eros from a primitive autoerotic fantasy into a true human capacity for love." In contrast, she interprets the two black men, "who want the woman to remain black," as negative images of a "regressive," "primitive" aspect of the psyche (1988: 160). Evidently, they personify the shadow, which von Franz encourages the dreamer to fight and defeat.

This interpretation dissatisfied and annoyed me. It seemed too conveniently formulaic, too complacently facile. What kind of ego, I wondered, would turn a beautiful black goddess white, evidently prevent her from seeking her mother's advice about whether she should keep seeing the dreamer, and adopt such an aggressive "better-dead-than-black" defense? This ego-defensive attitude did not seem to me so obviously "a true human capacity for love." During the intermission following this segment of the film series, I approached Boa and expressed my reservations and concerns. He merely remarked, as if this sufficed to resolve the issue, that the song "What Did I Do To Be So Black and Blue?" is about how one may be literally black on the outside but metaphorically white on the inside.

From a Jungian perspective, the function of the unconscious in dreams is to compensate a partial, prejudicial, or even defective attitude of the ego. Curiously enough, von Franz never entertains the possibility that this dream serves such a compensatory purpose. She assumes that the defensive, aggressive attitude of the ego is correct. Just as Jung, in his dream of the red-hot curling iron and the African-American barber who would turn his hair from straight to kinky, proposes an ego-defensive, non-compensatory (and, ironically, non-Jungian) interpretation, so von Franz offers a similar interpretation of this color-change dream. If the black woman, or black goddess, is an anima image, the dreamer refuses to relate to her unless she identifies totally with him, unless she turns into a white woman, or white goddess. The ego refuses to relate to the anima, the unconscious feminine aspect of the psyche, except on the unconditional terms that it imposes.

The ego of the dreamer is so defensive and so aggressive that it will apparently fight to the death to preserve the psychical *status quo*. If the two black men are shadow images, the dreamer refuses to relate to them unless it is to fight with them. If, as Jungians define "eros," it is the capacity to relate to others in both external and psychical reality, then this dream does not seem to me to indicate that the ego of the dreamer has that capacity. From a Jungian perspective, a rigid ego, rather than a flexible one, often imagines that it will just "die" if it changes. That is, the ego experiences the possibility of transformation as a mortal threat. For the ego of this dreamer, the dream constitutes just such a life-and-death situation. Paradoxically, the ego would rather fight to the death than die, or change. Edinger poses the problem of "what it means when a dream figure dies." The meaning is "very positive," in general. "The same is true, even more so, if one dreams of one's own death," Edinger says. "If one dreams that one's own ego has died, a big transformation is in line" (1994: 53). In this dream, the ego is willing to fight to the death, but this resolve is only apparently equivalent to being willing to die. The ego certainly does not acknowledge any vulnerability. It is not amenable to any experience of loss or any defeat. It is not a "dying" ego but a "killing" ego. The ego would fight, defeat, and, if need be, kill the shadow rather than relinquish the relation that it has with the anima.

A properly Jungian interpretation (that is, a compensatory interpretation) would challenge the dreamer to consider why the ego in the dream is so defensive, so aggressive—so resistant to the qualms of the anima, the black goddess who is so apprehensive about the prospect of going white. Rather than encourage the dreamer to inquire into and reflect on the possibility that the ego has a partial, prejudicial, or defective attitude, von Franz sides with the one-sided attitude of the ego. She uncritically supports the current position of the ego, in opposition to the trepidation of the anima. The black goddess has, as she says, a "problem" with the ego. The ego, however, evidently does not consider the fact that she is anxious about changing color, about going white—not just on her shoulder but eventually all over her body—to be problematic. If the ego had "a true human capacity for love," it would seem to me that it would have been responsive to and curious about the anxiety of the anima.

In the dream, the ego evinces absolutely no interest in how the black goddess feels about going white. It simply ignores the problem and maintains a one-sided, self-interested attitude. The ego is utterly unreceptive to the alternative perspective that the unconscious presents through the anima. The anima apparently feels that the relation with the ego is too close, too constant, that it needs to distance itself from the ego, or else the relation will become an unconscious identification. The ego in the dream is extremely possessive. In this case, the problem is not possession of the ego by the anima but possession of the anima by the ego. "Possession" is, in this sense, tantamount to unconscious identification. It seems to me that if the dreamer had "a true human capacity for love," the ego would be amenable to a relation of mutuality. As it is, however, the ego is indifferent to the concerns of the anima, the unconscious feminine aspect of the psyche. The dream is a very "masculine" dream, in which the ego is hardly sensitive to or solicitous of what the "feminine" may feel. The ego does not defend the anima against the shadow so much as it defends an exclusive possession of the anima by the ego against the shadow. The black goddess is a daughter who feels that she must consult the mother, who will advise her about "what to do." From a Jungian perspective, the mother in this case assumes the archetypal function of the "wise old woman," who might counsel an anxious young woman, or anima, who happens to be in the exclusive possession of a selfish, defensive, aggressive man, or ego.

Although von Franz does not offer a compensatory interpretation of the dream, she does offer what Jung calls an interpretation on the "subjective" level. She regards all of the figures in the dream as personifications of various aspects of the psyche. What interests her exclusively is the internal, psychical reality of the subject, the dreamer, not any objects in external reality such as white and black people, "race," or racism. In effect, von Franz offers a "structural" interpretation. If for Freudians the structures of the psyche are the id, ego, and superego, for Jungians they are the ego, anima, and shadow, as well as additional structures. For von Franz, the white "I" in the dream is a derivative personification of the ego; the black "goddess," a derivative personification of the anima; and the black "guys," a derivative personification of the shadow.

Although the interpretation that I have offered is a compensatory interpretation more consistent, I believe, with a properly Jungian perspective, which would problematize the defensive, aggressive attitude of the ego, it is also an interpretation exclusively on the subjective level—not on what Jung calls the "objective" level. An exhaustive interpretation of the dream would, it seems to me, require an interpretation on both the subjective and the objective levels. Such an interpretation would have to include an analysis not only of the relations between the ego, the anima, and the shadow but also of the relations between the dreamer, a white man, and black women and black men, as well as the relations between the dreamer and the issues of "race" and racism.

WESTERN MYTHOLOGY AND ALCHEMY

What, if anything, does this dream have to do with "racial" identity? We will never know for sure, because the question never arises for von Franz. It evidently never occurs to her that the dream might have anything to do with "race" or racism—or, for that matter, that the interpretation (and the theory that conditions the interpretation) might have anything to do with those issues. (I should perhaps emphasize that I do not mean to imply that Jungian analysis is intrinsically racist; I do not believe that it is.) Although the dreamer is white, although another figure in the dream is changing color, turning from black to white, and although two other figures in the dream are black, von Franz never wonders what and how the dreamer thinks and feels about white and black people. This omission seems to me significant, perhaps even symptomatic. We will never know what attitude the dreamer may have had toward the issues of "race" and racism, toward Africans, or toward people of a different skin color. All we know is that von Franz omits any consideration of "racial" identity in the interpretation that she proposes.

The dreamer is a white man. In the dream, he is in an "interracial" relationship with a woman who is black. From that, we might infer that the dreamer has a non-racist attitude toward black people—or at least toward black women, or at least toward beautiful black women. In addition, the dreamer regards the black woman as a goddess. For a white male who is merely human, the black female is divine. A white man does not just love a black woman—he deifies her, worships her. He does not regard her as inferior, or even equal, but as superior. (As long as she accompanies him, does he also regard himself as superior? In the presence of a "goddess," does he feel like a "god?") For the dreamer, "goddess" is a "pet name." Does the dreamer regard beautiful black women as "pets," the possession of whom he would defend to the death against black men? What, on the objective level, are the "racial" (perhaps even racist) attitudes that inform the identity of the dreamer?

The interpreter of the dream is a white woman, a Jungian analyst with a theoretical and practical interest in the application of what she calls "Western mythology" to dreams. She is a European woman who amplifies the images in the dream by recourse to Jewish and Christian mythology. She assumes that the myths of the Shulamite and the Queen of Sheba are immediately applicable to the image of the black woman in the dream. The assumption is that the transformation of a black woman into a white woman in Western mythology has exactly the same significance as the transformation of a black woman into a white woman in a dream— and that this transformation is a redemption. That the anima (rather than the ego) should be transformed or "redeemed"—and that this process should be symbolized by a color-change from black to white—seems to von Franz unproblematic. She does not question the positive value that Western mythology (as well as Jungian analysis and the ego of the dreamer) attributes to the color "white" or the negative value that it attributes to the color "black."

Von Franz also amplifies the images in the dream by recourse to Western alchemy. According to Jung, alchemy was the precursor not only of chemistry but also of "the most modern psychology"—that is, psychoanalysis (*CW* 7: 220, para. 360). The conscious attempt to transform external (or material) reality was simultaneously an unconscious effort to transform internal (or psychical) reality. In Western alchemy, the first stage in the transformational process is *nigredo* ("black"); most often, the last stage is *rubedo* ("red" or "golden-red"). Sometimes, however, the last stage is *albedo* ("white" or a union of all colors). Jung says that "*nigredo* or blackness is the initial state," which proceeds either "direct to the whitening (*albedo*)" or "to the one white colour that contains all colours," a state that many alchemists regarded as "the ultimate goal" (*CW* 12: 230–3, para. 334). Von Franz immediately applies this alchemical color sequence to the dream. Because alchemically "black" has a negative significance and "white" a positive significance, she assumes that the transformation of the black woman into a white woman is a positive transformation, in spite of the serious reservations that the black woman expresses to the white man.

Is it possible that a black woman might be right to be anxious about going white and a white man wrong to be indifferent to how she feels about it? Perhaps such a white man (under the possessive influence of whom a black woman tends to go entirely white) has a problematically masculinist, even racist, identity. Perhaps alchemically such an ego needs "blackening" at least as much as such an anima needs "whitening." In this case, however, there is no evidence that the dreamer has any capacity for such receptivity to the other, to the different. The white masculine (ego) would possessively transform the black feminine (anima) and defensively, aggressively fight and defeat the black masculine (shadow).

The problem is not just that alchemy is a European, Eurocentric, ethnocentric system but that the transformational process from *nigredo* to *albedo* is a sequence. (It is expectable, even perfectly predictable, that alchemists as white Europeans would value "white" as superior and "black" as inferior.) In alchemy, "blackness" and "whiteness" are *stages*. In at least some versions, *nigredo* is the first, lowest stage and *albedo* the last, highest stage. To the extent that Jungian analysis tends to regard the alchemical color sequence as a universal truth, one of the eternal verities, which requires no revision, it uncritically accepts and applies it as a developmental psychology: the psyche develops from black to white (or from black to white to red). If Jungian analysis were to theorize *nigredo* and *albedo* not as stages, however, but as *states*, it would relativize "blackness" and "whiteness." It would regard "blackening" or "whitening" as relative to the state of the ego (which might include issues of "racial" identity). If an ego were too black, it would need compensatory whitening; if it were too white, it would need compensatory blackening. The result would be that Jungian analysts would not immediately assume that any transformation from black to white is necessarily positive, as the alchemists evidently assumed, but that such a transformation might be negative—ego-defensive and non-compensatory. As psychologically astute as the alchemists may have been in many respects, there is no reason why contemporary Jungian analysts must adopt uncritically a color valuation that is absolute rather than relative. In fact, to the extent that "compensation" is fundamental to Jungian analysis, it is arguable that any absolutism is untenable.

Just as Freudian theories about wishes and Adlerian theories about inferiorities condition the practice of psychoanalysis and the interpretation of dreams, so, too, do Jungian theories about mythology and alchemy. "Racial" bias is not the only bias; there are also theoretical and practical biases in psychoanalysis. In addition, whether analysts employ the terminology of "intrapsychic" and "interpersonal" levels of interpretation, or whether they employ the terminology of "subjective" and "objective" levels of interpretation, both levels are essential to any interpretation that purports to be definitive. Although psychical reality is the ultimate reality in psychoanalysis, external factors, both personal and collective, such as the skin color of white and black people and issues of "race" and racism, are just as significant as any strictly internal factors. It is even problematic whether there are any strictly internal factors, in isolation from external factors. In this respect, color-change dreams always pose the question of the "racial" identity of the dreamer and all that it may imply unconsciously. The dreamer or other figures in the dream may change color for a variety of reasons, and the "racial" identity of the dreamer—what and how the dreamer thinks and feels not only intrapsychically and interpersonally about people of different skin colors but also *culturally* about "race" and racism—is a factor that psychoanalysts of all schools of thought have a responsibility to explore without prejudice.

Chapter 14

A color-change from brown to white to black

Not only "blacks" and "whites" change color in dreams. People of other colors—'brown," for example—may go both white and black, even in one and the same dream. I now wish to present an interpretation of just such a dream, one in which the dreamer first goes white, then goes black. The dreamer was a 34-year-old Mexican-American woman, a graduate student, who had moved from California to pursue a Ph.D. at a university in New York. She had the following color-change dream:

I am outdoors in a rural setting, playing near railroad tracks with my little dog-cat. Someone is there with me. It's my younger sister, but I feel that she is also other people besides herself. She's behind me, maybe on the other side of the tracks. I can't see her very well—she's more of a shadow. I am feeling very sad. I want to go away, to leave this sadness. A train comes down the tracks and stops in front of me. I climb onto the top of the train and sit facing forward with my dog by my side (looks like a dog but moves like a cat).

I'm riding on top of the train and feeling sad—lost, alone, depressed. After a while, I want to get off the train but don't know how. Turning around, I see my sister again and wonder that I did not see her climb onto the train. She seems to know how to help me off the train. She is slowing down the train. No, she is slowing down the time and space around us. She lifts her arms, and I rise up off the train. We—she and I—are moving at a different speed than the train. With her arms out-stretched, she floats me over the side of the train and onto the ground. As my feet touch the ground, I feel loose gravel and sense "real" time. The train speeds past on the tracks close to me. Wind whips my hair and clothes around slightly. I'm afraid of being blown against the train and crushed. My sister lifts my dog in the same way, while the train speeds past. My dog floats in air over the train and into my arms.

I'm standing next to the railroad tracks. The train has passed, and my sister is gone. It is sunset. The sun is bright, all is glowing. A warm breeze fills me with happiness. I am ecstatic, excited, and feeling somewhat light-

headed. I feel as though I'm still floating, gliding. My legs are weak and shaky. I feel the gravel underfoot as I turn to face the sunset. I'm wearing different clothes—I have on a long-sleeved brown shirt and a long skirt made of gauze or straw. I feel incredibly comfortable, calm. My hair is very long, voluminous, almost weightless. I am a white woman, with red hair. My face is round and freckled. Checking my reflection in a car window next to me to know that it is still me, I don't recognize myself until I smile and feel my cheeks puff.

I turn slowly to face the warm, glowing sunset and then turn to a man sitting on a crate next to me. An older man, perhaps 70, in a brown jacket. He is kind, gentle, and fair-skinned but of no particular race. I pull pictures out of my pocket. I want to show him what happened. I have maybe four pictures. They are of me on top of the train, my sister, my dog. Suddenly, I sense something strange from the pictures: my sister. What was she doing on the train when I didn't see her get on? Where did she get this power? Her involvement in all this makes me uneasy. I look down the tracks where the train disappeared.

I'm riding inside the train, waiting for something to happen. I want my sister to appear. I notice two little children clinging to a railing along the right side. They're cute little kids. Suddenly, a child appears. I notice that the kids are too perfect, too cute in their checks and bows. The other passengers notice the children and become concerned for them. I know that the children are not real, not what they appear to be. Another child appears. I feel that a hoax is unfolding, a huge conspiracy of some kind. I stand and ask the children where they came from. They are silent. I ask the passenger sitting next to me to ask the children where they came from. The children don't respond. I shout over to a little boy, "You, with the dots!" Yes, he knows that I'm speaking to him, but he doesn't respond. "Where did you come from?" He glares back at me. "Where are your parents? Show me where you were sitting." He moves away from the side of the train and walks hurriedly down the aisle past me. His twin sister lets go of the railing and follows him. The two children disappear into the door at the end of the aisle. Suddenly, all the children scatter—there are maybe ten or twelve of them. I point to the children as they start to disappear through the doors of the train. "Look! These children aren't what they seem!" I say to the passengers.

After a pause, I say: "There are many gods..." As I speak, I am turning into a man—a tall, big black man. My head is bald, and I'm wearing a fancy western suit. I am having trouble speaking. There is a lump in my throat. My throat is changing, my voice is deepening. I clear my throat, and in a new, deep voice I finish the sentence: "...but not all of us come from the same god."

When Freud interprets a dream, he follows a particular format. He first recounts a dream, *verbatim*, and then he conducts an "analysis" of the dream. He analyzes the dream by a piecemeal method. He asks the dreamer to provide "associations to each piece" of the dream (*SE* 4: 103). The pieces of the dream may be a word, phrase, or clause, which Freud italicizes for emphasis. Only after he presents each piece and the associations to it, does he offer a comprehensive interpretation of the dream. It is this format that I propose to follow.

ANALYSIS OF THE DREAM

A rural setting ... railroad tracks ... the other side of the tracks ... I am feeling very sad. I want to go away, to leave this sadness. A train comes down the tracks and stops in front of me. I climb onto the top of the train. As a child, the dreamer had, in fact, lived in a rural setting, "in the country, far away from folks." Although there were no other people around, "there were railroads all around us when we were kids." In that extreme isolation, the railroad had assumed a special significance. To the dreamer as a child, it had epitomized "connection." Because the railroad "was coming from one place and going to an entirely different place," it had implied "mobility," "another experience," "the future." The tracks were the "ideas" behind the train—"the hopes, the fears"—and the train was "the actual manifestation of all that." The dreamer said to me that she liked "the idea of going some place new." As a child, she had lived, as it were, "on the other side of the tracks." That is, as a Latina, or Chicana, she was from a "lower" social and economic class than Anglos. She had taken the train to "a better place" that she hoped would mean "concrete change, fundamental change in the situation." There was a possible pun in the dream: she had imagined that the way for her to change the situation was to become educated, or "trained." She had gone to a trade school, then to a community college, then to two state universities, and finally to a private university. She had left behind past sadness in hopes of future happiness. "I left home running away," she said. "I left because things were bad. I felt a victim of things over which I had no choosing. I didn't choose to be born where I was. I didn't choose to be poor. I know that I've been very angry, very sad. The sadness comes from a big hole in me."

My younger sister's behind me ... I can't see her very well—she's more of a shadow ... I want to get off the train but don't know how ... My sister seems to know how to help me ... She's slowing down the time and space around us. She lifts her arms, and I rise up off the train ... She floats me over the side of the train and onto the ground. As my feet touch the ground, I sense "real" time ... My sister lifts my dog in the same way ... My dog floats in air over the train and into my arms. The dreamer said to me that she and her younger sister had had a typical big sister–little sister relationship. "She's always been my little sister," the dreamer said. "She's always been a child. She's always been behind me in experiences. I now know that that's not true, but that's what I've thought, and I've hung onto that thought. Maybe for my own security I've wanted to keep her in that position, but I've gotten enough information when I've gone home to know that she's developed her world and has made her decisions about who she is as an individual. Now there's no more of this 'behind me.' " The night of the dream, her sister had telephoned her to tell her about a rather difficult intimate relationship. It was the first time that her sister had ever shared that sort of information. The dreamer had thought, "Wow, wonderful, great that she would decide to call me to tell me this and feel that it's her sister that she could tell instead of somebody else!" Instead of listening to her sister, however, the dreamer had "lectured her." Her sister had patiently replied that she hoped that the dreamer would "accept her as a person, as an individual with her own life, not tell her what to do or not to do, and simply hear what she had to share."

The dreamer realized that she had not been accepting. Her sister had to "point it out" to her. Toward the end of the conversation, the dreamer had thought, "Yes, she's right, she's right, I'm just doing this to her because she's my little sister. I have to back off. I've overstepped. I'm not treating her as an equal. I'm lecturing her because she's my little sister. She hasn't talked to me in a long time, and what right do I have to do this to her any more? I'm not listening, and she needs somebody to listen." The next day, when the dreamer awoke from the dream, she thought and thought about it. The dream, she said, made her feel different about her sister. She telephoned her sister to tell her about the dream and offer her an apology. "You helped me in this dream," she said. The dreamer acknowledged that her lecturing rather than listening and sharing was "about my problems, my hangups, my stuff, what I project onto you—and I realize that you have your life, and I'm sorry when I do this."

She realized that her projections onto her sister had distorted her perception of her, and the dream confirmed this fact. In the dream, she could not see her sister very well. Her sister was "more of a shadow." Perhaps the dreamer felt that her sister was more shadow than substance—or that a little sister was nothing more than the shadow of a big sister, who could continue unconsciously to belittle her. The dreamer was unfamiliar with Jungian theory and the archetype of the "shadow," but her sister served her in that capacity. Her sister functioned as a convenient object onto which the defensive ego of the dreamer could project, or cast like a shadow, the ostensibly inferior or negative aspects of the psyche.

In the dream, the dreamer wants to get off the train but does not know how. Her sister does know how and helps her get off the train. The dreamer is on a very "fast track," and her sister slows down space and time. In effect, her sister performs a miracle. She levitates the dreamer off the train and onto the ground. Her sister has knowledge and power that the dreamer had never previously recognized or appreciated. She "grounds" the dreamer in reality, in "real" time. She also levitates the dog off the train and into the arms of the dreamer. The dog is a "dog-cat," which "looks like a dog but moves like a cat." The dreamer had a cat at the time of the dream and had had both dogs and cats as a child. She had always had animals around her, "but sometimes I neglect them," she said, "and it bothers me that I do." Cats, she said, were "love," 'resources of life." Dogs were more difficult than cats because "they rely on people—they're more of an obligation." To the dreamer, dogs epitomized dependence. For her, they were "a stark reminder of how I have been irresponsible toward people as well as animals." In the dream, her sister returned love, resources of life, reliance on people, obligation, dependence, and responsibility to her arms.

The dreamer said that she felt that she was now "coming out of my own ego and my own little isolation." She was beginning to appreciate "where I came from and all my background as important." She meant that she had left behind her sister, her family, her home, her "racial" identity as a Mexican-American, just as she had left behind her dog-cat. "Yeah," she said, "I wanted to get away from it and forget all that, because I felt that it didn't contain any answers for me. I felt that all of these people were very superficial and one-dimensional and that they had nothing to show me." Subsequent experience, however, had gradually disabused her. "I have gotten off my high horse, and I have listened more and more. I'm still coming around, because I've thought that way for years and it's hard to stop thinking that way, but I know that it's not the right attitude, that it's not the truth."

It is sunset. The sun is bright, all is glowing . . . I turn to face the sunset . . . I feel incredibly comfortable, calm . . . I am a white woman, with red hair. My face is round and freckled. Checking my reflection in a car window next to me to know that it is still me, I don't recognize myself until I smile and feel my cheeks puff. At sunset, when day turns to night, the dreamer changes color: brown turns to white. As the dreamer elaborated the dream, she had turned into a big woman, healthy and positive. "In the dream, I've got this hair that I've always wanted," she said, "long hair, but it's red. I've got very fair skin, and I've got red freckles on my face. The woman interests me. She's the kind of person who doesn't have any difficulties. When I see certain white women like that, I think that they start with a clean slate. I look in a mirror, a car window, and I see her face, a white woman's face. I check, and I think, yeah, that's me." I asked the dreamer what it would be like for her if she suddenly, really, turned into a white woman. "In a way, it would be a relief," she said. "I think that there would be some kind of relief in being white—some kind of peacefulness. If I were white, I wouldn't feel the conflicts that I experience in being brown." These conflicts were "the different associations" that the dreamer had to various observations, such as the disparity between rich and poor in relation to "race" or color: "Very simply, even walking down the street and seeing some people who are well off and others who are not well off—seeing a homeless person and knowing that that person is usually a black person. Injustice and the history of it." Being brown had meant to her "mostly pain, for a very long time." It was "the pain—and the anger—of knowing that I, my family, and other people are suffering." She associated not only poverty but also illiteracy with being brown: "Knowing that it's a pleasure to read and that a lot of people whom I've grown up with don't know how to read, don't know how to write." White people took literacy for granted. They were arrogant. Illiteracy was "powerlessness" and a source of sadness for the dreamer.

What, I asked the dreamer, did it mean to be white? "There's a lot of insensitivity and ignorance associated with it," she said. "White people tend to think that there's only one way for the world to be, and they're very confident and comfortable about that." That one way seemed perfectly "natural" to white people. Again, I asked the dreamer what it would be like for her suddenly to turn white. "I think sometimes that if I could be white," she said, "I would just never have those conflicts, those emotions, and that history, and I could be calm. You know the saying 'Ignorance is bliss,' right? Well, I think that there would be some kind of relief. I can fantasize about that—about being at peace. Being white would mean that I could lift the burden of conflicts, emotions, and history and could feel relief."

I noted that in the dream the dreamer had turned into not just any white person but a quite specific white woman with red hair and freckles. "A person who has red hair is incredible," she said. "She has something that's unique and outstanding and that attracts a hell of a lot of attention, good and bad. I can relate to people who have red hair and freckles—or any kind of mark that they've had to carry up-front. A mark of that kind is something that's made them face and deal with who they are and the attention that they've gotten. It's made them struggle through this and come to who they are because of it." For the dreamer, there was, at least potentially, a very positive relation between physical characteristics and the formation of character through struggle.

The white woman in the dream was "not the standard white person that we see on television." She was a white person who had "some kind of connection with herself." She was a type of "Earth Mother." She was "in touch with the earth." The white woman "felt the sun and welcomed it." To the dreamer, the white woman in the dream was "the best of everything that I could pick out of a white person." The dreamer had felt "comfortable" being the white woman. In fact, she had "wallowed in it, it was such a good feeling." Although the dreamer had felt so good being white, she also noted that she "might have thought, 'What am I doing?'—because I had to check to see who I was."

The dreamer then said, "People have told me, 'You look like a white person.' When they say 'white person,' they're not saying 'freckle-faced, red-headed white person'—and I'm offended. They mean all of those negative things that I associate with a white person." Not many but some people had "accused" her of "looking white." Others had said that she was "turning white." What they had meant was that the dreamer was "losing touch with my community"—losing touch with her "racial" identity as a Mexican-American. The dreamer had begun to change when she moved away from home and went to college. Her way of speaking and thinking had begun to change. She no longer had "a heavy Spanish accent." She no longer had "the *lingo*, the barrio lingo." When she had returned home from college, she had "really *heard* it in my family." The change was "not something I had decided to do." She had not "gone and practiced." The change had occurred involuntarily, imperceptibly, unconsciously: "I just went home, and my ear had suddenly changed. I didn't feel that my family were talking wrong—I just *heard* them. I heard them differently, and they wondered whether, if my language had changed, my thoughts had also changed." The dreamer acknowledged that, in fact, her thoughts had changed: "I see the world differently now. I approach issues differently." At home "the lines were drawn" politically, with blacks and browns and liberal whites on one side and conservative whites on the other side. Family and friends had wondered whether, if the dreamer had changed the way she spoke and thought, "I would become—what do you call it?—an 'Uncle Tom.' We in the Mexican-American community have our own variety of that, you know."

I turn slowly to face the warm, glowing sunset and then turn to an older man, perhaps 70 . . . He is kind, gentle, and fair-skinned but of no particular race. I pull pictures out of my pocket. I want to show him what happened. I have maybe four pictures of me on top of the train, my sister, my dog. The dreamer, who has turned into a white woman and who will eventually turn into a black man, turns to a man who is "of no particular race." In the dream, the man serves the dreamer as a "non-racial" witness to—or as she said to me, "a reminder of"—what has happened to her.

I'm riding inside the train . . . I notice two little children, cute little kids, too perfect, too cute . . . I know that the children are not real, not what they appear to be . . . I feel that a hoax is unfolding, a huge conspiracy of some kind . . . I ask the children where they came from. They are silent. I ask a passenger to ask the children where they came from. The children don't respond. I shout at a little boy, "Where did you come from?" He glares back at me . . . The children disappear . . . I say to the passengers,

"Look! These children aren't what they seem!" The dreamer is now no longer the white woman with red hair and freckles but is again a brown woman on the train. The children, who are white and too cute, too perfect, introduce an issue of appearance versus reality, seeming versus being. They are too good to be true, too good to be believable. As a child, the dreamer had envied and resented white children because they were children of privilege. In the fifth grade, the dreamer had been removed from an elementary school that was 95 per cent Mexican-American and had been placed in a special program. "That's when I first realized the differences," she said. "I was put into a program with many white kids and some Asians. There were very few of us in the program, and we all felt as if we stuck out like sore thumbs. Everything about us— our speech, our education, our discussions about the world, the way we dressed—stuck out. Compared with the other kids, we were all far behind." The white children in the special program had been just like the white children in the dream: "They were dressed up in their polka-dots. They were all 'darling.' They just had that 'look,' you know. Real ego-centered, vicious kids." I remarked that the dreamer seemed angry. "Yeah," she said, "I was really *pissed*." She had known that the special program was an opportunity that she could not refuse, but she had also felt that it was an impossibility. She had felt the "pressure" to participate but had known that she "was going to suffer" and had not felt that she could "bring that suffering home and have my parents feel it." It was a problem with no solution: "Who was going to give me all those things? Who was going to be on my side?"

Later, as a graduate student, the dreamer had been a babysitter for a professor. "I went to her house," she said. "It was the first time that I had ever done any babysitting. I was in a white person's home, and I was curious to see what a professor's home would look like." What, she had wondered, were these white people like? "How did they live? What did they have?" They had had "little kids," and those children had had "rows and rows of books, spy novels, a room of art projects and doll houses— oh, so many things—and their own computer." The dreamer had gotten "really angry" at all the privilege: "They were exposed to so much. An *over*abundance of things—at a very young age. It was difficult for me, and the professor was a *social worker*. She should have been aware of how I might have felt about those things, but she would boast about her children: 'Oh, yes, she's taking art courses.' So I got really pissed." The dreamer had gotten angry, I suggested, because she had remembered the little girl that she had been and the things that she had lacked. "Yeah," she said, "and because I know so many kids who can't even *imagine* that. It's so far removed from their experience that they can't even entertain it. They don't know that the possibility exists, and if they do know about it, they know that it's so far out of their reach that they never give it a second thought."

In the dream, the dreamer demands to know where the children have come from. On the train, the dreamer, who is going to a destination, asks about the children, who are coming from an origin. What angers her is that this origin is a privilege. White children are really no better than brown or black children. They are only apparently better: just too cute, just too perfect. The injustice of the situation is a hoax or conspiracy that white people, white parents and white children, perpetrate when they refuse to acknowledge the arbitrary privilege of an origin that perpetuates inequality of opportunity.

I say, "There are many gods..." As I speak, I am turning into a man— a tall, big black man. My head is bald... I am having trouble speaking. There is a lump in my throat. My throat is changing, my voice is deepening. I clear my throat, and in a new, deep voice I finish the sentence: "... but not all of us come from the same god." Why, I asked, did the dreamer feel that she had turned into a black man? "In the dream," she said, "I was very uncomfortable with the things that I was saying. I was so judgmental, so hard. I was looking at these little kids and asking them where they had come from. I was uncomfortable with what I was doing, but I wanted to finish. I had to change, to become something that was very different from me." The dreamer could not be white or even brown to say what she was saying: "I had to be black, because I felt that what I was saying was critical, and it would take guts to say that to these white folks on the train. Because of the conflict, I couldn't be white. The black man was saying something to the white people, revealing something to them. He had to have a sensibility. He had to be black." I noted that the dreamer had turned not only into a black but also into a man. "Well," she said, "I sometimes think that men are arrogant—they just go through things and don't really think about the consequences. And that size. He was so big." Why, I wondered, did the black man have a bald head? "It was a shiny one, too," the dreamer said. "Shiny, shiny, shiny bald head. Well, he was headstrong. The guy had force, and I think that I saw that in his head. He was going to go ahead and butt heads, challenge them. It was a little too shiny, so maybe he wasn't really thinking. Head-strong but not really thinking." The black man would have been more thoughtful, I asked, if he had had hair on his head? "Not as headstrong," the dreamer said. "He was argumentative, and I associated that with his bald head. He was going to have a verbal confrontation with these people. He had this big head so that he would use his big brain. But it was so shiny. He had this ego-thing, you know, and I felt that it gave him strength."

In the middle of a sentence, the dreamer had changed from a brown woman into a black man. Not only her color but also her voice had changed. Her voice had deepened as she became a man. She had had trouble speaking because of a lump in her throat. "I got choked up," she said, "when I saw myself coming to an ultimatum. I choked. It was hurting me to do this, but, still, I wanted to get it out." A lump in the throat may be a constriction due to emotional conflict, but it may also be, in this instance, an indication of a change from female to male or a change from feminine to masculine. This dream is not only a color-change dream but also a sex-change or gender-change dream. As the dreamer goes black, goes male, goes masculine, she develops a lump in her throat, a larynx that enables her to speak with a voice of revelatory authority.

The dreamer says, "There are many gods, but not all of us come from the same god." As a black man, she answers the question that, as a brown woman, she had asked the white children. White children, brown children, and black children come from different gods. "I've always thought of gods," the dreamer said, "as associated with different worldviews or perspectives. For me, when I put that into context, it means that some people get *screwed* and other people get helped. I'm talking about rights and wrongs. All things are not equal. I'm saying that all things are not equal. In the dream, I'm talking about ideologies. Everything looks fine on the surface with these little pipsqueaks, and everybody's really cool about it, but I'm upset. I don't know where they're coming from. Some people come out of a certain worldview or perspective or ideology, and I have no idea what the logic is behind it. Where they're coming from, I have no idea. In the dream, I say, 'Let's recognize that we aren't all the same and that everything's not fine. There are different things going on here, and some of them are pretty damned serious.' "

INTERPRETATION OF THE DREAM

Is the motivation of this color-change dream a wish to be white—or a wish to be black? The dreamer does imagine that being a big, healthy, positive white woman would mean peace—relief from difficulty, conflict, and pain. She does imagine that being a big, bald black man would mean the courage to be critical, confrontative, and argumentative. Do these associations to "whiteness" and "blackness" mean, however, that the dreamer wishes that she were white or black? She does wish to have peace and courage, but does she actually wish to have white or black skin?

I asked the dreamer whether she had ever thought about turning black. "Not as much as about turning white," she said. "Color has been a major thing for me." Was she happy, I asked, with her own color? "I have mixed feelings," she replied. Had she ever wished not to be the color that she is? "No, never," she said. Then she paused. "Let me think about that." She paused again. "No," she said, emphatically. What she had wished for, she said, was "some of the privileges that come with being white," but she had never wished to be white.

What would it be like to be black, I asked, to have been black? "Ooooh, man, it would have been difficult, really difficult." If "white" meant privilege and "brown" meant deprivation and difficulty, then "black" meant even more deprivation and difficulty. In comparison with black people, she had had "a little bit of privilege" as a brown person. As a graduate student, she might be the only "person of color" in a class, but "if there's even one black person in the class, then *that* person is the 'person of color.' " The person of color always had "the burden of being different, being very different, and everything that has to do with 'different.' " As a brown person rather than a black person, the dreamer had had "an opportunity to be quiet, 'blend in' just a little bit, and get by." Being black would have intensified the experience of being different: "I wouldn't have kept quiet sometimes. I wouldn't have had the opportunity. I think that I would have *done* something really *radical*, out of anger, to hear some of the things that would have been said to me in class, directly at me—what white people say to black folks, what they imply." Sometimes, being brown was not being so different. "I'm a little bit"—the dreamer sighed—"*saved*. The white people are talking about me, too, but I'm spared just a little bit."

As a Mexican-American woman, the dreamer has a "racial" identity that is "brown"—between "white" and "black." Like Jung in Africa, she is in the minority in America. Unlike Jung, she does not feel panic at the prospect of changing color or "going white." She does, however, feel ambivalence about it. What concerns her is the old identity that she may lose if—or as—she gains a new identity. Just as Jung was afraid of losing "white" European identity in the presence of "black" African identity, she is afraid of losing "brown" Mexican-American identity in the presence of "white" American identity. The dreamer would like to be in a position consciously to pick and choose only those characteristics of the "other" that would enable her still to recognize the "self" that she has always known. She acknowledges, however, that she has already unconsciously both taken on and given up certain characteristics. The self has already assumed at least some of the coloration of the other. The dreamer is afraid that "racial" identity is all a zero-sum game, in which a gain (of unfamiliar or undesirable characteristics) on one side of the equation entails an equal or equivalent loss (of familiar or desirable characteristics) on the other side. What is at issue is the integrity of the self in contact with the other.

Did the dreamer "look white?" Was she "turning white?" Under the influence of the majority, from elementary school to graduate school, she had begun to "speak white" and "think white." She had noticed the change—she had heard the difference—and so had her family and friends in the barrio. Would she eventually be so "white" as to be unrecognizable? How much had she already changed, and how much more might she change? In the dream, she has a capacity for self-reflection on her psychical reality. When the dreamer changes into the white woman, she looks in the mirror to see who she is. Does she have the same identity—or a different one? The external appearance of the dreamer may seem different, but the internal reality is the same. On the surface she may seem different, but at a depth she is the same. "Racially," she may be a woman of a different color, but she is still essentially herself. What is that essence of identity that enables her to recognize herself? It is her smile. When the dreamer reflects on herself and smiles, she knows who she is.

The dream is an archetypal dream that employs what George Lakoff and Mark Johnson call the "life-is-a-journey" metaphor (1980: 44–5, 90–1). The dreamer comes from one place, her origin, and goes toward another place, her destination—her destiny. She has not come from the same place as whites. She has come from a place not of privilege but of deprivation. She journeys on a train, on a fast track of hopes and fears, toward connection, mobility, experience, and the future. Her sister, the shadow of all that she has left behind on the other side of the tracks as inferior or negative, is there to help her when she wants or needs to get off the train. A kind, gentle person of no particular "race," a "non-racial" person, helps her remember what she has experienced on the train. As day turns to night, brown turns to white, the dreamer reflects on herself, smiles at herself, in the mirror of identity. Brown again, the dreamer gets back on the train. She realizes that all is not what it seems to be. Then brown turns to black, female turns to male, and the dreamer, not without difficulty, speaks the truth: "There are many gods, but not all of us come from the same god." This is not a monotheistic but a polytheistic revelation. The psyche of the dreamer evidently exemplifies what Hillman calls "polytheistic psychology" (1981). The America of the dreamer is not the America of *e pluribus unum*—"from many, one." It is an America of "from many, different." For the dreamer, the truth of America is not unity but multiplicity—"multiracial," multicultural differences. In spite of appearances, in spite of checks and bows and polka dots, everything is not fine. Where someone comes from, what god someone comes from, what worldview, perspective, or ideology one comes from, what class one comes from, what culture one comes from, and what "race" or color one comes from are collective factors that exert a profound influence on individual identity.

What, I asked the dreamer, did she feel about the current "racial" situation? "I think that it's a major issue," she said. "A lot bigger than people even think it is. Some people think that it's already been blown out of proportion—that everything is reduced to 'race'—but it's an even bigger problem. It's huge. It's a manifestation, one great manifestation, of the *human* problem that just appears in this way." What did she mean by the human problem? "The problem of connecting outside ourselves," she said. "Because there's not the barest kind of connection right now, 'race' becomes a huge issue. It becomes a huge barrier. It doesn't have to be at all, but it is, because there's not even the slightest connection between us and anything outside ourselves—the *world*." The issue of "race" would not be so big if people had any connection at all with a world different from the one that they happen to inherit and inhabit. "It's incredible," the dreamer said, "to see a completely different world, a different way of being that can exist, that does exist. It's hard for some people to imagine that sort of thing, but I know what it's like—to feel *disconnected* from the world. When I was a child, I didn't know that there were all these white people. I thought that America was a Mexican country. I thought that Spanish was the dominant language. I thought that everybody lived as we did. Now, when I go home, I see an entirely different world, that same world. I can see that there's a different way to look at things, a different way to live. That experience has helped me in a lot of ways." Had the experience helped her, I asked, because it had enabled her to see the other in a certain way? "Because it enabled me to entertain the very possibility that there *is* another side . . . to *everything*," she replied. "I have seen another side. I have lived another side. I have a memory of the other side. It enables me to think things in an entirely different way. It's a pretty serious way of growing up, it's not an easy way, but that's really living, that's really living. So I don't wish to be white. I don't really know what it's like, but I do know what being around it is like."

I do not regard this interpretation as exhaustive. The dream is quite complex and not, it seems to me, reducible to a formulaic interpretation, either Freudian or Jungian. This color-change dream does, however, demonstrate that "race," racism, and "racial" identity are significant collective issues in the cultural unconscious of at least some dreamers—and not merely derivatives of some other, ostensibly more basic, strictly personal reality. From the associations that the dreamer provides, it seems obvious to me that what motivates the dream is not a wish to have white skin— or black skin. There are wishes (for lack of a better word) in the dream: a wish to have the peace (and privilege) that the dreamer associates with "whiteness" and a wish to have the courage that she associates with "blackness." These "wishes," however, seem to me less causes of an effect (or motives of the dream) than means to an end, which is a very serious proposition about "racial" identity, multiplicity, and difference in contemporary America. If the function of the unconscious is to compensate the one-sided attitudes of the ego, to present to the ego other-sided perspectives, then what this dreamer says about the capacity to experience different worlds and "to entertain the very possibility that there *is* another side" is, as the dreamer says, an issue of decisive importance—is, in fact, "the *human* problem" of a connection with an "other" outside the "self."

Samuels says: "I must say that I cannot see why one has to feel good about being a man; I feel ambivalent about it" (1993: 198). Similarly, the dreamer does not see why one has to feel good (or bad) about being a "white," a "black," a "brown," or any other color; she feels ambivalent about it. From the panic of the white European Jung to the ambivalence of the brown Mexican-American dreamer may not seem much progress toward an authentic multicultural imagination, but it may be an accurate account of where we are, if not of where we ought to be.

Chapter 15

Old Man River

As I conclude this book, I experience a sense of just how incomplete this particular account of "race," color, and the unconscious is. I wonder about the general applicability and utility of what one "white" man, an American, a New Yorker, in the 1990s has written. If I remain certain about anything, it is that issues of "race," racism, and "racial" identity deserve more attention than they have received from psychoanalysis. The "raciality" of the unconscious requires additional exploration. So far, psychoanalysis has given short shrift to the multicultural imagination. Although this is a psychoanalytic book, I do not believe that psychological analysis is either the only or the best way to interpret "race," racism, and "racial" identity. I would not "psychologize" these issues—as if psychical reality were primary and social, political, economic, and other realities secondary. Equal opportunity may be a potential, but privilege and deprivation are actualities. I simply happen to be a psychotherapist with an interest in psychical reality.

For George Herbert Mead, the decisive terms are "mind," 'self," "society," and "others" (1934). For me, they are "psyche," "self," "culture," and "others." I agree with Mead that mental reality is fundamentally a social reality—or, as I prefer to say, psychical reality is fundamentally a cultural reality—a relation between self and others. "When psychoanalysis moves away from the clinical context," Jean Laplanche says, "it does not do so as an afterthought, or to take up side-issues. It does so in order to encounter *cultural phenomena*." According to Laplanche, psychoanalysis is not a narrow clinical but "a broad cultural movement" (1989: 11–12). For me, the clinical *is* the cultural. Psychoanalysis does not so much move away from the clinical context in order to encounter cultural phenomena as it encounters cultural phenomena *in* the clinical context. From a psychoanalytic perspective, what Mead calls "significant others" may be either external others or internal others. The issue for me is how the ego, the "I," or the self-image, can relate in a non-defensive, receptive way to other-images, whether they be external or internal.

Some whites believe that they were the first people to develop an ego. They have variously described this development in evolutionary or historical terms. They tend to believe that we were once all unconscious or "primitive." At some moment, these whites assert, they developed an ego and became conscious or "civilized." The presumption has been (and I contend that it continues to be) that non-whites—and especially blacks—may have soul and body, but they have little or no ego; they are simply not as conscious as whites. From this perspective, non-whites are still benighted and have yet to be enlightened—if, in fact, they can be. The historicist believes that it is only a matter of time until they are enlightened; the evolutionist believes that, for all intents and purposes, they cannot be, will never be, because they are different and inferior not merely in degree but in kind, not by culture but by nature—that is, by "race." A variation on this theme is the contention by Richard J. Herrnstein and Charles Murray (1994; Jacoby and Glauberman 1995; Fraser 1995) that on a "bell curve" blacks are "racially" less intelligent than whites.

I do not mean to imply that all whites always regard blacks as different and inferior. In fact, some whites regard blacks as different and equal, sometimes even different and superior. Consider the following "Old Man River Dream," in which one of my patients, a white woman, imagined me, her therapist, as a black man:

> *We are going down river in a boat. In the dream, you don't look like you. You have a blue-black face. You're a large man, big. You're like Paul Robeson in build. You're wearing a black-and-white checked shirt. You're in the stern, I'm in the bow. I'm flooded. It's as though the boat for me is a piece of felt, with water all through me. I'm apprehensive that I'll get nipped by a snake or alligator. You don't seem to be bothered by the process.*

The dreamer free associated as follows:

> The black man epitomized strength and mystery. There was something unfamiliar yet attractive about him. He was not threatening or frightening. He was like a riverboat captain on the waters of the Mississippi. The boat was like a lily pad, that sometimes floated above the water, sometimes floated below the water, but that was not going to sink. I wasn't sinking, but I wasn't dry. It was as if the black man was saying, "Don't worry, Sugar, it's OK. I know where I'm going." It was as if you were saying that there is not as much reason to panic as I do: you know these waters.

The dream is obviously a transference dream. The therapist and the patient are metaphorically together "in the same boat." Certain psychoanalysts, perhaps especially alchemical Jungians, might wonder about the riverworthiness of the boat as a suitable container for the therapeutic process, because it is evidently such a porous, leaky vessel. The black man is a strong, mysterious other-image of a navigator, or archetypal guide, through the waters of the unconscious, which are flooding and soaking but not sinking the self-image of the dreamer through *feelings*, through material that is (as the dreamer says) "felt." Jung would probably interpret the saturation alchemically, as the *solutio* stage of the therapeutic process, in which the waters of the unconscious—frequently in the image of a "deluge" but also typically in the image of a "sea, lake, river, spring" dissolve the defensively egocentric attitudes of the dreamer (*CW* 14: 272, para. 364). In this instance, the ego may be apprehensive about possibly dangerous contents of the unconscious (a snake or alligator), but at least it is not so defensive as to be unreceptive to the guidance, through the transference, of a knowledgeable black man. (Perhaps I am not merely a white man after all.)

Both Freudian and Jungian analysts have recently begun to address the issue of what I call the fantasy principle. Castoriadis speaks of the "radical imagination"; Hillman speaks of the "imaginal." Of the two, Hillman seems to me to offer a more comprehensive account. Although Castoriadis modifies the dictum "Where id was, there ego shall be" to "Where ego is, id must also appear," he retains the ego–id (or ego–imagination) opposition. He does not seem to consider the ego itself to be an image. For Castoriadis, the ego still apparently exists in opposition to the imagination. For Hillman, however, the ego is merely one image among many images, with which it coexists (Adams forthcoming). Thus he speaks of the "imaginal ego," an ego that appreciates that "it too is an image" (1979: 102). Hillman does not oppose the ego to the imagination; he relativizes it and includes it in the imagination. From this perspective, the ego is simply a self-image in relation to other-images. In effect, both Castoriadis and Hillman advocate a non-defensive ego, or self-image, that would be receptive to other-images—as the ego of the dreamer is receptive to the black man.

Many blacks are, of course, just as defensive as any whites are about "race" or color. For example, recourse by some blacks to the collective solidarity of "racial" identity may be either an effective strategy and tactic or merely an evasion of the responsibility and opportunity for an individual identity. It seems to me obvious that blacks have had much more justification than whites to be "racially" defensive, since whites have tended to be so offensive. The demand by many blacks for "respect" says it all. The fact remains, however, that blacks ultimately encounter the same dilemma as whites: how eventually to develop a self-image that is less defensive in relation to other-images.

A certain "African style" has continued to exist *sub rosa*, under duress, in spite of prejudice and discrimination—and in spite of slavery. In terms of cultural atrocities, slavery qualifies as one of the extreme traumas. The physical and psychical dislocation of slavery remains an issue for many blacks who strive to establish an effective identity, both collective and individual. For some, the existence of an ethnic tree that survived forcible transplantation, in spite of slavery and all efforts to sever the roots, and that expansively influences contemporary cultural experience dignifies the struggle for identity. For others, it matters not so much whether such a tree and such roots exist—they will invent them. To the extent that some blacks have recently attempted to establish an "Afrocentric" identity, they have contrived a "narrative truth" rather than a "historical truth" (Spence 1982). This "truth" serves a quite specific purpose, which is to abolish any sense of positional inferiority relative to whites.

Among the most extreme versions of this effort is the account that Michael Bradley (1991) provides of the evolution of European whites, or "ice" people (who are by nature emotionally cold, aggressive, and racist), from African blacks, or "sun" people (who are by nature emotionally warm, non-aggressive, and non-racist). Bradley even cites Freud, who (in an essay that he ultimately decided not to publish) hypothesizes that under the catastrophic impact of the Ice Age, Europeans became "generally *anxious*" (1987: 14)—or neurotic. Another extreme version is the one that Elijah Muhammad of the Nation of Islam offers. According to him, European whites evolved from African blacks by the efforts of a mad black scientist, Mr Yakub, who bred (or "grafted") whites from blacks. Over a period of 600 years, this eugenics project gradually browned, reddened, yellowed, then finally whitened the black followers of Mr Yakub. The result was a "race" not of humans but of "devils." These devils, Elijah Muhammad says, "were really pale white, with really blue eyes." He considers these "the ugliest colors" (1965: 116). Not only does Elijah Muhammad reverse the colorist aesthetic that devalues black in opposition to white, he also reverses the racist prejudice that dehumanizes blacks as apes. He says that some whites attempted to breed themselves black again—but with only partial success: "A few were lucky enough to make a start, and got as far as what you call the gorilla." The entire "monkey family," he says, derives from European whites (1965: 119). Such "truths" are, of course, simply a reversal of the spurious "racial" purity notions of white supremacists. The effort is perfectly predictable: if some whites fantasize superiority over blacks, then some blacks will, with a vengeance, fantasize superiority over whites—and in terms virtually identical with those that whites have historically misapplied to blacks. There is a certain irony to these pseudoscientific evolutionary accounts. Some contemporary geneticists conclude that we all were once "black"— or at least African: that we all share common ancestors, an "Eve" and an "Adam" from whom we descended "out of Africa," respectively, 200,000 years ago and 188,000 years ago (Wilford 1995, 23 November: A,

1 and 28). (This is a genetic, not a "racial," hypothesis.) Afrocentrists contend that we have all descended out of Africa not only genetically but also culturally. They assert that Western culture (or, more specifically, Western philosophy) is a legacy that the Greeks stole from the Egyptians, who, in the Afrocentric version of events, were black (James 1954; Bernal 1987, 1991). Mary Lefkowitz (1996; Lefkowitz and Rogers 1996) argues that this is simply an unscholarly preference for a mythical rather than a historical account of cultural priority.

I conclude this book in the year of the O.J. Simpson trial and the Million Man March—two events that have demonstrated once again to "whites" and "blacks" how fraught an issue "race" or color can be in America. What would we do without "race" or color as an issue not only in America but also in Europe, in Africa, and in other cultures? Can we imagine a discourse that eschews "black" and "white" categories? Do not these categories, even when we apply them for positive purposes, with the best of intentions, simply reiterate and reinforce the very opposition that produces the problem in the first place? "Race" does "matter," as Cornel West insists (1993), but will it matter less and less (unless, that is, we continue to "racialize" discourse)? Shelby Steele has argued that good ends never justify bad means. He maintains that affirmative action, or "racial" preferences, have been unnecessarily divisive. According to him, the uncritical linkage of "black skin to deprivation and white skin to privilege" has artificially fostered ill will toward African-Americans. He says that "race remains a dangerous shorthand whether the intentions are good or bad." The rhetoric of "good intentions—diversity, cultural identity, multiculturalism, pluralism"—which he acknowledges are "worthy ideas," deflects attention from the real issues, which are "persistent inequality, the proliferation of demagogues and a relentless racial politics that erodes more national common ground every day." Steele concludes: "America suffers as much today from a well-intentioned identification of its citizens by race as it does from old-fashioned racism" (1995, 24 October: A, 27). This position is similar to that of the sociologist William Julius Wilson (1980), who argues that inequality is increasingly a function not simply of "race" but of class, or an "underclass." Although Steele is often categorized as a "conservative" and Wilson as a "liberal," they both seem to privilege economic inequality as the primary issue. Can we be confident, however, that equality in that one sense would mean an end to racism?

From the evidence that patients present to me in dreams or in the therapeutic dialogue, it seems to me that we are all, white and black, in transition toward a discourse of difference rather than opposition, one that emphasizes culture rather than nature. If so, such a transition will not be without difficulty. There is a certain paradox to racism. I mean that as long as we categorize people by nature, as long as we simplistically regard psychical differences as a function of physical differences, we can avoid, postpone, or minimize conflicts, controversies, and confrontations over culture—that is, over the life-styles of people. The differences in life-styles between people are much greater than any differences in "races"—and potentially much more contentious. An example would be the protests of Alice Walker against the cultural practice of clitoridectomy and infibulation as an inhuman and immoral act. Walker courageously exposes the defects of a cultural relativism that would be utterly nonjudgmental toward certain life-styles. Once culture or ethnicity rather than nature or "race" becomes the issue, however, we are suddenly in a difficult position: I mean that we are in a position that has to acknowledge that any truly significant differences in life-styles between people are cultural *preferences*, not natural *orientations*. Until recently, "race" or color has seemed a matter of natural *fact*. In contrast, ethnicity is a matter of cultural *values*. (Perhaps it is no accident that not only the "character" issue but also the "culture" issue has suddenly assumed such prominence in the political reality of contemporary America.) We may not like—in fact, we may detest—certain life-styles, and since life-styles are by definition arbitrary and conventional, *any* such practices (not just extreme examples like female genital mutilation) may suddenly become topics of radical contention. It is precisely this problem of *practices-as-preferences* that seems to me to pose not only an opportunity but also the most difficult challenge for contemporary cultural studies—and for any psychoanalysis that aspires to be authentically multicultural.

Conflict over very real cultural differences can be just as intense as any conflict over merely apparent, ostensibly significant natural differences. "Ethnic cleansing" on the basis of cultural differences can be just as vicious, just as violent, just as genocidal, as " 'racial' cleansing" on the basis of natural differences. Even if we were to abolish racism (or colorism), we would still have to contend with "ethnicism." Entreaties to tolerate or celebrate differences by an appeal to cultural relativism may be necessary, but they may also be facile. I do not believe that racism will vanish, but I do believe that "race" or color will gradually seem less and less relevant as a category, and ethnicity will seem more and more significant. An end to racism would not necessarily mean an end to conflict; it might even mean an increase in it. To become conscious of the diversity of diversity is to become conscious of an innumerable number of cultures and the incredibly vast differences between them. I do not believe that the psyche is by "human nature" bound to categorize phenomena oppositionally—or conflictually. It is difficult but by no means impossible for the psyche to categorize phenomena differentially. Oppositional categorizations, whether on the basis of nature or culture, require less effort than differential categorizations. It is easier unconsciously to reduce complex differences to simple oppositions and then projectively to typify the self as superior and the other as inferior—and much harder consciously to discern and comprehend the virtually infinite variety of differences. I do, however, believe that some if not all of us can develop a relatively receptive, non-defensive ego and the capacity for a differential, multicultural imagination. If enough of us do, then perhaps we will be able to make a decisive difference.

Colorism is a variety of essentialism. The assumption is that an outer appearance (skin color) is an indicator of an inner essence. The essentialist fallacy effectively restricts (I would say, condemns) all individuals—"white," "black," or whatever color—to a collective "natural" identity: to a *singular* psyche rather than what Samuels calls a plural psyche. It is this "singularism" that the playwright Suzan-Lori Parks considers especially pernicious, particularly as it affects African-Americans: "As there is no single 'Black Experience,' there is no single 'Black Aesthetic' and there is no one way to write or think or feel or dream or interpret or be interpreted." There is, she emphasizes, no "one way of being" (1995: 21–2). These are wise words not only for "blacks" but also for "whites" and for people of every other color, as well as for psychoanalysts and psychotherapists: there are many ways to be, many ways to interpret and be interpreted—many more than we have yet even begun to imagine.

Bibliography

Adams, M.V. (1982) "Ahab's Jonah-and-the-Whale Complex: The Fish Archetype in *Moby-Dick*," *ESQ*, 28, 3: 167–82.

Adams, M.V. (1983) "Whaling and Difference: *Moby-Dick* Deconstructed," *New Orleans Review*, 10, 4: 59–64.

Adams, M.V. (1984/85) "Getting a Kick out of Captain Ahab: The Merman Dream in *Moby-Dick*," *Dreamworks*, 4, 4: 279–87.

Adams, M.V. (1988) "Madness and Right Reason, Extremes of One: The Shadow Archetype in *Moby-Dick*," *Bucknell Review*, 31, 2: 97–109.

Adams, M.V. (1991) "My Siegfried Problem—And Ours: Jungians, Freudians, Anti-Semitism, and the Psychology of Knowledge," in A. Maidenbaum and S.A. Martin (eds) *Lingering Shadows: Jungians, Freudians, and Anti-Semitism*, Boston and London: Shambhala, pp. 241–59.

Adams, M.V. (1992) "Image, Active Imagination, and the Imaginal Level: A *Quadrant* Interview with Robert Bosnak," *Quadrant*, 25, 2: 9–29.

Adams, M.V. (forthcoming) "The Archetypal School," in P. Young-Eisendrath and T. Dawson (eds) *The Cambridge Companion to Jung*, Cambridge: Cambridge University Press.

Adams, M.V., and Sherry, J. (1991) "Appendix A: Significant Words and Events," in A. Maidenbaum and S.A. Martin (eds) *Lingering Shadows: Jungians, Freudians, and Anti-Semitism*, Boston and London: Shambhala, pp. 357–96.

Adler, A. (1916) *The Neurotic Constitution: Outlines of a Comparative Individual Psychology*, trans. B. Glueck and J.E. Lind, New York: Moffat, Yard.

Albers, J. (1975) *Interaction of Color*, New Haven, CT, and London: Yale University Press.

Anderson, D. (1991, 13 October) "The Braves' Tomahawk Phenomenon," *New York Times*, 8, 1.

Anonymous (1993 April) "Short Cuts: Finding the Hairstyle That Best Suits You," *EM*, pp. 58–9.

Anzieu, D. (1989) *The Skin Ego: A Psychoanalytic Approach to the Self*, trans. C. Turner, New Haven, CT, and London: Yale University Press.

Associated Press (1993, 11 August) "Accused Slayer of a Surgeon Says 'Fake Aryan Beauty' Angers Him," *New York Times*, A, 11.

Associated Press (1993, 26 August) "Beaten Trucker Recalls Little," *New York Times*, A, 17.

Baldwin, J., Perl, A., and Lee, S. (1992), *Malcolm X* [screenplay], in S. Lee with R. Wiley, *By Any Means Necessary: The Trials and Tribulations of the Making of Malcolm X*, New York: Hyperion, pp. 169–312.

Baring, A., and Cashford, J. (1991) *The Myth of the Goddess: Evolution of an Image*, London and New York: Viking.

Barthes, R. (1968) *Elements of Semiology*, trans. A. Lavers and C. Smith, New York: Hill & Wang.

Begg, E. (1985) *The Cult of the Black Virgin*, London: Routledge & Kegan Paul.

Berg, C. (1951) *The Unconscious Significance of Hair*, London: George Allen & Unwin.

Berger, P., and Luckmann, T. (1966) *The Social Construction of Reality: A Treatise in the Sociology of Knowledge*, New York: Doubleday.

Berke, R.L. (1991, 12 October) "Thomas Accuser Tells Hearing of Obscene Talk and Advances; Judge Complains of 'Lynching,' " *New York Times*, 1, 1 and 9.

Bernal, M. (1987) *Black Athena: The Fabrication of Ancient Greece, 1785–1985*, New Brunswick, NJ: Rutgers University Press, vol. 1.

Bernal, M. (1991) *Black Athena: The Archaeological and Documentary Evidence*, New Brunswick, NJ: Rutgers University Press, vol. 2.

Bernstein, J. *et al.* (1991) "Jung and Anti-Semitism (Workshop)," in M.A. Mattoon (ed.) *Personal and Archetypal Dynamics in the Analytical Relationship: Proceedings of the Eleventh Annual International Congress for Analytical Psychology, Paris, 1989*, Einsiedeln: Daimon Verlag, pp. 459–500.

Bhabha, H.K. (1984) "Of Mimicry and Man: The Ambivalence of Colonial Discourse," *October*, 2: 125–33.

Birren, F. (1961) *Color Psychology and Color Therapy: A Factual Study of the Influence of Color on Human Life*, Secaucus, NJ: University Books.

Black Rock Coalition (1990) *The History of Our Future* [audiotape], Salem, MA: Rykodisc.

Boas, G. (1990) *The Cult of Childhood*, Dallas, TX: Spring.

Bonham Public Schools—(1910) *Rules and Regulations, Course of Study, and Directory for Session of 1910–1911*, Bonham, TX.

Bosnak, R. (1988) *A Little Course in Dreams*, Boston and Shaftesbury, MA: Shambhala.

Boss, M. (1977) *"I Dreamt Last Night . . .": An Approach to the Revelations of Dreaming—and Its Uses in Psychotherapy*, trans. S. Conway, New York: Gardner.

Bowers, K.S., and Meichenbaum, D. (eds) (1984) *The Unconscious Reconsidered*, New York: John Wiley & Sons.

Bradley, M. (1991) *The Iceman Inheritance: Prehistoric Sources of Western Man's Racism, Sexism and Aggression*, New York: Kayode.

Brooke, R. (1991) *Jung and Phenomenology*, London and New York: Routledge.

Brunner, C. (1986) *Anima as Fate*, trans. J. Heuscher, Dallas, TX: Spring.

Campbell, J. (1959) *The Masks of God: Primitive Mythology*, New York: Viking.

Campbell, J. (ed.) (1971) *The Portable Jung*, trans. R.F.C. Hull, New York: Vintage.

Cardinal, M. (1983) *The Words To Say It*, trans. P. Goodheart, Cambridge, MA: VanVactor & Goodheart.

Castoriadis, C. (1987) *The Imaginary Institution of Society*, trans. C. Blamey, Boston: MIT Press.

Chaudhuri, U. (1994) Personal communication.

Child, C.M. *et al.* (1928/1966) *The Unconscious: A Symposium*, Freeport, NY: Books for Libraries.

Cleaver, E. (1968) *Soul on Ice*, New York: Dell.

Cohen, M.N. (1960) *Rider Haggard: His Life and Works*, New York: Walker & Company.

Conrad, J. (1899/1971) *Heart of Darkness*, ed. R. Kimbrough, New York and London: W.W. Norton.

Dalal, F. (1988) "Jung, a Racist," *British Journal of Psychotherapy*, 4, 3: 263–79.

Davis, F.J. (1991) *Who Is Black? One Nation's Definition*, University Park, PA: Pennsylvania State University Press.

De Angulo, X. (1977) "Comments on a Doctoral Thesis," in W. McGuire and R. F.C. Hull (eds) *C.G. Jung Speaking: Interviews and Encounters*, Princeton, NJ: Princeton University Press, pp. 205–18.

Diamond, S. (1974) *In Search of the Primitive: A Critique of Civilization*, New Brunswick, NJ: Transaction.

Dilthey, W. (1976) *Selected Writings*, ed. and trans. H. P. Rickman, Cambridge: Cambridge University Press.

Du Bois, W.E.B. (1903/1993) *The Souls of Black Folk*, New York and Toronto: Alfred J. Knopf.

Ebony (1993 April).

Edinger, E.F. (1985) *Anatomy of the Psyche: Alchemical Symbolism in Psycho-therapy*, La Salle, IL: Open Court.

Edinger, E.F. (1994) *Transformation of Libido: A Seminar on C.G. Jung's Symbols of Transformation*, ed. D.D. Cordic, Los Angeles: C.G. Jung Bookstore.

Eliade, M. (1958) *Birth and Rebirth: The Religious Meanings of Initiation in Human Culture*, trans. W.B. Trask, New York: Harper & Brothers.

Elkins, S.M. (1959) *Slavery: A Problem in American Institutional and Intellectual Life*, Chicago: University of Chicago Press.

Ellenberger, H.F. (1970) *The Discovery of the Unconscious: The History and Evolution of Dynamic Psychiatry*, New York: Basic Books.

EM [*Ebony Man*] (1993 April).

Emerson, R.W. (1836/1971), "Nature," in R.E. Spillier and A.R. Ferguson (eds) *The Collected Works of Ralph Waldo Emerson*, Cambridge, MA: Belknap Press of Harvard University Press, vol. 1, pp. 1–45.

Erikson, E.H. (1968) *Identity: Youth and Crisis*, New York: W.W. Norton.

Erikson, E.H. (1969) *Gandhi's Truth: On the Origins of Militant Nonviolence*, New York: W.W. Norton.

Fairbairn, W.R.D. (1990) *Psychoanalytic Studies of the Personality*, London and New York: Tavistock/Routledge.

Fanon, F. (1967) *Black Skin, White Masks*, trans. C.L. Markmann, New York: Grove.

Firth, R. (1973) *Symbols: Public and Private*, Ithaca, NY: Cornell University Press.

Fraser, S. (ed.) (1995) *The Bell Curve Wars: Race, Intelligence, and the Future of America*, New York: Basic Books.

Freud, S. Except as below, references are to the *Standard Edition* (*SE*), by volume and page number.

Freud, S. (1985) *The Complete Letters of Sigmund Freud to Wilhelm Fliess, 1887–1904*, ed. and trans. Jeffrey Moussaieff Masson, Cambridge, MA, and London: Belknap Press of Harvard University Press.

Freud, S. (1987) *A Phylogenetic Fantasy: Overview of the Transference Neuroses*, ed. E. Grubrich-Simitis, trans. A. Hoffer and P.T. Hoffer, Cambridge, MA, and London: Belknap Press of Harvard University Press.

Freud, S., and Abraham, K. (1965) *A Psycho-analytic Dialogue: The Letters of Sigmund Freud and Karl Abraham, 1907–1926*, ed. H.C. Abraham and E.L. Freud, trans. B. Marsh and H.C. Abraham, New York: Basic Books.

Gadamer, H-G. (1975) *Truth and Method*, New York: Seabury.

Gates, Jr, H.L. (1986) "Editor's Introduction: Writing 'Race' and the Difference

It Makes," in H.L. Gates, Jr (ed.) *"Race," Writing, and Difference*, Chicago and London: University of Chicago Press, pp. 1–20.

Geertz, C. (1973) *The Interpretation of Cultures: Selected Essays*, New York: Basic Books.

Geertz, C. (1983) *Local Knowledge: Further Essays in Interpretive Anthropology*, New York: Basic Books.

Giago, T. (1994, 13 March) "Drop the Chop! Indian Nicknames Just Aren't Right," *New York Times*, 8, 9.

Goldstein, K. (1969) "Concerning the Concept of 'Primitivity,' " in S. Diamond (ed.) *Primitive Views of the World*, New York and London: Columbia University Press, pp. 1–19.

Gordon, P. (1991) "The *Free Associations* Interview: Cornelius Castoriadis Interviewed by Paul Gordon," *Free Associations*, 2, 24: 483–506.

Greenwald, J. (1988, 15 August) "Prejudice and Black Sambo," *Time*, p. 25.

Griffin, J.H. (1960) *Black Like Me*, Boston: Houghton Mifflin and Cambridge, MA: Riverside.

Gutheil, E. (1951) *The Handbook of Dream Analysis*, New York: Liveright.

Haggard, H.R. (1991) *The Annotated She: A Critical Edition of H. Rider Haggard's Victorian Romance*, ed. N. Etherington, Bloomington and Indianapolis, IN: Indiana University Press.

Hall, G.S. (1905) "The Negro Question," *Proceedings of the Massachusetts Historical Society*, 2, 19: 95–107.

Hallpike, C.R. (1979) *The Foundations of Primitive Thought*, Oxford: Clarendon Press.

Harris, H.W., Blue, H.C., and Griffith, E.E.H. (1995) *Racial Ethnic Identity: Psychological Development and Creative Expression*, New York and London: Routledge.

Harris, J.C. (1955), "The Wonderful Tar-Baby Story," in *The Complete Tales of Uncle Remus*, comp. R. Chase, Boston: Houghton Mifflin, pp. 6–8.

Helms, J.E. (ed.) (1990) *Black and White Racial Identity: Theory, Research, and Practice*, Westport, CT, and London: Praeger.

Henderson, J.L. (1990) *Shadow and Self: Selected Papers in Analytical Psychology*, Wilmette, IL: Chiron.

Herbert, B. (1996, 12 February) "Affront to Black People," *New York Times*, A, 15.

Hernton, C.C. (1965) *Sex and Racism in America*, New York: Grove.

Herrnstein, R.J., and Murray, C. (1994) *The Bell Curve: Intelligence and Class Structure in American Life*, New York: Free Press.

Hillman, J. (1972) *The Myth of Analysis: Three Essays in Archetypal Psychology*, Evanston, IL: Northwestern University Press.

Hillman, J. (1975) *Re-Visioning Psychology*, New York: Harper & Row.

Hillman, J. (1979) *The Dream and the Underworld*, New York: Harper & Row.

Hillman, J. (1981) "Psychology: Monotheistic or Polytheistic," in D.L. Miller, *The New Polytheism: Rebirth of the Gods and Goddesses*, Dallas, TX: Spring, pp. 109–42.

Hillman, J. (1986) "Notes on White Supremacy: Essaying an Archetypal Account of Historical Events," *Spring*, 46: 29–58.

Hillman, J. (1992) Remark at workshop on "Alchemical Psychology" at New York Open Center, 15–17 February.

Hillman, J., with Pozzo, L. (1983) *Inter Views: Conversations with Laura Pozzo on Psychotherapy, Biography, Love, Soul, Dreams, Work, Imagination, and the State of the Culture*, New York: Harper & Row.

hooks, b. [Watkins, G.] (1992) *Black Looks: Race and Representation*, Boston: South End.

Horney, K. (1937) *The Neurotic Personality of Our Time*, New York: W.W. Norton.

Jacoby, R., and Glauberman, N. (eds) (1995) *The Bell Curve Debate: History, Documents, Opinions*, New York: Times Books.

James, G.G.M. (1954) *Stolen Legacy*, New York: Philosophical Library.

Jones, E. (1953) *The Life and Work of Sigmund Freud: The Formative Years and the Great Discoveries, 1856–1900*, New York: Basic Books, vol. 1.

Jones, E. (1955) *The Life and Work of Sigmund Freud: Years of Maturity, 1901–1919*, New York: Basic Books, vol. 2.

Jordan, W.D. (1968) *White over Black: American Attitudes toward the Negro, 1550–1812*, Chapel Hill, NC: University of North Carolina Press.

Jung, C.G. Except as below, references are to the *Collected Works* (*CW*), by volume, page number, and paragraph.

Jung, C.G. (1963) *Memories, Dreams, Reflections*, ed. A. Jaffe, trans. R. and C. Winston, New York: Pantheon.

Jung, C.G. (1973) *Letters: 1906–1950*, ed. G. Adler and A. Jaffe, trans. R.F.C. Hull, Princeton, NJ: Princeton University Press, vol. 1.

Jung, C.G. (1976) *The Visions Seminars*, Zurich: Spring, vols. 1 and 2.

Jung, C.G. (1977) *C.G. Jung Speaking: Interviews and Encounters*, ed. W. McGuire and R.F.C. Hull, Princeton, NJ: Princeton University Press.

Jung, C.G. (1984) *Dream Analysis: Notes of the Seminar Given in 1928–1930*, ed. W. McGuire, Princeton, NJ: Princeton University Press.

Jung, C.G. (1988) *Nietzsche's Zarathustra: Notes of the Seminar Given in 1934–1939*, ed. J.L. Jarrett, Princeton, NJ: Princeton University Press.

Kallen, H.M. (1956) *Cultural Pluralism and the American Idea: An Essay in Social Philosophy*, Philadelphia: University of Pennsylvania Press.

Kennedy, A. (1987) *People Who Led to My Plays*, New York: Theatre Communications Group.

Kennedy, A. (1988) *Funnyhouse of a Negro*, in *In One Act*, Minneapolis, MN: University of Minnesota Press, pp. 1–23.

Klein, D.B. (1977) *The Unconscious: Invention or Discovery? A Historico-Critical Inquiry*, Santa Monica, CA: Goodyear.

Kluger, R.S., and Kluger, H.Y. (1984) "Evil in Dreams: A Jungian View," in M.C. Nelson and M. Eigen (eds) *Evil: Self and Culture*, New York: Human Sciences Press, pp. 162–9.

Kohler, W. (1927) *The Mentality of Apes*, trans. E. Winter, London: Routledge & Kegan Paul.

Kohut, H. (1971) *The Analysis of the Self*, New York: International Universities Press.

Kohut, H. (1977) *The Restoration of the Self*, New York: International Universities Press.

Kohut, H. (1978) *The Search for the Self: Selected Writings of Heinz Kohut 1950–1978*, ed. P.H. Ornstein, Madison, CT: International Universities Press, vol. 1.

Kohut, H. (1984) *How Does Analysis Cure?*, ed. A. Goldberg with P.E. Stepanksy, Chicago and London: University of Chicago Press.

Kovel, J. (1970) *White Racism: A Psychohistory*, New York: Pantheon.

Kriegel, L. (1990, 3 May) "Academic Freedom and Racial Theories," *New York Times*, A, 27.

Krige, E.J., and Krige, J.D. (1943) *The Realm of a Rain-Queen: A Study of the*

Pattern of Lovedu Society, London, New York, and Toronto: Oxford University Press.

Kris, E. (1952) *Psychoanalytic Explorations in Art*, New York: International Universities Press.

Labaton, S. (1996, 11 June) "Suspects are Held in 2 Fires at Black Churches in the South," *New York Times*, B, 7.

Lacan, J. (1977) *Ecrits: A Selection*, trans. A. Sheridan, New York: W.W. Norton.

Lacan, J. (1978) *The Four Fundamental Concepts of Psychoanalysis*, ed. J-A. Miller, trans. A. Sheridan, New York: W.W. Norton.

Lahr, J. (1993, 28 June) "Under the Skin," *The New Yorker*, pp. 90–4.

Lakoff, G., and Johnson, M. (1980) *Metaphors We Live By*, Chicago and London: University of Chicago Press.

Laplanche, J. (1989) *New Foundations for Psychoanalysis*, trans. D. Macey, Oxford and Cambridge, MA: Basil Blackwell.

Lee, B. (1988) "Straight and Nappy," in S. Lee with L. Jones, *Uplift the Race: The Construction of School Daze*, New York: Simon & Schuster, pp. 154–57.

Lee, S. (1988) *School Daze* [screenplay], in S. Lee with L. Jones, *Uplift the Race: The Construction of School Daze*, New York: Simon & Schuster, pp. 182–327.

Lee, S. (1993) *Malcolm X* [videotape], Burbank, CA: Warner Home Video.

Lefkowitz, M. (1996) *Not Out of Africa: How Afrocentrism Became an Excuse To Teach Myth as History*, New York: Basic Books.

Lefkowitz, M.R., and Rogers, G.M. (eds) (1996) *Black Athena Revisited*, Chapel Hill, NC: University of North Carolina Press.

Lévi-Strauss, C. (1952) *Race and History*, Paris: UNESCO.

Lévi-Strauss, C. (1966) *The Savage Mind*, Chicago: University of Chicago Press.

LeVine, R.A., with Strangman, E., and Unterberger, L. (1966) *Dreams and Deeds: Achievement Motivation in Nigeria*, Chicago and London: University of Chicago Press.

Lévy-Bruhl, L. (1910/1985) *How Natives Think*, trans. L. Clare, Princeton, NJ: Princeton University Press.

Lévy-Bruhl, L. (1921/1966) *Primitive Mentality*, trans. L. Clare, Boston: Beacon.

Lichtenberg, J.D. (1984) "The Empathic Mode and Alternative Vantage Points for Psychoanalytic Work," in J. Lichtenberg, M. Bornstein, and D. Silver (eds) *Empathy*, Hillsdale, NJ, and London: Analytic Press, vol. 1, pp. 113–35.

Lind, J.E. (1914) "The Color Complex in the Negro," *Psychoanalytic Review*, 1, 4: 404–14.

Lind, J.E. (1917) "Phylogenetic Elements in the Psychoses of the Negro," *Psychoanalytic Review*, 4, 1: 303–32.

Lipsyte, R. (1991, 18 October) "How Can Jane Fonda Be a Part of the Chop?" *New York Times*, B, 10.

McDougall, W. (1939) *The Group Mind: A Sketch of the Principles of Collective Psychology with Some Attempt to Apply Them to the Interpretation of National Life and Character*, Cambridge: Cambridge University Press.

McGuire, W. (1995) "Firm Affinities: Jung's Relations with Britain and the United States," *Journal of Analytical Psychology*, 40, 3: 301–26.

Mailer, N. (1957) "The White Negro: Superficial Reflections on the Hipster," *Dissent*, 4, 3: 276–93.

Malcolm X, with Haley, A. (1965) *The Autobiography of Malcolm X*, New York: Grove.

Malcolm X. (1989) *Malcolm X: The Last Speeches*, ed. B. Perry, New York, London, Sydney, and Toronto: Pathfinder.

Mannoni, O. (1964) *Prospero and Caliban: The Psychology of Colonization*, trans. P. Powesland, New York and Washington: Praeger.

Marriott, M. (1994, 26 June) "Afro Days Are Here Again," *New York Times*, 1 (Style), 31 and 33.

Martin, C. (1993) "Anna Deavere Smith: The Word Becomes You: An Interview with Carol Martin," *TDR*, 37, 4: 45–62.

Mead, G.H. (1934) *Mind, Self, and Society: From the Standpoint of a Social Behaviorist*, ed. C.W. Morris, Chicago: University of Chicago Press.

Medin, D., and Ortony, A. (1989) "Psychological Essentialism," in S. Vosniadou and A. Ortony (eds) *Similarity and Analogical Reasoning*, Cambridge: Cambridge University Press, pp. 179–95.

Melville, H. (1850/1987) "Hawthorne and His Mosses," in *The Writings of Herman Melville*, ed. H. Hayford, A.A. MacDougall, G.T. Tanselle, *et al.*, Evanston, IL, and Chicago: Northwestern University Press and Newberry Library, vol. 9, pp. 239–53.

Melville, H. (1851/1988) *Moby Dick; or The Whale*, in *The Writings of Herman Melville*, ed. H. Hayford, H. Parker, and G.T. Tanselle, Evanston, IL, and Chicago: Northwestern University Press and Newberry Library, vol. 6.

Merwine, M.H. (1993, 24 November) "How Africa Understands Female Circumcision," *New York Times*, A, 24.

Miller, J.G. (1942) *Unconsciousness*, New York: John Wiley & Sons.

Mingus, C. (1971) *Beneath the Underdog*, ed. N. King, New York: Alfred A. Knopf.

Mitchell, J. (1974) *Psychoanalysis and Feminism*, New York: Pantheon.

Mitchell, S.A. (1993) *Hope and Dread in Psychoanalysis*, New York: Basic Books.

Montagu, A. (1952) *Man's Most Dangerous Myth: The Fallacy of Race*, New York: Harper & Brothers.

Morrison, T. (1992) *Playing in the Dark: Whiteness and the Literary Imagination*, Cambridge, MA, and London: Harvard University Press.

Muhammad, E. (1965) *Message to the Blackman in America*, Chicago: Muhammad Mosque of Islam No. 2.

Myers, I.B., with Myers, P.B. (1990) *Gifts Differing*, Palo Alto, CA: Consulting Psychologists Press.

Nazario, S.L. (1990, 12 September) "Identity Crises: When White Parents Adopt Black Babies, Race Often Divides," *Wall Street Journal*, A, 1 and 8.

Osgood, C.E., Suci, G.J., and Tannenbaum, P.H. (1957) *The Measurement of Meaning*, Urbana, IL: University of Illinois Press.

Osofsky, G. (ed.) (1969) *Puttin' On Ole Massa: The Slave Narratives of Henry Bibb, William Wells Brown, and Solomon Northup*, New York, Evanston, IL, and London: Harper & Row.

Oxford English Dictionary.

Parks, S-L. (1995) "An Equation for Black People Onstage," in *The America Play and Other Works*, New York: Theatre Communications Group, pp. 19–22.

Parrinder, G. (1967) *African Mythology*, London: Paul Hamlyn.

Pasteur, A.B., and Toldson, I.L. (1982) *Roots of Soul: The Psychology of Black Expressiveness*, Garden City, NY: Doubleday.

Patterson, O. (1995, 7 August) "Affirmative Action, On the Merit System," *New York Times*, A, 13.

Patton, P. (1992, 8 November) "Who Owns 'X'?" *New York Times*, 9, 1 and 10.

Perls, F.S. (1992) *Gestalt Therapy Verbatim*, ed. J. Wysong, Highland, NY: Gestalt Journal.

Propp, V. (1968) *Morphology of the Folktale*, ed. L.A. Wagner, trans. L. Scott, Austin, TX, and London: University of Texas Press.

Rainville, R.E. (1988) *Dreams across the Life Span*, Boston: American Press.

Redfearn, J.W.T. (1985) *My Self, My Many Selves*, London: Academic Press.

Reed, I. (1972) *Mumbo Jumbo*, Garden City, NY: Doubleday.

Reich, W. (1949) *Character Analysis*, trans. T. Wolfe, New York: Orgone Institute Press.

Reik, T. (1949) *Listening with the Third Ear: The Inner Experience of a Psychoanalyst*, New York: Farrar, Straus.

Ricoeur, P. (1967) *The Symbolism of Evil*, trans. E. Buchanan, Boston: Beacon.

Ricoeur, P. (1970) *Freud and Philosophy: An Essay on Interpretation*, trans. D. Savage, New Haven, CT, and London: Yale University Press.

Roland, A. (1988) *In Search of Self in India and Japan: Toward a Cross-Cultural Psychology*, Princeton, NJ: Princeton University Press.

Rosenthal, A.M. (1993, 12 November) "Female Genital Torture," *New York Times*, A, 33.

Roubiczek, P. (1952) *Thinking in Opposites: An Investigation of the Nature of Man Revealed by the Nature of Thinking*, London: Routledge & Kegan Paul.

Russell, K., Wilson, M., and Hall, R. (1992) *The Color Complex: The Politics of Skin Color among African Americans*, New York, San Diego, CA, and London: Harcourt Brace Jovanovich.

Rustin, M. (1991) *The Good Society and the Inner World: Psychoanalysis, Politics and Culture*, London and New York: Verso.

Sachs, W. (1947) *Black Anger* [retitled *Black Hamlet*], Boston: Little, Brown & Company.

Sacks, D. (1992, 29 July) "The Cutting Edge of Multiculturalism," *Wall Street Journal*, A, 10.

Said, E.W. (1978) *Orientalism*, New York: Pantheon.

Samuels, A. (1988) "Letter to the Editor," *International Journal of Psychoanalysis*, 69: 551–2.

Samuels, A. (1989) *The Plural Psyche: Personality, Morality, and the Father*, London and New York: Routledge.

Samuels, A. (1991) "National Socialism, National Psychology, and Analytical Psychology," in A. Maidenbaum and S.A. Martin (eds) *Lingering Shadows: Jungians, Freudians, and Anti-Semitism*, Boston and London: Shambhala, pp. 177–209.

Samuels, A. (1993) *The Political Psyche*, London and New York: Routledge.

Sandomir, R. (1993, 5 May) "Beyond the Fringe: The Boldly Bald," *New York Times*, C, 1 and 12.

Schutz, A. (1962) *Collected Papers: The Problem of Social Reality*, ed. M. Natanson, The Hague: Martinus Nijhoff, vol. 1.

Schutz, A. (1964) *Collected Papers: Studies in Social Theory*, ed. A. Brodersen, The Hague: Martinus Nijhoff, vol. 2.

Segaller, S. (1989) *The Wisdom of the Dream: Inheritance of Dreams* [videotape], Chicago: Films, Inc., vol. 2.

Segaller, S., and Berger, M. (1989) *The Wisdom of the Dream: The World of C.G. Jung*, Boston: Shambhala.

Shapiro, D. (1965) *Neurotic Styles*, New York and London: Basic Books.

Shapiro, D. (1981) *Autonomy and Rigid Character*, New York: Basic Books.

Shapiro, D. (1989) *Psychotherapy of Neurotic Character*, New York: Basic Books.

Shapiro, D. (1993, 12 April) Personal communication.

Shils, E. (1967) "Color, the Universal Intellectual Community, and the Afro-Asian Intellectual," *Daedalus*, 96, 2: 279–95.

Sloane, P. (1989) *The Visual Nature of Color*, New York: Design.

Smith, A.D. (1994) *Twilight: Los Angeles, 1992*, New York and London: Doubleday.

Snead, J. (1990) "European Pedigrees/African Contagions: Nationality, Narrative, and Communality in Tutuola, Achebe, and Reed," in H.K. Bhabha (ed.) *Nation and Narration*, London and New York: Routledge, pp. 231–49.

Sontag, S. (1978) *Illness as Metaphor*, New York: Farrar, Straus & Giroux.

Spence, D.P. (1982) *Narrative Truth and Historical Truth: Meaning and Interpretation in Psychoanalysis*, New York and London: W.W. Norton.

Steele, R.S., with Swinney, S.V. (1982) *Freud and Jung: Conflicts of Interpretation*, London and Boston: Routledge & Kegan Paul.

Steele, S. (1995, 24 October) "Race and the Curse of Good Intentions," *New York Times*, A, 27.

Storch, A. (1924) *The Primitive Archaic Forms of Inner Experiences and Thought in Schizophrenia*, trans. C. Willard, New York and Washington: Nervous and Mental Disease Publishing Co.

Swales, P.J. (forthcoming) "Freud, Filthy Lucre, and Undue Influence."

Terkel, S. (1992) *Race: How Blacks and Whites Think and Feel about the American Obsession*, New York: New Press.

Todorov, T. (1984) *The Conquest of America: The Question of the Other*, trans. R. Howard, New York: Harper & Row.

Todorov, T. (1986) " 'Race,' Writing, and Culture," trans. L. Mack, in H.L Gates, Jr (ed.) *"Race," Writing, and Difference*, Chicago and London: University of Chicago Press, pp. 370–80.

Todorov, T. (1993) *On Human Diversity: Nationalism, Racism, and Exoticism in French Thought*, trans. C. Porter, Cambridge, MA, and London: Harvard University Press.

Torgovnick, M. (1990) *Gone Primitive: Savage Intellects, Modern Lives*, Chicago and London: University of Chicago Press.

Treece, J.B. (1986, 13 October) "Nakasone's Ugly Remark Says a Lot about Today's Japan," *Business Week*, p. 66.

Turner, V. (1967) *The Forest of Symbols: Aspects of Ndembu Ritual*, Ithaca, NY, and London: Cornell University Press.

Van der Post, L. (1955) *The Dark Eye in Africa*, New York: William Morrow & Company.

Van der Post, L. (1975) *Jung and the Story of Our Time*, New York: Pantheon.

Von Franz, M-L. (1972) *The Feminine in Fairytales*, ed. P. Berry, Irving, TX: Spring.

Von Franz, M-L., with Boa, F. (1988) *The Way of the Dream*, Toronto: Windrose Films.

Walker, A. (1992) *Possessing the Secret of Joy*, New York, San Diego, CA, and London: Harcourt Brace Jovanovich.

Walker, A. (1993) *Possessing the Secret of Joy*, New York: Pocket Books.

Walker, A., and Parmar, P. (1993) *Warrior Marks: Female Genital Mutilation and the Sexual Blinding of Women*, New York, San Diego, CA, and London: Harcourt Brace & Company.

Wallerstein, R.S. (1988) "One Psychoanalysis or Many?" *International Journal of Psychoanalysis*, 69: 5–21.

Watkins, M. (1986) *Invisible Guests: The Development of Imaginal Dialogues*, Hillsdale, NJ: Analytic Press.

Werner, H. (1957) *Comparative Psychology of Mental Development*, New York: International Universities Press.

West, C. (1993) *Race Matters*, Boston: Beacon.

Whitmont, E.C., and Perera, S.B. (1989) *Dreams, A Portal to the Source*, London and New York: Routledge.

Whorf, B.L. (1956) *Language, Thought, and Reality: Selected Writings of Benjamin Lee Whorf*, New York: Technology Press of Massachusetts Institute of Technology and John Wiley & Sons.

Whyte, L.L. (1960) *The Unconscious before Freud*, New York: Basic Books.

Wilford, J.N. (1994, 25 January) "Gifts Keep Alive Search for Other Life in Universe," *New York Times*, C, 5.

Wilford, J.N. (1995, 23 November), "Genetic Sleuths Follow Clues to Elusive Ancestral Adam," *New York Times*, A, 1 and 28.

Williams, L. (1991, 30 November) "In a 90's Quest for Black Identity, Intense Doubts and Disagreements," *New York Times*, 1, 1 and 26.

Wilson, W.J. (1980) *The Declining Significance of Race: Blacks and Changing American Institutions*, Chicago and London: University of Chicago Press.

Winnicott, D.W. (1971) *Playing and Reality*, London: Tavistock.

Wolfe, G.C. (1992) *The Colored Museum*, in W.B. Branch (ed.) *Black Thunder: An Anthology of Contemporary African American Drama*, New York: Mentor, pp. 1–44.

Young-Eisendrath, P. (1987) "The Absence of Black Americans as Jungian Analysts," *Quadrant*, 20, 2: 41–53.

Zack, Naomi (1993) *Race and Mixed Race*, Philadelphia: Temple University Press.

Zahner-Roloff, L. (1990) "Dreams in Black and White: Living in the Sunset Hour of Time," in G. Saayam (ed.) *Modern South Africa in Search of a Soul: Jungian Perspectives on the Wilderness Within*, Boston: Sigo, pp. 19–45.

Name index

Subject index

acting 179, 186–190
acting out 129, 187
active imagination: *see* imagination
affirmative action 9, 37, 244
Afrocentrism 49, 168, 173–4, 176, 197, 243–4
AIDS/HIV 2, 196–7
Alamo xiii, xvii
albedo 219, 223–4
alchemy 219–24, 241
analytical psychology 8
anima 201, 203, 215–24; whitening of 223
anti-Semitism xx–xxi, 41–4
appearance versus reality 17, 19, 39, 77, 81, 91, 193, 203–4, 208, 227, 232–3, 237, 245
archetypal: Hillman's definition of 24; images versus archetypes 45, 104–6, 165; and stereotypical 39–40; *see also* archetype(s)
archetype(s): of bad instincts, ego darkness, uncivilized savage, "Negro" 165; as categories of the imagination 44; and collective representations 59; compared to Kantian categories 44–5; of lowest values 166; as natural versus cultural categories 45–6; as phylogenetic prototypes, or schemata 44–5; versus archetypal images 45, 104–6, 165; *see also*, archetypal, collective dimension of psyche, *and* collective unconscious

bald head 86, 92–6, 227, 234; *see also* hair *and* shaved head
barbarism 67, 145

barber 74–5, 83–4, 183, 220; *see also* hairdresser
basic rule 17, 192–3
bell curve 241
black(s): aesthetic 246; being 149; celestial figures 121; compared to simians 125, 136, 146–8, 243; experience 246; negative value of 223; potential superiority of 156–7; as signifier of id 53; what it means to be 234–6; *see also* blackness
black–dark–night associations 20–2, 34, 82
black goddess 218–22
black–primitive–instinctive associations 51–2
Black Rock Coalition 204
blackness: "African" 22; deliteralizing 149–50; impact of, on English 19–20; literal 220; moral versus "racial" 32; Melville on 31–2; negative aesthetic and moral values of 20; negative associations of 25–6, 34, 132–3, 136–8, 166–7; positive associations of 136–7; relativizing 224; shades of 27; test 207; "Thanatos" 22, 137, 140; and unconsciousness 150–3; *see also* black(s)
Bonham, Texas xiii–xix
boundaries 131–2, 180–1
Brown vs. Board of Education xiv
brutality 114–15, 139, 145–6, 178

castration 76; female 168; of "Negro" 164
categories: in terms of colors 14; differential versus oppositional 245; Kantian 44; natural versus cultural

10–11, 45–6, 244; "racial" xix, 159, 244; uninformative 10–11
civilization: and chance 100; Conrad on 69–70; European, white 152; Freud on 52, 153–4; Jung on 114, 144–5; Lévi-Strauss on 99–100; not synonymous with rationality 59; van der Post on 152; and white breasts 162
clitoridectomy 168–9, 174, 245
clitoris 162, 168, 172, 174
collective dimension of psyche xviii; redefinition of 45–47; *see also* archetypal *and* archetypes
collective representations 56–57
collective unconscious 46, 163; acquisition of contents of, by individual through culture 165; African-Americans as proof of 101–4; as cultural 40, 46, 165; as cultural imposition 167; Fanon on 165–7; Freud on 44; as human, not "racial" 101; Jung on 44–5; as "Greek" 102–3; versus personal unconscious 44; as purely formal, categorical 104; same in man of another "race" 118; *see also* archetypal *and* archetypes
color(s) 18; -attentive 159; -blind 159, 205, 208; as "catching" 115, 117; and culture 35; delusions 123–4; hair 99; -hypersensitive 159; -imaginative 159; no opposite 198; and religion 120–2, 125–8; sequence in alchemy 219; theory 33–6; *see also* complex: color
color-change dreams: 3–4, 211–12, 218–19, 226–7; definition of 1, 211
color complex: *see* complex
colorism 13–14, 17–18, 245–6; in alchemy 219; of some blacks 18; as phobia 154
communication: nonviolent versus violent confrontation 23; and translation 23
communicative intercourse 24
communicative solution to racism 23
compensation: in dreams 210, 220; for inferiority 122, 124, 211; for one-sided ego attitude 127–9, 135, 238
complex: color xxii, 91, 120, 124, 130, 138–9, 195; black ("Negro") 126–7,

138, 140; blood 122; Christ 126; definition of 120; ego- xxiii; equality 163; hair 91; inferiority 122, 139, 160–3; Moses 126; psychoexistential 161; "racial" 120; racist 120; sexual 120; superiority 124; white 126, 140
Copernican Revolution 19
conscious–unconscious opposition 28, 152–3
consciousness 152–3, 181–3; and going other 183
constructs: arbitrary 14; theoretical 152
contagion 84, 112–18
"contentual" unconscious: *see* unconscious
contiguity 51
contradiction: law of 54–6
cross-cultural psychoanalysis xx
cultural: context 165; dimension of psyche xx; factors xx, 39; hybridization 23, 175; ingraining 47; preferences versus natural orientations 245; relativism 107, 168, 176, 245; unconscious 40, 46, 165–7; values 245

"dark continent" 70, 142
decentering: earth, ego, white 19
deconstruction 198
delusion of reference 194
depth psychology xviii, 4, 8, 166
derivative(s) 38–9, 41, 78, 193–4, 214, 221–2; versus reality responses 40
difference(s) 6; as almost the same but not quite 117; within blackness and whiteness 27; celebrate, tolerate 245; color 13; contrast but neither compete, contradict, nor oppose 26; cultural xx, versus natural 11, 245; decisive 246; in degree between African and European 151; as descriptive versus evaluative category 11; discourse of 244; disappearance of physical 22–3; and empathy 186, 191; in equality 23; ethnic versus "racial" 158; Freud on minor, or small 13; indifference to 23, 168; infinite variety of 245; between Jews and "Aryans," Germans, Christians, Europeans 41–44; Jung on cultural 50; in kind 241; versus oppositions 153; not